Across The Years

BY VIRGINIUS DABNEY

Across The Years

MEMORIES OF A VIRGINIAN

Virginius Dabney

1978
DOUBLEDAY & COMPANY, INC.
GARDEN CITY, NEW YORK

ISBN: 0-385-12247-0
Library of Congress Catalog Card Number 77-15147

To my wife
thanking her for saying "yes"
fifty-six years ago

Contents

Foreword

After I had retired from the editorship of the Richmond *Times-Dispatch*, and had written *Virginia: The New Dominion* and *Richmond: The Story of a City*, Miss Sally Arteseros, my accomplished editor at Doubleday, encouraged me to write my reminiscences. I agreed, but did not wish to attempt anything as pretentious as an autobiography. It was my hope to give a picture of the world in which I grew up about three quarters of a century ago—so different in dozens of ways from the far more hectic and complicated world of today—and to record some of the memories that have intrigued, inspired or amused me.

"Always scribble, scribble, scribble, eh, Mr. Gibbon?" was the inane comment made on one occasion by the Duke of Gloucester to the masterful chronicler of Rome's decline and fall. Without in any sense comparing myself to Gibbon, except in this one particular, I too am continuing to scribble. It is what I enjoy doing. Whether the results in this instance are worth the reader's attention is for others to determine.

Almost anyone who has spent nearly half a century as an active journalist in one of the most fascinating eras in world history, as I have, will have had interesting experiences. He will also, in all likelihood, have come into contact with various men and women who made that era notable.

Some of my friends whose careers have revolved about writing have kept it up after retirement. Others, a minority, say that they are glad not to be bound any longer to their typewriters, and are content to sit and contemplate the ceiling or whatever else is within range. This last does not appeal to me in any degree. So long as my health remains acceptably good, and I have enough of my "marbles" to continue functioning, I prefer to remain busy, preferably putting words on paper.

In doing so I attempt, not always successfully, to distinguish between the authentic and the spurious, the genuine and the false. I try to spare the reader a choice such as confronted John Randolph of Roanoke in a tavern. Said Randolph to the waiter, "If this be tea, bring me coffee, or if this be coffee, bring me tea."

Insofar as the present work is concerned, I have, over the years, kept a number of diaries, notebooks and scrapbooks. Hence the production of this memoir was a relatively simple task. Little research was necessary, since so much of the book is based on personal experiences and recollections.

Certain opinions that I express herein—as for example with respect to some so-called modern art, and concerning what I regard as obscenity—will be considered by many to be out of tune with the best current thinking. So be it; these are my views.

Yet I am convinced that we must not cling too tenaciously to all the standards of the past, many of which are necessarily outmoded. I have always been impressed by the words of that notable Virginian, Landon Cabell Garland, first chancellor of Vanderbilt University, who said, "Men never amount to much until they outgrow their fathers' notions." A similar thought was expressed by Thomas Jefferson when he wrote, "Laws and institutions must go hand in hand with the progress of the human mind. . . . We might as well require a man to wear still the coat which fitted him when a boy, as civilized society to remain ever under the regimen of their barbarous ancestors."

I trust that in these reminiscences I have maintained a reasonable sense of proportion and a proper sense of values. There was a Richmonder, now dead, whose value judgments were positively grotesque. He seemed bemused by the power and prestige of great wealth, and remarked to me one day, "The really great Americans were men like J. P. Morgan, Charles M. Schwab and John D. Rockefeller. George Washington, Thomas Jefferson and Patrick Henry wouldn't be one-two-three with those fellows." Such idiocy deserves to be recorded.

Perhaps I have helped in this memoir to acquaint other sections of the United States with a few truths concerning Virginia and the South. The misconceptions are legion. A rather trivial example of this was seen in the musical *Shenandoah*, which ran for years in New York during the 1970s, and was purportedly based on events in the Shenandoah Valley of Virginia during the Civil War. Every scene showed hanging moss, whereas there is exactly as much hanging moss in the Valley of the Shenadoah as there is around Niagara Falls. A small thing in itself, but symptomatic of larger misconceptions.

My editor, Miss Arteseros, has insisted on my using the personal pronoun in this book more frequently than I like to do. Time and again, in commenting on a passage in the manuscript, she would say, "This is your *personal* memoir, and you must write it in the first person." So I would dutifully insert "I" at various points. Incidentally, she has made extremely helpful suggestions with all of my Doubleday books. This is directly contrary to the experience of a friend of mine who has written a number of distinguished works under another publisher's imprint. He remarked that his publisher had never been of the slightest help. If he had Sally Arteseros as his editor, it would almost certainly have been a different story.

I am much indebted to my sister, Alice Parker, and her husband, John C. Parker, who read a number of the chapters and made extremely helpful criticisms and suggestions. Others who have been good enough to read portions of the manuscript and to make valuable criticisms are Staige D. Blackford, Jr., John E. Leard, Overton Jones and J. Harvie Wilkinson, Jr. My daughter, Mrs. James S. Watkinson, not only did a professional job of typing the entire work, but offered incisive suggestions for improving the writing. Miss Mary Morris Watt, chief librarian at Richmond Newspapers, was helpful, as always, as were the members of her staff and the staffs of the Virginia Historical Society, the Virginia State Library and the Richmond Public Library. Alf Goodykoontz, managing editor of the Richmond *Times-Dispatch*, and Marvin Garrette, assistant managing editor, gave me timely assistance. I wish also to acknowledge my special indebtedness to the *Times-Dispatch*, since I have drawn freely on my writings for that newspaper over the years. In addition, my thanks to the Boston *Herald-American* and to the *Magazine of Albemarle County History* for the use of material contributed to them by me.

Finally, as with my other books, I desire to express my gratitude to my wife. She has read the entire manuscript with a critical eye and no inhibitions in stating her opinions. Words are inadequate as I seek to make clear my sense of obligation to her.

Virginius Dabney

Richmond, Virginia

1

In the Beginning

THE TWENTIETH CENTURY was only thirty-nine days old
when I appeared on this spinning planet, February 8, 1901. The
event occurred in my parents' home at the University of Virginia,
which had not then been annexed by the neighboring town of
Charlottesville.

The comfortable but undistinguished frame house in which I
first saw the light—hardly anybody was born in a hospital in those
days—is still there, albeit somewhat enlarged. Situated at 1602
Gordon Avenue, corner of Ackley Lane, it was serving in the middle and late 1970s as the Central Outpatient Clinic of the Blue
Ridge Comprehensive Community Health Center. The house was
built by my father, Richard Heath Dabney—at that time the one
and only professor of history at the University of Virginia—
following his marriage in 1899 to my mother, Lily Heth Davis of
Albemarle County, Virginia. My sister Lucy, two years my junior,
also was born there.

I spent my first six years at 1602 Gordon Avenue, but my recollections of that era are decidedly dim. A salient event which my
father related to me afterward, but which I do not recall, was the
whaling he gave me for hitting my similarly youthful cousin, Edward Hickson, in the head with a tin can. Perhaps I was intent
upon mayhem or perhaps it was an accident. Edward was not
seriously wounded, but I gather that Father thought Edward's
mother had to be appeased. This was the only time in my life that

1

my father chastised me physically, although I probably deserved it often.

The world of 1901 was, of course, a vastly different world from the one that we know today. The overwhelmingly rural United States contained only 76 million persons, slightly more than one third of the present population; there were no airplanes and practically no automobiles; radio, television and the income tax all lay in the future. A dollar was most emphatically a dollar, as witness the advertisement of a Boston, Massachusetts, boarding house: "Turkey dinner, 20¢, supper or breakfast 15¢"; or that in the Omaha, Nebraska, *World-Herald*, "Sugar 4¢ lb., eggs, 14¢ dozen." The United States had won the war with Spain, Admiral Dewey was the national hero and Vice-President Theodore Roosevelt would soon became President, upon the assassination of William McKinley. Carry Nation, the Kansas cyclone, was wielding her trusty hatchet with devastating effect on the glassware of the saloons, and the Woman's Christian Temperance Union of Richmond was planning "gospel temperance meetings in many churches," looking to the ultimate adoption of national prohibition. Negroes were being lynched in various sections of the nation; there were 107 of these barbarities, with blacks usually the victims, in 1900, and 107 more in 1901. On the day after I was born, the local press reported that at Leavenworth, Kansas, a "miserable wretch" accused of crime was burned at the stake by a mob.

How did I acquire the name Virginius, which sounds like that of a Roman senator? This question is frequently asked. I was named for my grandfather, Virginius Dabney, who in turn was named for the state of Virginia. His father, Thomas Smith Gregory Dabney, was so distraught over leaving his beloved native state in 1835 to settle in Mississippi that he called his just-born son Virginius. Thomas Dabney was the subject of a notable book, *Memorials of a Southern Planter*, by his daughter, Susan Dabney Smedes. The work was highly praised by reviewers, went through a number of editions and was so greatly admired by William E. Gladstone, the British prime minister, that he arranged for an

English edition. (Alfred A. Knopf brought out a new American edition in 1965, edited by Fletcher M. Green.)

My grandfather, Virginius Dabney, was a captain on the staff of General John B. Gordon in the Civil War, and after the conflict operated boys' schools in Middleburg, Virginia, Princeton, New Jersey, and New York City; he wrote a most favorably reviewed novel, *Don Miff*, that went into four printings in six months; served as adviser to New York publishers and was an editorial writer on the New York *Commercial Advertiser*.

Virginius Dabney's first wife, my grandmother, was the daughter of James E. Heath, who was said by Edgar Allan Poe in 1841 to be "almost the only person of any literary distinction in Richmond." He wrote a largely forgotten novel and play which were of some note at the time. He was also editorial adviser and in effect the first editor of the *Southern Literary Messenger*. Heath's father, John Heath, was the first president of Phi Beta Kappa when it was founded at the College of William & Mary.

Mother was a great-granddaughter of John A. G. Davis, who, as the thirty-eight-year-old chairman of the University of Virginia faculty, was fatally wounded in 1840 by a rioting student. Davis had come out of his residence in Pavilion X, East Lawn, to try to remove the mask of a youth who was taking part in the firing of guns and general disorder. The student shot him and he died two days later. Davis's wife, the former Mary Jane Terrell, my great-great-grandmother, was the granddaughter of Dabney Carr and Martha Jefferson, sister of Thomas Jefferson.

We moved in 1907 to another frame house on the summit of what was called Preston Heights, about a quarter of a mile from our previous abode. Stucco was applied to the exterior of the house many years later. It is there today, 703 Rugby Road, the property of Mr. and Mrs. E. L. Hogshire. Known as Edgewood, it stood in 1907 on a tree-shaded tract, and the whole property was ten acres in extent. It fronted on Rugby Road from Edgewood Lane to a point somewhat beyond the present Wayside Place, and extended downhill toward the rear in the direction of the present Emmet Street or Route 29.

There was a carriage house where the surrey was kept, and beneath it was the ice house, which was filled annually, if and when the large pond across Rugby Road from Edgewood froze. Not long after my arrival in the new dwelling, I frightened my parents practically out of their wits by falling into the seventeen-foot-deep hole, which had no ice in it at the time. The trap door in the carriage-house floor leading to the ice house below was usually closed, but on this particular occasion it was open, and the hinged wooden cover was propped up with a stick. I couldn't be satisfied until I had peered into the abyss. In the process, the stick was jarred loose, and the trap door fell, hitting me in the back and propelling me head over heels into the opening. Far from knocking me unconscious, the seventeen-foot fall merely caused me to bawl loudly enough for the Negro handyman to come running. He hurried down the ladder and carried me up. How I managed to escape serious injury is a mystery, but except for a few bruises, I was not hurt. I don't know whether I landed on my head or on some other part of my anatomy. If on my head, my nonadmirers might be inclined to say that this explained divers of my aberrations in later years.

Albemarle is one of the most beautiful and historic of Virginia's counties, and from our new home we had a striking view of the Blue Ridge Mountains, standing like a purple wall against the sunset. In another direction Thomas Jefferson's Monticello—Italian for "little mountain"—looked serenely down. The county's landscape is either rolling or mountainous, and from its red soil have sprung some of the nation's great men. In addition to Jefferson, whose spirit broods over all, there was George Rogers Clark, the intrepid "Hannibal of the Northwest," whose conquests there were chiefly responsible for the award of that vast region to the United States in the treaty of 1783 following the American Revolution. Other natives were Jack Jouett, Jr., whose forty-mile ride from Cuckoo Tavern to Monticello saved Governor Jefferson and most of the Virginia legislature from capture by the British, and Meriwether Lewis of the famous Lewis and Clark Expedition to the Pacific Coast.

Our dwelling, built in the latter part of the nineteenth century, was comfortable but by no means luxurious. In the "sitting room"

4

was the usual horsehair-covered sofa, redolent of the Victorian era, and on a wall was *The Burial of Latané,* which hung in hundreds of Virginia homes. The engraving showed the simple ceremony at the newly dug grave of gallant young Captain Latané, the only man killed in "Jeb" Stuart's spectacular ride entirely around McClellan's invading army in 1862.

In the more formal "parlor" across the front hall from the sitting room were two chairs that had graced the Tuileries palace in Paris during the reign of Marie Antoinette. They were purchased in the French capital by James Monroe for Thomas Jefferson. My great-great-grandfather, John A. G. Davis, got them when Monticello's furnishings were auctioned off following Jefferson's death. Toward the rear of the house was Father's study, with its huge bookcase and his desk in the center, piled high and chaotically with miscellaneous books, papers and other material.

The area of Preston Heights in which our house stood was far more sparsely settled than it is today, for it is now completely built up. There was a large water tank immediately across Rugby Road from Edgewood, and from it to the pond below and all the way to Grady Avenue on the south there stretched a large field covered with broom sedge. Near the center of this field was a tall and handsome pine, up which we boys liked to climb. We also played baseball in the broom sedge surrounding it.

Adjoining Edgewood on the north was Rugby, the capacious home of former Confederate General Thomas L. Rosser, a residence in the Victorian style, surrounded by smaller dependencies, many large trees and numerous acres. Peacocks adorned the grounds. The Rosser dwelling is still there, but it is closely hemmed in by numerous houses. The peacocks have long since gone to their reward.

As for Edgewood, all that remains of its original ten-acre tract is the wide yard that surrounds the house. The rest was divided by my father in the 1930s and 1940s into twenty-two building lots and sold for residential purposes. Every lot but the one occupied by the Unitarian Church contains a dwelling today.

Rugby Road in my early youth was unpaved, and dust and mud vied for supremacy, depending on the weather. There were no sidewalks—only a few planks here and there—so that our accustomed travel on foot to the university, half a mile away, or to more distant Charlottesville, was a bit difficult. However, walking for one's usual errands and excursions was taken for granted. Our surrey, pulled by a somewhat spavined steed appropriately named Andantino, was mainly for the ladies. A jangling trolley car from downtown terminated opposite the university's Rotunda. Later the line was extended to a point on Rugby Road more than a quarter of a mile from our home. It was useful for trips to Charlottesville, which then had a population of about 6,500. The city now contains about 40,000 persons.

An all-important member of our household during those early years was Roberta Becks, a Negro woman of great reliability and pleasing personality who cared for Lucy and me. Nanna, as we called her for some unexplained reason, was my cherished friend and constant defender. She was never too busy to minister to my childish wants, however irrational or absurd.

Nanna was the mother of several children without benefit of matrimony. They had arrived long before she became a part of our entourage. Curious as to the process by which she acquired these individuals, and as yet not made privy by my father to the essential facts concerning the birds and the bees, I asked her if it were possible to have children without being married. I put this query to her several times, but without satisfactory results.

"Go 'long chile," she would say. "Ef I told you dat, you'd know much as I do."

When I was married many years later in Richmond, Nanna was an honored guest at the wedding and reception. She all but conceded that she was more responsible for my rearing than my parents. When our first-born arrived, we brought Nanna to Richmond as the child's nurse. She was really too old by that time to be anything like as useful as in former days; my wife said she waited on Nanna more than Nanna waited on her or our infant daughter.

Our much-loved nurse remained with us for a couple of years. One of her favorite sayings was, "Don't bother 'bout de stars,

Lawd, just gimme de crown!" We were all saddened by the news of her death.

At Edgewood there were at least two greatly valued cooks over the years, Eliza Brooks and—much later—Leonard Goode. Lewis Washington, who worked the vegetable garden, made the fires in the grates, looked after the horse, etc., was another black mainstay for decades. First contact with him came when he turned up one day at Edgewood and told my father that he had just been released from the penitentiary after serving a term for murder. He asked for a chance to make good, and Father hired him after looking into his record. They remained firm friends in this relationship until Washington's death decades later. He married and begat thirteen children, several of whom were in the Dabney family's employ at one time or another.

One of my earliest recollections is of a steady "thump thump" in the kitchen on Sunday mornings where Lewis Washington was beating the dough for beaten biscuits. The dough was spread on a thick wooden board and he belabored it with a wooden mallet shaped like a baseball bat, only shorter. The resulting biscuits were delectable.

My early education was obtained entirely at home. I did not attend any school until 1914, when I entered the Episcopal High School, near Alexandria, Virginia, at age thirteen. Prior to that time my teachers were my father and my Aunt Lucy—Lucy Minor Davis, a sweet maiden lady who lived with my parents. We always called her "Tee"; don't ask me why.

My schooling in reading, writing and arithmetic began at an early age, with Aunt Lucy in charge. She was in her late sixties at the time. A devout Episcopalian, Tee was zealous in her desire to introduce me to the Scriptures. When in the course of our biblical excursions we encountered such subjects as concubines and circumcision, I sought enlightenment from her concerning their meaning, but she was not very helpful. In fact her replies to my queries were so vague as to leave me as much in the dark as ever. This, however, is decidedly by the way. I owe her an immense debt of gratitude for the devotion with which she addressed her-

7

self to my enlightenment and the uncounted hours she expended in that enterprise.

Aunt Lucy was extremely intelligent and widely read, and was a walking encyclopedia of the history and literature of England and Scotland. She had a deeply affectionate nature and a profound understanding. Greatly beloved by everyone, she was consulted by various relatives and friends, who trusted her good judgment. Possessed of a gentle sense of humor, she proclaimed herself "a total abstainer but not a fanatic." In order to prove the totality of her abstinence she would take an occasional glass of wine.

When my father was paying court to my future mother in the late nineties, Aunt Lucy is reported to have been disturbed by these attentions to her great-niece because my father was not a religious man. She had been the only teacher my mother ever had, and she also had given my Aunt Alice her only instruction. (Southern women seldom went to college in those days; aside from everything else, most of them could not afford it.) Heath Dabney married Lily Davis, of course, despite Aunt Lucy's misgivings, but as the years passed Tee came to love and respect my father for his many fine qualities. That affection and respect was returned by him in full measure.

Aunt Lucy taught both my mother and me, not to mention my sister Lucy, who was named for her, and my still younger sister Alice; thus she taught two generations of Dabneys and Davises. She also undertook the occasional instruction of John Staige Davis, Jr., my cousin—who lived nearby. I seized the opportunity to hide in a closet immediately behind the stool on which John Staige was sitting, and kicked him from his perch now and again. Tee was much mystified, and never caught on to the reasons why her pupil kept losing his balance.

In January 1908, Father inaugurated his own special brand of instruction in foreign languages, with me as the willing guinea pig. He began with German, in which he was especially fluent, since he had spent three years in Germany getting his Ph.D. I was almost seven years old at the time. A year later we began studying French, in which Father was also fluent.

His theory in teaching languages was that an American boy or girl should learn a foreign tongue in the same way that he or she first learned English, i.e., by conversation and reading, *not* by memorizing tiresome, difficult grammatical rules. The process should begin early, he said, long before high school.

We started off with the simplest reading materials. Father read me *Der Struwwelpeter* (*Slovenly Peter*) in German and translated it, after which he had me read the original German. I then had to learn by heart the meanings of a list of simple German words and translate simple German sentences from a German book devoted to grammar and conversation. We used only the conversation.

After finishing the above, I read aloud, without translation, after hearing Father read them aloud, selections from three readers used by German children to learn their own language. By the end of a year, I had read, in German, Andersen's and Grimms' *Fairy Tales* and Aesop's *Fables*, plus other material for a total of about 1,500 pages. Similar instruction in French was equally successful. As a result of my father's remarkably effective pedagogical innovations, I had a tremendous advantage over students of German and French who had been taught by conventional methods. Furthermore, I understood and enjoyed what I read. In school and college I breezed through the courses in French and German, thanks to my superior instruction—not to any special ability on my part.

However, when Father used the same technique in attempting to teach me Greek, the results were something else. I managed to pass the courses at Episcopal High and the University of Virginia, but with mediocre grades at the latter institution. Yet the basic soundness of the instructional method seems obvious. Many schools now are using some of the same principles. In fact, about twenty years ago I wrote an article, by request, for one of the public school journals, describing the process by which I was taught foreign languages.

I never took Latin. Father decided to start me off in Greek, since he felt that there was more interesting material in that language for a boy. He said I could pick up Latin later on my own, if desired. The desire never took hold of me.

In addition to finessing Latin, I did not study English grammar, even for a single day. This was pursuant to Father's theory that it is far more important and useful to read, write, speak and listen to good English than to learn boring rules of grammar or to memorize declensions and conjugations.

Episcopal High School required English grammar in the lower forms. Father sent Willoughby Reade, head of the school's English department, letters that I had written home from Boy Scout camp, and he put me in the fourth form when I entered, which meant that I skipped all the grammar. I have never regretted this, nor do I grieve over having studied no Latin. I can't see that either omission has handicapped me to any appreciable degree.

Commenting on the often expressed view that an understanding of Latin is essential to a proper understanding of English, Father disagreed strongly. He felt, moreover, that neither Latin nor Greek should be a requirement for the B.A. degree. This despite his own great facility in both languages. His feeling was that unless a student could read Latin or Greek easily and appreciate the beauties of its literature, studying either of them was a waste of time. He quoted the headmaster of famous Harrow School in England as saying that the amount of Greek taught by Oxford and Cambridge universities is "of no use to the boys whatever, and takes them from studies which they prefer."

In tutoring me at home, away from the other boys who were attending either public or private schools, Father was taking the risk that I might not be congenial with my youthful contemporaries and might not become one of the gang. Fortunately it didn't seem to cause any problems. I saw a lot of the boys of my own age in the afternoons, and played football, baseball, tennis, marbles and other games with them. I was a much better athlete at that stage than I was at any time thereafter. For example, there was a Boy Scout track meet in the summer of 1913 on Lambeth Field at the University of Virginia between the Scouts of Richmond, Charlottesville and the university. I was twelve years old, and I competed against boys of twelve, thirteen and perhaps fourteen—I can't recall. The still older boys had separate events. In the younger group, I won the 50, 100, 220 and 440-yard dashes. One strange thing about this is that I don't think I entered another track meet at any subsequent time. I began growing weedlike a couple of years later, and whatever speed I had departed from me.

Boys in the community with whom I was most intimate were John Staige Davis, Jr., later a prominent physician in New York City and a widely known huntsman; Henry B. ("Skinny") Gordon, who would serve several terms in the Virginia House of Delegates; Francis E. ("Bussie") Howard, later a brigadier general in the U. S. Army; Marion P. ("Pat") Echols, a colonel on General MacArthur's staff in World War II, whose collarbone I broke as a boy when I tackled him in an impromptu football game; and C. Venable ("Hippo") Minor, who served a term as president of the Virginia State Bar. A slightly older member of the group was Edmund Minor Wilson, a cousin of Edmund Wilson, the writer, and one of the most original fellows I ever knew. He died all too young.

Before I went off to Episcopal High I was inducted, with mysterious rites, into a society called Zeta Iota Pi, which had been organized by somewhat older boys of the university community. What the letters Zeta Iota Pi stood for, if anything, I never found out. This occult brotherhood had a rousing yell and a whistle. I can give the whistle to this day, and I can also recall the yell:

> *Zeta Iota Pi, fee fo fi;*
> *Meow, scat! Zeta Iota Pi.*

Occasionally we held what was called a *soirée*. It revolved about ginger ale, potato chips and similar condiments. The thought never crossed our minds in our wildest moments that we might celebrate with potations even slightly alcoholic. The organization faded out in a couple of years.

The inauguration of Woodrow Wilson as President of the United States in 1913 was a major event of my youth. Our troop of Boy Scouts went to Washington "to keep order" along Pennsylvania Avenue, or so it was said. The Reverend Beverley D. Tucker, Jr., rector of St. Paul's Episcopal Church at the university, afterward bishop of Ohio, was our beloved scoutmaster. After we had performed our function, such as it was, in Washington, and the parade and ceremonies had finally ended, we repaired, exhausted, to the Union Station. Our train, like most of the trains, was hours late. So we lay down on the station floor and went to sleep. Suddenly at some time after midnight we were roused and told to board our coach. In a semistupefied condition we hurried to the steps leading down to the platform. I was only half awake, and when I reached the top of the stairs I stumbled and fell headlong all the way to the first landing. My fellow Scouts thought I had smashed a few bones, if not my skull, but I seemed in those days to have a genius for falling into ice houses or down flights of steps and emerging largely unscathed. In this instance, unfortunately, I fell down the wrong steps and had to pick myself up and go back to the right ones. But I arose from my plunge with no breaks or sprains.

However, I must confess that a couple of years before my epoch-making dive in the Washington depot I took another with less satisfactory results. I was galumphing down dusty Rugby Road on Andantino, our somewhat scruffy carriage horse, when he took it into his head to turn abruptly leftward into Gordon Avenue. I was unaware of his intention until it was too late, with the result that I took a header and broke my right arm just above the wrist when I hit the ground. It was soon healed.

I was never a good rider in my youth, and I did no riding at all in later years. My Uncle Staige Saunders, who was a great "kidder," but who knew whereof he spoke in this instance, said my bouncing and jouncing style of riding was such that he could see the Blue Ridge Mountains between me and the horse.

While I am recording my early mishaps of one sort or another, I must mention what happened when I was climbing around on the not quite completed stadium at Lambeth Field. My foot slipped and my mouth came down on the corner of a concrete step. One of my upper front teeth was knocked out, another was cracked and my lower lip was badly cut. I picked up the tooth from the ground and walked home, bleeding profusely. I must have been a gory sight when I walked into the room where my mother was sitting. She washed the blood from my face, and we drove in the surrey to see Dr. Harry L. Smith, the family dentist.

He kept my tooth overnight, and told me to return the next day. At that time he stuck the tooth into my mouth and put a brace on it, in the hope that it would grow back. *Mirabile dictu*, it did, thereby making medical history as of that time. My case was cited for decades in the University of Virginia Medical School. However, I knocked the tooth out several years later playing basketball, so it had to be replaced with an artificial one. The scar where I cut my lip is still there.

My father was wont to remark that he didn't see how boys ever grew to manhood, in view of the manner in which they fell out of trees, off of bicycles or down steps, slashed themselves accidentally with pocket knives, ran around in the cold without proper clothing, experimented with firearms, broke through the ice while skating, and so on.

One perilous pastime of my youth was the shooting off of firecrackers at Christmas and on the Fourth of July. This was legal in those days, and the wonder is that some of us didn't get our hands or fingers blown off. The small firecrackers were not lethally dangerous, but the "cannon crackers" were another story. We would light these and throw them as far as possible before they went off with a reverberating roar. Christmas and the glorious Fourth would not have been half as much fun without them.

I learned to swim at an early age, thanks to my older cousin, Preston Lockwood of St. Louis, who took me to the pool in the basement of the university's Fayerweather Gymnasium for lessons. The pool was dank and dark, and bullfrogs, so the story went, had grown to maturity in its dim recesses. It wasn't long before I was able to paddle around there on my own. When I felt entirely at home in the water, I began going to the old reservoir on the lower reaches of Observatory Mountain near the university. This was the favorite community "swimmin' hole" in summer. It was patronized exclusively by males, including some university students and numerous boys, large and small. It never occurred to us to wear anything while swimming or diving there, despite the fact that the reservoir was only a relatively short distance from the road. It was in the woods, so that the gamboling nudists could not readily be seen. Presumably the ladies of the community who might be taking walks in that area to admire the mountain laurel maintained a discreet distance. They surely must have heard the loud shouting.

A sensation of the year 1910 was Halley's Comet. It completes its circuit every seventy-six years and will be seen again in 1986. This was the comet that flashed alarmingly across the sky late in the year 1606 when the Jamestown settlers were preparing to embark from London for Virginia. Such a portent in that era was supposed to be ominous in the extreme. When Halley's Comet returned in 1910, for its fourth circuit since the 1606 appearance, there was some lurid stuff in the press. Almost anything might happen, it was said, when the earth passed through a million miles of the comet's tail at a speed of 2,500 miles a minute. There was no basis, of course, for these dire speculations. My parents waked my sister Lucy and me one night and took us out into the yard to view the dazzling celestial phenomenon with its brilliant tail extending across the heavens.

Another excitement was when the circus would come to town. We would go down to Main Street in Charlottesville and wait long hours for the parade to pass. It was always late, but it would finally come into view with its clowns, its beautiful ladies in spangled tights, its ponderous pachyderms and its fierce animals pacing back and forth in their cages. Always there was one vehicle with its shutters closed to pique the crowd's curiosity. And always, of course, there was the steam calliope bringing up the rear with its shrill tootling.

On a much smaller scale was the divertissement provided when a monkey and organ grinder came occasionally to our neighborhood. This was a rare and unpredictable event, but suddenly in our front yard the organ grinder, usually Italian, would appear with his monkey on a leash. All the kids would rally 'round, and the monkey would gobble a banana or munch an apple, if either was forthcoming, picking fleas from his hide the while. The organ grinder would accept any small coins that were offered and move on down the road.

The newly invented motion pictures were other excitements of the time. A nickel would get you in, if you could dig one up, and another nickel would provide peanuts or candy. A lady played the piano during much of the silent show, but she had to retire periodically to rest. Mary Pickford, Pearl White, House Peters, Charlie Chaplin, Francis X. Bushman and Theda Bara were among the matinee idols.

The collection of baseball cards (cards that came in packages of certain brands of cigarettes, especially Piedmonts), with pictures of big league baseball players on them, was one of my special interests. I knew the name and batting average of virtually every player in the National and American leagues. Like all such collectors, I sought vainly and constantly for a picture of Honus Wagner, the star shortstop of the Pittsburgh Pirates and the league's leading hitter. We didn't know that Wagner had told the makers of Piedmonts to take him out of their collection since he didn't want to be associated with the sale of cigarettes. A mere handful of the Wagner pictures got into circulation. One of them turned up in 1975, and the finder said he was holding it for $3,000.

Given my interest in the stars of the diamond, it was an annual thrill when the Washington Senators of the American League came to the University of Virginia for early spring training. This lasted only a few years, for the weather there was too uncertain and not warm enough. But I was able to see such immortals as Walter Johnson and Eddie Ainsmith, the famous battery which made baseball history. Ainsmith, a powerful and extremely agile man, caught Johnson for many years. The latter, a tall, broad-shouldered, brawny Kansan with blazing speed, made an amazing record of wins, losses and strike-outs with the perennially second-division Washington club.

Another early diversion was attendance at the performances of Shakespeare presented by the Ben Greet Players, an English company which provided outdoor plays on college campuses. This was my introduction to Shakespeare on the stage.

Our home, Edgewood, was a hospitable one. My mother, in particular, loved to entertain, and somehow managed to do it constantly, despite our small means. There was almost a stream of guests, either staying in the house or joining us for meals. Like many Virginia women of her generation, Mother hardly ever entered the kitchen and knew nothing whatever about cooking. She always had a cook to perform that office.

Belles who came to the university dances were frequent guests in our home. Two of the most beauteous and charming were Beatrice ("B") Crawford, later Mrs. Merritt T. Cooke, and Sarah Hamilton, later Mrs. Stephen Booth McKinney. It was nothing to have half a dozen palpitating students in our parlor at one time, sitting figuratively at the feet of one of these beauties. My father used to marvel at the ease with which B Crawford or Sarah Hamilton would make what were called "goo-goo eyes" at each one of the swains in turn, giving each the impression that he was "it," when, as likely as not, none of them was.

There was no such thing in that era as the "going steady" of later years, when a young man and girl would see nobody else for an entire weekend, and also would dance with one another exclusively. By contrast, in the early 1900s there was a constant shifting of dates, and at dances there were cards specifying the youth with whom the girl would start each dance. But then, for the belles a line would form, and there would be a series of "breaks" before the music stopped. In other words, each belle would dance with quite a number of individuals before the next dance on the card came up. Of course there were always a few "sad birds" who got no breaks at all.

A favorite and quite swank method of dating was to hire a horse and buggy from a downtown livery stable. The equipage would be delivered by a young black boy. The lady in the case, perhaps in a "peach basket" hat and wearing a corsage of violets, and her sharply dressed escort, in peg-top trousers and the type of stiff collar later made famous by Herbert Hoover, would climb into the buggy and traverse either the three-mile or the nine-mile circuit—two drives in the vicinity of Charlottesville. Usually the barefoot young black sat on the back of the vehicle throughout the drive, facing the rear with his legs dangling. This last invariably cramped the style of any ambitious suitor.

Ladies were sufficiently daring in about the year 1910 to raise their skirts from the level of the ankle bone to that of the shoe top. Another evidence of advancing civilization was seen when it became possible to use the term "leg" instead of "limb." Then too there was the emergence of the "peek-a-boo waist." It had embroidered perforations which permitted glimpses of female epidermis upon the arms and "as much as two inches below the nape of the neck." Some clergymen were outraged.

Women were not yet smoking in appreciable numbers. In fact, New York City passed a law in 1908 forbidding them to smoke. This caused the New York *Herald* to headline the fact that several women were seen puffing cigarettes in a carriage en route to the opera.

I was not concerned with such matters at that stage of my career, although when I reached my teens I did occasionally puff on corn silk wrapped in a piece of paper—a horrendous smoke which scarified the tongue and couldn't possibly have been anything but an ordeal.

Certain comic strips attracted me, especially one called "Us Boys." Its principal character was Eaglebeak Spruder, a tough guy who wore his cap either backwards or sideways. This seemed to give him a special and indefinable charm.

Scoutmaster Tucker took the university troop on two summer camping trips, lasting about a week, one on the North River near Lexington and the other on the Cowpasture near Millboro Springs. I never got enough to eat on the former trip, and I don't think the others did either. The cuisine was better managed the second time around. A dire calamity on the second trip occurred when Hippo Minor, who in his early years was vastly overweight, got the worst case of poison oak I ever saw. We fished and swam and took hikes both years, and the Cowpasture seemed to me, at age thirteen, to be a powerful and impressive stream. What was my astonishment when I saw it some forty years later, and found it to be hardly more than a good-sized creek.

For ten straight years, from 1907 to 1917, I spent part of each summer at oak-shaded Caryswood, the farm of my great-uncles and -aunts near Evington, Virginia, a small hamlet on the Southern Railway some eighteen miles below Lynchburg. The house was built in the 1850s.

Getting to Evington from Charlottesville was, in itself, an adventure. I always traveled in the reeking, cinder-strewn day coach, and my rations were a couple of hard-boiled eggs, plus maybe a sandwich and a chicken drumstick and gizzard. The highlight of the trip was the tunnel just outside of Lynchburg. I usually choked on the smoke, but there was a thrill in passing through the murky tube.

I was one of four boys, all cousins, who sojourned together at Caryswood, and our simple bucolic amusements and diversions doubtless have little appeal for the younger generation today. We cut "bee trees" to get the honey, gigged frogs, went 'coon hunting —but usually caught only 'possums—made cider, filled mudholes in the country road with rocks, swam "nekkid" in Flat Creek and played tennis on a "court" which was merely a level place on the front lawn with a net stretched across it. Since there were no backstops, we must have chased those tennis balls thousands of miles.

John Staige Davis, my cousin from the university, and Edward Hickson, a relative from South Carolina, referred to above, were two of the quartet of boys at Caryswood, and William H. Irvine, later a leading member of the Virginia House of Delegates, was the other. Edward Hickson has practiced medicine for many years at Rustburg, the county seat of Campbell County, in which Caryswood is located.

We boys slept in the two-story "office" in the yard, along with Uncle Staige Saunders, a delightful bachelor who ran the farm. He was on the first floor and we on the second. Our sleeping was done on two hard double beds, with mattresses made of something closely resembling bricks or paving blocks. We scorned the effete facilities of the big house, and used the privy behind the barn. Since there was no tub or shower in the office, our ablutions were performed with considerable frequency in one of the various swimming holes, albeit without soap.

Uncle Staige dubbed us boys "professors," and provided each of us with a "chair." I was libelously charged with bathing less often than I should, so I became "Professor of Conservation of Natural Resources."

The professors engaged in activities which might seem to their counterparts today to be worse than useless. For example, we decided that we would walk to Lynchburg, which is twenty miles by road. We didn't intend to do anything spectacular after we got there, but we set forth at dawn. At about midday we arrived, went to two movie shows and caught the train back to Evington.

On another occasion we organized a camping and fishing expedition to Otter River, some six or eight miles distant. Our wagon train was a formidable one, and after hours of arduous travel, we reached a swampy portion of the stream. But before we could hook a single catfish, squadrons of mosquitoes approximately the size of turkey buzzards descended upon us and began operating on the exposed portion of our anatomies. We spent a miserable night, amid the whining of those dive bombers, and returned, scratching violently, to Caryswood.

The hay loft under the roof of the Caryswood barn was among our regular hangouts. John Staige Davis went to sleep there in broad daylight and slid, snoring, down the hay pile and through the outside door on the second floor. He hit the ground with a thud—apparently on his head. We assured him that if he ever committed, say, an ax murder, he could count on us to testify that his brain had been heavily damaged in his youth.

Automobiles were nonexistent in the Caryswood area for the greater part of the decade when I was a sojourner there. We traveled the three miles to Evington on horseback, in a buggy or a wagon, or on our feet, which were always bare until about the year 1913. The trip took most of the morning or afternoon. The rutted country road passed through a number of farms, and several gates had to be opened and shut, lest the bulls wander or the billy goats stray. When we got to Evington we collected the mail and usually dropped in at one of the two small stores for a bottle of pop and to hear the latest gossip. After sixty years I can still smell the pungent odor that permeated those premises, a combination of chewing tobacco, leather, rubber and cheap candy.

Generally speaking, we boys did not use the "big house," except at meals. These powerful and greatly relished repasts were enlivened by the napkin-ring sharpshooting of Uncle Staige. Everybody had a napkin ring in those days, and while the table was being cleared for dessert, Uncle Staige would collect the rings and begin trying to make one after another jump over the flowers in the center. His technique was to press down on the ring with his forefinger, thus causing it to bound upward. Aunt Mary, at the other end of the table, always shook her head sternly in disapproval but with scant results.

Nobody fires napkin rings across the table at Caryswood anymore, for the old place was sold when the last of the Saunderses died. It looks much as it did half a century ago, although the coming of the motor age has wrought important changes. Whereas in earlier days the dirt road crossed the lower part of the yard, and neighbors or transients would exchange greetings from their surreys, buggies or wagons, the modern hard-surface highway is farther from the house and out of sight of the front porch.

But while the aforesaid friendly neighborliness is missed, Evington and Caryswood have been brought much closer together, and places that were almost inaccessible are now within easy motoring distance. It is no longer necessary to drive through cow pastures, opening and shutting gates, and the trip from Caryswood to Evington, which took about an hour in earlier times, can now be made in about four minutes. We have here in microcosm the transformation that has taken place throughout most of America.

Yet as I look back across the years, I see four boys—hatless, coatless and shoeless—strolling down a winding lane, making footprints in the dust.

A rare opportunity to spend the summer of 1912 in and near Paris came in the form of an invitation from Father's half-brother, Thomas Lloyd Dabney. Paralyzing sinus headaches had forced his retirement from the Metropolitan Opera in New York, and he was teaching voice at Sèvres. Under the stage name of Lloyd d'Aubigné he had sung the role of Don Jose in *Carmen* regularly opposite the great Calvé, and had been recognized as one of the Met's finest tenors. When he invited Father and me to visit him for the summer in his villa at Sèvres, we leaped at the opportunity.

The mighty *Titanic* hit an iceberg in April, and went down in the North Atlantic with a loss of 1,517 lives, the worst marine disaster in history. I well remember when Mother came into Father's study, where I was having my daily French lesson, and gave us the shocking news. However, I can't recall that any of us felt apprehension about making the crossing to France. Father and I boarded the train for New York on June 7.

In the smoker we saw some professional gamblers playing cards. Three of them won a lot of money from the fourth, whereupon the latter, evidently suspecting skulduggery, pulled a gun. He informed them that if they didn't return the money in five minutes he would shoot. "You're gonna give it back!" he shouted. They did. The episode is recorded in the diary that I kept throughout the trip.

Uncle Tom had tossed off a request that we bring him two rocking chairs and an ice-cream freezer. We spent hours at Wanamaker's in search of these articles and on the docks trying to get them aboard the *Chicago* of the French Line, on which we were to sail. It was a major chore, the magnitude of which my uncle evidently had not grasped. In addition to all else, I wrote, "the porter didn't have any sense." We finally got the articles on board.

I also described for posterity the following notable nonevents: "We didn't go up in the Singer Building because they charged fifty cents apiece to go up in it. We didn't go up in the Woolworth Building because it wasn't built."

Father had resolved that from the time when we set foot on the *Chicago* we would speak nothing but French. This pious and commendable resolution was forgotten in about fifteen minutes. Nothing further was heard of it.

The trip across the ocean to Le Havre was pleasant in every way, and the sojourn of two months in and near Paris was unforgettable. Father was solicitous throughout for my well-being and happiness. He took me to several circuses as well as to a number of motion-picture shows. Most of all he guided me to the Louvre for countless visits, and to every other important museum in Paris, as well as to all of the principal sights. Sèvres, which is on the Seine, is just a few miles upstream from Paris, and we went into the city on the *bateau mouche* practically every day. It was a liberal education for an eleven-year-old boy.

No greater Francophile ever existed than Father, and he reveled in his daily contacts with the French people, whom he felt to be probably the most civilized on earth. He liked to tell of an incident he witnessed in Paris in 1885 as illustrative of that people's intensity of feeling and their unwillingness to compromise when a principle seemed to be at stake. Evangeline Booth was addressing a crowd, and she exhorted them, "*Cherchez Jésu, cherchez-lui!* [Seek Jesus!]" Whereupon a Frenchman leaped from his seat with clenched fists, and walked down the aisle toward the speaker yelling, "*Jamais! Jamais!* [Never! Never!] *Vive Voltaire! Vive Rousseau!*" Before the evening was over another member of the audience behaved similarly. This appealed to Father, who himself was incapable of remaining silent when he felt called upon to speak out on any subject.

On our daily visits to Paris, we noted the fishermen of the Seine, who sat imperturbably along the riverbank. Not one ever had a nibble during the entire two months, as far as we could observe. Sitting and gazing at the flowing stream may have been their way of relaxing, and it could be that none ever expected to catch anything. On my subsequent visits to Paris over the years, there always seemed to be a fisherman or two sitting on the bank with a rod and line, gazing intently at the water, but never getting a bite.

One of the memorable experiences of our trip was the military review at the Longchamps race track on July 14, Bastille Day. We had tickets, courtesy of the Spanish ambassador, and we arose at five-thirty in order to get to the eight o'clock opening.

When President Fallières of France arrived at that hour, he was given a twenty-one-gun salute, after which the review began. Here were some of the crack units of the French Army. First came thirty-five thousand infantrymen, wearing the traditional horizon-blue uniform with red trimmings. Some were on bicycles, the 1912 version of motorized divisions. There were also pontoon bridges and a few primitive airplanes. Next came the artillery, pulling the far-famed French 75s. And finally the cavalry rode past, making a brave show in their striking uniforms and on their fine mounts. A great cavalry charge, kicking up clouds of dust, was the climactic event.

We were witnessing the last gasps of a world that was dying. Cavalry charges were rapidly becoming obsolete, and in slightly more than two years the Germans would be smashing their way toward Paris, and only the "miracle of the Marne" would save the city. The cataclysm that began in the late summer of 1914 would bring death to millions and change the map of Europe, toppling the Hohenzollerns, the Hapsburgs and the Romanoffs from their thrones. Little did we dream that all this lay in the near future.

Our experiences with the French during the trip were almost uniformly pleasant. True, a waiter who spilled nearly half a bottle of Normandy cider insisted that we pay for the whole bottle, which seemed unreasonable. And there was one other disagreeable incident.

We were at the Hagenbeck Circus and were looking at a monkey in his cage. A man standing near asked Father for his umbrella. Father handed it to him, and the man proceeded to poke at the animal through the bars. The monkey promptly grabbed the umbrella and bit two holes in it. Making no apologies, the man handed the umbrella back to Father without a word. The latter, understandably, was not amused, and pointed to the two holes. All he got from the man was a shrug in the Gallic manner and the words *"Ah oui."*

Father wanted to bring Mother some especially nice presents. He got a bolt of handsome cloth for her to use in having a dress made and one or two other things of that nature. But the gift that he considered most important was an expensive and typically French bronze statuette of a young girl, with flowing garments, perhaps eighteen inches high. It was a charming thing, but wholly unsuited to our home, since it belonged in a mansion with fountains. Mother evidently realized this as soon as she saw the *objet d'art*, for she kept it on a table in her and Father's bedroom. It was out of place there, too, but at least it was out of sight. I never knew what Mother said to Father on the subject, or how she explained keeping the statuette upstairs. If Father was badly upset, as he probably was, he said nothing to me on the subject.

When our visit to Sèvres was over, we took the train for Rouen, stopping off overnight and getting a hasty view of the churches and other sights. On reaching Le Havre, we found that *La Lorraine*, the ship on which we were to travel back to the United States, would be a day late in sailing. So we went to Trouville, across the Seine's mouth from Le Havre, for a brief visit.

En route to New York on board ship Father told me that Mother was "expecting." The actual arrival of the baby was not anticipated for two or three months, but the excitement surrounding our return on the night of September 3 was such that the child was born early the next morning. Alice Saunders Dabney, afterward Alice Dabney Parker, arrived weighing slightly in excess of four pounds. Fortunately it was possible to build up her weight gradually so that her premature birth brought no serious danger to her health. She would be a joy to her parents throughout their lives.

2

Father, Mother—and Lucy

ALICE'S BIRTH HELPED markedly to assuage my parents' grief over the tragic loss of my sister Lucy, who had died some eight months before in her ninth year. Lucy's death was the end of a long and agonizing ordeal for my father and mother.

At age seven she had suddenly been found to have diabetes, which was nothing less than a death warrant in that era, before the discovery of insulin. No child had ever survived diabetes, and from the moment when Lucy's illness was diagnosed, it was realized that her case was hopeless.

When Dr. John Staige Davis first informed Mother that Lucy had this fatal malady and could live only a short time, Mother went to bed for two days. She pretended to Father that she was simply indisposed, but she was in fact prostrated. When she finally summoned the strength she informed Father and they battled it through together.

No hint of the seriousness of Lucy's condition was ever given to her or to me during the entire period of her illness. How my parents managed to preserve their cheerful outward demeanor for nearly two years when this heavy load lay on their hearts is more than I can understand.

Lucy was a pretty, obedient and intelligent child with large brown eyes and a sweet and lovable disposition. She made friends with young and old, and was a great favorite with the entire community, especially after it became known that she had some sort of disability, the terrible seriousness of which was not generally realized. Musically talented, she also wrote well for a child of her age. In the last Christmas of her life she got fifty-five presents and thanked each donor with a separate note.

Although limited to a rigid diet which eliminated all bread, fruit and sugar, and hence all ice cream, cake and candy, Lucy did not complain. Her self-control and discipline would have done credit to any adult. She carried on her normal activities and was exceptionally cheerful and affectionate.

Father and Aunt Lucy taught her every day, just as they did me. Father said in later years that he watched in anguish as she began losing weight and gradually fading away.

Tests were made of her condition at periodic intervals, and my parents awaited the results in a fever of apprehension. On February 10, 1912, she began feeling unwell, and the doctor was sent for. Later in the day she had 102 degrees of temperature, and that night her breathing became difficult and could be heard all over the house. Next day she seemed at first to improve, but the heavy breathing began again. Her mind wandered as the fever mounted.

In the afternoon, she suddenly said to our mother, "Look at them, Mother, don't you see them?" "What, darling?" Mother asked. "Oh Mother, the angels, don't you see how near they are?"

I happened to enter the room soon afterward and found Mother in tears. She tried bravely to smile. It was the only time in my life that I ever saw her cry, and I felt instinctively that calamity was near.

It was. Lucy's breathing became more and more labored. Early the next morning before I had arisen Father and Mother came into my room and got into bed with me. Mother said, "We came to tell you that Lucy left us quietly in the night." They were both in remarkable control of their emotions. Even Father, who normally was much the more emotional of the two, seemed relatively calm.

I sobbed quietly when I received this news, although I was halfway expecting it. Lucy and I had been quite congenial and we seldom fought, but being two years older, I, of course, considered myself superior in every way. Father asked me that day or the next if I wished to see Lucy once more. I said I did not, and Father said he thought I was right in wanting to "remember her as she was in life." He and Mother felt that I ought not to go to the funeral, so I went to "Skinny" Gordon's for the day.

Lucy was buried in the University Cemetery. On her tombstone were engraved the words "Part of the Morning Light."

After Mother's death in 1973 at age ninety-eight, we found in her desk a manuscript in her handwriting entitled "Memoirs of Lucy Davis Dabney." It had apparently lain there for sixty-two years, and none of us knew of its existence. There are hardly any interlineations or corrections, for Mother always wrote with great speed and facility. Copied after her death on a typewriter, it ran to more than twenty double-spaced pages.

This is an extraordinary piece of writing, especially for the restraint with which Mother describes the faint hope and deep despair which alternately gripped her and Father during the ordeal lasting nearly two years. Before Lucy's illness, Mother had been keeping a record of the little girl's doings and sayings, but had allowed it to lapse. The memoir written after Lucy died opens as follows:

"I hardly know what Lucy's age was when I discontinued this brief history of her life . . . and it is hard to take it up again when that life is ended and the rest must be 'she was' instead of 'she is,' 'she did' instead of 'she does.' My impression is that when the last page in this little book was written Lucy was nearly five, and the four years that have passed since showed hers to be a character of such remarkable strength and sweetness that, fresh as her beautiful traits are in all our minds when she has only left us three months, I fear that I may not do them justice. In telling of her I will seem to describe a child so unusual that I know I will be thought to be influenced by my natural feelings of partiality, but I take refuge in the belief that it would hardly be possible to represent her as more perfect than she was—and that the rare combination of self-control, consideration for others, tact and personal charm was such that no one who knew her could feel that I am overdoing it in my picture of her."

Numerous specific examples follow, illustrating the exceptional self-control, sweetness and maturity of this little child. It may well be that Mother exaggerated somewhat while trying not to, but there can be no question that Lucy was remarkable in many ways.

My parents, Lily and Heath Dabney, were crushed by her death, Father perhaps even more than Mother, for such tragedies caused him intense emotional trauma. He remarked to me more than once in after years that he had been in an "agony of grief" over Lucy's death.

In the spring of 1912 the already-mentioned invitation came from Thomas Dabney in France for Father and me to visit him for the summer. Almost certainly Mother was also invited. In any event, she insisted that we go, as it would give Father a change of scene and help him to recover his usual calm and happy disposition. It was, furthermore, a rare opportunity for me. So we went, as described in the preceding chapter.

Throughout his eighty-seven years of life my father exhibited the salient characteristics of the old-fashioned Virginian—chivalry and courtesy, adherence to the principle of *noblesse oblige* and a sense of honor that was paramount above all.

A man of personal charm, an excellent raconteur and mimic, he also loved outdoor sports, and was a good tennis and golf player. In addition, he was chess champion of the University of Virginia faculty. His musical talent was considerable and he played well on the violin. Good music moved him so deeply that he sometimes could not sleep after a concert, and even stayed awake all night. He had a good baritone voice, which he employed in both amateur musicals and the shower bath. He wrote incisive prose and witty verse, and served as editor of the *University of Virginia Magazine* in his student days. And although he seldom took more than one or two drinks, he was a convivial companion, and loved to gather 'round the flowing bowl with friends.

His mother died when he was born and his first wife died when she gave birth to their only child, who likewise failed to survive. Hence motherhood was nothing less than sacred to him. He could scarcely mention the death of his mother or his first wife without tears in his eyes. My mother was his second wife.

One of Heath Dabney's notable characteristics was his candor, his straightforward approach to every issue, his unwillingness to compromise or equivocate. He would not remain silent when he felt that an overriding principle was at stake, or when he thought he might be deemed, by his silence, to be acquiescing in some cause or program that he felt to be wrong. On more than one occasion he risked dismissal from a student body or faculty because of his outspokenness.

For example, when he was a student at the University of Berlin, Heinrich von Treitschke, the famous Prussian chauvinist, was one of his lecturers. The *Herr* professor was positive that he knew the answers to practically everything, and he made some ridiculous statements concerning the United States. Dabney could not let these assertions go unchallenged, and he wrote von Treitschke a tart comment in which he said, in effect, that the professor's statements were nonsense. He thought he would be dismissed from the university, but nothing happened.

After winning his Ph.D. a couple of years later at Heidelberg *multa cum laude*, the highest mark given, Dabney began his teaching career as head of the Department of History at Indiana University. Here he again risked condign punishment when he defied David Starr Jordan, the university's president. Jordan had said to the assembled teaching staff that "the *conscientious* members of the faculty attend chapel regularly." Dabney had not been regular in his attendance, and he felt that Jordan had insulted him. He fired off a letter to the president in which he declared, "Under no conditions will I enter your chapel." Again he thought he was going to be discharged, but nothing more was heard of the matter.

Dabney had been awarded his M.A. by the University of Virginia in 1881. At that time, the University of Virginia M.A. was among the toughest anywhere. It required that the applicant take the highest class in each subject, with no electives. But the only document bearing upon my father's scholastic record at the institution found among his papers after his death related not to his excellent marks in various courses but to his truly extraordinary cutting of classes during the session of 1879–80. A report to his father by James F. Harrison, M.D., chairman of the faculty, sets forth that Dabney cut modern languages no fewer than seven times during the previous month and history eight times. Chairman Harrison commented, "Mr. Dabney should be strongly admonished by his father to regular attendance upon the lectures." His father was mild in his admonishment, perhaps because he and Heath were so devoted to each other. "How is this?" he wrote to his son on the latter's report. "As well as I can remember, I don't think I missed three lectures a year." Heath's reply is lost to posterity. However, he must have mended his ways, or he would never have gotten his degree and gone to Germany for advanced study.

While at the University of Virginia, Dabney became an intimate friend of his fellow student Woodrow Wilson. Father got Wilson into his fraternity, Phi Kappa Psi. The fraternity wanted to have a *soirée,* but never during Father's three years at the institution could they find a time when "everybody had a dollar." Such was the poverty of that post-bellum collegiate generation.

Ray Stannard Baker describes Dabney in his biography of Wilson as the latter's "best friend at the University of Virginia." The two men remained on cordial terms, although Dabney saw little of Wilson after he entered the White House. Many years after Wilson's death, Margaret Axson Elliott, Wilson's sister-in-law, wrote that Dabney was one of five men who "belonged in the inner citadel of his [Wilson's] heart."

The extensive correspondence between Wilson and Dabney after they left the university is in the Alderman Library there. The only letter Wilson wrote Dabney which is not in that collection was dispatched to him when the author of these reminiscences was born. Evidencing the easy relations and spirit of persiflage that governed their friendship, Wilson's congratulatory letter opened with the salutation "O, Thou Very Ass!"

This was more than two decades after their university years, and it was characteristic of Wilson in his relations with those whom he found congenial. Despite prevalent notions, he possessed keen humor and a sense of the ridiculous. When he visited my parents at Edgewood during his term as governor of New Jersey, I was a boy of ten or eleven. I hung around Father's study door listening to the hilarious anecdotes that Wilson was telling. Woodrow Wilson is one of the most misunderstood men in American history, for he is almost universally regarded as humorless and austere. True, he did give that strong impression to persons whom he disliked, and he did not suffer fools gladly. Furthermore, his personality underwent a complete change for the worse in the last years of his life, following his illness and paralysis. This was the chief cause of his breaks with several old political and personal friends, a fact that should be borne in mind.

After making an intensive study of Wilson's personality and human traits for a chapter in the book *The Greatness of Woodrow Wilson*, edited by Em Bowles Alsop (1956), I described him there as follows:

"A man who danced hornpipes on station platforms while campaigning for the presidency and jigs in the White House after his election . . . loved limericks, wrote some good ones himself and recited nonsense verse on many occasions; was one of the best story-tellers of his time. . . ." He was also a mimic of rare talent, and he doubled as a successful football coach at two universities while serving as professor.

When Heath Dabney thought he was about to be fired from Indiana University, he informed Wilson of his apprehension, and Wilson wrote the University of Virginia urging that institution to prepare a place for him to land, if the occasion should arise. It didn't, but he was offered a position on the faculty at Charlottesville in 1889, and his ambition was realized. He spent the rest of his life on that faculty, retiring at age seventy-eight.

Dabney was an interesting and stimulating lecturer. He was also a no-nonsense taskmaster—kind, considerate and understanding with the student who was willing to work, but never showing favoritism or passing a student who had not made the necessary grade.

A football star flunked one of Dabney's history examinations, and came to see his professor in a belligerent mood. When Father told him that he couldn't do anything about his grade, since he had clearly failed, the gridiron hero threatened to "take it to the dean." "Take it to the dean and be hanged!" said Father. That was the end of that.

The late Winston Babb of the Furman University history faculty told me in 1965 that he owed to Professor Dabney's thoughtfulness and kindness the fact that he was able to get his M.A. on schedule in 1936. Babb had a serious illness midway through the year in which he planned to graduate, and was in the hospital for a month. He could never have completed the requirements in that year, he declared, had not his seventy-six-year-old teacher come over to the hospital several times a week for three weeks, sat by his bed and worked with him on the course. Babb was greatly moved by this. He said he knew some people ranked professors by the number of books they wrote, but that "Your father's action meant more to me than any number of scholarly works."

Dabney's tremendous work load at the university, where he taught all the courses in history for several decades (1889–1923) and all the economics for nine years of that time (1897–1906), while serving for eighteen as dean of the Graduate School (1905–23), prevented his doing much original research or writing. In 1888 he published *The Causes of the French Revolution*, a highly regarded work based on lectures delivered by him at Washington & Lee University two years previously. In 1898, *John Randolph: A Character Sketch* appeared. Thereafter his published writings consisted almost entirely of articles or letters in the newspapers. He was asked by Johns Hopkins University to write a history of Reconstruction and by the Thomas Y. Crowell Company to write a life of Robert E. Lee, but he was never able to finish either book, owing to his overwhelming burden of work. The enormous amount of time he devoted to teaching his children languages also helped to make such creative writing extremely difficult.

Dabney was conservative in his views on economics. When William Jennings Bryan ran for the presidency in 1896 on a platform that included "free silver at 16 to 1," Dabney regarded this supposed panacea for the nation's ills as economic madness. In opposing Bryan, he was thrown into association with Joseph Bryan of Richmond, the leader of the Palmer and Buckner "gold bug" forces and no relation of William Jennings.

Joseph Bryan had been a friend of Dabney's for several years, and the latter had been a guest at house parties at Brook Hill, the Stewart estate near Richmond, where numerous Bryans were always in evidence. It was at a Brook Hill house party that Dabney met his future wife, Lily Davis of Willoughby, Albemarle County.

Bryan's sons were students in Dabney's classes at the University of Virginia, and they were on a footing of complete congeniality with "Uncle Dabs," as they called him. Their aunts, the Stewart ladies, invited him and his wife regularly to their lavish Christmas house parties, lasting several days or a week. The large Brook Hill residence was festively decorated for the occasion, mint juleps and other libations were in great profusion, the food was delectable, the ambience delightful. All and sundry were summoned to the dining room in the reverberating baritone of the Negro butler. His intonation of the word "Lun-n-n-n-ch!" was memorable.

Original verse by various members of the group was read at the house parties, songs from such operettas as those of Gilbert and Sullivan were warbled and diverse other varieties of entertainment were provided by the assembled guests.

One of Dabney's more notable productions was his fervent apostrophe to Scotch whiskey, inspired by the King William V.O.P. brand, delivered at a Brook Hill house party in January 1900.

It is too long to be quoted in full, but three lines provide the general theme:

> *Milk is for babes; for men, SCOTCH is the pap,*
> *The juice of liberty—aye, freedom's sap.*
> *Let's put all Caledonia on tap!*

It did not appear seemly for a university professor to be publicly identified with such verses, so Dabney did not sign the copy

which Joseph Bryan had printed and framed. It hung in the bar
of Richmond's Westmoreland Club for thirty-seven years, and
when that organization closed its doors, the framed poem was
transferred to the bar of the Commonwealth Club.

Uncle Dabs was welcomed to a Brook Hill house party at
Christmas, 1903, in an amusing bit of verse by Charles Cotes-
worth Pinckney, Jr. It is a parody on T. R. Ybarra's *Lay of Ancient Rome* and follows:

*An Ode in the Latin Tongue to the Genial
and Erudite Professor*

Oh, welcome to our Dabibus,
He, Hot-Stuff is you bettum,
Come rest your toga on a rack
And light a cigarettum;
Observe his diamond studibus
And elegant cravattum,
His maxima-cum-laude shirt
And very stylish hattum.

When he was young he used to bet
Upon the racing equi,
He got there sometimes, and again
He got it in the neckqui;
And I have heard at times he winked
At puellas on the Forum
And to their great delight hath made
Those Goo-Goo oculorum.

S.P.Q.R. and V.O.P.
Welcome, thrice welcome Dabibus,
It adds much to our Christmas cheer
If we can just you habebus.

The contributions that Dabney made to the general gaiety of
the Brook Hill house parties led sixteen of the participants to give
him a handsome sterling-silver loving cup, with bone handles,
holding about half a gallon, and inscribed "To 'Uncle Dabs,'

From His Nephews of the Apollinaris Club"—the name face-
tiously adopted by the Brook Hill group.

From the beginning, Dabney was an all-out foe of state-wide
prohibition as well as of the Eighteenth Amendment and the Vol-
stead Act. He did not regard such enactments as within the
proper purview of legislative bodies, and was a national director of
the Association Against the Prohibition Amendment. While he
recognized the harmful effects of overindulgence, and had nothing but contempt for men or women who got drunk, he felt that
temperate, sociable drinking had positive benefits. A drink or two,
he believed, tended to break down barriers between strangers and
promote pleasant social intercourse.

The correctness of the latter theory would seem to have been
borne out by the friends he made when crossing to Europe alone
on a transatlantic liner in 1933. He began exchanging pleasantries at the brass rail with one of the male passengers, and the result was that Father and this man, together with several other
congenial spirits, never went to bed before 2 A.M. throughout the
voyage. Father, who was then seventy-three, sang songs and told
jokes with "the boys," as he put it, until far into the night.

He was jovial, witty and outgoing, although those who did not
know him sometimes got the impression that he was of a stern
disposition. This was because he had unusually thick, bushy and
mobile eyebrows, so that the merest furrowing of his brow often
appeared to be an ominous frown.

Heath Dabney wrote an article for *Commerce and Finance* of
New York, at the editor's invitation, expressing the view that the
Eighteenth Amendment was an unconstitutional outrage. In the
piece he referred to "this unconstitutional sumptuary statute,
masquerading under the aegis of the Constitution, and upheld by
a strange alliance of preachers, moonshiners, bootleggers, manu-
facturers of 'soft drinks' and other seekers after the dollar." *Commerce and Finance* distributed copies to 280 daily newspapers and
twoscore magazines and periodicals. The Anti-Saloon League
demanded in its official organ that Dabney be fired from the University of Virginia faculty on the ground that his statement

35

"proves his lack of capacity to be a professor of history in any school or university." The sentiment was echoed in the Virginia General Assembly by Samuel Adams, member of the House of Delegates from Halifax County. Nothing came of it, of course.

Heath Dabney was always gallant toward the fair sex. He said that, as far as he could recall, he had never told but one lie, "and that was to protect a lady." He preferred ladies who were shapely, saying jocosely, "I don't like girls who rattle in my arms." He abhorred the skinny women in the fashion advertisements and said, "They look like cockroaches."

Lady Russell, who, under the name "Elizabeth" wrote *Elizabeth and Her German Garden*, was a frequent dinner or luncheon guest at Edgewood during her and Father's latter years. Pretty, attractive and witty, she flirted with him and said he reminded her of her first husband, whom she called "The Man of Wrath." There was one especially memorable meal when Lady Russell brought her dog into the Edgewood dining room, picked ticks from his hide during the repast and dropped them one by one into her glass of water.

Her sudden death occurred a few weeks later. It prevented a chess game that she and Father had scheduled.

Father was always devoted to children, and they returned his affection. His five grandchildren, who were his special favorites, all called him "Fofo." Father had a way with children. In 1933 he was in a garden in Rothenburg, Germany, and he saw a small German boy whom he didn't know. He got into a conversation with the child and soon had him laughing and calling him Fofo.

"I adore children, and I think they know it and like me," he once remarked; and when the children in question were his own or his grandchildren, his devotion was doubly great.

He was never too busy to read to his grandsons and granddaughters, to tell them stories or to play with them. He would sing them the most nonsensical songs or recite the most ridiculous rhymes.

The birth of his grandson and namesake, Richard Heath II, in 1941 was the cause of great rejoicing on his part. A few friends around the university were invited in for libations in honor of the occasion. Father, who was eighty-one, sought to become acquainted with little Heath as promptly as possible. In 1947, a few months before he died, he remarked to me that he wanted so much to know six-year-old Heath better, and he added sadly, "I've got so little time."

Professors are proverbially absent-minded, and Father was no exception. A notable example was when he addressed the assembled university students and faculty on his correspondence with Woodrow Wilson. After a few opening remarks, he reached into his pocket for the letters. Lo and behold, he had left them at home! A howl went up from the audience, and Father was deeply embarrassed. However, he was so familiar with the letters that he was able to go on with his address.

His absent-mindedness was also reflected in his automobile driving. For years he did not want a car, since the tires on the early models went flat and the cars had other defects. At that time he regarded automobile travel as the most uncomfortable mode of transportation known to man and declared, "I infinitely prefer an oxcart." Finally, when automobiles had been perfected and Father could assemble the money (his highest salary throughout his career was $6,000), he purchased one. Soon he was zooming around the university and Charlottesville at speeds that terrified the natives.

Probably the most unforgettable episode involving his driving occurred one day when he endeavored to park the car in his garage. Instead of stepping on the brake, he stepped on the accelerator, with the result that the car took out the whole back of the garage and dropped over into a three-foot-deep trench at the rear of the structure. Father was depressed for days. After the building had been put back together, a railroad tie was placed inside it and in front of the rear wall to prevent a recurrence.

Another incident involving Father's virtuosity as a chauffeur occurred when he was driving back alone from Hot Springs, where he had undergone massage treatments for sciatica. It was a hot July day and he was about seventy-five years of age. En route to

Charlottesville, he had a flat tire. He got out and pumped it up laboriously in the heat, and set out again. Once more the tire went down, and he repeated the performance. A third flat caused him to pump it up a third time. Finally he arrived at Edgewood, drenched with perspiration and pretty well exhausted. "Didn't you have a spare tire?" someone inquired. "Oh yes," was Father's cheerful reply, "but I was saving it for an emergency."

At about this time his driving became so erratic that we feared for his life and that of others on the road, so we prevailed upon him to stop driving entirely. He didn't want to, but he agreed.

Father's strength and physical endurance were remarkable. He was about five feet ten inches tall, an inch shorter than that in his latter years, weighed about 165 or 170 and was "tough as a pine knot." When he was fifty-six and I was sixteen, we swept snow from the ice on the pond across Rugby Road, preparatory to filling our ice house. I thought I was in pretty good physical condition, but Father just about ran me into the ground as he brushed the snow from the glittering surface at a dizzy pace. I ended with my tongue hanging out and he was not even out of breath. His stamina was also evident when, occasionally fearing that he was late for his class, he would tuck his book under his arm and jog over to the university, a distance of half a mile.

In World War I, he and I made a minor contribution to the war effort by rising at five o'clock on a number of mornings in June 1917 and raking rocks from our garden in order to prepare it for planting. Once more his endurance was greater than mine.

Upon the outbreak of the war, he was made vividly conscious of the lectures he had heard in his student days in Berlin under the bellicose Prussian, von Treitschke. They helped greatly to convince him that Germany had launched the war deliberately in a grab for world power. Dabney had seen young Germans packing von Treitschke's classroom and absorbing his appeals to the Kaiser to overrun any small country that Germany might need. The Dutch empire struck von Treitschke as especially tempting, and he exhorted "the young giant, Germany" to "take Holland, and we'll have an empire ready-made." So when Germany invaded

Belgium in 1914, it seemed logical to assume that she was following his advice.

While no one can condone the atrocities that the Germans undoubtedly committed in Belgium, Dabney was mistaken in believing that they were solely guilty of starting the war. He did not have access at the time to the archives that were thrown open after the close of hostilities and which showed a much more complex picture, with other powers sharing in the war guilt.

If Father was moved by one thing more than any other during the conflict, it was the courage of the French Army, especially at Verdun. His voice would tremble as he spoke of the thousands who laid down their lives before forts Vaux and Douaumont. Mention of the "Watchword of Verdun—*On ne passe pas!*" sometimes reduced him to tears.

Father spoke before the end of hostilities at various important meetings in New York and Philadelphia, usually for the purpose of arousing sentiment on behalf of the League of Nations. Ex-President William H. Taft presided over these gatherings.

Dabney also addressed several such meetings after the war. At one such assemblage in New York an amusing incident occurred. Taft slipped a cog in introducing Father, for he referred to him as "a very eminent divine." Several of Father's intimate friends were in the audience, and they were in stitches, for they were aware that he probably hadn't been inside a church for twenty years. Father rose to the occasion, saying, "I greatly appreciate the introduction Mr. Taft has given me. I knew he was the Unitarian Pope, but I was not aware that even the Unitarian Pope could elevate me to the lofty status of a very eminent divine." He then went on with his speech. When he sat down, Taft responded jovially. "Of course," said he, "I erred in describing Dr. Dabney, but since he has pronounced me the Unitarian Pope, I hereby confer upon him the rank of archbishop."

Heath Dabney was in advance of his time in his advocacy of a League of Nations with powers of enforcement, but he was ultraconservative in some other directions. For example, he was steadfast in his opposition to the admission of women to the University of Virginia. It was his feeling that the university was distinctly masculine in its intellectual and social climate, and that the admission of women would be harmful. He disagreed strongly with my editorial advocacy of a federal antilynching bill in the 1930s, since he saw such a bill as an invasion of states' rights, and he was also highly skeptical of the ability of most blacks to benefit from a college education. Yet in his last years he agreed with my campaign, launched in 1943, for the abolition of segregation on Virginia's streetcars and buses.

Dedicated as he was to the well-being of his students, and willing as he was to go the last mile with any of them who revealed a desire to improve their minds, he was unhappy over what he took to be most students' lack of interest in their studies and their failure to acquire a general education. At Indiana University he was shocked when he asked sixty sophomores to name the opposing sides in the Battle of Marathon and only two could do so. He came sadly to the conclusion that most students had no zeal for learning. "As far as I can tell," he remarked on more than one occasion, "the average student doesn't want to learn anything whatever." Yet if the name of one of his former pupils happened to come into the conversation, he would almost invariably refer nostalgically and with obvious affection to this perhaps once wayward and inattentive youth as "one of my old students."

Evidencing his ability to laugh at himself, he kept a letter written him by one of his dissatisfied pupils at Indiana University. It follows:

> Prof. Dabney
> Kind Teacher
> I am only to glad to drop history, so from this time I will not be under your instruction, Which I regret, But I detest the study.
> > With the best wishes of one of your studients.
> > I remain your's ect.

The foregoing was merely one of a collection of extraordinary documents that he had in his archives, and that he brought out fairly frequently for the amusement of guests. He had, for example, a list of answers on historical subjects given by public school teachers who were examined at the University of Virginia in the summer of 1909. Here are a few samples:

Q. Give some of the characteristics of the American Indian.
A. Some said they did not come from Adams and Eves. Some said they come from the North, some from the South. Some said they even come up from under the ground.
Q. Mention some of the chief events of President Theodore Roosevelt's administration.
A. He served his term out and was not assassinated.
Q. Tell what you can of the Missouri Compromise.
A. Missouri promaced us all the land all a long the Atlantic coast to Florida back west to the River. So we taken it.

The teachers were asked to name three prominent Virginians and write a paragraph about each. The three "Virginians" chosen by one teacher were Thomas Jefferson, Abraham Lincoln and Columbus.

A prize exhibit in Father's collection, which he delighted to read to guests, was a letter from an Italian immigrant, living in the New York area, to a company from which he had ordered a pump. This memorable communiqué follows:

Dear Mr. ———

I got de pump, but why for god's sake dont you send me no hanle. My customer he yell like hell by de wheel, de pump she no go. What de hell I go do? Please send de hanle at once.

Yours truly,
Antonio Scalminio

P.S. Since I write dese letter I find de goddam hanle in de box. Excuse *me!*

Gilbert and Sullivan's operettas were among his prime favorites. He could sing or recite many of the famous songs, and when the D'Oyly Carte Company came over from England, he went regularly to Washington with friends to attend one or more of the performances.

Heath Dabney even sang Gilbert and Sullivan numbers on the golf course, notably at Buena Vista Springs, Pennsylvania, where he visited several times as the guest of Fred S. Valentine of Richmond. When he made a good score he would dance about the green and warble one of his favorites from the operettas. The caddies were so amused that they came to look forward to these diversions. The songs that he usually sang on these occasions were "Tit-Willow," especially if he made a birdie, or "He Remains an Englishman."

Edgewood during these years, and long before, was a hospitable home for our relatives, both old and young. It was characteristic of that era for sisters, cousins and aunts to sojourn for weeks, months and even years with their kin. Aunt Lucy Davis was with us at Edgewood until her death in 1925. Mother's sister, Alice Chancellor Davis, lived there until her marriage in 1917. At least two young male relatives were at Edgewood throughout their college careers. Other kinspeople and friends, especially from Caryswood, frequently stayed for days or weeks. All this takes no account of the innumerable guests who came for meals.

David A. Booth, an English-born student at the university who lived at Edgewood for several years, wrote an extraordinarily perceptive and well-done article about Father for the university *Alumni News* (November 1956).

"His home was a continual coming and going of friends, both young and old, famous and unknown, who came to visit, to stay, to live," Booth said. "On his retirement, many students wrote, recalling Sunday night suppers in his gracious home, the long talks on the moonlit porch, or in the garden on a summer's evening."

Booth went on to declare that "for many years there was no one at the university who typified more completely the ideals for which the university stood than Heath Dabney." He added that Dabney "was just and candid, integrity was his strength and honor his virtue. He was thoughtful of others, without affectation, and liberally endowed with the quality so lacking in so many of us, the quality of wisdom."

At age seventy, Dabney submitted his resignation from the faculty, as is required. But President Alderman replied that he had no idea of accepting it. So he continued to teach for eight more years, for a total of forty-nine at that institution. By then the burden of lecturing and correcting examination papers had become great and he remarked frequently upon the fact. His family saw that it was time for him to retire, but he was reluctant to do so. Apparently he wanted to fill out a half century on the university faculty. However, he finally agreed to hand in his resignation.

To his surprise, he found that he was quite content with his new-found leisure. He still spoke with fondness and nostalgia of his "old students" and was never happier than when being greeted by one of them on the university grounds or in his home. But he did not yearn to return to the classroom.

He lived another eight years, happy in his family and his friends. David Booth has given us a vignette:

"He could still be seen walking towards the Alderman Library, dressed in tweeds, cane in hand, an old hat covering his snow white hair. His neighbors vied with each other to pick him up in their cars and take him down Rugby Road, such was the love that he inspired."

One day in February 1947, Heath Dabney fell down a steep flight of cellar steps. He was never the same again, and his physical and mental powers began to fail markedly. On May 16, 1947, he died. He was buried in the University Cemetery near his own father and his little daughter Lucy.

Tributes poured in from many directions in the form of letters, telegrams and editorials in the press. A letter from one of his "old students," a Rhodes scholar, is typical of many:

"Not only did Doctor Dabney make history live again, but in addition to his superlative attributes as a teacher, his own charm and personality will always keep him alive and vivid in my memory."

Another said that "with the possible exception of my own father, he had more influence in forming my point of view in life and the world in general than anyone," while still another declared that "he had a greater influence on my intellectual development than any other person."

The Norfolk *Ledger-Dispatch* summed up his career as follows:

"The real measure of such a remarkable man is to be found in the quality of his scholarship, in the respect for intellectuality which his teaching and his direction of graduate students gave, in the play of his rich personality on thousands of lives, and in his contribution to his chosen subject of history, to the life of the mind in Virginia and the South, and in the nation too. The whirlwinds which have swept through the world in the years of Dr. Dabney's retirement, powerful though they were, could not shake the monument of achievement and influence which such a life represents."

Father was almost fifteen years older than Mother, and Mother lived twenty-seven years after his death, until age ninety-eight. She remained at Edgewood, and nearly always had a university student as a roomer. Relatives were frequent guests. Her sister Alice, Mrs. John S. White, was widowed at about the time of Father's death and moved next door.

Mother and Aunt Alice had grown up at Willoughby (sometimes spelled Willowby), the thousand-acre farm in Albemarle County acquired after the Civil War by their grandfather, Captain Eugene Davis. He built the house in 1871. It is considerably changed and the surrounding land has been cut up for land development. Davis served as a captain of cavalry in the Civil War and was taken prisoner at Yellow Tavern. He was confined in Elmira Prison, New York, where he suffered extremely from hunger and cold. Sometimes reduced to eating rats, he also found it necessary on one occasion to sleep with a fellow prisoner who had smallpox in order to keep from freezing. Miraculously he did not contract the malady.

Eugene Davis's brother, the Reverend Richard T. Davis, chaplain in a Confederate cavalry regiment, may have set some sort of record, for "he charged at the head of the regiment in every battle, not armed cap-a-pie like the warrior Bishop of Beauvais, but armed with his Christian fortitude. . . . He had neither weapons of offense or defense." The foregoing is from a published account written by a member of the regiment.

Mother and Aunt Alice were the daughters of Eugene Davis's

son, James Maury Morris Davis, and the former Alice Fleming Saunders of Caryswood, the old Saunders place described in the previous chapter. Jim Davis enlisted at fifteen as private in the Confederate Army and served until the close of hostilities in the famous First Virginia Artillery, Rockbridge Battery. He then matriculated at the University of Virginia.

Judging from his surviving likenesses, Jim Davis was certainly not handsome, quite the contrary. However, he seems to have been exceptionally charming. His attractive personality and, later, his great ability as a lawyer are attested on every hand in letters of the period. His popularity with his fellow students at the university—most or all of whom had just been mustered out of the Confederate forces—is evident in the following passage from the memoir that John Stewart Bryan, publisher of the Richmond newspapers and president of the College of William & Mary, wrote concerning his father, the distinguished Joseph Bryan:

"Jim Davis . . . was as brilliant as he was amusing. . . . His room was by common consent the chosen gathering place of a large coterie of friends who became a select band by cutting their names on his study table." (This much-whittled-on piece of furniture is in my library today, and one of my most prized possessions. Thirty-three of my grandfather's fellow students carved their initials on it.) Joe Bryan, who had just come out of John S. Mosby's famous troop of cavalry raiders, was the most artistic whittler of the group. He was perhaps Jim Davis's most intimate friend. In 1870 they began practicing law simultaneously in Richmond, and Davis was happy to let Bryan operate out of his office temporarily, while both of them slept there behind a screen.

Davis's marriage to Alice Saunders was short-lived, for soon after their second daughter was born, his wife died. He was almost prostrated with grief, but remained outwardly cheerful to an amazing degree, as is apparent from many surviving letters. Yet he insisted on visiting Alice's grave in Hollywood Cemetery every day for years, no matter what the weather. When he contracted tuberculosis, some believed it was brought on, or at least aggravated, by his visits to the cemetery.

45

Joe Bryan went with him on a trip to Florida, hoping that this would benefit him, but all efforts to cure his disease were futile. When he died in 1883, a legal career that had attracted extraordinary praise was cut short.

During his last illness, his friends gave touching evidences of concern. Bryan was constant in his attentions, and Thomas Nelson Page, the novelist, wrote offering to come and nurse him at Willoughby. When he died, Joe Bryan wired, "Special train will arrive in Charlottesville after twelve to bring remains and party here on time. Buy no tickets all expenses paid here." Bryan, by then, was well-to-do, but for him to send a special train seventy miles and back to bring his friend's body to Richmond for burial was a truly amazing testimonial of affection.

James Davis's two little daughters, aged eight and seven—my mother and aunt-to-be—were reared at Willoughby by their grandfather, Eugene Davis, and his unmarried sisters, Lucy and Elizabeth. Davis operated a large dairy farm, and supplied a broad area of the community with milk. He was widely beloved and admired, and a kindly counselor and benefactor to many.

Joseph Bryan said Eugene Davis "spent an hour in prayer at noon each day and was the best man I ever knew." He had suffered one personal tragedy after another, beginning with the murder of his father on the university grounds by a rioting student, which left his mother with seven children. His young wife, the former Patsy Morris of Green Springs, Louisa County, died when she was only twenty-three after the birth of their third child. All three of their children died young, the first at age seven, the second at age thirty-six and the third at twenty-seven. Despite these endless sorrows, Eugene Davis carried on with unflagging courage and humor. His letters are shot through with originality, liveliness and wit.

Several young male relatives lived at Willoughby for years, during their student days, at no cost whatever to them, and walked two and a half miles daily to the university and the same distance back. No automobiles whisked them around the university grounds from one class to another, as seemed to be an essential element of student life almost everywhere a century later.

Eugene Davis died in 1894 while on his knees at prayer. My mother, then nineteen, never held it against him that he disapproved of dancing and theater-going, and she loved him so deeply that when he died, as she put it years later, "I thought I would never smile again." The tributes that poured in for this private citizen who had never been widely known or famous were extraordinary. One newspaper account said that his funeral "was perhaps the largest ever witnessed in this city," while another described it as "one of the largest ever seen in this county." Professor Francis H. Smith of the University of Virginia, writing in that institution's *Alumni Bulletin*, said that the funeral procession was "nearly a mile in length," and that one would have surmised that it was not the funeral of a private citizen but "someone in high office or perhaps some beloved Confederate general."

Additional light is expertly shed on the characters and personalities of many Davises and Morrises in "Eugene Davis—a Biographical Sketch, and Letters of the Davis and Morris Families, 1824–1893, Selected and Edited by Alice Dabney Parker," on file at the University of Virginia's Alderman Library. Eugene Davis's wife, Patsy Morris, who died young, was one of many members of the Morris family who lived in the Green Springs area of Louisa County. She lived at the place known as Green Springs, while other members of the Morris family were at Hawkwood and Grassdale. This area was the center of much controversy in the 1970s involving plans for a penal institution there and for the digging of vermiculite, both of which were deemed by many to be extremely damaging to that beautiful, unspoiled section of Virginia.

The religious heritage transmitted by Eugene Davis and his whole generation to their descendants was kept alive by my mother, to the extent that she was a regular attendant at church throughout her life. But such a thing as praying for an hour at noon each day, as Eugene Davis did, was rare in the nineteenth century and practically unknown thereafter. Davis family letters to and from Willoughby show a constant concern for the spiritual lives of the writers, to a degree well-nigh nonexistent in similar cir-

cles in our own day. It is one of the things that differentiate the
nineteenth century sharply from the twentieth.

My mother was extremely fond of people, and she loved parties.
I have seldom seen anyone who enjoyed them so much, or who
derived such pleasure from having guests staying in the house or
coming for meals. This was true both before and after my father's
death. Father was decidedly gregarious, but not quite to the
same extent.

Fortunately, there were almost always a couple of much-
cherished black factotums to carry on in the kitchen and around
the place. Mother had never had to do any cooking, with the result that, as already noted, she knew absolutely nothing about it.
When she was approximately ninety, there was a brief interim
when no kitchen help was available. She wrote us cheerfully that
she was subsisting mainly on applesauce and potato chips.

Her love of people was seen in the fact that if she went to a
party of any kind, she would move about as much as possible. In
her last years, when she was in her eighties or even her nineties, I
would suggest that she sit down, but invariably she refused. She
was afraid she would thereby fail to see some person or persons
whom she wanted to see—probably not for any particular reason
but merely to chat. And she was determined to chat with the
maximum number of her friends.

Those friends were legion. She had a great gift for attracting
people to her and holding them. On her travels she often struck
up acquaintances with strangers, corresponded with them thereafter and exchanged visits with them. They might be members of
the English aristocracy or persons of a much lower social status.
In the latter category was the hall porter at a London hotel where
Mother stayed several times. She invited him to visit her in Virginia. He came to this country some years later, made it a point to
include Charlottesville in his itinerary and took a meal at Edgewood. He was treated, of course, like any other guest.

A friend or chance acquaintance arriving in Charlottesville had
only to telephone Mother to be invited immediately to be her
guest for an indefinite stay. Her characteristic greeting was "Oh,

my *dear*, where are you? When are you coming to me?" How her domestics put up so cheerfully with this sort of thing is something of a mystery. The house might be full already, but Mother seemed to feel that there was always room for more. If the newly arrived person or persons happened to be British, so much the better. Mother was as partial to the English as Father was to the French. So long as she could visit England, which she did many times, she was entirely willing to forgo visiting any other country.

Always younger than her years and anxious to remain so, Mother did not relish the idea of being called "Grandma" or "Granny" by her grandchildren. When our first-born was old enough to speak to her, my wife made the excellent suggestion that "Nona," Italian for "grandmother," be the form of address. Mother approved the proposal with alacrity, and was "Nona" thereafter to all her grandchildren. (In Italy they spell it *nonna*, but we did not know that.)

Her friendships embraced all age groups. A succession of ten or more university students stayed at Edgewood as roomers after Father's death, and her rapport with these young men was exceptional. At least one, who was always strapped for funds, borrowed money from her and, I regret to say, seems never to have paid it back. But this was decidedly untypical, and nearly all of these students corresponded with her after they were graduated, telling of their progress, their marriages and their children. Some brought the children to see her. When she died there were touching expressions from several concerning the great influence she had been in their lives.

Mother was a voracious reader. For decades she belonged to the University Book Club and was a member of the committee that chose the new books to be bought and circulated. As time went on, the novels became more and more earthy in their love scenes and in the printing of material that in earlier days had been completely beyond the pale. Mother shook her head sadly, but the Book Club remained up to date in its selections.

Mother's generosity to relatives who really had no claim upon her was amazing. A tenth cousin, or a cousin by marriage, would be found to be in financial straits, and Mother would send him or her a check from her none too ample means. The fact that the person was, vaguely, "a relation," however remote, was sufficient, she felt, to warrant this monetary assistance. Similarly, her Negro servants, who were paid the modest going wage, could count on her for more than modest assistance in case of emergency. For example, a man who had been in her employ for years had large hospital bills. She paid them unhesitatingly in full.

Mother was a dedicated fighter for good causes, such as the preservation of old neighborhoods and the retention of as many trees as possible along Charlottesville streets. When well into her nineties, she appeared at City Council meetings on behalf of trees and the preservation of early Charlottesville.

She was a devoted worker at the University Hospital, and for years was president of the Hospital Circle. One important phase of her duties was to conduct an annual rummage sale.

Arrangement of funerals for poor families of her acquaintance was another of her good deeds. She knew how to see that everything was done decently and in good order, but as inexpensively as practicable.

An exceptionally interesting letter writer, she wrote with fluency and ease. She was punctilious in sending thank-you notes to the numerous persons who invited her to functions of one sort or another. To illustrate: she spent eight days with us in Richmond in March and April 1963. Then eighty-eight years old, she went to ten luncheons, dinners or teas and declined five additional invitations for lack of time. When she left, ten thank-you notes were piled neatly on my desk, ready for mailing.

Five years later, when she was ninety-three, Mother and Mrs. Thomas J. Wertenbaker, widow of the widely known history professor at Princeton, flew to London for a two-week stay. After their arrival, they found that they were to be chauffeured about in the Rolls Royce of an English friend who insisted on transporting them to the five nighttime London shows for which they had tickets. When they left the United States, they had had no idea how they would get to and from these theatrical performances, but they took off anyway. One might say that they landed on their feet.

On Mother's ninety-fifth birthday, Dumas Malone, author of the definitive life of Thomas Jefferson, and his wife, Elisabeth, gave her a party in their home at the University of Virginia. Dr. Malone offered the following toast.

"I claim the privilege of proposing a toast to our guest of honor. I do not emphasize the fact that this is her birthday, for in her case birthdays don't count. She has the spirit of eternal youth, and her joy in life has not diminished perceptibly with the passing years. . . . We are fortunate that she could find a place for this party in her crowded social program. She is quite at home in the modern world. This is the more remarkable because she is the personal embodiment of the best traditions of this ancient commonwealth. We salute her as a great lady and take this occasion to remind her that she is very dear to all of us. Let us drink to Mrs. Dabney."

It was shortly after this that Mother began failing perceptibly, as was inevitable. Her hearing and eyesight became quite bad, and her general health declined. As with almost all persons who reach extreme old age, she grew more positive in her opinions and less tolerant of disagreement. At times she was alert mentally and at other times not.

But she was determined until the last few years of her life to have as many guests as possible, especially on Sunday. She could no longer follow the table conversation closely because of her deafness, but she loved to have friends around her. The constant presence of a woman companion made it possible for her to remain in her own home, which she was most anxious to do.

When death finally came, St. Paul's Church at the university was virtually filled, despite a pouring rain, and many went to the cemetery in the deluge. Messages came from far and near.

"A great lady who reminded us of more gracious times" and "the end of an era" were two of the recurrent themes in these letters of condolence. She had been instrumental in founding the Charlottesville Chapter of the English-Speaking Union, and numerous contributions were received to help finance that organization's Lily H. Dabney Exchange Student Scholarship, named some years before in her honor. The trustees of the Episcopal

High School near Alexandria, Virginia, who were in session shortly after her death, passed formal resolutions in gratitude for her having been a "friend and counselor" to so many E.H.S. boys. Several young people who had known her requested small souvenirs, such as a handkerchief or a book. Peter Taylor, the nationally known short-story writer and poet, a member of the University of Virginia English faculty, contributed a poem, *Three Heroines*, to the *Virginia Quarterly Review* and dedicated it "To the memory of Lily Heth Dabney, another of my heroines."

In nothing have I been more fortunate than in my parents. I shall always to be grateful for the example they set for me and the stimulus they provided. When I think of the loving care and the cultural advantages that were afforded me, and contrast these with the bleak surroundings and cultural desert into which a slum child is born, I cannot fail to count my blessings.

3

School Days, School Days . . .

IT WAS THE afternoon of September 14, 1914, and my father and I were walking the three miles from Alexandria to the Episcopal High School, where I was enrolled for the coming session. We had arrived by train from Charlottesville, and Father decided that we would go out to the school on foot instead of hiring a conveyance. A three-mile walk was nothing unusual in those days, but it did seem slightly bizarre for us to be making our initial appearance in this fashion at Episcopal High. On top of all else, we weren't supposed to be there until the following day. I never knew why Father chose to show up twenty-four hours ahead of schedule. One other boy also jumped the gun by an entire day with his father, but they didn't arrive on foot. This was John Taylor Lewis, Jr., of Cedar Grove, Clarksville, Virginia—my friend for more than sixty years.

The trunk which bore my belongings came out to school in a wagon. It was the same battered piece of luggage that had served my father back in the seventies when, as a youth, he had visited his grandfather, Thomas Dabney, at the old family place, Burleigh, near Jackson, Mississippi. Thomas Dabney, an extremely prosperous cotton planter, had been ruined by the Civil War, but he carried on gamely during Reconstruction in the face of terrible adversity.

As Father and I walked out to E.H.S. I do not recall that I was particularly apprehensive, although I was aware that I would probably be homesick, like virtually all the other "rats," or first-year boys. En route to the school we passed through what was known as Mudtown, a collection of squalid shacks obliterated many years later by the explosive expansion of Alexandria and the whole adjacent region of northern Virginia across the Potomac from Washington. In 1914 the school grounds were surrounded on three sides by open fields, and on the other by the Virginia Theological Seminary. Today the three sides are closely built up, and E.H.S. is a 130-acre oasis in the middle of a conglomeration of trunk highways, supermarkets and high-rise apartments.

Many years ago it came to be known as "the High School," possibly because it was the only high school in Virginia for decades after its founding in 1839 by Episcopal clergymen and laymen. The term is less used today, partly perhaps because of the jeers that it evoked from students or alumni of other preparatory schools, who referred to it laughingly as "T.H.S."

Sometimes called a "Dixie Eaton," Episcopal High is undoubtedly one of the foremost preparatory schools in the United States. The physical equipment today is superlative, but until a short time ago it was not in the top bracket; for many years, in fact, the facilities were distinctly Spartan. Prior to 1914 the boys were breaking ice on their buckets in the morning. When I arrived in the fall of that year, advances had been made through construction of two new dormitories, a gymnasium, an athletic field and twelve tennis courts. The dormitories actually had hot and cold running water, showers and "electric lights throughout," as stated in the school's advertising. Yet the living quarters of the boys in those new structures were decidedly austere.

Each boy had what was really a stall, with a green curtain hanging across the entrance. The stall was about six feet wide, and there was a bed, a small rush-bottom chair with no arms and a wooden press for clothes. The stall had a window in one end, but no electric light and no desk. The only light at night was in the ceiling of the long corridor on which the bunks faced. It was hoped that the boys would use these quarters for sleeping purposes only, and would stay out of them in the afternoons when classes were not being held. Athletic, literary or other activities were supposed to engage their attention each day after school. Everybody had to attend study hall at night.

The school trustees and administrators were not being parsimonious in providing these limited facilities. They simply did not have the money to do more. Tuition for each of my three years was $400. Despite this low figure, lack of funds almost prevented me from enrolling for the session of 1914–15. It was only because my father got an increase in salary at the last minute that he was able to send me off to school.

But if the living quarters and recreational facilities at E.H.S. in 1914 were somewhat primitive by latter-day standards, they were almost luxurious compared with those available to the boys before the Civil War. In that era, furthermore, the rod was not spared, either for misbehavior or unsatisfactory recitations. Young delinquents stood huddled by one of the few stoves in the place, awaiting summons to the headmaster's office. They usually had put on extra jackets and stuffed socks or padding into the seats of their pants to deaden the blows. At least one headmaster, the Reverend John Peyton McGuire, who presided over the school on the eve of the Civil War, was so nearsighted that he was unaware of these protective arrangements. Certainly he flailed the lads right lustily, and "the noises that came from within were not comforting to those on the waiting list," as one account had it.

The headmaster who took office in 1845, the Reverend Edwin A. Dalrymple, not only believed heartily in physical punishment, but achieved a measure of immortality by putting into effect some of the most amazing rules ever heard of. One of these reads as follows: "No student shall eat butter and molasses at once or at the same meal, nor shall any student waste in any way or leave uneaten or conceal to avoid eating. . . ." Also: "No student shall sing any Negro or low song or chorus or tune in the boys' parlor or elsewhere." There were other regulations that almost matched these in imbecility.

When the school opened in 1839, there was no course in English, but much emphasis on Latin, Greek and mathematics. English was added four years later, but few took it. E.H.S. offers no courses in Greek today.

But in other directions the curriculum has expanded remarkably, and the faculty numbers about thirty-three, compared with twelve when I was a student. Enrollment has jumped from about 180 to 280. Among the courses added are public speaking, music, art, dramatics, Russian language (five courses), Russian history and communism, public affairs, Asian history, computer programming, aviation, economics, archaeology, theology, international relations and typing. Tuition is approximately ten times what it was in 1914, yet it falls far short of meeting all costs.

The list of courses offered in the early years of this century was small, and the faculty too, but most of the basic subjects were taught, and the level of instruction in those subjects was extremely high. There were no Ph.D.s on the teaching staff, and none of the "masters," as they were known, had ever attended a school of education. But a good, solid schooling could be had by any pupil willing to study.

This was largely due to the fact that E.H.S. had a great headmaster in the person of Archibald R. Hoxton, and a cadre of six teachers—chosen by his predecessor, Launcelot M. Blackford—who remained with Headmaster Hoxton through the thirty-four years of his incumbency. These men, often termed the "Old Guard," had the following names and sub rosa nicknames: Willoughby ("Wiley Boley") Reade, John M. ("Dreamy") Daniel, Richard P. ("Dick" or "Cap'n Dick") Williams, Jr., Grigsby C. ("Shack") Shackleford, Robert L. ("Bob" or "Twit") Whittle and Francis E. ("Nick") Carter.

"Archie" Hoxton (known to the boys as "Flick" when he wasn't listening) was a man whom everybody respected. He was the embodiment of all that was fine in the school, its traditions and its honor system. When the centennial observance was held in 1939, alumni from far and near came, but if a single one had so much as smelled a cork, the fact escaped this observer. We were all loath to take even one drink, for fear of wounding Mr. Hoxton's feelings.

Launcelot Blackford, Archibald Hoxton's predecessor, was more widely read than he. A Confederate veteran who had fought under Stonewall Jackson, Blackford was about as unmilitary-looking a young man as one would be likely to see. A beloved figure, Dr. Blackford impressed his highly cultured personality upon the boys and brought the school along in difficult days when there was always a grievous lack of funds. He managed somehow to go abroad several summers to study the English schools and European civilization in general, and strove to cultivate in the boys a love of good literature. Always a stickler for proper speech, he is reputed to have said, when a physician attending him pronounced the word "abdomen" with the accent on the first syllable, "Ah, I believe the word is ab*do*men." On another occasion when things were not going too well he observed, "I deem it treason to repine."

It would have been impossible to imagine Flick Hoxton expressing himself in such terms. His words were simple and direct, like his straightforward and forceful personality. One of the most brilliant athletes in University of Virginia history, he was a superlative quarterback and shortstop. Yet, as he told me once, he weighed a bare 137 pounds in college, and that much only if he had his "mouth full of shot." There were stories of his legendary feats on the gridiron in outwitting or evading gargantuan opposing linemen, and of an unassisted triple play on the diamond. His astounding quickness was obvious as he taught his class in mathematics, for he could break a piece of chalk at the blackboard and catch both pieces before they hit the floor.

Many headmasters are disliked, since it is they, in the end, who must enforce discipline. I never knew a boy who actively disliked Flick Hoxton, although many stood in awe of him, and would rather have had a physical thrashing than a dressing down in his office. Corporal chastisement had been abandoned long since, of course.

Headmaster Hoxton was a fine administrator who insisted on topflight scholastic performance. He was able to pilot the school through its severe financial stringencies and to provide it with far better physical facilities than it had when he took over. His able and attractive son, Archibald R. Hoxton, Jr., is a worthy successor today.

The six masters who served on the E.H.S. faculty throughout

the senior Hoxton's years live in the minds and hearts of Episcopal High alumni—or "old boys," as they are called. It is astonishing to reflect that five of the six were in their late twenties or early thirties in 1914, and that Archie Hoxton was only thirty-nine. To the boys they all seemed "as old as God," as one former student expressed it.

When at age thirteen I arrived on what was known as "the Holy Hill"—apparently because of the adjacent Virginia Theological Seminary—my long and unusual first name attracted immediate attention. The result was that I was instructed by various older boys to add other names, so as to make my cognomen even more impressive. Thus I ended up with Virginius Theopidus Sempronius George Washington Jim Jeffries Abraham Lincoln Hannibal Artaxerxes Dabney. It got to be a regular ritual: "Boy, what's your name?" and I would reel off "Virginius Theopidus Sempronius . . ." I am still addressed occasionally by friends as "Theopidus" or "Sempronius."

Before I went away to school, I was known to the other boys as "Ninus" (pronounced Ninnus), which could have originated in somebody's futile attempt to say "Virginius." I must have been a solemn youngster, for when one of my uncles greeted me jovially with the words "Hello, ginger ale!" I replied without cracking a smile, "I call myself Ninus." My solemnity was remarked on by my parents, and my mother told me many years later that I had been exasperating in my lack of expressions of appreciation for presents given me and other favors done, in contrast to my appreciative and outgoing younger sister Lucy. For example, when Father told me in the summer of 1914 that he had succeeded in finding the money to send me to E.H.S. that fall, he expected me to be overjoyed. Inwardly I was, in fact, much pleased, but outwardly I was inexplicably phlegmatic and unresponsive. Father was quite naturally puzzled and annoyed.

My grandfather, for whom I am named, was always called "V" by his friends, and after I had departed for boarding school, Father wrote Archie Hoxton saying that it would please him greatly if I too could be called "V." So the headmaster began calling me that, and soon everybody else followed suit. V it has been ever since.

As a rat, I was required every morning to wake up Allison Palmer of Orlando, Florida, an older boy in a neighboring stall, with the following salutation: "Hi thee up, m'lord, it is time to arise. Seven-fifteen is tolled by the morning belfry." Every boy had to be in his place in the dining room on the stroke of seven-thirty, more or less fully dressed. There was hot competition to see who could stay in bed longest and still make it to breakfast without getting "stuck" demerits for being late. Fabulously fast times, some of them in seconds rather than minutes, were recorded.

Everybody complained loudly about the food, as is seemingly inevitable at all boarding schools. We paraded around the grounds on Saturday nights singing "Proc, Proc, Proc, the boys are starving . . ." a heartfelt appeal addressed to the proctor, George C. Stewart, who was responsible for supplying the food.

True, the meals were not exciting, but how could they be? A hundred and eighty ravenous boys had to be filled up three times a day, and the job was done about as well as could be expected, given the low tuition. There was undoubted monotony in the menus, especially in view of the fact that the same thing was served on each day of the week, so you knew that you would get scrambled eggs for breakfast every Tuesday and hot dogs for lunch every Wednesday. A none-too-inspiring variety of molasses known as "treacle," pronounced "trickle," was served at all three meals the year-round, and was not conducive to gastronomic joy. There was a simple dessert each day, and the term for it was "boss." The chief form of gambling around the institution was to bet a "week's boss" or "two weeks' boss" on this or that. A favorite bet was whether the progeny of any teacher's pregnant wife would be a boy or a girl. I won two weeks' boss when I bet that Mrs. Hoxton's second child would be a boy; he is now the headmaster.

The origin of the term boss is lost in the mists of antiquity. It was used at Locust Dale Academy in Madison County during the 1870s, when my father-in-law, T. Wilber Chelf, was a student there.

My allowance during my first year at school was twenty-five cents a week, which was less than most boys received. (It went up to $2.00 a month in my senior year.) I kept a diary and recorded my expenditures. "Went to the store and spent .10" occurs several times. Such an outlay was a momentous event. The store was owned by "Vic" Donaldson, and was a couple of hundred yards beyond the athletic field. An individual whom everybody called "Bun"—Vic's brother-in-law, I believe—was in charge. Vic also operated wagons and buses, the latter being available to boys going to Washington or Alexandria. He was commonly regarded by the boys as little short of a highway robber, probably with no justification whatever.

I could go to the store occasionally and spend five or ten cents, but transportation on the bus to the Washington trolley stop was out of the question. I always walked the two miles to the suburban station at Lloyd's and two miles back on the return trip.

Unlike the plan at most schools, our weekly holiday was—and still is—on Monday, rather than Saturday, and we were permitted to go to Washington on one Monday a month, if we had no demerits. These last had to be worked off by walking around the quarter-mile track, a mile per demerit. Some boys spent most of their Mondays walking 'round and 'round.

When I went to Washington with one or more friends, it was almost always for such raucous diversions as a vaudeville show at Keith's or a visit to the zoo. There was also the Gayety, which was considered quite risqué, but today would probably be about on a par with the First Baptist Sunday School. We usually grabbed a snack at something called the Washington Lunch, spending anywhere up to thirty cents. I managed to hoard a few dollars beyond my weekly allowance, thanks to gifts at Christmas or on my birthday. In my second and third years I was somewhat more affluent, and was able to attend an occasional baseball game of the Washington Senators. Since I was a monitor in my senior year, I could go to Washington every Monday, if I could afford it. I saw Ty Cobb try to steal third with a Detroit base runner already on the bag and almost get back to second. The play was so close that Ty protested vehemently when he was called out, so vehemently, in fact, that he was thrown out of the game by the umpire.

Once when my mother was visiting at E.H.S., she told me that she would be glad to take John Staige Davis, Jr., and me to Washington on the following Monday. She asked once or twice if I had spoken to John Staige about it, and found that I had not. Finally, when she brought it up again, she said in later years that my response was, "You're no worse than anybody else's mother, but . . ." In other words we preferred to go by ourselves. I find the phrasing attributed to me rather shocking, but cannot deny its accuracy. Mother seems to have taken it in stride, for she laughed about it often.

On Mondays when Washington was out of the question, financially or otherwise, several of us would go to the store and make buckwheat cakes on the kerosene stove, flipping them into the air and catching them in the pan. It was my first and last culinary accomplishment.

The Confederate tradition was strong at Episcopal High, since most of the boys were from the South. Robert E. Lee was therefore one of their idols, but in the annual polls taken to decide the school's favorite historical character, Lee sometimes lost to Cleopatra.

One of my hair shirts at school was the directive that I practice regularly on the violin. Prior to my matriculation I had taken lessons at the university and had revealed absolutely no talent for the instrument. Father hoped vainly to make a musician out of me, for he and Aunt Lucy played violin and piano duets for diversion at Edgewood. His father was also musical, not to mention his half-brother, Uncle Tom of the Metropolitan Opera, and his charming half-sister, Aunt Sue, who was so gifted as a pianist that she could have been a professional. But none of this musical virtuosity percolated down to your humble servant. By contrast, my sister Alice, who played the organ in church for many years, is musically talented.

Since Father still had hopes for me, I dragged my violin along when I went off to school. There were no facilities whatever for practicing, since no courses in music or music appreciation were in the curriculum at that time. I had to find an empty classroom in the afternoons and scrape and screech away. The noises were horrendous and audible over a wide area. My friend Johnson McGuire told me he thought I was probably the worst performer in the history of civilization, and I agreed with him. By the latter part of that session I had put my violin in storage for good. It was painful to disappoint my parents, but by then they were convinced.

In view of my lack of talent, the school's failure to provide courses in music and music appreciation did not trouble me, but it was a serious deficiency. So was the absence of emphasis on the importance of going to Washington for cultural purposes. It was not until the end of my senior year that I visited the Congressional Library, the Capitol, the Supreme Court and the House of Representatives, all in one day. And that was the extent of my acquaintance with those institutions during my three years at E.H.S. I never thought of going to any art galleries or concerts. Today there is a great deal of stress in the school catalogue and from the administration on the importance of taking advantage of the symphonies, plays, galleries and other attractions of Washington. And special opportunities are afforded the boys to do so.

We had no library at the school, and I hereby confess, to my genuine embarrassment, that it never occurred to me that we needed one. We were in school until the early afternoon five days a week, and in study hall five of the seven nights. A library was not something that I felt the need of; such a thing as reading on the side, in addition to my class assignments, never crossed my mind. I managed to get a prize each year for "excellence" in all my studies, and concluded—wrongly and stupidly—that nothing else in the way of reading was needed. The Joseph Bryan Memorial Library was not presented to the school by Mr. Bryan's family until long after I had graduated.

There were three literary societies, one of which, the Wilmer, was for boys under fifteen. I was in that one for two of my three years. While these organizations were called "literary," they were mainly for social purposes. Each had a few dog-eared books which seemed to be used mainly as missiles. I can scarcely recall ever seeing anybody reading one of them. The two senior societies did have annual reading, declaiming and debating contests, which were important events.

I was president of the Wilmer Literary Society for two of the three terms in my second year, but this signified nothing insofar as literary accomplishments were concerned. Nor was I a literary light in other directions. I got on the staff of the *Monthly Chronicle* for one term my second year, but never was able to survive the competition thereafter. I was not on the staff of the annual. The deep interest in journalism that I acquired later was largely absent at this stage.

In athletics, baseball and tennis were my sports. I played second base on the baseball team my senior year and was a reasonably good fielder but was certainly no Babe Ruth with the bat. I won the Baltimore Polytechnic game with a home run, but struck out three times in the important final game with Woodberry, and on the whole was a weak hitter. "Pat" Callaway, the coach, had joined the E.H.S. teaching staff that session, and this was for me the beginning of a warm friendship of more than half a century with that admired and beloved instructor of youth. Few teachers of boys have had a deeper impact on their characters and their careers.

I was the school's singles tennis champion at age fifteen, and won the final championship match 6–1, 6–3, 6–0. In fairness it must be said that my opponent, Johnson McGuire, was off his game or the score would not have been so one-sided, if, in fact, I would have won at all. Tennis was my favorite pastime—as it has been ever since—and I played as often as possible. The endurance of youth is astonishing. Once, when I was fourteen, I played eight or nine sets of singles in one day. Seven of them were close and hard fought, and in either one or two additional sets I won two weeks' boss from another boy.

Whatever prowess I showed on the cinder path in the Boy Scout track meet of 1913 had evaporated a few years later, and I did not go out for track at E.H.S. By then my feet were too big and got tangled up when I ran. I weighed 153 pounds and was a quarter of an inch under six feet a month before my sixteenth birthday and six months before my graduation. Despite my height, I did not put on long pants until Easter, 1916. The other boys ragged me for months to know if I ever intended to discard my knee breeches.

All six of the teachers known as the Old Guard were favorites of mine, and I had one or more classes under each. There was a particular problem with Grigsby C. Shackleford because of my inability to keep a straight face when he leaped about the classroom in demonstration of mathematical truths. He was a superior math teacher, especially because of his deep involvement in his subject. For example, instead of choosing a point on the blackboard in the normal way, he would shout "Take ANY point!" and throw a piece of chalk at the board. From that locale as a starter he would proceed to elucidate the problem in the most animated fashion. Mathematics appealed to him as such a beautiful science that he could not restrain his enthusiasm. I described one such episode in a letter to my parents as follows: "Gosh, I came near laughing again at 'Shack' yesterday. It was much harder for me to keep from laughing at him then than it was to understand the math. He was jumping around and he hit his shin on the 'rostrum' and nearly lit on his bean, and I pulled my eyeshade way down and laughed like the Dickens. He didn't see me." Shack's gyrations were for me a perennial problem, and I wore the eyeshade regularly to his class in the hope of concealing my mirth. I was not always successful. Despite it, he was extremely kind, and when he saw that I was having trouble with the course, he invited me to his home, so that he might try to solve my difficulties. I went and was deeply grateful.

Episcopal High's honor system has always been its special pride. It is not a system in name only, as at some schools, but a living, breathing part of the institution's life. Lying, stealing and cheating are banned, under the code, and each boy is honor bound to report any fellow student guilty of these infractions. Although the school today is larger than in former years, and the students come from more diverse backgrounds, Headmaster Archibald R. Hoxton, Jr., says that "the honor system is functioning as well today as it probably ever did." During my three years at E.H.S., one boy was expelled for cheating. Decades later I saw his name in a list of financial contributors to the school—remarkable evidence of the hold that Episcopal High has on its "old boy," even one who suffered the ultimate penalty at its hands.

During my years on the Holy Hill it would never have occurred to any of us in our most hysterical or irrational moments to refuse en masse to go to chapel or to class. But the atmosphere of the 1960s and 1970s, both in high school and college, has been in glaring contrast to that of half a century before. The boys at E.H.S. staged a chapel boycott at the time of the turmoil in the colleges, and a boycott of classes for one day in 1976. The excuse given on the latter occasion was that classes were being held on a regular Monday holiday "with no apparent justification."

Another aspect of life at Episcopal nowadays that contrasts completely with the situation prevailing in earlier eras is the presence of blacks among the matriculates. For some years now there has been an average of from six to nine blacks in school at each session, and the headmaster states that "on the whole they have done very well." One was head monitor and another was chairman of the Honor Committee. They have also starred in athletics. It would have been inconceivable in 1914–17, of course, to have so much as thought of admitting Negro youngsters to E.H.S. The fact that they are there is one more evidence of changing times.

One thing that never changes at E.H.S. is the school's athletic rivalry with Woodberry Forest School near Orange, Virginia. In football, it is the oldest uninterrupted rivalry between prep schools in the South, and celebrated its seventy-fifth anniversary in 1975. The number of wins for each in football and other sports is almost even. There has always been a high caliber of sportsmanship in the E.H.S.–Woodberry games, no matter whether the maroon and black of Episcopal or the orange and black of Woodberry emerges on top. The E.H.S. colors were black and blue until the late nineteenth century, at which time it seemed desirable to choose a color scheme that was less susceptible to jokes from opposing teams.

Dances are held at Episcopal High several times a year. In my day the dance steps were of a conventional nature, such as waltzes and two-steps. Mark Sullivan wrote in *Our Times* that in 1911 there was the "fox trot and the horse trot, the crab step and the kangaroo dip, the camel walk and the fish walk, the chicken scratch and the lame duck" not to mention "the snake, the grizzly bear and the bunny hug." These sound not unlike some of today's more amazing terpsichorean diversions, but back in the early days of the century the hops in Episcopal High's Stewart Gymnasium —now replaced by a much bigger gym—were on the ultraconservative side.

The declaration of war on Germany by the United States Congress in April, 1917, caused a stir in the school, but in view of the long period of rising tension between President Woodrow Wilson and the German Government, it had been more or less expected. We seniors realized that we might be going into the service, although since I was only sixteen, I did not envision enlistment in the near future. We had followed the course of the war in Europe on the school bulletin board for years. John M. ("Dreamy") Daniel, who taught history and government, put pins in the map to show the movements of the armies. In the spring of 1917 we did some elementary drilling.

It is fantastic to recall that such persons as David Starr Jordan, then president of Stanford University, and Norman Angell, the British author, were saying shortly before World War I burst upon mankind that such cataclysms were no longer thinkable. Jordan declared that "great international wars are practically at an end," while Angell told all and sundry that "far from these great nations being ready to fly at one another's throats, nothing will induce them to take the immense risks of using their preposterous military instruments if they can possibly avoid it." Yet Sarajevo and the fateful assassination of Austria's Archduke Franz Ferdinand by a Serbian terrorist loomed almost immediately ahead.

The tremendous carnage at Verdun and along the Somme was duly noted at E.H.S., but it all seemed so far away that we boys found it hard to comprehend the full horror of what was happening in Europe. There were other things on our minds.

Among them were the amusing antics of two fellow students,

W. Thornton Martin and Charles C. Wertenbaker. Martin later became the "Pete" Martin of *Saturday Evening Post* fame, pungent interviewer of countless celebrities, and author. His bosom pal, Wertenbaker, later wrote several books, including *Before They Were Men*, which dealt with E.H.S. "Wert" was also a leading member of the *Time* magazine staff, and was awarded the Medal of Freedom for his work as a correspondent in World War II. Martin and Wertenbaker spent many of their waking moments in efforts to outwit the school authorities, and were often in hot water. Despite their undoubted talents, they set no scholastic records, for their interests lay elsewhere. They spent almost countless Mondays walking off demerits.

Wertenbaker's famous trick of getting up in study hall to sharpen a pencil, somehow throwing a book at himself, which hit him in the back of the head, and then looking around indignantly illustrates their ingenuity. Everybody in that part of study hall, except Wertenbaker, would be stuck numerous demerits, but all would get them off on stating that they did not throw the book. Martin and Wertenbaker also vied with one another in trying to set speed records getting out of bed at the last minute and dressing for breakfast. They arrived at times wearing two garments, mostly unbuttoned, and unlaced shoes.

Pete Martin must have surprised a few people at Episcopal in 1947, thirty years after his departure, by producing a moving and well-written tribute to Willoughby Reade upon the retirement of that veteran faculty member. Obviously Wiley Boley made a deep impression on Pete, although hardly anybody, least of all Mr. Reade, would have suspected that the harum-scarum youth who sat in his class had his mind on anything except trying to beat the rap in almost every conceivable way. Martin's tribute is reproduced in *The High School*, the excellent history of the institution by Richard P. Williams, Jr., published in 1964.

There is a happy medium in the matter of grades and demerits, and the Martin–Wertenbaker duo erred in both directions by getting too many demerits and not enough respectable grades. My late friend Verne Bickelhaupt, of Richmond, recognized that high grades were always desirable, but that getting no demerits at all could have its unfavorable aspects. So he gave his grandson, Verne Morland, fifty cents for every A grade in school, provided he didn't always get A on deportment. Grandpa Bickelhaupt wanted to be certain that young Verne didn't become a teacher's pet.

Martin and Wertenbaker were certainly not teacher's pets; on the contrary, they were occasional habitués of "Egypt," the dank cavern in the basement of the gym where the bolshevik element was wont to congregate, cuss "the establishment" and smoke. This group was often in conflict with the nonsmoking athletes who preferred to gather upstairs in the main school building and warble such ditties as "Down by the Old Mill Stream" and "When You Wore a Tulip." There was a cleavage in the student body roughly along these lines, although many of the younger boys were only vaguely conscious of the fact. Each group tried to elect the final presidents of the two senior literary societies, perhaps the school's highest honor. The bolsheviks were occasionally triumphant, despite the glamour always surrounding star full-backs and tackles.

The boy who got the most astounding grades at E.H.S. during my years there, and did it with comparatively slight effort, was Littleton M. Wickham. He was brilliant in both math and languages, a rare combination, and carried off practically every scholarship medal and prize in the place. He was scornful of athletes, and his friend Minor Wilson accused him jokingly of having played halfback on the tennis team at the Money School, a small academy he had attended. A dedicated snob, as he himself was the first to admit, he was descended from Charleston, South Carolina, aristocracy and John Wickham, the famous defense attorney in the Aaron Burr treason trial of 1807.

After graduating in law at the University of Virginia, "Lit" Wickham taught for a few years at Episcopal High and then began practicing law in Richmond. He would spend hours rummaging through dictionaries and other reference books in search of precisely the right word or phrase for a legal brief, when such exactitude was by no means that important. Given a jury case by his firm, he invariably lost it because of his top-lofty attitude toward the jurors. An intellectual, he made no bones about it and wanted everybody to know it. Wickham gave up the law after some years and repaired to his ancestral estate, Woodside, near Richmond, where he collected a large library in various languages and spent most of his time amid his books. A unique achievement, or so it would seem, was his reading all the known works of Homer, Virgil, Dante and Rabelais in the original. He also was incredibly well read in English literature but scorned American authors and paid no attention to their writings.

When St. Mary's Episcopal Church, to which he belonged, invited worshipers of all faiths to attend a certain service, Wickham stood at the door as the Methodists, Baptists and adherents of other denominations entered and said to each, "I am a member of this church and I want you to know that you are not welcome here."

This was inexcusable, but Littleton Wickham was *sui generis*. He had a coterie of loyal friends who understood his eccentricities and appreciated his remarkable qualities. He didn't care tuppence what anybody else thought of him. In his last years he attracted a group of young college graduates who came frequently to Woodside for the purpose of enjoying his stimulating conversation and profiting from his enormous fund of knowledge. His funeral was largely attended, not only by persons from Richmond and environs but from more distant points.

Wickham was against nearly all the changes that had taken place in the past several decades, if not since the Civil War. He didn't go quite so far as a gentleman with the incredible name of Mountjoy Cloud, who visited the University of Virginia from time to time. Cloud, a native Mississippian, said he wished he had been born in 1835 and been killed in Pickett's charge at Gettysburg. If Lit Wickham didn't take quite such extreme positions as Mountjoy Cloud, he was typical of those Virginians who are said to revere the past, regret the present and fear the future.

A number of the boys who were at Episcopal High from 1914 to 1917 were conspicuously successful in later life. A partial list would include:

The Reverend Arthur L. Kinsolving, University of Virginia Rhodes scholar, who served as rector of famous Trinity Episcopal Church, Boston, and fashionable St. James Church, New York.

William L. Marbury, distinguished Baltimore attorney, a fellow of Harvard College for twenty-two years, chairman of the Maryland Commission on Higher Education and chancellor of the Episcopal Diocese of Maryland.

Dr. Johnson McGuire, nationally known cardiologist, head of cardiology at the University of Cincinnati, where he established the Johnson McGuire Cardiac Laboratory.

Dr. Benjamin M. Baker, University of Virginia Rhodes Scholar, another nationally known cardiologist and member for a time of the Johns Hopkins medical faculty.

Dr. John Staige Davis, Jr., head of the arthritis clinic at St. Luke's hospital, New York, for thirty-eight years, and associate attending physician at Bellevue Hospital for decades.

Bishop Richard H. Baker, rector of the Church of the Redeemer, Baltimore, for twenty years and then bishop of North Carolina.

Dr. Staige D. Blackford, professor of internal medicine at the University of Virginia Medical School and organizer of the Eighth Evacuation Hospital in World War II, in which he served overseas as a lieutenant colonel. He died all too soon in 1949, aged fifty.

J. Willcox Dunn, a star athlete at E.H.S. and the University of Virginia, with no time there for journalistic pursuits, won the Elijah Lovejoy Award for Courage in Journalism in 1958. He founded the *Princess Anne Free Press* at Virginia Beach in 1952 and promptly took out after the local political machine, despite suits in the courts and physical threats. For ten years "Bill" Dunn financed his paper's regular and continuing deficits from his own modest resources, until the burden finally became too great and publication was discontinued.

Such men as these have been turned out for many generations at Episcopal High. It is a school that stands for integrity and honor, wisdom and learning, mental discipline and physical development. Needless to say, not all who attend go out from its halls exhibiting these virtues, but a large number exemplify in substantial degree the principles for which E.H.S. stands. It is a rare boy indeed who does not leave this old school equipped to be a better man.

4

Along the Lawn and Ranges

I T NEVER OCCURRED to me that I would go to college anywhere but at the University of Virginia. This is something of a confession, since I should have wondered at least once whether it would not be best for me to pursue my studies in an atmosphere other than the one in which I had been born and raised. Not that there was anything inherently wrong with that atmosphere; on the contrary, there was much to commend it. But I should have addressed the question of whether a change would be beneficial and broadening. I didn't, and my parents seemed equally sure that the institution where I had grown up was the place for me. Financial considerations could well have played a part in their decision.

The only debate was over whether I was too young to enter college. During my final year at Episcopal High I tended to believe that I was, and I wrote my father and mother asking if I could remain at the school for another year and take graduate courses. Actually, this would have made little academic sense, since I was graduating, and a graduate of E.H.S. in those days took subjects on the first-year college level. There were only about six or eight graduates each year. My parents saw no reason for me to delay my college education, despite the fact that I was some two years younger than the other freshmen—or "first-year men," as they are called at Virginia. I acquiesced in their decision, took "advanced standing" examinations at the university on the subjects that I had completed at Episcopal and saved a year in getting my degrees.

I lived at home during my college career, which enabled my parents to keep a weather eye on me. In view of my youth and lack of sophistication, my mother put me on a pledge not to touch alcohol during my freshman year, 1917–18. The University of Virginia has a reputation for free and easy drinking, which I believe to be much exaggerated. The fact that it was the prohibition era had little bearing, since the Eighteenth Amendment was only a slight deterrent to anybody desirous of bending a convivial elbow, at Virginia or elsewhere. The motto of Virginia students was "Prohibition is better than no liquor at all."

The University of Virginia is often said to be the most beautiful institution of higher learning in America. The architectural genius of Thomas Jefferson, its founder, flowered in this, the last work of his life. He drew inspiration from Greek and Roman prototypes and from the work of the great Italian architect Palladio. The central core of the buildings, the Rotunda, Lawn and Ranges, stands today almost exactly as it was in Jefferson's time.

The Rotunda, modeled after the Roman Pantheon, is at the head of the rectangular Lawn, a lovely stretch of green bordered by venerable trees. Five two-story pavilions, no two of them alike, stand on each side of the Lawn, linked together by long low rows of one-story rooms for students. White columns complement the red brick of the buildings. Paralleling these structures but separated from them by gardens, and linked to them by serpentine walls, are East Range and West Range. These are quite similar to their counterparts, East Lawn and West Lawn, and provide additional quarters for students. Jefferson termed the whole an "academical village." In modern terminology it is the "Grounds," never the "campus," and the "G" is always capitalized.

Professors have always lived in some of the Lawn pavilions, although my parents never did. Father thought there would not be enough privacy. I was on the Lawn often during my early youth, however, since some of those professors' sons and daughters were my friends. My first dancing classes were in the Echols' home, and I ate ice cream and cake at Hippo Minor's birthday parties. The Lawn was also a convenient place for simple games such as "prisoner's base," especially on summer evenings when the fireflies glowed and the great tree trunks and rows of white columns furnished hiding places in the dim light.

The only building in Jefferson's original group which does not survive today is what he called the "anatomical theater," used for surgical operations. Long years afterward it was known as the "stiff hall" and we boys gave it a wide berth. "Pickled" cadavers were kept there for use of the medical students. Fraternity initiations sometimes included making a "goat" enter the building at night and pull one of the corpses out of its vat. The three-story brick structure was demolished in the late 1930s to provide space for the new university library.

As a boy I watched some of the famous and venerable professors strolling about the Grounds. Conspicuous among them was white-haired Dr. John W. Mallet, the internationally known English-born chemist, a Fellow of the Royal Society and member of the Chemical Societies of France and Germany. As an officer in the Confederate forces, Mallet devised the method whereby the Confederacy's vanishing nitre supply for explosives was replenished. It was done by saving human urine throughout the South. Carts made the rounds in scores of communities, collecting the night's urine and hauling it to boiling vats, where the urea was extracted and then shipped to Augusta, Georgia, for the manufacture of gunpowder. That plant was said to be always only a few days ahead of the army's requirements.

Another emeritus professor was Dr. Francis H. Smith, who had begun his teaching career at the university in 1853 as professor of natural philosophy. When I first saw him, in the early 1900s, he was in his nineties—he lived to be ninety-nine. Dr. Smith could be seen taking the air on the Lawn near his home. During his teaching career he was often voted the most popular of all the professors.

Milton W. Humphreys, emeritus professor of Greek, was perhaps as close to a universal genius as any faculty member in the institution's history. Widely recognized as a Greek scholar, he also taught Latin in two universities, Hebrew in one and botany in another. He wrote French and German fluently, and contributed in those languages to periodicals in Paris and Berlin. Humphreys also taught courses in advanced mathematics in two universities and astronomy in one. He was offered the chair of physics in another. In the Civil War he was a Confederate artilleryman, and, as a recognized authority on ballistics, contributed to the highly technical *American Journal of Artillery*. Professor Humphreys was on the Washington College faculty under the presidency of Robert E. Lee before coming to the University of Virginia.

Charles A. Graves, long a member of the university's law faculty, also taught at Washington College under Lee. His subjects there had been modern languages and English. The versatility of some of these professors was amazing; they were able to instruct in entirely unrelated disciplines. Dean William M. Thornton of the University of Virginia School of Engineering had taught Greek at Davidson College. My father, as already noted, was not only the sole professor of history at the university for thirty-four years, he also gave all the courses in economics for nine of those years. Fortunately there was no "publish or perish" doctrine in that era. Professors who carried crushing teaching loads found original research and writing to be almost impossible. There were, of course, no sabbatical leaves.

Another familiar figure about the Grounds was Henry Martin, the Negro bell ringer. He was employed in and around the university from 1847 until 1868, and was head janitor and bell ringer from 1868 until 1909. He died in 1915, probably aged ninety-nine. Nattily dressed "Uncle Henry," who always wore a cravat and stiff collar, rang the Rotunda bell about a dozen times a day, summoning the students to class, until the bell was destroyed in the Rotunda fire of 1895. Then he switched to the chapel bell, and again was extremely conscientious and efficient in carrying out his duties. Professor C. Alphonso Smith wrote a delightful interview with Martin for the 1914 *Corks and Curls*.

The interview quoted Uncle Henry as saying that he was born at Monticello in 1826, that his mother "belonged to Mr. Jefferson" and that "she married his body servant." Space does not permit extensive quotation from the interview, but a few extracts follow:

"Yes, sir, I was bell-ringer at the University for fifty-three years and P'fessor, I been as true to that bell as to my God. . . . They don't seem to pay much 'tention to the bell now, but I had to wake up the cooks and the dormitory students. . . .

"I can't read, but I've had fifteen children and I made 'em all learn to read and write; not any more. Politeness beats learnin'. Politeness ain't never sent a man to the penitentiary, but I know plenty o' colored folks that went there 'cause they knowed too much. . . .

"This bell they got now, it sound just the same for a funeral as for a game o' football; but when I rang it everybody knew what I was ringin' it for. There's that bell now. It don't seem to me to say nothin'. It just hollers."

Reminiscing concerning the Civil War, Uncle Henry said, "Durin' the war I nursed hundreds right there in that Rotunda, and when I go in it now, I ain't studyin' 'bout the books I see. No sir, I'm thinkin' on the soldiers that I seen layin' on the floor. It didn't make no difference how much they was sufferin', they didn't make no noise. No sir, they lay right still a-lookin' straight up at the ceilin'."

Another relic of bygone days at the university was Temperance Hall. Dr. Paul B. Barringer, a former chairman of the faculty, writes in his memoir, *The Natural Bent*, that the Temperance Society, responsible for the hall's construction, was "one of the most popular institutions at the University" in the years following the Civil War. Barringer termed it "notable for its sensible handling of a difficult problem." Before and after the war there were prominent advocates of temperance on the university faculty. Not only so, but they proselyted vigorously for the cause. Among the leaders were William Holmes McGuffey, author of the famous McGuffey Readers; William Barton Rogers, later the founder of Massachusetts Institute of Technology; John B. Minor, renowned professor of law, and John A. G. Davis, chairman of the faculty.

Temperance Hall, which was torn down in 1914, was a two-story brick building at what has been known to generations of

Virginia students as "the Corner." The hall was on the second floor, while the first floor was occupied by the post office, an Express office and a bookstore. Dr. Barringer wrote that in the postbellum years, "A young fellow who found himself drinking too much . . . sent in his name, and, in the presence of his fellow reprobates, took the pledge for the rest of the session or for some other designated period, and kept it."

Not only Temperance Hall but the Temperance Society was nonexistent at the university when I entered in 1917. The amount of drinking was considerable, but I believe it to have been no worse than in many other centers of higher learning. The reputation acquired by the university for excessive tippling was due in large measure to the fact that drinks were hoisted more publicly there than in many places. For example, the Eli Banana ribbon society paraded around the Grounds on Saturday nights, beating on a drum and singing:

> *Eli Banana, the starry banner,*
> *We are drunk boys, yes every one;*
> *It's not the first time nor yet the last time*
> *That together we'll get out on a hell of a bum,*
> *bum, bum.*

Other University of Virginia societies had drinking songs, but none was so rowdy in my time as this one, or made so much public noise. A somewhat earlier group calling itself the Hot Feet was equally raucous, but its riotous orgies got completely out of hand, and it was disbanded by the university authorities in the early 1900s. In its place arose the IMP Society, certainly no band of teetotalers, but more discreet in their behavior.

Charles Wertenbaker published a novel, *Boojum*, in 1928 which had literary merit but gave a grossly distorted picture of boozing at Virginia. The book had the students drinking literally morning, noon and night, and pictured them as interested in practically nothing else. No human beings could have survived after consuming such colossal quantities of alcohol as Wertenbaker described. The book helped to create the image of a rum-soaked university.

During prohibition almost the only alcoholic potation available at the institution was corn whiskey, occasionally aged but most of the time not. This product of moonshine stills burbling happily in the coves of the Blue Ridge or the swamps of Tidewater was full of fusel oil when raw, and might also contain dead mice, bugs or whatnot. In the words of one imbiber, "When you take a swig of it, you have all the sensations of having swallowed a lighted kerosene lamp."

A favorite method used by Virginia "studes" in consuming this "white lightning" was to pour it into a Mason jar, which might or might not contain ice, wrap a bath towel around it and drink it straight. If the drinkers wanted to be especially fancy and could find any mint, they would stick a few sprigs into the concoction and call it a mint julep.

I was no longer on a drinking pledge with my mother during my second year, and I made a spectacle of myself when I was initiated into the T.I.L.K.A. ribbon society. A loving cup containing some sort of alcoholic beverage was passed around before the dinner. I was almost totally inexperienced in such matters, and was told that the liquid was wine. Actually it was whiskey and water. After I had taken several swallows, we were summoned to the table. En route my head began whirling and I was barely able to get to my seat. I was nauseated as well as dizzy, and was hauled from the table by colleagues. They got me into a back alley where I managed to lose what was on my stomach. They then conveyed me to a nearby boarding house and put me to bed. I awoke the next morning feeling great, and took off for Episcopal High School with the freshman basketball team, of which I was manager.

The episode had repercussions. For some weeks or months I was greeted derisively by friends intoning "They told me it was wine," and by others who called me "Whiskey." I informed Father of the embarrassing occurrence, and he was not too dismayed. I never told Mother; she would have been immeasurably shocked and grieved.

This was in the fall of 1918, when World War I was rushing to its climax. The conflict had a drastic impact on the university from the time when our belligerence was formally declared in April 1917. Many of those who were graduated in June entered the service, and some didn't wait for graduation. Enrollment for the following session, 1917–18, fell from 1,064 for the previous session to 700. Students who were already enrolled were urged by the authorities to stay in school until called. Those who were eighteen years old drilled on the Lawn as members of the Students Army Training Corps (SATC) under the command of Colonel James A. Cole U.S.A., ret. The colonel, known as "Whispering Jimmy," rattled the windows as he rasped his commands in a throaty bellow that could be heard for roughly a quarter of a mile.

Since I was under eighteen, I was ineligible for the SATC, but I and others in my age bracket had our own unit and drilled with the rest. We called ourselves the Infants' Training Corps (ITC). I rose to the exalted rank of corporal.

Like nearly all American males of that era, I was anxious to get into the service. In early November 1918, I couldn't stand it any longer, and my seventeen-year-old friend Charlie Ferguson and I decided to go to Washington and see if we couldn't get into something. It was November 6, and we were about to set out on the night train, when Father persuaded us to wait until the next morning, since there seemed to be no point in our starting off at midnight. Next day came the false armistice report, and that stopped us. The war ended with the real armistice on November 11.

The curriculum for 1917–18 had included some special wartime courses. For instance, I took Military Science B1. By the autumn of 1918 most of the courses were of that character. Mine included Automobiles, Military German, Sanitation and Hygiene and something called War Issues Eng. Lit. After the November Armistice and the December examinations, the curriculum reverted to normal. The veterans began pouring back in the autumn of 1919, and they kept coming throughout the succeeding months. By the session of 1920–21, there were on the Grounds, in the inimitable phrase of Dean Paul Minton of the Virginia Commonwealth University School of Arts and Sciences, 1,700 "skins full of students."

I was no Einstein in the classroom as a freshman, but I did considerably better thereafter, being elected to Phi Beta Kappa and the Raven Society, also scholastic, in my third year. Father chose my freshman courses for me, which was probably a mistake. They were second-year college Greek, third-year college French, physics and astronomy. I had had no French for three years, I had never found either Greek or mathematics congenial to my disposition and here I was, at age sixteen, with three out of four courses involving those disciplines. True, Father arranged for me to by-pass advanced calculus by substituting astronomy. Professor "Reddy" Echols was wont to term this substitution "the loophole for the feeble-minded," but I was only too happy to leap through that loophole.

I made a halfhearted attempt to get on the reportorial staff of *College Topics*, the student newspaper, but was unsuccessful. Later I became an assistant editor for two years of the annual, *Corks and Curls*, the name of which has often been misinterpreted to mean "wine and women." Actually it has no such connotation. In earlier days a student who flunked a course was said to have "corked," while one who made a high mark was said to have "curled."

The dreadful influenza epidemic in the fall of 1918 played havoc with the university. We students, like many others throughout the United States, wore white masks over our faces in the hope of avoiding the pestilence. I managed to escape entirely, but Professor William Harry Heck, who was lecturing to us in the course on sanitation and hygiene on how to escape the flu, contracted it and died. Many students were ill and some did not recover.

Wheatless, meatless and porkless days were decreed by U. S. Food Administrator Herbert Hoover. By this means shipments of food to the Allies were approximately trebled. If anybody complained because of these slight deprivations, I did not hear of it.

In contrast to certain manifestations of recent years, especially in the late 1960s, the attitude of the students toward the university authorities was altogether respectful. Undergraduates in my time never thought of making demands on the president or the deans, much less staging sit-downs around the Grounds, marching on the president's office or threatening to shut down the institution. It would have been altogether unthinkable for a group of belligerent students to have entered the sanctum of President Edwin A. Alderman or Dean James M. Page with a list of demands. The emphasis in the period 1917–21 was all the other way. Professors and students tipped their hats to one another when passing on the sidewalk, and the students were deferential at all times.

There was an almost pathological fear on the part of the students lest they do what was termed "sticking your neck out." Incredible as this must seem, it was sticking your neck out if you spoke up in class and answered a professor's question to the group as a whole. It was likewise regarded as bad form to do reading for the course above and beyond the assignment and to let that be known. I well remember my indignation when a fellow student said out loud in class that he had done some extra reading. When I found out later that I had made a better term grade than this man, I rejoiced idiotically for no other reason than that I felt he got what he deserved for having gone so far beyond proper bounds.

This tradition of not sticking your neck out had other ramifications. A freshman who had won an athletic letter in high or prep school was not supposed to display the fact by wearing the sweater right-side-out on the athletic field; it must be worn wrong-side-out. I am ashamed to say that I complied. This unbelievable nonsense with respect to sweaters seems to have lasted only a few years.

There was also a temporary aberration as to shirts and ties. For at least one whole year the only good form at Virginia was to wear a white shirt and a solid black four-in-hand tie. This stylistic edict reportedly came down from Yale. At all events, one saw herds of students wearing nothing but white shirts and black ties, the over-all effect being that of a morticians' convention. I was one of the sheep who trotted along in complete conformity. However, I did exhibit a glimmer of intelligence when one of the senior brothers in my fraternity, Delta Kappa Epsilon, gave me some fatherly counsel concerning the wearing of a hat. First-year men were supposed always to wear hats. My brother in D.K.E. said he would advise me to keep the headgear on until Christmas of my second year, lest I be thought to be sticking my neck out. I ignored his advice.

Nearly thirty years after I had left college, I picked up the *Cavalier Daily* for November 18, 1950, and my eye fell on a discussion of the same old problem involving the sticking out of one's neck. It was a column by Curt Bazemore and Staige Blackford, and it could have been a description of the precise situation that prevailed after World War I. "When a professor asks a question," wrote Bazemore and Blackford, "or tries to provoke a little discussion about something, he almost has to get down on his knees and plead with the students to make an answer or to get lukewarm participation. . . . If a man should ever have the audacity to speak out in the classroom unless he is questioned directly, his fellow-students ask, 'Well, just who is this guy trying to show off how much he knows?'" The columnists deplored that so many undergraduates are "stifled in the air of enervation and mired in the mud of conservatism."

The foregoing could not be written today. There still is probably more reluctance on the part of the students to speak up in class than at many institutions, but less than they showed a quarter of a century ago. The over-all institutional climate has undergone a spectacular change. Enrollment has grown to approximately 15,500 in 1976–77, including thousands of women and hundreds of blacks. The student body is so diverse and so cosmopolitan that the intellectual and social climate has undergone a dramatic metamorphosis. Necks are stuck out in ways that were not dreamed of in former days. The changes that have occurred are good in some respects but certainly not in all.

On the plus side scholastic standards are much higher, and admission to the university is far more difficult. The faculty includes many greatly distinguished members. The institution has achieved national stature and is no longer looked down on as "the country club of the South." Whereas half a century ago something like 30 per cent of the first-year men were dropped by the end of their initial session, this figure has shrunk to less than 2 per cent. In recent years hundreds were on the Dean's List at all times, but requirements for this listing were made more stringent in 1977.

As on practically every campus in the land, coats and ties for men gave way in the late 1960s and early 1970s to sport shirts and blue jeans, while mustaches, beards and long hair proliferated. When the girls arrived in 1970, they wore faded, often patched, blue jeans and stringy hair. Skirts were seldom seen. This situation changed in the middle and late 1970s, until coats and ties are more often worn, as are skirts. Mustaches and beards have become less prevalent.

Rules governing contacts between the sexes have done a 180-degree turn in the past fifty years. Whereas in the 1920s no reputable girl would have thought of entering even the ground floor of a fraternity house at any time, many have no inhibitions today about going upstairs. Furthermore, university rules permit round-the-clock visitation of members of the opposite sex in dormitory bedrooms. This sexual revolution has spread to the entire country. Steadily shifting mores plus readily available contraceptives and legal abortions have wrought a revolution of the most far-reaching character.

University dances in my time and for many years thereafter were held in the gymnasium and were "pledged," i.e., no student could attend who had had a drink of anything alcoholic since noon of that day. This pledge was observed 100 per cent. There was a case where a student who had had "too many," and apparently didn't know what he was doing, went on the floor and danced. He was expelled by the Honor Committee, a penalty which may have been too harsh. Everybody went to the dances in the gym, and there was no competition from parties in the fraternity houses. Gradually this changed, and more and more students took their dates to fraternity dances where there was no pledge against drinking, and chaperones, if any, were few and far between. There was partying upstairs as well as down. This went on long before women were admitted to the university on the same basis as men. A few years after they were let in, all rules against visitation in the dormitories were abandoned. At least one Episcopal clergyman in the community was a leader in breaking down the barriers against dormitory visitation, incredible as this must seem. He also differed sharply with the university's renowned honor system.

During the first half of the century, Easter Week, the week following Easter Sunday, was the social peak of the year. There was a dance in the gymnasium every night from Monday through Saturday. The Elis, T.I.L.K.A.s, Beta Theta Pis, PK and German Club and *Corks and Curls* each gave a dance, and in one of my years, the IMPs did likewise. The problem of going to all these affairs, which lasted until three o'clock in the morning on week nights (the IMP dance lasted until five), was a bit staggering. One was supposed to attend classes, of course. I came down with fever at the end of one Easter Week simply from excessive strain and loss of sleep.

I invited several girls to the dances during my final three years, and was more or less infatuated with a couple of them. One day in the spring of 1920 my mother, who chaperoned regularly at these affairs, remarked to me that she was greatly impressed by the charm, good looks and fine manners of Douglas Harrison Chelf of Richmond, who was attending the dances and visiting her former Sweet Briar classmate Anna Fawcus on University Place. This was the sort of girl, said Mother, that she wished I would take a fancy to. Such a parental remark, under nearly all circumstances, would have guaranteed that I would head immediately in the opposite direction. However, I was beginning to be of the same mind myself. We had our first dates in the spring of 1920.

"Doug" Chelf was then in her fifth year of attending the hops at Virginia Military Institute—which may be some sort of record —not to mention similar functions at various other citadels of higher learning. You had to get in line at dances in order to have the pleasure of a brief whirl around the floor with her. It was obvious, therefore, that the competition was going to be something special. I addressed myself to the problem as intensively as I could, but it was not until the following session, 1920–21, my last, that I felt that I was making headway. I invited her to all the dances that year, and she always stayed with Anna Fawcus, who was a distant cousin of mine and extremely popular herself. The modern generation of collegians will be amused to learn that we were wont to have a cup or two of hot chocolate at Anna's after the dances. Not exactly the conventional picture of preferred *divertissements* at the University of Virginia.

When Doug was at the university I saw her at all possible times, and when she was back in Richmond I was often miserable, as is evident from various poignant notations in my diary. I also recorded there on several occasions that I was having difficulty concentrating on my studies.

Easter Week for at least the first third of this century was decorous in the extreme by comparison with later carryings-on. The girls were perfumed and powdered and wore formal evening dresses; the boys donned their white ties and tails and visited the barber shop. Contrast this with the mud-spattered orgy of recent years. Known as "Easters Weekend" rather than "Easter Week," it came in March or April, but had no direct tie-in with Easter. The boys and girls wore old clothes, and a good thing, too, for they deliberately slithered around in artificially created mud holes, getting the gunk in their hair and eyes, all over their clothes and down their necks. While indulging in this unique form of romantic relaxation, they consumed "grain alcohol drinks . . . straight from large fruit juice cans," to quote the Richmond *Times-Dispatch* correspondent on the scene. By 1976 the debauch had gotten so out of control that the university authorities ordered it discontinued.

It was amazing to find the supposedly much more sedate University of Richmond students similarly splashing and sliding around in artificially created mud on their campus in March of 1976—perhaps minus the grain alcohol. The idea was obviously catching on, and there was no way of knowing what other excruciating collegiate gambols might be in the offing.

"Streaking," namely running at top speed across the campus in the nude, was a great fad at some men's and women's colleges during the session of 1973-74, and there were streaking incidents at the University of Virginia's Easters Weekend that year.

Possibly these latter-day streakers got the idea from the Virginia student who "at high noon one day in 1895 on a bet ran from the Rotunda to the cemetery and back wearing nothing but boxing gloves and track shoes" (*Alumni News*, December 1963). The same publication advises that "in 1887, it took seven hours of engineering ingenuity to remove a cow placed on the Rotunda roof by students." Just what type of ingenuity got the bovine up there is not made plain. Another cow was somehow placed atop the Rotunda in the mid-1960s, but it has been many years since these animals wandered about the Lawn. The *Alumni News* also brings tidings that "the faculty minutes of 1866 said cows belonging to students were not to be permitted on the Lawn except during the hours of 6 to 8 A.M. and 4 to 6 P.M., when it was permissible to bring them in for milking."

In Thomas Jefferson's time cows may have mooed about the Lawn, but women were forbidden to be seen there. Nowadays the place is not only thronging with women but it is the focal point of the institution.

When I was a student, Dr. Edwin A. Alderman, the prestigious president of the university, could be seen strolling to or from his office. He had been president of the University of North Carolina and Tulane, and was a person of immense dignity. Probably the most eminent Southerner of his era, after the passing of Woodrow Wilson, he was a polished orator and a personality of great potency and considerable charm. Usually he found it difficult to unbend and, in the words of his biographer, Dumas Malone, "frequently he appeared unduly conscious of his presidential state." Malone goes on to relate that "younger members of the faculty who might have been called by their first names with entire propriety were sonorously addressed as 'Doctor'; and a recent bride could hardly conceal her astonishment when greeted with 'Good morning, Madam.'" These pomposities were visible to all.

Once when there was a discussion in faculty meeting of bringing some distinguished speaker to the university, Alderman suggested that Lord Kelvin be invited. "But Lord Kelvin's dead," physics Professor Llewellyn Hoxton interjected. "Oh yes, in a general way," Alderman replied unblinkingly, and in his most resonant tone.

Despite his rather obvious idiosyncrasies, Dr. Alderman was liked and respected by many professors and students. He told me on one occasion of an amusing episode at the U. S. Naval Academy. He had just been appointed to the academy board, and the admiral who was then superintendent was showing him around. When they arrived at the library, they looked in the door and saw a vast and almost empty room, with a few attendants at desks. "We try to keep the boys out of here as much as possible," the admiral declared proudly.

The university boasted of other unusual characters besides Alderman. For example, there was Professor Armistead M. Dobie of the law faculty, later appointed to a federal judgeship. His triphammer rhetoric reminded one of a machine gun, and he said of himself, "Ten thousand words a minute are just his daily feed." When one heard Dobie lecturing to his class or haranguing the students in Cabell Hall, it brought to mind the exclamation of Shakespeare's King John, "'Zounds! I was never so bethump'd with words."

Dobie's exhortation to the students before the annual football game played in those days with Georgetown University in Washington, was famous. It got so many laughs that he repeated it at successive rallies each year in Cabell Hall. Dobie would charge up and down the rostrum, waving his arms and shouting in his high-pitched voice, "I want you Virginia men to make the welkin ring for the Orange and Blue tomorrow afternoon during that gridiron classic with Georgetown, and in such stentorian tones as to make a broadside from the Atlantic Squadron sound like the dying groan of a consumptive gnat!"

On a different level were the simple but genuinely moving words of Professor William H. Echols when he addressed the students on the entry of the United States into the First World War. Echols, as my father often said, "looked like a Norse Viking." About six feet four, broad-shouldered, deep-chested and sandy-haired, his physical presence was immensely impressive. "War is nothing but mud and blood," he told the students. But he was not trying to discourage them from enlisting—quite the contrary. He was urging them to follow the example of James R.

McConnell, a University of Virginia student who had joined France's Lafayette Escadrille in 1916. McConnell was badly injured in a plane crash in France, but insisted on going back on patrol, although in great pain and hardly able to turn his head. "He might as well have been wearing horse blinders," one fellow pilot said. The result was inevitable. His bullet-riddled body was found in the wreckage of his plane just behind the St. Quentin Canal.

Echols reached the climax of his inspiring address with the words ". . . and Jim McConnell, whose spirit flies somewhere in France, to show you the way." "Every man in that audience wanted to enlist the moment Reddy Echols sat down," Father would say, his voice shaking with emotion.

Since the Secretary of War urged all who were in college to stay there until called, this kept the institutions of higher learning in business; otherwise they would have been in a state of near collapse. When undergraduates were inducted into the Student Army Training Corps, they became members of the armed forces.

Life remained fairly normal at the university, although the daily drills and the altered curriculum made it obvious that a war was in progress. That winter was one of the bitterest on record, and ice and snow remained on the ground for six weeks. Walking to classes down slippery Rugby Road was a strenuous form of exercise. I fell and tore my pants grievously.

When spring finally came, I went out for baseball, and played second base on the first-year team. We defeated Woodberry twice but for some reason did not play Episcopal. There were other games.

During those years college baseball was second only in popularity to football, and there was much interest. Today it is often hard to get even a few dozen people to turn out for college baseball games, although interest in the big league clubs remains high.

Commercialization of football was almost completely nonexistent at Virginia in my day. For a few years in the late nineteenth and early twentieth centuries professional coaches from the North had been hired, but it was decided to return to the alumni coaching system. Under this arrangement, some alumnus who had starred in football returned for a few months in the fall and tried to whip the team into shape. He was paid his expenses. But in 1920 the decision was reached to go back to professional coaching, and Dr. Rice Warren, an alumnus, was brought in. Since that time only professionals have been employed.

In 1919 the coach was Harris Coleman, captain of the famous 1915 team that beat Yale and almost beat Harvard with all-American Eddie Mahan in the Harvard backfield. The heaviest man on the Virginia eleven of 1915 weighed not more than 200 pounds, the backfield averaged around 170 and nearly every man played sixty minutes. There are only sixteen players in the official team photograph.

Athletic scholarships did not exist then at Virginia, if indeed they existed anywhere. Today alumni and others in almost every institution that aspires to gridiron glory raise at least $1 million annually for such scholarships. The Virginia team was more successful under the alumni coaching system than it has been in nearly all the subsequent years. One reason is that in this era of huge athletic budgets and absurd hippodroming, the University of Virginia raises much less money for athletic scholarships than most. It also maintains high entrance and eligibility standards. College football today has degenerated in many areas into hardly less than a racket.

My baseball career at Virginia was not a glamorous one. After playing second base on the first-year team, I was at the same position in two varsity games the following year, but did not get a letter. I was taken on the southern trip, which involved an amusing episode. We were en route to Athens, Georgia, where we were to play the University of Georgia. Early in the morning we had to change trains, after a considerable wait, at a whistle stop called Lula. Some of the boys started a crap game on the station platform, and before they knew what was up, the sheriff had grabbed them and was threatening to haul them off to jail. Fortunately our coach, Ed Smith, a University of Virginia alumnus who had just come back from the war, shrewdly got into a conversation with the sheriff and found that the latter's son had also fought overseas. Smith was a smooth and voluble talker, and by the time he got through buttering up the sheriff and complimenting him on having such a heroic son, the mollified lawman let everybody off.

The following spring I sat on the bench until near the end of the baseball season. I was obviously not highly regarded by the coach—Harry Spratt, who had played with the Boston Braves—and I saw little prospect of getting into any games. The coach may well have been right. However, tennis had just been officially recognized as a minor sport at the university, and I knew I could make the tennis team. So I dropped baseball and played in the two remaining matches of the season, against V.M.I. and the Country Club of Virginia. I was fortunate in winning my singles in both of them. In 1920–21 I played throughout the season, and won singles matches against Penn, Navy and the Country Club of Virginia, while losing to V.M.I. When the season ended I was at the top of the University of Virginia tennis ladder. Dave Jarvis, the captain, was a better player, but I challenged him and managed to defeat him, 6–4, 5–7, 6–4. He never challenged me back, so I remained a precarious number one.

During the spring of 1920 I pitched for the Dekes in the interfraternity baseball games, and we won the championship. I didn't have much on the ball as a pitcher; a fast ball—not very fast—and a "roundhouse" curve completed my repertoire. But I did have good control, and could put the ball where I wanted it. There were four games, I pitched the full nine innings in each and didn't allow a single earned run in any of them. The catcher was Robert R. Parrish, then a scrub but later captain of the university team, which helps to explain such success as I had.

Also during that spring my good friend Richard H. Baker and I sold ice-cream cones at several of the varsity baseball games to make a little extra cash. We charged ten cents per cone, which some regarded as highway robbery, but it was impossible to make anything at all unless we did so. We carried on our enterprise at four games and each of us cleared a grand total of $28.50.

"Dick" Baker, later the Episcopal bishop of North Carolina, and I had my father's history class together, and when the class in the basement of the Rotunda was over we would often repair to

Johnny LaRowe's pool room at the Corner and shoot a game or two of pool. In fact, my diary shows that I often engaged in this form of indoor sport with various friends. I was never very good at it, but found it relaxing.

I applied for a Rhodes scholarship during the spring of 1920. The prize went to my close friend Arthur Lee Kinsolving, afterward rector of Trinity Episcopal Church, Boston, and St. James Church, New York City. As matters turned out, I was not sorry that I lost, for the following summer in Richmond I became so enamored of Miss Chelf that I lost all desire to leave for Oxford in the fall. My situation was reminiscent of that described by John Rolfe when he spoke of his love for Pocahontas, the Indian Princess: "To whom my hartie and best thoughts are, and have a long time bin so intangled, and inthralled in so intricate a laborinth, that I was awearied to unwinde my selfe thereout."

The most important single aspect of life at the University of Virginia has long been the honor system, which goes back to 1842. Lying, cheating and stealing are banned under the code, with expulsion for infractions.

As vice-president of the Academic Class for 1919–20, I served on the Honor Committee during that session whenever a member of the class was accused of a violation. Only one student from the class was expelled during that year, while another was brought before the committee but not convicted. I was the accuser in the latter case, for I was sure that I saw this man looking over his neighbor's shoulder during a quiz and copying the neighbor's paper. The accused denied it, of course, and since there was no incontrovertible proof and it was barely possible that I had been mistaken, some members of the Honor Committee were unwilling to vote for conviction. I had no hard feelings toward them because of this.

In this connection, let it be carefully noted that there is much misunderstanding concerning one crucially important aspect of the University of Virginia honor system. I refer to the fact that it is the obligation of any student who witnesses cheating or any other violation *to confront the suspected person and demand an explanation.* If the explanation is unsatisfactory, the suspect must appear before the Honor Committee of students to answer the charge. This is widely, and mistakenly, described as "talebearing" or being a "tattletale," something that nearly all children are warned against by their parents. This is *not* talebearing, but almost precisely the opposite.

The most striking example I can think of to prove the vitality of the university's honor system is contained in the bequest of a student who was expelled under its terms. When this man entered the armed forces of the United States soon after the outbreak of World War II, he wrote the president of the Honor Committee expressing his "lasting belief in Virginia and her honor system" and advising that he had put into his will a bequest of $10,000 to the University of Virginia.

There is understandable concern today with respect to the future of the system. With the student body roughly ten times as big as it was in my day, and with thousands of students attending who were never exposed to the operations of an honor system, there are unquestionably problems, but there is confidence that the system can be maintained.

One of the enjoyable aspects of college life for me was membership in the Delta Kappa Epsilon Greek letter fraternity. I joined along with half a dozen others from Episcopal High. The fraternities furnished nearly all the student leadership at that time, but this is by no means the case today, and they have declined in prestige.

Apparently we University of Virginia Dekes were favorites of James Anderson Hawes, the general secretary of D.K.E. for twenty-six years. This middle-aged gentleman, who hiccuped slightly when he talked, made us periodic visits, and sought to keep us in the straight and narrow. Other chapters addressed him respectfully as "Mr. Hawes," but we always called him "Jimmy," and were much less deferential. If on Sunday he would say, with a slight hiccup and knocking the ash from his cigar, "Well, which of you boys is going to church with me?" some would go and some wouldn't. He seemed to like this attitude, for we were told

that when visiting other chapters he always mentioned the one at
Virginia as among his favorites. There were two other favorites—
the one at Yale, his alma mater, and whichever chapter he happened to be visiting. Jimmy invariably addressed us on the glories
of D.K.E. It appeared that Dekes had won World War I, in the
person of General Peyton C. March, army chief of staff and
member of the lodge; they discovered the North Pole in the person of Robert E. Peary, also a member, and performed other
prodigies. During the First World War, Jimmy operated the
Deke Club in the Grand Hotel in Paris, where brethren back
from the front could sustain themselves with something more
stimulating than coffee and doughnuts. Jimmy was evidently inde-
pendently wealthy, and being a bachelor could afford to devote
his time to visiting fraternity houses. It is a rather incom-
prehensible way to spend one's career.

I did not belong to the mysterious Seven Society at the university. Founded there in 1905, the organization has made many
financial contributions to various university causes. These always
involve the numeral 7 in some way. The *Cavalier Daily* describes
a typical donation.

"In 1958 the rector of St. Paul's was sitting in his study wondering how to pay for chapel repairs, when a stone crashed through
his window with a note plus $2.77 payment for the broken win-
dow. The note told him at seven minutes past seven to take 77
steps east from the Rotunda, alter his course by 77 degrees and
walk another 77 paces and 7 inches. Following his instructions the
rector found $177 for chapel repairs."

Not all members of the Seven Society are males, and names of
those who belong to the occult order are not revealed until after
death. The membership of Miss Mary B. Proffitt, secretary to
Dean Ivey F. Lewis, also a Seven, was made known after Miss
Proffitt's passing. The Sevens always make a donation to the university on Founder's Day, April 13, the birthday of Thomas Jefferson. When I delivered the Founder's Day address in 1970, it was
announced from the platform that the Sevens were making a donation in honor of my mother, who was in the audience.

A number of students at Virginia in my time became famous in later years. Several at Episcopal High who made names for themselves were mentioned in the previous chapter, and they were my fellow students at the university. There were others. Julian Green and I were in a class together, but I knew him only by sight. He impressed me as an introvert, quiet and withdrawn. Born in Paris of American parents, he remained an American citizen, although he has spent most of his life in France. He spells his first name "Julien" in most of his books. No one in 1920 could have predicted his brilliant career as a writer and his election in 1971 to the French Academy, the first non-Frenchman ever elected to that extremely select group. Green is a homosexual, as he declares with complete frankness in his book *Terre lointaine*. Colgate W. Darden and J. Lindsay Almond, future governors of Virginia, were in the university during my time there, but I did not know either of them then. Henry J. Taylor, the syndicated columnist, was a Deke and a good friend. Douglas Arant, later a *magna cum laude* graduate of the Yale Law School, president of the Alabama State Bar Association and leader in Birmingham's civic and cultural affairs, was another fellow student. So was C. Waller Barrett, in later years the university's greatest benefactor of all time. The fortune in shipping that he accumulated after leaving college was used to give the Alderman Library the finest collection in existence of rare original manuscripts and first editions in American literature, 400,000 items valued at $15 million. Waller Barrett has made other significant contributions to cultural advancement by writing books, serving as chairman or trustee for leading libraries or library-related organizations in various parts of the country and on boards of educational institutions. T. Munford Boyd, totally blind, was one of the most popular and admired members of the student body and made Phi Beta Kappa. After graduation he served as judge of the Juvenile and Domestic Relations Court in Charlottesville. During World War II he was on the legal staff of the War Production Board, later served as advisory counsel to the Virginia Code Commission and is the author of two well-received books on legal subjects. He was for many years a leading member of the University of Virginia law faculty.

Three men who subsequently became college presidents were

students at Virginia when I was there. They were: Henry H. Hill, president of Peabody College for Teachers, Nashville, Tennessee, and also of the American Association of School Administrators and the American Association of Colleges for Teacher Education; Frank R. Reade, president of Georgia State College for Women, Valdosta, Georgia; and Peyton N. Rhodes, president of Southwestern College at Memphis. Also there was W. Horsley Gantt, later a student under the great Pavlov in Russia, and founder at Johns Hopkins University of the Pavlovian Laboratory for the Study of Neurophysiology, which he headed for many years; and Thomas J. Michie, who became a U. S. District judge.

Edward R. Stettinius, afterward Secretary of State, was prominent and popular as a student at Virginia during my time, but no scholar by any stretch of the imagination. He remained in school for a couple of years after I left, and I assumed that he had graduated. The fact is, however, that he never came within hailing distance of doing so. Yet he got an honorary degree much later from Oxford University. The case of Stettinius was in one respect typical of a fair number of students at Virginia in that era. The institution was in dire need of funds, and allowed some undergraduates to remain just about as long as they could pay the tuition, provided they didn't rob a bank or violate the honor system. No such situation exists today. Those who fail to make the required grades are promptly dropped.

There was a sheet at the university called the *Yellow Journal,* which appeared during each of several years while I was in college, and which delighted in needling as many students as possible. "Silence Is the Journal's Thunder—to Be Ignored Is Ignominy" was the reverberating slogan. Nobody knew who the editors were, although some pretty good guesses could be made. A favorite gambit, always included, was a list of members of a nonexistent organization called "I Phelta Thi." The roster consisted of about 50 per cent swingers and 50 per cent total innocents. The latter were much embarrassed while the former probably felt complimented. A sample news item described an imaginary fistfight between two prominent students, who were named. They were taken to the hospital, so the item ran, but "Doctors report that there is no hope, both will recover."

When I received my B.A. degree in June 1920 there was the usual procession down the Lawn, but it was unique in one respect. The band imported to lead the march didn't know what tune to play as the professors and graduates moved toward Cabell Hall. Robert I. Boswell, a waggish fellow who was a topflight baritone soloist with the University Glee Club, came forward to supply the needed information. With tongue in cheek, he hummed a few bars of that ribald ditty "The Bastard King of England." The band took up the tune right lustily, and the class of 1920, with President Edwin Anderson Alderman leading the way, marched down the Lawn to an air that, it seems safe to say, had never been heard before under similar circumstances.

One of the most unusual examinations I ever took was the final exam in my M.A. French class. Professor Richard H. Wilson, a picturesque and original instructor, told the class to write as much or as little as they desired, and on any subject, just so they wrote in French. There were six members of the class, and nobody knew what anybody else's subject was. By an extraordinary coincidence five of us chose the same theme—*l'amour*. I got 94; interpret it as you like. We had been reading French novels all year.

I picked up a bit of extra cash correcting French papers one session and history papers another, but I also worked each summer while in college. In the summer of 1918 I was a "bolter" in the shipyard of the Newport News Shipbuilding & Dry Dock Company. The American Army was blasting its way through the Argonne, the marines were winning further fame in Belleau Wood, and "Smash the Kaiser!" signs decorated the shipyard. In helping to produce warships we felt that we were making a modest contribution to the war effort. I bolted together parts of the battleship *West Virginia* and a destroyer. A record-breaking heat wave struck in early August, and it was hotter in that shipyard than I have ever imagined. There was metal on all sides in the torrid sun, metal hot enough to blister one at the touch, and in addition rivets were being heated red hot in stoves. The mercury hit 110 degrees in the shade, and the shipyard shut down for an entire day, war or no war. Langley Field also ceased to function.

I worked the following summer with the DuPont Engineering Company at Pontiac, Michigan. It was building five hundred houses there for employees of the Oakland Motor Car Company. I had two outdoors jobs which totaled thirteen hours a day and I gained fourteen pounds. Niagara Falls was a stop on the way home, and I got back with $250, which to me was a fortune.

In the summer of 1920 I was given a clerical post in Richmond with the Terminal Storage Corporation, thanks to its president, William J. Parrish, whose sons were my college-mates. Mr. and Mrs. Egbert G. Leigh, Jr., wanted somebody to sleep in their house at 504 West Franklin Street while they were summering at their country place, Piedmont. I was happy to perform this office. It was a lovely house, with every comfort. The only trouble was that the Leighs' long-haired dog had left regiments and battalions of fleas all over the ground floor. I would begin sprinting when I entered the front door, and go up the steps to my room three at a time in order to prevent the ravenous insects from attaching themselves to my person. The effort was often unsuccessful.

Mr. Leigh was one of the most charming and cultivated conversationalists I ever knew. He had never been to college, since his father was unable to send him, but he had read widely and he expressed himself in beautiful English. I greatly enjoyed talking with him on almost any subject when he was in town. The only theme that got me into trouble with him was Woodrow Wilson, whom he deeply despised. Before I became aware of his feeling, I said something complimentary to Wilson. It evoked an explosion from the other end of the sofa that left me shaking. Mr. Leigh's antagonism toward President Wilson extended to the latter's family and entourage. For example, his opinion of Wilson's son-in-law William G. McAdoo was precisely as follows: "When I say unto you that McAdoo is a hatchet-faced son-of-a-bitch, I use the term advisedly."

Mr. Parrish gave me another summer job in 1921, this time in the office of the Fulton Brick Works, so I was again in Richmond and again in the Leigh home.

By that time my pursuit of Miss Douglas Chelf was ardent and relentless. She lived with her parents at Dumbarton, in an attractive house, Lake Lodge, overlooking Staples Mill Pond, and almost next door to Dumbarton Grange, the home of James Branch Cabell. Neither dwelling is there any longer. Douglas' father, T. Wilber Chelf, an insurance executive, had been in the retail drug business, first as a partner of Cabell's father, Dr. Robert G. Cabell, under the name of Cabell & Chelf. Wilber Chelf had won a gold medal in college for excellence in chemistry, and when the University College of Medicine was founded in 1893, under Dr. Hunter McGuire, young Chelf was named its first teacher of chemistry. He served for one session.

Mrs. Chelf, a pretty and vivacious lady, was the daughter of Robert B. Green, and the great-granddaughter of Patrick Gibson, business partner of George Jefferson, cousin to Thomas. The family has a letter from Thomas Jefferson, dated 1811, concerning the proposed appointment of Gibson to a diplomatic post at Lisbon. Jefferson expressed "sincere respect and esteem" for Gibson, as he did on other occasions, but was against his being given the post, since in 1811 we were on the verge of war with Great Britain, and Gibson had been born in Scotland. He was not chosen.

In seeking the hand of Doug Chelf I was in competition with various V.M.I. men. In order to see her I had to journey far out on the streetcar line to the Lakeside stop, where she or her parents would meet me in their automobile and transport me to Dumbarton. Usually I would take my departure before Mr. and Mrs. Chelf's bedtime, and someone would drive me to the streetcar. If I couldn't tear myself away by that hour, I would walk the mile or so to the car stop. Perseverance paid off, and we became engaged on July 13. We have always regarded the number thirteen as lucky. Our daughter Lucy was born March 13 many years later, and our son Heath passed the crisis in a near-fatal illness on November 13. In addition, I was elected president of the American Society of Newspaper Editors on July 13.

The commencement program at the university in 1921, when I received my M.A., was an exceptional one, since the institution's centennial was being celebrated. The observance was supposed to have taken place in 1919, but was postponed because of disturbed world conditions following the war of 1914–18. The program lasted for four days, and eminent speakers from the United States and Europe participated. There was a pageant, "The Shadow of the Builder," in which Father took the prominent role of Socrates. We graduates walked down the Lawn twice to the McIntire Amphitheatre—once to hear Sir Auckland Geddes, the British ambassador, and John Bassett Moore of Columbia University, later judge of the World Court, and again to get our degrees. Dr. Alderman was the speaker on the latter occasion.

My four years at the University of Virginia were at an end. They had been passed in the proverbial ivory tower. I had been fully aware of World War I, of course, while it was in progress, for it affected my daily life, but after the war ended, events overseas or in the city, state and nation engaged my attention only at rare intervals. Woodrow Wilson's fight for the League of Nations did not enlist my concern to the extent that it should have, despite the fact that my father was addressing important audiences in the East on the League's behalf. I paid little attention to what was going on in the political circles of Richmond and Washington. Although I was twenty years old when I finished my college education with an M.A. degree, my view of the world around me was essentially immature and parochial. Fraternity matters, college elections, sports events and Douglas Chelf were in my thoughts. I read the sports pages but not the editorials. It never occurred to me that I should read any books, except those assigned me in class, and I was oblivious to the magazines. True, the parallel reading in some of my courses was extensive, but I felt that once this and other class work was done, it was wholly unnecessary to do any extracurricular reading or study.

In amplification of the above reference to parallel reading, be it noted that in the month of January 1921, in the M.A. course in American literature, I read the following novels: *The Last of the Mohicans, The Scarlet Letter, The House of the Seven Gables, The Virginia Comedians, Horseshoe Robinson, The Yemassee, Edgar Huntly, The Grandissimes, The Turmoil* and *The Voice of the People.* This was not a typical month, but it serves to show that I was doing a good deal of parallel reading in my courses, especially those in English, taught by Dr. James Southall Wilson and Dr. John C. Metcalf, two particularly inspiring teachers.

From time to time during my college career I would be told by some student that he had made a high grade in this or that course "without cracking a book." In other words, he claimed that he had done no studying at all. It may be that some of these boasts were based on fact, but I am constrained to believe that nearly all of them were buncombe. Certainly in my own case I was never able to make any such claim. I would occasionally cut a class, and on two successive days in Easter Week, 1920, I cut all my classes. But, generally speaking, I was conscientious in attending the lectures and carrying out the assignments.

The race problem did not exist for me during my college career, and I gave it no thought whatever. In that era nobody of stature, North or South, was advocating anything more drastic for the southern blacks than better facilities and opportunities within the framework of "separate but equal." As far as I was concerned, the Negroes were "in their place," and that was that. I had only kindly feelings toward them, and abhorred the lynchings that were still occurring, mainly in the Deep South, but I felt no righteous indignation over the obvious discrimination against them in areas of education, health, housing and job opportunities.

The Jewish problem, if there was one at Virginia, was of minor dimensions, not only for me but for everybody. True, the small group of Jewish students had two fraternities of their own, but they were not banned from the ribbon societies or other similar student organizations. Isadore Oppleman, a star athlete, was elected to these organizations and was prominent and popular, as was Michael B. Wagenheim, whose forte was college publications. I knew of no antagonism toward Jewish students as a group.

Over-all, the University of Virginia in the 1920s was a quite different institution from that of the 1970s. Half a century ago the student body and faculty were much smaller, more homogeneous and more intimate. The boys were better groomed and wore coats and ties, although the raccoon coats so prevalent in the Ivy

League were nowhere to be seen. There were practically no married students; the vast majority had no thought of matrimony until after graduation and the acquisition of an adequately paying job. Only a handful of undergraduates had automobiles, and the virtually all-male student body did not go away on weekends, in contrast to the mass exodus that occurred in later years. On Sundays I always took a couple of friends to my home for dinner.

Today we see a vastly bigger university that contains many more of the topflight public school graduates, and hence is more representative of the state as a whole. The percentage of private school graduates is much smaller than it was in the 1920s. Women and blacks make up a large proportion of today's student body. Entrance and degree requirements are higher, and the boys who, in the old days, couldn't get into Harvard, Yale or Princeton, or who flunked out there and came to Virginia, can't get into Virginia anymore. The university's laboratory and other physical equipment is greatly improved. Endowment and state appropriations have become more adequate, and faculty salaries are far more competitive with those in the wealthiest universities. We have today a quite different institution, but unquestionably a great institution.

After taking liberal arts courses at the university for four years, and graduating with the B.A. and M.A. degrees, I had not reached any conclusions as to what sort of career I wished to pursue. Journalism had not appealed to me and I was groping. During my final year at Virginia I was invited by Archibald R. Hoxton to teach French and algebra at Episcopal High during the session of 1921–22. This seemed an excellent way to spend a year, since it would give me more time to decide on next steps. I accepted.

5

The Plunge into Journalism

I FELT STRANGE and out of place when I arrived at the Episcopal High School on September 21, 1921, ready to begin my adventure in pedagogy. This uneasy sensation is recorded in my diary. In addition to the fact that I had never done anything of the sort before, I was wondering if my youth would make it difficult for me to control the boys, some of whom were almost as old as I.

First-, second- and third-year French was my principal subject, and I was a bit rusty, as I had had no French at the university for about a year. So I brushed up during the week preceding my arrival at E.H.S. Thanks to the superior instruction that I had enjoyed long before from my father, I was able to keep a few jumps ahead of my pupils without undue difficulty.

I signalized my arrival on the Hill by accidentally sleeping through breakfast the first morning I was there—certainly an inauspicious beginning. As a teacher I was supposed to be setting an example of punctuality and attention to business for the wayward youths under my care.

Sensing my discomfort, one of the older boys, E. P. Winston ("Jelly") Richardson, whom I had known years before, inquired politely if I would like him to wake me each morning. His bunk was in Blackford Hall, where my room was, and he said he could quite readily knock on my door on the way to his morning shower. I accepted with alacrity. Jelly Richardson was not only a fine young fellow, but one of the best baseball pitchers ever to

102

wear the uniform at Episcopal High. Furthermore, he was the brother of Margaret Richardson, a pretty and attractive girl with whom I had had an ultrajuvenile romance from about age eleven to age fifteen. The Richardsons, who lived in Wilmington, Delaware, visited each summer at the Rosser place, Rugby, adjoining Edgewood.

My dismay at sleeping through breakfast was somewhat lessened that night when I was in charge of study hall and had no difficulty keeping order. A couple of days later full classes began, and I recorded in my diary that I "got along better than I expected." From that time on there was generally smooth sailing.

It was particularly pleasant to be with my former teachers once more—the six members of the so-called Old Guard, most of whom, still in their thirties, I could now bring myself to call by their first names. With Mr. Hoxton such a liberty was unthinkable. There were also the younger teachers, with all of whom I was congenial. Those already on the faculty were "Charlie" Tompkins, "Pat" Callaway and "Dick" Cocke, while two others, Murrell ("Shorty") Edmunds and C. G. Gordon Moss, were newcomers like me.

Richard Hartwell Cocke was the other teacher of French, and I enjoyed especially my association with him. One of the Cockes of Bremo on the James River, he was not only delightful personally, but also well read and possessed of marked literary and musical ability. We formed a lasting friendship.

Charlie Tompkins was another exceptional personality—chuckling, smoking his pipe and talking in his deep voice. Coach for many years of football and track, Charlie became something of an E.H.S. institution.

Reference has been made in a previous chapter to Pat Callaway, coach of the baseball team on which I played in 1917. It was a special dividend of my year as an instructor to be with him once again. His homespun personality and dry wit endeared him to everyone.

Shorty Edmunds coached basketball and was active in dramatics. Extremely conservative in his views at that time, he was metamorphosed some years later into a left-wing liberal, as well as a talented novelist and poet. At Episcopal he was a lively and ebullient spirit, probably stricter in the classroom and the gymnasium with the prominent athletes than he would have been had he not wanted to demonstrate that, despite his small stature, he was not afraid of anybody. And he wasn't.

Gordon Moss arrived at E.H.S. fresh from Washington & Lee University, a fact which, with my sophomoric prejudices, I feared would make it impossible for me to be *simpático* with him. I soon found that he was neither a "parlor python" nor a "lounge lizard," although I had been silly enough to imagine that practically all W & L men were such. They had similarly irrational opinions of Virginia men. Nevertheless, Gordon and I hit it off well. A third of a century later, as a member of the Longwood College faculty, he would stand firmly and courageously, in the almost hysterical atmosphere of the massive resistance era, against the closing of the Prince Edward County public schools. Some of his statements were undoubtedly extreme, but he did not flinch under the heavy pressure.

Early in the session at Episcopal High I awakened to the fact that I was far behind in my reading, so I set out to remedy this deficiency. I read a number of classics, such as *Henry Esmond, Vanity Fair, Adam Bede* and *A Tale of Two Cities,* plus a good deal of Shakespeare and such contemporary novels as *The Age of Innocence, This Side of Paradise* and *If Winter Comes.* Dick Cocke introduced me to the writings of H. L. Mencken, whom I found highly stimulating and amusing. As best I can recall, I had never heard of him or the *Smart Set*—of which he was co-editor— although his famous essay on the South entitled "The Sahara of the Bozart" had evoked howls of indignation from all corners of the former Confederacy.

I succeeded in persuading my fiancée to attend the various school dances. We were not much older than the members of the senior class, and she got her usual "rush" on the dance floor.

I was still floundering in my effort to decide on a profession or business. My experience as a teacher was enjoyable and rewarding, but I did not wish to make teaching my career. I had halfway determined to try to land a job in Richmond's huge tobacco industry, although I viewed the prospect without enthusiasm. Father was not pressuring me in any way, but was trying to help me make a final decision. During the winter he wrote to inquire if I had ever given any thought to journalism. Strangely, I had not, but when I began thinking about it, the idea became increasingly attractive. Soon I was writing John Stewart Bryan, publisher of the Richmond *News Leader*, asking for an appointment. I went to Richmond in March, and Mr. Bryan offered me a reportorial job, effective July 1. Although I was without newspaper experience, and reporters were then being hired at $15 a week, he promised me $20, and said he would make it $30 at the end of one year. From that time on, I knew that I wanted to be a newspaperman.

Mr. Hoxton invited me to return to Episcopal High the following session, but I declined, for I could hardly wait to begin work on the *News Leader*. As soon as commencement was over I went to the University of Virginia and spent three weeks with my parents. I rented a typewriter and began trying to learn the rudiments of typing. Regrettably I developed the hunt and peck technique, and have always wished that I had taken a brief course in the touch system. A course in shorthand also would have been helpful, but it is a startling fact that practically no American reporters, then or since, have taken shorthand. Today, with tape recorders readily available, it is no longer so necessary, but accuracy would be greatly increased if newspapermen were able to take down statements verbatim.

I reported at the *News Leader* on the appointed day, July 1, 1922. The paper was housed in a somewhat ramshackle structure on the east side of Eighth Street just north of Main. This building was torn down when the *News Leader* moved in 1924 to its new headquarters at Fourth and Grace, and the area was used for a parking lot. Subsequently it was the site for part of the Bank of Virginia building.

There was no elevator in the *News Leader*'s aging abode, and one walked up creaking steps to the second floor, where the news and editorial offices were located. I reported to Robert M. Lynn, the managing editor, who referred me to William J. Robertson, the city editor, my immediate boss. He gave me a desk and a typewriter. The item with which I began my newspaper career was one or two paragraphs long, and dealt with the arrival on the Richmond market of the famous Hanover cantaloupes. I was so totally uninformed on the fundamentals of journalism that I didn't even type the piece in double space, but used single space. This did not endear me to city editor Robertson, who must have wondered how this stupid oaf ever got past the front entrance, much less was hired.

However, I was eager to learn, and I hoped to make up in zeal what I lacked in experience. Everything about the job seemed fascinating; in fact it opened up a whole new world. Having been immured in my ivory tower at the university and Episcopal High, I had lost contact with everyday affairs. Now, as a reporter assigned at one time or another to police courts, higher courts, city hall, the Capitol, churches and pretty much every other agency that produces news, I was receiving a liberal education. In fact, I learned more about the world around me in my first six months on the *News Leader* than I did at any other similar period of my life. There's nothing like newspaper reporting to teach one what really goes on in a community.

The paper ran a rather primitive operation by present-day standards. Office boys carried copy to the composing room in their hands, since pneumatic tubes for that purpose were some years in the future. Reporters walked to their beats or took a streetcar. No reporter had an automobile of his own, nor was there an office car for use of the staff. During the 1930s, O. O. McIntire, a syndicated columnist, wrote proudly, "I know newspapermen who drive to the office in their own cars." There weren't any such in Richmond in 1922, and mighty few elsewhere.

A possible exception was Dr. Douglas S. Freeman, who had been editor of the *News Leader* for the preceding seven years when I joined the paper, and who probably had a Model T Ford. He did not publish any of his renowned historical and biographical works until 1934, but he was celebrated already for his knowledge of the Civil War and for the manner in which he had commented editorially on the campaigns of World War I and compared them in detail with those of the War of the Sixties. I confess that this seemed to me to be a far-fetched exercise. In World War II he sought to do the same thing, but with much less success in that conflict's global theater of operations. Which brings to mind the story told me in the 1940s by the Reverend R. Cary Montague, the delightfully human and lovable city missionary for the Episcopal Church. He said he asked his ninety-year-old father if he had read Dr. Freeman's comments that day on the war in the Pacific, and his father replied, "Certainly not! I don't give a damn what General Lee would have done on Wake Island."

Douglas Freeman was as brilliant a man as I have ever known, and his capacity for work was unrivaled, as far as my experience goes. The combination made it possible for him to turn out an almost unbelievable volume of editorials, book reviews, speeches, articles and books. He arose about 2:30 A.M., worked at his home until around 4:30 A.M. and then went to the office, arriving a couple of hours ahead of everybody else. His time was budgeted precisely all day, and included two news broadcasts over the radio. Recreation for him was at a minimum, indeed almost nonexistent. Freeman sometimes took walks in the vicinity of his home or puttered around the garden—every such activity was rigidly scheduled—and in his last years took piano lessons. But work was to him far more important than relaxation, and his daily routine would have been back-breaking for anybody else. He almost never attended social functions.

Although Freeman was only in his late thirties when I came on the paper, his manner was that of a man in his sixties or seventies. He went out of his way to be friendly with me, even to the extent of addressing me as "my sweet boy" when I was forty years old and he was in his fifties. I almost wondered if he was going to pat me on the head.

While Freeman had general supervision over the news and editorial departments of the paper, he was generally concerned with more lofty matters than assignments of the various reporters. City editor Bill Robertson was looked to for this. Bill was a big bear of a man, gentle, refined and soft-spoken, the exact opposite of

"Hildy Johnson," the rip-roaring, profane news executive of the motion picture *The Front Page*.

Soon after I joined the staff, Mr. Bryan, the publisher, asked if I would come to live at his home, Laburnum. He said he was away a good deal, and he wanted somebody in the house with Mrs. Bryan. I declined as politely as I knew how, for I was aware of the talk it would cause around the office. The other reporters would assume that I was some sort of fair-haired boy. But Mr. Bryan insisted, and said he was going to call up my parents in Charlottesville if I persisted in my refusal. So I finally accepted. I was at Laburnum for about a year, until I was married, and the Bryans were delightfully hospitable.

I made a grievous mistake when I had been on the paper less than three weeks. Bill Robertson told me to go to the State Corporation Commission and find out why the Negro-operated and -owned Mechanics Savings Bank had just closed its doors. In view of my total lack of experience, I should not have been given this assignment. I went to the commission's offices and talked with Chairman Berkley D. Adams. He told me that valuable securities had been taken from the bank's portfolio and worthless securities substituted for them. Adams didn't forbid me to quote him, but said, "I wouldn't use this if I were you." I naïvely imagined that his advice would be followed by the paper, and took no notes. When I got back to the office, I wrote nothing. Pretty soon city editor Robertson asked, "Where's that bank story?" "Mr. Adams said he thought it best not to publish anything" was my guileless reply. "What!" exclaimed Robertson. "Can you write the story?" "Sure," said I. "Well, get busy," said Robertson.

I thought I remembered what Adams had told me, but I made a crucial blunder. I wrote that Adams said valuable securities had been taken from the bank's portfolio *by* John Mitchell, Jr., president of the bank, and worthless securities substituted for them. Mitchell was probably the most prominent black citizen in Richmond, publisher of the *Planet*, the Negro weekly, as well as president of the bank. Of course Adams had said no such thing.

When the paper appeared that afternoon with my inaccurate bank story on page one, there was a first-class uproar. Adams quite properly denied that he had attributed the bank's closing to skulduggery on Mitchell's part. I was given a good raking over the coals by managing editor Lynn, who, although a mild-mannered gentleman like city editor Robertson, said very positively that my mistake was a bad one, as it certainly was. J. St. George Bryan, one of the owners of the *News Leader*, told me that we were wide open to a substantial libel suit. I had visions of being fired.

I wasn't, but for a solid year—until the statute of limitations on libel had run out—I was miserable. "Don't get your daubers down," Dr. Freeman admonished me, using an expression that I had never heard. What saved the situation was the finding by the state bank examiner that the bank had closed because of "an unsound credit and investment policy, mismanagement, falsification of records and dishonesty." This pretty well solved my problem, and no suit was filed. But the episode taught me a lesson that I never forgot. It was that one should always take absolutely accurate notes on important conversations involving possible libel, and never try to quote such a conversation from memory. The vital importance of accuracy *under all circumstances* was another lesson that was borne in upon me.

As the newcomer on the reportorial staff, it was logical that I should be given several of the lowliest tasks. Somebody had to type two or three columns of church notices each week for the Saturday paper, and this devolved upon me. It was decided to have a daily column and weekly feature on doings of the Elks, Moose, Odd Fellows, Owls, Woodmen of the World, Masons, et al., and I got this boring assignment. Many years later I found that I had been more or less embalmed for posterity by Emily Clark in her book *Stuffed Peacocks*, since I was the unnamed "slim and serious youth" who dealt with these cryptic matters at the opposite end of the large office telephone booth from Miss Clark. She was the society editor of the paper, and was occupied in gathering news of weddings, engagements and tea parties while I was recording the doings of the Elks and Shriners.

But my principal assignment, and one that was excellent training for so lamentable a greenhorn, was what was known as "News of Southside and Chesterfield." South Richmond had been annexed by the city, but was nevertheless in a slightly separate category, being on the south side of the James River, with courts and other institutions of its own. I was assigned to go daily by streetcar to that area and report what I found in the way of news. My first stop was the undertaker's, where I had my first view of a corpse. The gentleman in charge regaled me with stories of the enormous number of caskets that were shipped in during the flu epidemic of 1918. Police Court and Hustings Court, Part II, were next on my itinerary. I found them intriguing, as I had never been inside any court. Old Police Court Justice Maurice chewing his quid and spitting tobacco juice was typical of many judicial functionaries in that era. I had never known such persons before, nor had I viewed a police blotter. I also gathered church news, and was interested to learn of the B.Y.P.U. and the Epworth League, both of which were new to me. I awakened to the fact that Baptist churches have such unromantic names as First, Second and Main Street, whereas Episcopal congregations are usually named for saints.

Despite advice given me by a one-time reporter on the New York *Herald* that it would be all right to smash the window of a photographic establishment and lift a picture that had been denied me, I smashed no windows. The former *Herald* reporter was then a prominent insurance man in Charlottesville and a friend of my family. He had counseled me as quoted above, as I prepared to enter journalism, and had said, "I think the paper would stand behind you in such a situation," i.e., if I broke a window to steal a picture. I have never ceased to wonder how he could have given me such preposterous advice.

Possibly in New York or Chicago such methods were condoned on certain papers, although I doubt seriously if the management of the New York *Herald* would have done so. Certainly nothing of the sort would have been countenanced in Richmond. Nor were the newsrooms of Richmond papers redolent of whiskey in the 1920s, as seemed to be the vogue in some cities. A Richmond reporter would not hesitate to call up a bootlegger and order a case or a jar of corn delivered to his home, but if there were whiskey bottles around the *News Leader*, I never saw them. Once an empty half pint was found on the premises, and there was quite a storm. No drinking whatever took place during office hours. This was in direct contrast to the situation that prevailed only a few years before on that great organ of moral enlightenment, the Richmond *Virginian*, founded in 1910 by the Rev. Dr. James Cannon, Jr., later Bishop Cannon, and his fellow crusaders, for the purpose of securing the adoption of state-wide prohibition. The *Virginian's* city room "reeked with whiskey," according to several reporters who worked there.

No doubt there was a certain amount of boozing during the period 1910–20 on the "wet" and unregenerate Richmond papers which competed during those years with the "dry" *Virginian*, but when I came on the *News Leader* in 1922 the situation there was under strict control. And I doubt if drinking during office hours in the 1920s was much of a problem on the *Times-Dispatch* and *Evening Dispatch*, the other local papers. However, on a morning daily, where many of the staff work until late at night, opportunities for libations are greater than on one published in the afternoon, such as the *News Leader*.

It is difficult to say whether newspapermen, by and large, have been more prone over the years to drink excessively than members of other professions or businesses. I can only testify that I know of altogether too many talented journalists whose careers have been wrecked by drink.

The quality of ardent spirits vended by the bootleg fraternity was uneven, needless to say. The story is told of a man who changed bootleggers and, being uncertain whether the new consignment was drinkable, decided to send a sample to a laboratory. It had a good amber color, but he wished to be careful. His fears were justified, for the laboratory reported, "Your horse has diabetes."

My own bootician, who shall be nameless, was more reliable. He was wont to deliver my order in a suitcase adorned with labels from various transatlantic steamers and many of Europe's leading hotels. I lost track of him after repeal. Some twenty years later I was sitting in my office when a man came in who looked vaguely familiar. "You probably don't recognize me," said he. Suddenly I realized who he was, and called his name. "I'm with the Richmond Y.M.C.A. now," he explained. And he asked me for a contribution.

Ideas as to what constitutes obscenity were far stricter in the 1920s than those prevailing today. This is vividly illustrated in the attack on the novel *Jurgen* by James Branch Cabell. John S. Sumner and his New York Society for the Suppression of Vice filed proceedings against *Jurgen* on grounds of obscenity. The court rejected this contention, and rightly so. I read *Jurgen* again recently, and it is mild indeed by comparison with many of today's novels and plays. It contains veiled references, *double entendres* and oblique descriptions, but nothing explicit, no four-letter words. Cabell's allusive prose conveys erotic images for those who try to understand what he has in mind. But the over-all impact of the book's so-called obscenity is as nothing compared to that in any number of recent novels.

In journalism, the Hearst papers had been preoccupied for decades with sex and crime, but the tabloids arrived in the twenties to plumb new depths of sensationalism. Someone said that patrons of the Hearst sheets couldn't read without moving their lips, whereas purchasers of the picture-filled tabloids couldn't read at all.

The three Richmond papers were conservative in make-up and news treatment, although the rival afternoon papers, the *News Leader* and *Evening Dispatch*, did use large front-page headlines to attract street sales. Such sales were important in those days. Also, an extra was published when there was exceptional news, since radio was in its infancy and television was far in the future.

Wage scales on newspapers, North and South, were entirely too low. Vacations were for a maximum of two weeks, and if you became ill and were out for two weeks, you got no vacation. Furthermore, the work week was six days, and there was no such thing as overtime. You stayed on a story until you wrapped it up. I was so absorbed in my job that I gave little thought to these things, but when the Newspaper Guild was organized in the early 1930s, I joined, and remained a member until I was named chief editorial writer of the *Times-Dispatch* in 1934. The guild then became a labor union and, while guilty of inexcusable excesses which resulted in the deaths of several fine newspapers, served a real need. Wages and working conditions were vastly improved as a result of the pressure it exerted.

Douglas Chelf and I were married October 10, 1923, in Grace Episcopal Church at the corner of Foushee and Main streets, a church that has since been demolished. The Reverend W. H. Burkhardt, rector of Grace Church, and the Reverend Beverley D. Tucker, Jr., rector of St. Paul's, officiated. The reception was at the home of Dr. and Mrs. Paul W. Howle, 1015 West Franklin Street. Mrs. Howle was the bride's aunt, and Dr. Howle was our family's beloved physician until his death thirty-one years later.

We eluded any rice-throwing groomsmen by getting the train for New York stopped at Greendale, the next station north of Dumbarton. On arriving in Gotham early the next morning we went to the Hotel Collingwood for a stay of several days, and then to Pocono Manor, in the Pennsylvania mountains, for several more. In New York we promptly bought tickets on a rubberneck bus and toured Manhattan. Glenn Hunter in *Merton of the Movies* and Grant Mitchell in *The Whole Town's Talking,* two theatrical hits of that year, were next on our agenda. Manhattan was a thrilling place in those days, and one could walk about the streets at any hour of the day or night without fear of being mugged or murdered. For an aspiring newspaperman it was especially fascinating, since all the famous newspapers were on the stands—the *World,* the *Herald,* the *Tribune,* the *Evening Post,* the *Sun* and the *Times,* not to mention a number of others. Only the *Times* and the *Post* (totally changed) remain from this list. New York City, furthermore, is far less attractive than it was half a century ago. The streets are dirty, taxi drivers and bellhops are often rude and many of the people one meets on the street are unpleasant. Times Square, in 1923, was pretty much the hub of everything, with the tower of the *Times* in the center and theaters all over the area. The tower and the theaters are there today, but the square and its immediate environs have become a veritable cesspool of vice, perversion and pornography, disgusting and also dangerous.

When we arrived at Pocono Manor we found that it was operated by Quakers, and that in order to purchase cigarettes one had to do business with a devious character behind the barn. I was smoking in those days, and I made contact with this individual.

We returned to Richmond, and to a flat on the second floor at 820 Park Avenue, since obliterated to make way for a building of Virginia Commonwealth University. It was the home of Wyndham R. Meredith, a prominent lawyer and charming gentleman of the old school. The principal trouble with the flat was that it was under a tin roof, and of course there was no air conditioning. I doubt if we could stand such temperatures today.

The following summer I was assigned to cover the national marble championships in Atlantic City, all expenses paid by the Scripps-Howard Newspapers for myself and my wife. Scripps-Howard was sponsoring the tourney. Our dear friend John Archer ("Nick") Carter—practically all Carters are called Nick—had covered the elimination matches in Richmond, and was supposed to follow up in Atlantic City, but for some reason was unable to go. We were charged with accompanying both the Richmond and the Petersburg champs to the scene of battle. They had never been on a train or in a hotel. On the sleeper they spent the night crawling up and down between the upper and lower berths, and when we arrived at the rooms in the hotel, one of them inquired, "Do we cook our meals up here?" Both were eliminated from the competition early in the action, but we remained until the tournament was over. The highlight of the trip, as far as I was concerned, was a telegram I got from city editor Earl Sowers—Bill Robertson had gone to another paper—congratulating me on my "excellent work."

During the winter or early spring of 1925 I was invited by the James Branch Cabells to meet Hamilton Owens, editor of the Baltimore *Evening Sun*. Owens was lining up correspondents in various states who would write signed articles for that paper's editorial page, and he asked me to come to Baltimore for a discussion. I did so, and it was the beginning of an association that was a turning point in my journalistic career. H. L. Mencken was contributing articles regularly to the editorial page of the *Evening Sun*, and I was to fill this same spot occasionally, if I could produce the kind of material desired.

I lost no time in sending in a contribution entitled "Poor Old Virginia." The title was a quotation from the then governor, E. Lee Trinkle, who was bemoaning the use of that phrase by persons critical of the state. The gist of my piece was that Virginia was indeed in a sad plight, and that Trinkle was pursuing a "Babbittic 'boost, don't knock' program." I went on to quote a memorable statement made by him at the Democratic National Convention of 1924, when he seconded the nomination of Carter Glass for the presidency: "No one can point the finger of scorn at Carter Glass—except with pride!"

I wrote the foregoing, and a good deal more like it in that article, although at the time I was assigned as a reporter to Governor Trinkle's office, and was dependent on him for news of his administration. When the piece appeared in the *Evening Sun*, it aroused considerable comment in the Virginia press, most of it adverse. Douglas Freeman summoned me to his office for a mild dressing down, which could have been a lot worse. But I was not transferred to another assignment, and Governor Trinkle was not furiously miffed when next I saw him, although he did say that I ought to "get out of the state" if I felt that way about it. He was having an almost perpetual feud with the press, and this was just one more grievance in a long series.

At that time practically all state offices were located in the Capitol and two other structures in Capitol Square, and one of those, the new State Office Building in the southeastern corner of the square, was only about two thirds full. As a reporter, I visited these offices daily, and wondered whether all that space would ever be needed by the Commonwealth. Slightly more than half a century later there were several additional state-occupied structures near the square as big as the above-mentioned State Office Building, plus a large State Highway Building and annex, two substantial hotels that had been bought and converted, along with a commodious life insurance company headquarters, the

Federal Reserve Bank building, and numerous other structures here and there, as well as much rented space. And the end was not yet. True, Virginia's population had doubled since the mid-1920s when I was assigned to Governor Trinkle's office and other state offices, and the vast growth of the federal government made necessary the addition or expansion of numerous state agencies. But the proliferation of the state's own departments and bureaus seemed to be absolutely endless. Consider the staggering fact that whereas the state's general fund appropriations for the 1946–48 biennium were approximately $100 million, for 1977–78 they are $3.7 billion. Current expenditures, in other words, are thirty-seven times as large as those of thirty years ago.

I continued writing for the *Evening Sun*, several articles a year for some six or seven years. These inevitably came to Mencken's attention, and I was astonished to find myself mentioned as an ornament of southern journalism in a book review by Mencken in the August 1926 *American Mercury*. This could only have been based on my *Evening Sun* pieces. In the same year I submitted an article on Virginia to the *Mercury*, and it was accepted. This was in the heyday of the magazine's fame, and almost every young newspaperman was anxious to appear in its pages. I was walking on air for days after the note of acceptance arrived. However, I was never able to land anything else in the *Mercury* during Mencken's editorship.

The "Bad Boy of Baltimore" made his famous southern tour in 1926, accompanied by Paul Patterson, publisher of the Baltimore Sunpapers. When they reached Richmond, Cabell gave them a dinner at his home, and I was invited, along with six or eight others. When I was introduced to H.L.M. he opened wide his china-blue eyes and exclaimed, "I thought you were an old man!" I have never understood this. He may have confused me with my grandfather, for whom I am named, and who died in 1894. Grandfather was a novelist and editorial writer in New York, and Edward P. Mitchell, editor of the New York *Sun*, wrote of him admiringly in his reminiscences.

The contrast between the public image of Mencken, wielding

his meat ax and belaboring the "booboisie" and pretty much everything else, and the friendly, thoughtful man who did many quiet kindnesses was well illustrated in an episode that followed the Cabell dinner. I had brought with me Ernest Boyd's little book on Mencken, in the hope of getting the subject thereof to autograph it. He and Cabell both signed it "in Cabell's house, with all good wishes," and Mencken said that if I would mail it to him, he would get Boyd to sign it too. I mailed it, and in due time it came back with Boyd's signature—a unique souvenir of a well-remembered occasion.

At about this time I found that I had a slight heart condition. It did not appear to be terribly serious, but I was told to curtail my tennis. My heart was behaving strangely and missing beats, and my life insurance went up somewhat in cost. I was smoking about ten cigarettes a day, and sometimes a pipe instead of a cigarette. I asked four doctor friends if they thought that amount of smoking was the cause of my problem, and all said they didn't think so. Then I happened to mention the matter to Dr. St. George Tucker Grinnan, a leading pediatrician. He said at once that smoking was undoubtedly the villain, and that I should abandon all use of tobacco. I did so, and in a few months my heart was back to normal; so was the rate on my insurance. Whatever the truth of the claims and counterclaims with respect to cigarettes and cancer, there can be no question that in my case tobacco was harmful. I shall always be grateful to Dr. Grinnan for telling me so.

I resumed tennis, and was runner-up several times in both singles and doubles for the city and country club championships. I came closest in 1927, when I lost to J. Pinckney Harrison for the city title. The match went to five sets, took over three hours and was played with the thermometer in the nineties and extremely high humidity. Every set was 6–4. Since I survived that, and have been playing regularly ever since—approximately half a century—it seems clear that my disability was only temporary.

I received a legacy of about $2,500 in 1927 from my great-aunt Sarah Eggleston. European travel was extremely cheap then, and my wife and I decided to blow the entire amount and take the grand tour, if I could get a leave of three months from the paper. I got it, and we sailed in August on the *Majestic*.

After landing at Southampton, we did an intensive tour of England and Scotland, and then crossed to the continent. There we covered most of France and Italy, as far down as Naples, and returned via Switzerland and the Rhine. We were young then, and so thrilled and excited by this opportunity to savor the glories of Europe that we rested for exactly one day out of three months. The remainder of the time we tore around at a punishing rate—morning, afternoon and often at night. When we boarded the *Majestic* in November for the return voyage, I had lost no less than fourteen pounds, but it had been completely worthwhile. Furthermore, if I had invested the $2,500 in the then booming stock market, I would probably have lost it in the great crash that came two years later.

In 1928 I accepted a job on the Richmond *Times-Dispatch* which carried with it more money and more stimulating work than had been offered me on the rival *News Leader*. The morning paper's offer was no doubt due, in part, to the fact that in addition to the article in the *American Mercury* I had landed others in the *Nation, Scribner's* and *Plain Talk*. The last-named publication had appeared only shortly before, and was edited by G. D. Eaton, who usually signed his writings G.D.E. In view of the tone of his magazine it was said that the initials evidently stood for "God Damn Everything."

The *Times-Dispatch* was housed in a barnlike structure on Seventh Street south of Main. The building was known as "the stable," since the Railway Express kept horses there in former days. It was not a palatial establishment; I was excited, nevertheless, by the opportunity afforded me.

The bitter presidential contest of 1928 between Alfred E. Smith and Herbert Hoover was in full swing when I joined the *Times-Dispatch* in June of that year. My newly acquired responsibilities called for a signed article each Sunday on the editorial page, and I was also chief political reporter. I devoted a whole series of Sunday pieces to the support of Smith's candidacy. My sympathies have seldom been so strongly engaged on behalf of any candidate as they were in his. The moribund Ku Klux Klan had been given new life by the nomination of a Roman Catholic for the presidency. Bishop James Cannon, Jr., the extremely able and slippery Methodist prelate, mobilized his myrmidons in behalf of Hoover in a blatant attack on Smith's religion. Yet Cannon claimed repeatedly that he was fighting Smith solely because of his stand against prohibition.

In my *Plain Talk* article, I had dealt with the anti-Catholic crusade then raging against the presidential candidacy of Govenor Smith. I had managed to lay my hands on copies of eight or ten of the most virulent anti-Catholic sheets that were mushrooming in all parts of the country, and quoted some of the absurd canards being broadcast in their columns. Among these was the flat statement that the Pope was responsible for starting World War I; that "more than one hundred thousand young men in this country are being informed that it is their Christian DUTY" to kill all Protestants; that the Catholic Church does not recognize the validity of marriages between Protestants, "thus branding millions of worthy American men and women as libertines and harlots"; and that the same church has made and sold in America "millions of bottles of the infamous Benedictine, favorite beverage of the underworld, used in dives and brothels for the corruption and destruction of men and women."

The foregoing is the sort of nonsense that the supporters of Al Smith had to combat in the campaign of 1928. Altogether too many people swallowed this balderdash, with the result that Smith lost Virginia by 24,000 votes and the nation by a wide margin. A generation later the religious issue was put to rest for good by the election of John F. Kennedy as President, and it is difficult for those who did not experience the Hoover–Smith campaign to realize how malignant were the emotions aroused at that time by this so-called issue.

My wife and I had remained at 820 Park Avenue for only one year, and then had moved to an apartment in a new building at 11 North Linden Street just north of Main. We were there for a couple of years, after which we moved to a comfortable one-story frame house at 6005 Howard Road, Westhampton, generously given to us by Mr. and Mrs. Chelf, my wife's parents. We would remain there until 1939.

In order to produce a signed article of 1,200 to 1,500 words each week for the *Times-Dispatch*, I had to formulate my opinions and my philosophy in a more precise manner than I had previously done. My thinking was considerably influenced by H. L. Mencken —to a greater extent, in fact, than by anyone except my father. Mencken's questioning of many accepted beliefs appealed to my youthful mind. His ferocious attacks on individuals and institutions generally regarded as sacrosanct intrigued me. I had no idea of following him blindly, but he made me think.

During my first six years in journalism it had gradually been borne in upon me that there were serious injustices in our society, with the result that I came to be regarded at that stage of my career as something of a "parlor pink." Despite my previous indifference to the plight of the Negro, I became his advocate. I urged that literate blacks be given the franchise, but I did not favor the elimination of the segregation system, since I did not feel that the blacks were ready for this. I espoused the cause of the Scottsboro, Alabama, defendants—blacks who were convicted and sentenced to die for a crime they did not commit. I helped to defeat "barber bills" whereby white barbers were trying to eliminate black competition. In another sphere, the brutality with which some owners of textile mills and coal mines in the South fought the attempts of their employees to organize for better wages and working conditions aroused my indignation, although I did not defend the unions in all things. The tactics used by certain union busters to break strikes included shooting strikers in the back. I also crusaded against antievolution bills, such as were passed in Tennessee, Arkansas and Mississippi, and against intersectional animosity. I wrote frequently on politics in state and nation, and also on historical subjects. These Sunday articles appeared regularly from 1928 until late in 1934.

After the Hoover–Smith presidential campaign, during which Bishop Cannon had been on the front pages constantly as the chief spokesman for the anti-Smith forces in the southern states, the Methodist prelate became an even greater storm center. A whole series of grave charges were filed against him, by persons both inside and outside the Methodist Church. These included gambling in illegal New York bucketshops—shady brokerage houses—hoarding flour during World War I, committing adultery and failing to account for many thousands of dollars contributed through him to the anti-Smith campaign. All this seemed to make Cannon an admirable subject for a book, and I began researching his career. After I had collected the material, I took three months' leave from the paper, without pay, in order to complete the writing. I was afraid that if I didn't finish the job with all possible speed, somebody would get ahead of me. It should be noted that Bishop Cannon at that point was a national, even an international, figure. Mencken called him "the most powerful ecclesiastic ever heard of in America," and a man "whose merest wink" could "make a President of the United States leap like a bullfrog." William R. Hearst, the newspaper publisher, who spent much time and money trying to undermine his influence, said he had "the best brain in America, no one excepted." Cannon's brain was in fact so sharp that the combined efforts of all those who detested him were insufficient to convict him on a single one of the above-mentioned charges. He got off in the courts and also before the church tribunals that tried him. Yet a large number of Methodists and others were never convinced of his innocence.

When I finished the manuscript and submitted it to publishers, the bishop was under fire from various directions, but the charges against him had not been finally disposed of. He was the center of an almost unprecedented uproar, but I got a long series of rejections for my manuscript. There were at least two reasons for this. In the first place, I had written the book in much too great haste, and it was not well done. In the second, there was the very real danger that Cannon would sue. His almost regular practice was to file suit against a newspaper, magazine or book publisher for some large amount, ranging from several hundred thousand dollars to a million, and then settle for a few thousand. Most of the defendants preferred to make such an out of court settlement, even if they felt confident that they could win the case, since a modest payment would be less expensive than a prolonged court battle. Cannon would certainly have sued any publisher who brought out my book, and such a suit would presumably have stopped the sale of the book, at least until the case was decided in the courts.

The great crash of 1929 came while I was on leave and working intensively in the attic at 6005 Howard Road on my Cannon manuscript. It was important that I recoup my lost three months' salary by selling my biography of the bishop, but I was unable to get it published for another twenty years, when I had rewritten it from beginning to end and Cannon had died. By that time interest in his lurid career was at an extremely low ebb.

With the onset of the Great Depression I was unable to find means of recovering the three months' salary that I had forgone. Not only that, but along with nearly everybody else fortunate enough to have a job in those grim days, I had a couple of salary cuts before the prolonged ordeal was over. A compensating factor was the steady drop in living costs.

Our first-born, Douglas Gibson, a daughter, had arrived in June, and the exchequer was strained by this addition to the family, although our joy far exceeded our concern over any related financial problem.

However, there was a ray of sunshine when a letter arrived from the University of North Carolina Press inviting me to write a book on liberal movements in the South from the American Revolution to the present. An advance royalty of $200 was offered. This was no princely sum, but do university presses today pay an advance under any circumstances? Most of them require a subsidy by the author of several thousand dollars, at least. The invitation from Chapel Hill was accepted, and I plunged into the task with enthusiasm. I worked extremely hard and spent just about all my spare time for nearly two years researching the subject and writing *Liberalism in the South.* It appeared in October 1932 at or near the very bottom of the Depression. The book was favorably reviewed both North and South, and William Soskin, literary editor of the New York *Evening Post,* formally predicted that it would win the Pulitzer Prize for history. Of course it didn't; neither did it sell. The first printing of, I believe, 1,500 copies was finally exhausted and there was no second printing. A partial explanation for the manner in which the work was ignored by the book-buying public may perhaps be found in the fact that so many people, especially in the South, were dead broke. (Some forty years later, the book was reprinted by a New York reprint house, as were my next two books.)

Meanwhile, back at the *Times-Dispatch* I was bored and frustrated. I was writing occasional editorials in addition to my Sunday article, but reporting was beginning to pall. I had been at it for about a decade and the excitement and novelty had gone out of it. I saw no likelihood of important advancement on the paper. There had been two vacancies in the post of editor, and each time the management got somebody from New York who knew little or nothing about Virginia. I sounded out Arthur Krock, chief of the New York *Times* Washington Bureau, in the hope that he might have an opening. I had been writing signed "Watchtower Correspondence" for the *Times* from Virginia since 1929 (and would keep it up until 1948), so he was somewhat familiar with my work. But the Depression was still far from over, and Krock said he could not offer me anything.

I learned that several newspapermen had received grants for study in Germany and Austria from the Oberlaender Trust of the Carl Schurz Memorial Foundation, which was seeking to promote better relations between the United States and the German-speaking countries. I determined to apply. It would enable me to get away for a few months and to decide on my next steps. I went to Philadelphia for an interview, and was informed soon thereafter that a grant of $2,200 had been approved. This was to cover a six months' stay. Nowadays such a sum would be ludicrously inadequate, but in 1934 prices in Europe were at rock bottom, the dollar was strong and $2,200 was enough for my wife and me. We would have to supplement it somewhat, in order to take along our four-year-old daughter, but this could be managed. I arranged to write my weekly article for the *Times-Dispatch* editorial page from Europe, and also to mail in editorials.

It was a fascinating time to be in Central Europe—almost too fascinating—as Adolf Hitler had come to power in Germany the year before. There were periodic reports in the press that Americans were being slapped in the face and otherwise maltreated by the Nazis for not saluting as they walked past memorials to Nazi heroes, and some of our friends thought we were more or less out of our minds to be going to Germany at such a time, but there seemed to be no real cause for alarm. We sailed in March 1934 to be in Europe until September.

The Oberlaender Trust did not wish me to interview Hitler or to be subjected to the intense Nazi propaganda that was immediately applied to any visiting journalist. It accordingly announced that I was coming over to study "German periodical literature," and every effort was made to camouflage the fact that I was in reality studying the whole political and military situation. I went once to the Prussian State Library on Unter den Linden and looked at a few magazines—and that was the extent of my six months' "study of periodical literature." As a matter of fact, I couldn't see the two journals that I specifically requested, *Harper's* and the *Nation*. They were *verboten* to the public, since they contained articles highly critical of the Nazis.

We were in Berlin six weeks, Vienna six weeks, Munich eight weeks, Berchtesgaden two weeks and Bonn two weeks, with side excursions to many other places, including Prague, Budapest and Nuremberg. It was indeed an exciting experience, and one that meant much to both of us. An intelligent, well-educated German Fraülein, Annaliese Clarenbach, had been recommended to us, and was available to travel with us and look after our little girl. We were able to afford this by staying in pensions and watching our budget carefully. Everything in Germany and Austria was unbelievably inexpensive. For example, at our fine pension in Berlin the four of us had two rooms and a bath, with three excellent meals, for the well-nigh incredible sum of $6.00 a day over-all. Our dollars went unusually far because the Oberlaender Trust had arranged that they should have a special value in relation to the mark, but prices were amazingly cheap for all Americans.

I heard Hitler speak at the Tempelhof Airfield in Berlin on May 1, the German Labor Day, before what was said to be the biggest crowd in the history of the world—two million people. I had an excellent seat in the press box. In view of the hysterical pro-Hitler ovations that I had read about, I anticipated a similar demonstration on this occasion. The field was surrounded by gigantic pylons bearing the swastika, and there were hundreds of enormous Nazi flags. A musical build-up with thousands of marching soldiers and storm troopers preceded the formal program. The Nazis, with their great ability to put on dramatic and colorful spectacles, seemed to have organized this one in a manner to achieve the maximum response.

Finally the announcement came over the loudspeaker: "*Achtung! Achtung! Der Fuehrer!*" Hitler appeared hatless and giving the Nazi salute as he stood beside the chauffeur of a car that swept across the field while the band played his favorite march, the stirring *Badenweiler*. Other cars followed with Goebbels, Goering and lesser lights. Strangely enough, the huge crowd was almost completely silent. Hitler and the others mounted the reviewing stand, and Goebbels limped forward on his club foot to introduce the speaker. He was greeted by polite handclapping. When Hitler walked to the reading desk, he too received only nominal applause. His subject was "Labor and Unemployment," not exactly a rouser, but the apathy with which his address was received was remarkable. Hitler was interrupted eighteen times during his forty-minute speech, but only two or three of these plaudits seemed genuinely spontaneous and at all loud. I thought surely there would be a tremendous ovation when he sat down, and took out my watch to time the applause. It lasted exactly seven seconds. The program closed with the playing of the *Horst Wessel* song, composed by Horst Wessel, a Nazi brawler who consorted with prostitutes and pimps, and was murdered by Communists.

The frosty reception given the Fuehrer was extremely puzzling. It was not until two months later that I found what seemed to be at least a partial explanation.

My wife and I were in an Alpine cafe at Berchtesgaden on the night of June 30. Germans at the same table kept whispering to one another in low tones that a number of persons somewhere had been shot. They seemed agitated and our curiosity was aroused. After the program of music, dances and songs of the Bavarian Alps was over, other Germans stood about discussing these mysterious events. When we got back to our pension, the proprietress told us there had been an announcement over the radio that Hitler had smashed a "small conspiracy," that seven persons had been shot and others taken into custody.

Next day, Sunday, the *Berchtesgadener Anzeiger* got out an extra, which I still have. It is printed on one side of a sheet of paper, like a handbill, with the names of the seven "conspirators" who were shot, and a few other alleged facts—the official Nazi version of what had happened. There was much interest on the part of the citizens of Berchtesgaden in all this, and they stood in the streets reading the *Anzeiger*. But there was absolutely no disorder or obvious excitement.

Not until a couple of days later, when the English newspapers arrived, did we discover the magnitude of Hitler's June 30 "blood purge" or "night of the long knives," as it came to be known. The Nazis had murdered not seven but several hundred, perhaps a thousand, Germans on the pretext that they were involved in a plot of some kind. Possibly a group of them were up to something, although no evidence was ever presented. Hitler simply announced later that there was a plot against his leadership, and that he had no alternative but to crush it. Many of those murdered were people Hitler didn't like or who had opposed him at one time or another. Some were shot at their desks, others were found dead in rivers or swamps and about 150 were stood up before firing squads in Berlin's Lichterfelde Barracks. The last-mentioned victims of the Fuehrer were ranking members of the *Sturmabteilung,* or S.A., the brown-shirted storm troopers. Ernst Roehm, the scar-faced head of the S.A., had made no secret of his desire to see that organization become the nucleus of the German Army, with himself in command. However, no evidence was forthcoming that anything in the way of a conspiracy was about to be sprung by Roehm. The latter, a notorious homosexual, had been Hitler's fellow fighter for Nazidom since the early days of the movement, perhaps the closest of all his friends at the time of the movement's beginnings. Other Nazi leaders—although not Hitler, apparently—shared Roehm's weird sexual propensities. Hitler was fully aware of this, but when he decided to murder his former comrades, he professed to be shocked by their perversion.

The undercurrent of hostility between Hitler and the Brown Shirt leadership apparently explains, at least in part, the chilly reception the Fuehrer got at the Labor Day observance in Berlin. Half a million Brown Shirts were immediately in front of the speaker's stand, and hence in a position to lead the applause or to dampen it. The S.A. was far from enthusiastic, as was clearly evident to those of us in the press box. The lurking antagonism that was obviously present at that time burst forth in the wholesale murders of the S.A. leaders and others on June 30.

The North American Newspaper Alliance sent me a cable about a week after the "blood purge" asking me to give them the inside story of that sanguinary affair. I was not in a position to do this, as I had no idea myself at that stage just what the inside story was. Furthermore, if I had tried to find out, given my altogether limited knowledge of the situation and my almost nonexistent contacts, I might well have gotten myself shot, or at a minimum have been thrown out of Germany. I wanted to complete my six months in Central Europe, an invaluable experience for my future work, and then to express myself freely and frankly concerning the Nazi atrocities.

Jews were being sharply discriminated against in 1934, of course, despite loud denials from certain quarters. They were being insulted, humiliated and exiled, and some were beaten up. There were appeals in the Nazi-controlled press for "Aryan" Germans not to patronize Jewish business establishments. Also, there was a venomous campaign against the Jews in *Der Stuermer*, the principal anti-Semitic sheet. However, few imagined then that the Nazis would begin exterminating them in murder camps at Dachau, Buchenwald, Bergen-Belsen, Auschwitz and the rest.

Signs forbidding Jews to enter certain localities were rare in 1934. We saw only one such sign, and that was outside Dinkelsbuehl, the charming picture-book town. We arrived there on a rickety railroad train pulled by a tiny, comic-strip type of locomotive, with a coal stove in the middle of each coach and a pipe leading from it through the roof. As we walked to the town from the railroad station we saw a placard on a telephone pole which said, in German, "Jews Not Wanted—City Council of Dinkels-buehl." This made us so angry that we almost turned around and left. I photographed the sign so as to have it as evidence on our return to the United States.

While we were in Berchtesgaden a letter came from Charles P. Hasbrook, publisher of the *Times-Dispatch*, offering me the post of chief editorial writer of the paper, with assurance that if my work was acceptable, I would be given the title of editor. I accepted by return mail, needless to say. This was the opportunity I had been waiting for. Had it not come, I would have left the *Times-Dispatch* as soon as I could find something to my liking elsewhere. Hasbrook informed me that Vincent G. Byers, editor of the paper and former managing editor of the New York *Evening Post*, was resigning October 1, 1934, and that I was to take over my new job on that date. I couldn't have been more pleased.

A few weeks after I received these glad tidings we feared that a general European war was about to break out. Chancellor Dollfuss of Austria was shot by Austrian Nazis in his office. He was refused the service of either a physician or a priest, and was left to bleed to death. We had seen Dollfuss a short time before at a ceremony in front of the Vienna City Hall. A pleasant-looking man, only five feet tall, he was accompanied by Cardinal Innitzer, who was often with him on ceremonial occasions. Dollfuss was a Fascist, but he was grimly determined, if possible, to prevent his native land from being crushed beneath the jackboots of the far more menacing German Fascist to the north.

We were in Rothenburg, the delightful old dream-city on the Tauber River, when the news came that the Nazis had murdered Dollfuss. Almost exactly twenty years had elapsed since Archduke Franz Ferdinand of Austria had been assassinated at Sarajevo, with catastrophic consequences for mankind. Would this latest murder of an Austrian leader bring a new world war? We hurried back to Munich. Mussolini rushed troops to the Italo-Austrian border, indicating his determination to prevent Hitler from seizing Austria. Whether *Il Duce* would have stood firm if *Der Fuehrer* had decided to move is anybody's guess. But Hitler evidently did not regard the time as ripe, and the situation calmed down.

The trip to Rothenburg from which we had rushed back was one of many that we were able to take, thanks to our confidence in Fraülein Clarenbach, the exceptionally able and reliable companion for our little girl. We could leave for several days and feel entirely at ease, sure in the knowledge that our daughter was being well cared for.

Nick and Evelyn Carter were on a European trip, and in late August they arranged for a stopover at our Munich pension. We enjoyed showing them some of the sights, which included sojourns in the Hackerbräu Bierhalle and the Hofbräuhaus, where we had dinner. At these two watering places Nick and I each consumed, during the afternoon and evening, a total of four liters, or just over one gallon, of beer. Since we were in the beer capital of the world, we felt obligated to do justice to the occasion. The Carters left a couple of days later for the United States.

We stopped in Paris en route home. Little Douglas and Fräulein Clarenbach had an unpleasant experience in a shop. The lady in charge of the store was all smiles when she saw a supposedly rich American tot and her companion come in. But when she found that only one franc (four cents) was to be spent, she immediately became so rude and disagreeable that little Douglas was in tears and did not wish even to walk by that shop again. Her mother and I had several encounters with rude, even abusive and profane, salespeople during the ten days that we were in Paris. This was in glaring contrast to our experience during six months in Germany and Austria. The invariable good humor and good manners of the German and Austrian salespeople, no matter whether one spent four cents or $40, could not fail to impress. In fairness to the French, we have found them to be much more prepossessing on some subsequent trips. In fact, a few years ago, there were several instances of quite extraordinary kindness and politeness on the part of both French men and women.

We said good-bye to Paris and Fraülein Clarenbach on September 23 and boarded the boat train for Cherbourg. It was necessary to go out to the *Bremen* on a tender, and there was a high wind. Douglas "Sr." was holding on to little D. as they went up the swaying gangplank, with the result that the former's brand-new Rue de la Paix hat blew off into the sea. It was a calamity from which we were slow to recover.

However, the rest of the trip was quite pleasant, and we were excited at the prospect of going home. When we reached Richmond on the sleeper from New York on September 28, I picked up the *Times-Dispatch* and read, to my consternation, that Charles Hasbrook had resigned as publisher of the paper. I wondered whether I was still to be chief editorial writer, and visited the paper promptly for the purpose of finding out. The answer was altogether reassuring. I was not only to be chief editorial writer, but they wanted me to get to work the next day, instead of October 1, as originally planned. This put me in something of a bind, as my personal affairs were in a state of chaos after an absence of half a year, but I acquiesced gladly.

On my arrival at 6005 Howard Road, sporting the mustache that I had turned out overseas, the Alex Parkers' cook was much impressed. "I declare, Mr. Dabney," said she, "you really looks like a man with that mustache. When you left here, you didn't look like nothing but an overgrown boy." However, my mother objected so vehemently to the mustache that I shaved it off almost at once.

The trip had been a wonderful experience from every standpoint, not least for the invaluable background it afforded me concerning events and personalities in Central Europe, especially Hitler and the Nazis. What I had seen and heard stood me in particularly good stead when Hitler seized Czechoslovakia and Austria, and the world moved closer and closer to war.

I managed somehow, along with my brand-new editorial duties, to write three comprehensive signed articles on Nazi Germany, the first of which appeared forty-eight hours after our arrival and the others on the two following days. In these I expressed the view that the Nazis were preparing for war. I also sought to analyze their entire program, its brutalities and intellectual obscenities.

When I left for Europe the preceding March, I had been frustrated and discouraged, but now I was full of zest for my new job. It didn't really matter how hard I had to work; it was fun.

6

On the Eve of Armageddon

MANY MILLIONS OF Americans had lost their jobs by the autumn of 1934 when I took over the editorial page of the *Times-Dispatch*. The country was close to the bottom of the Great Depression. President Franklin D. Roosevelt had put through a whole series of legislative enactments designed to cope with the crisis, some of them sound and others not. My first inclination was to support virtually his entire program, but I come to see later that a good deal of it was specious and wasteful.

Mark F. Ethridge, who had made a fine editorial reputation on the Macon, Georgia, *Telegraph*, and then joined the staff of the Washington *Post*, was chosen publisher of the *Times-Dispatch* late in 1934, succeeding Charles Hasbrook. U. S. Senators Harry F. Byrd and Carter Glass of Virginia were attacking most of FDR's program vigorously, and Ethridge shared my dismay at this. The *Times-Dispatch* was especially critical of Byrd for these repeated attacks, and he became much concerned, even angry. He and I had been on friendly terms ever since he entered the governor's mansion eight years before, but he evidently felt that I was trying to undermine him politically. He did not communicate with me directly, but had some wrathful exchanges with Ethridge. The paper continued to criticize him when we felt that he deserved it, but the criticism was moderated later when we saw that Byrd was right in some of the severe things he said concerning the laws passed by Congress at Roosevelt's instigation.

Harry Byrd had been sending me a Christmas basket of apples

ABOVE, Richard Heath Dabney, father of Virginius Dabney, and member of the University of Virginia faculty for forty-nine years, at approximately age sixty-five. His unshakable integrity, constant concern for his students, and keen sense of humor were perhaps his principal characteristics.

RIGHT, Lily Heth Dabney, mother of Virginius Dabney, is shown in her middle or late eighties. She lived to be ninety-eight, and flew to London for a two-week stay when ninety-three. She loved people, and her greatest pleasure was to entertain relatives or friends in her home.

ABOVE, Lucy Minor Davis, maiden gr[e]
great-aunt of the author, who taught him ev[e]
thing except languages until he went o[ff]
school at age thirteen. She was widely read [.]
greatly beloved. Like nearly all women of [her]
generation, she never went to college.

LEFT, Thomas Lloyd Dabney, half uncle of [the]
author, who had been a Metropolitan O[pera]
star near the turn of the century, singing u[nder]
the name of Lloyd d'Aubigné, is shown du[ring]
the war of 1914–18 with his French Army [fil-]
leul, Louis Grave. Dabney was teaching v[oice]
at his villa in Sèvres outside Paris, and he ch[ose]
several soldiers from the French Army to be [his]
filleuls and come to his villa from the tren[ches]
for rest and recreation.

Virginius Dabney aged three and a half, after two summers at Nahant, Massachusetts. Before going there he had been extremely sickly. (*J. E. Purdy & Co., Boston*)

Lucy Davis Dabney, sister of the author, who died of diabetes at age eight before the discovery of insulin. A remarkable child, she never complained because of the rigid diet prescribed for her, and was cheerful and happy until her inevitable death.

Boy Scouts at the University of Virginia about 1913. Front row, left to right, John A. Lile, William T. Moseley, Marion Patton Echols, V. Dabney and C. Venable Minor. Rear row: Henry B. Gordon, John Staige Davis, Jr., the Reverend Beverley D. Tucker, Jr., afterward Episcopal Bishop of Ohio, and Jack Nevin.

Baseball team at Episcopal High School in 1917. From row, left to right: Johnson McGuire, first base; Musco Burnett, third base; J. Willcox Dunn, shortstop and captain; V. Dabney, second base; Philip M. Harding, catcher Second row: Lee Trenholm, outfield; Asbury Hodgson pitcher; Francis E. Carter, manager; Patrick A. Callaway coach and for many years the most beloved member of th school faculty; Lawrence A. Balliere, outfield; Christian V. Holland, catcher. Rear row: John C. Page, pitcher, and Simon Seward, outfield.

Douglas Harrison Chelf of Richmond, shown when she was attending the dances at the Virginia Military Institute for five straight years. She became Mrs. Virginius Dabney in 1923. *(Homeier–Clark, Richmond)*

City room at the Richmond *News Leader* in 1924, a typically cluttered newsroom of the era. On the left, in the group of five: foreground, left to right, Allen Cleaton and R. L. C. Barret; behind them, Earl Jones, office boy; Roy Fitzgerald, and Dr. Douglas S. Freeman, editor. In right rear of room, at typewriter, Hugh Rudd, and Scott Hart. Proceeding toward the front: office boy, name unknown; V. Dabney, Roy C. Flannagan, John Riis, Earl Curtis, office boy; Leroy R. Cohen and city editor Earl Sowers, at desk with mustache; from his left, John Archer Carter, Zach Woodall and Lee E. Cooper. *Faris–Dementi Studio, Richmond)*

Virginia newspaper editors, all of whom had trained under John Stewart Bryan, then publisher of the Richmond *News Leader*, were entertained at luncheon in 1936 by Dr. Douglas S. Freeman, editor of the *News Leader*. Left to right: Dr. Freeman, J. St. George Bryan, Louis I. Jaffé, Norfolk *Virginian-Pilot*; John Stewart Bryan, Douglas Gordon, Norfolk *Ledger-Dispatch*; V. Dabney, Richmond *Times-Dispatch*; William B. Smith, Roanoke *World-News*, and Robert Glass, Lynchburg *News*.

Roberta Becks, nurse of Virginius Dabney, is shown caring for his first child, Douglas G. Dabney. This competent and conscientious woman was an indispensable and highly valued member of the two Dabney households for decades. *(Boice)*

V. Dabney in Dinkelsbühl, Germany, on the six-month trip to Germany and Austria made in 1934 by himself, his wife and their daughter under a grant from the Oberlaender Trust. He is wearing the mustache he grew at that time, but it was not at all luxuriant and is hardly visible. Note Nazi swastika in background.

from his extensive orchards each year since about 1928, and he continued to do so throughout his public career, even when I was attacking his role in Washington. When he retired, we were on the best of terms.

In 1936 Ethridge accepted an offer from the Louisville *Courier-Journal,* and John Dana Wise, publisher of papers in Columbia and Spartanburg, South Carolina and Augusta, Georgia, was brought in to succeed him. Wise gave me the title of editor and our relations were excellent for several years. But he became increasingly domineering as time passed—of which more anon.

Even as editor, I was in charge of only the editorial page, with no responsibility for the rest of the paper. This was the arrangement that I greatly preferred. I was and am an editor and writer, not an administrator or executive. Many editors have charge of the entire paper, but most of these have little time to write anything themselves. I wanted to write.

When I assumed my post as chief editorial writer, I had only one editorial operative to assist me. He was William B. Southall, an attractive man with a slight stutter who had been wounded with the U. S. Marines at Belleau Wood. "Senator" Southall, as he was known, was a fairly effective performer, but he was notoriously lazy. For example, when he arrived at the office in the morning, he would snap on his desk light and then disappear for anywhere from a half-hour to an hour. He had a certain facility in turning out editorials, but not if they were on complex subjects requiring research. He seldom read anything except the Richmond papers and the New York *Times.* We took a dozen of the better magazines, but if Southall ever looked at one of them, I never detected him in the act. Nor could I ever find that he was reading any book. In addition, he annoyed me by throwing paper and other debris on the office floor, with the result that the area around his desk looked like the residue of a minor hurricane.

The job of getting out seven editorial pages a week is a sufficiently demanding task for two alert and energetic writers, but when one of them is working halfheartedly about five or six hours a day, the thing becomes impossible. I began looking around for a replacement, and found him in William Shands Meacham, editor of the Danville, Virginia, *Register*. Meacham had made a reputation in Danville as an authority in several fields, and, in addition, had a graceful and practiced editorial style. He came to Richmond and Southall went back on the reportorial staff. In partial extenuation of Southall's lackadaisical editorial performance it should be noted that he had been passed over several times for promotion to chief editorial writer, and this doubtless tended to crush his spirit.

I commented frequently in the paper on Adolf Hitler's increasingly bellicose actions, which were usually accompanied by loud protestations that he wanted only peace. *Der Fuehrer* made a whole series of patently false statements on this subject, beginning with the one issued after the death of President von Hindenburg: "We ask only that our present frontiers shall be maintained, and believe me we shall never fight again, except in self-defense." This transparent untruth was followed by "Germany neither intends nor wishes to interfere in the internal affairs of Austria, to annex Austria or to conclude an Anschluss." Then there was that other memorable declaration: "The Sudetenland is the last territorial demand I have to make in Europe."

It seemed obvious to me, thanks largely to my six months in the citadel of Naziism, that Hitler was trying to lull the rest of the world to sleep while he prepared his *Blitzkrieg*. I wrote a series of editorials analyzing the Nazi movement and record, in the light of my observations in Central Europe and the Fuehrer's book, *Mein Kampf*, in which his sinister plans were fully set forth.

Austria was seized, of course, in March 1938, and then in September of that year Nazi Germany's campaign to take over Czechoslovakia reached its crescendo. Poor befuddled Prime Minister Chamberlain of Great Britain held a series of ominous conferences with Hitler in Germany, during which the German dictator constantly raised the ante and Chamberlain as regularly backed down, on the assumption that he was achieving "peace in our time." The shattering climax came at Munich, when Czechoslovakia, the land of Masaryk and Benes, was betrayed by her allies, Britain and France, and handed over to the tender mercies of the Nazis.

I wrote a series of outraged editorials on these tragic events which brought what was probably the largest reader response ever evoked by any series of mine. The editorial "The Sell-Out to Hitler," which appeared on September 20, 1938, following the capitulation of Britain and France in the face of Germany's sword rattling, may have been the best editorial I ever wrote. It filled the entire editorial space, and the favorable reaction surpassed anything of the sort in my experience. It opened as follows:

"The year 1938 will mark the beginning of the end of the British Empire, the decline of France as a world power, and the rise of a German Empire far mightier than that of Charlemagne. Those are the fateful conclusions to which we have been driven by the events of yesterday in London and Paris, where the British and French governments capitulated ignominiously and completely to the demands of the Nazis, and set about the business of dismembering not only the last obstacle in Hitler's path to the Black Sea, but the last stronghold of freedom in the heart of Europe. . . ."

My thesis was that if Britain and France had told Hitler that they would declare war if he did not take his hands off of Czechoslovakia, he would probably have backed down. "He knows," I wrote, "that Germany today cannot stand a prolonged struggle with powers that can blockade his coasts and shut off his supply of raw materials." (The full text of this editorial appears in the Appendix.)

I worked almost around the clock on my editorials of 1938 and 1939, dealing with the approach of another world war; hours meant little in those days. Such merit as the editorials possessed derived, I believe, from this, and from the further fact that there was emotional content in them.

On the other side of the fence was Thomas Lomax Hunter, a *Times-Dispatch* columnist who wrote under the caption "As It Appears to the Cavalier." Hunter was pro-German all the way. He was a fine stylist in both light verse and prose, well read in the classics, but abysmally ignorant concerning the issues that con-

fronted the world in those parlous times. In any controversy involving France and Germany, the Teutons were always right, according to "the Cavalier." In fairness, Hunter did not actively
espouse the cause of the Nazis, but he was supremely confident
that most of the criticism leveled at them was based on unsub-
stantiated rumors and half-truths. The fact that I had been in
Germany and Austria for six months during Hitler's rise, whereas
he had never been to Europe, meant nothing to him. He was at
his best in writing about rural Virginia, and some of his columns
on this subject are classics of their kind. He was also a relentless
and highly effective critic of prohibition, so much so that he almost drove the drys wild. But he annoyed me dreadfully with his
pontification on subjects about which he knew hardly anything.
We sometimes took issue with him editorially.

A member of the paper's reportorial staff who died in his early
thirties in 1936, and whose death was a loss to journalism, was
Adoniram Judson Evans, Jr., known to all as "Jud." Jovial, witty,
highly original in both his writings and his conversation, Jud
Evans was blimplike in his physical contours. I shall always be indebted to him for terming me the only married man he had ever
known "who doesn't have that whipped look." When Jud came
down with his final illness, he failed, with characteristic lack of
foresight, to call a doctor until it was too late.

At about this time I had an interview with Huey P. Long, the
self-styled "Louisiana Kingfish." Long was causing a nation-wide
sensation with his "share the wealth" program. By dint of
demoniac energy, consummate ability and uninhibited dema-
goguery, he had turned Louisiana into a one-man dictatorship, and
was eying the White House. He was promising over coast-to-coast
radio hookups that he planned to see that any man who needed it
would get a $5,000 homestead and a $2,000 income. His "every
man a king" broadcasts in the depths of the Depression were
bringing him the almost incredible total of 15,000 to 30,000 letters a day. An obviously worried President Roosevelt was wincing
under his attacks.

I was curious to meet this man who was causing such a tremendous stir in political circles, and one day when I was in Washing-

ton I sent my card in to him and requested an interview. Huey was hungry for publicity, and he consented to meet me in a room off the Senate floor. I took my wife with me, and also our friends the Dumas Malones. In a few minutes the Kingfish rushed in, with hair disheveled and waving his arms like a windmill. "Sit down, lady!" he said to my wife, as he almost pushed her into a chair.

It appeared that Long had chosen to put on a hick act for our benefit. He used bad grammar and spoke in an accent that sounded as though it had oozed up from the Louisiana cane-brakes. We were in the process of asking him a few questions when somebody came in with a note. He glanced at it and rushed out, still waving his arms and never pausing to say good-bye. He impressed all of us as crude and vulgar to the nth degree.

Shortly afterward he was on the Senate floor, shouting furious criticism of Postmaster General James A. Farley, one of Roosevelt's right-hand men, and professing in the most sanctimonious terms to be shocked at something or other that he said Farley had done. Long's assault on the postmaster general was delivered in faultless prose and without the bogus down-home accent that he had employed in his conversation with us.

If this ruthless and brilliant man had not been assassinated the following year, he might have become this country's first dictator. He had furnished the blueprint in Louisiana.

In 1935 my sister, Alice Saunders Dabney, was married to John C. Parker, a Franklin, Virginia, attorney, later president of the Virginia State Bar and chairman of the Virginia Constitutional Convention of 1956. They have two charming and able daughters —Alice Fleming, now Mrs. Reginald E. Rutledge, Jr., and Elizabeth Williamson, now Mrs. James C. McColl. Both girls were graduated from Sweet Briar College after making fine records. Alice Fleming, mother of two, is the Reverend Fleming Rutledge, curate of Christ's Episcopal Church, Rye, New York; and Betsy McColl, mother of one, has been winning tennis tournaments for years in Virginia and South Carolina. Fleming Rutledge, ordained as a deacon, did not seek ordination to the priesthood until the ordination of women had been approved by the General Convention of the Episcopal Church.

During the middle and late 1930s the *Times-Dispatch* was deeply involved editorially with the enactment by the Virginia General Assembly of a law governing the hours worked by women in industry. There had been no Virginia legislation on this subject since 1890, and we were the first paper to advocate remedial action. I wrote a number of Virginia editors urging their support. Several of them were glad to give it, and at the session of 1936 we got the measure through the House, only to see it killed by one vote in a Senate committee. By the time the session of 1938 convened, overwhelming sentiment had been built up for the bill, and it went through both branches of the General Assembly with hardly any dissenting voices. It provided a nine-hour day and forty-eight-hour week for women in place of a ten-hour day and sixty-hour week, with certain exceptions. The new law was not perfect, but the U. S. Department of Labor pronounced it the best on the subject in any southern state. The *Times-Dispatch* was credited with a large degree of responsibility for its enactment.

I was named by federal authorities to a committee of citizens to study the wage scale in the canning industry and make recommendations. At a hearing on the subject in New York, after listening to both sides, we voted to raise the minimum wage to 40 cents. This was undoubtedly warranted, but it was apparent that the other members of the committee on which I served were all left-wingers, including a Communist. One member, a professor from the University of Texas, was nothing less than insulting to the representatives of the canning industry. When an elderly canner said mildly that if the wages were pushed too high he might have to close down, this professor snarled, "What do you mean by threatening us," I could not refrain from saying, "I don't feel that I have been threatened. The gentleman is simply stating his side of the case." This hearing afforded me an insight into the technique used by the Roosevelt administration to push up wages in the various industries. In most cases, as in this one, the raise in the pay scale was justified, but the system made wage hikes practically inevitable. The supposedly nonpartisan citizens' committees were stacked with liberals and radicals.

An agency known as the Southern Policy Committee was formed at about this time, largely through the efforts of Francis P. Miller, a former Rhodes scholar and world traveler who later ran for governor of Virginia and was almost elected. It included educators, clergymen, editors and businessmen. I was asked to join the group, which would focus on southern problems, and attempt to find solutions. At the first meeting in Atlanta in 1935, farm tenancy was singled out as the South's prime problem, and we passed resolutions and set in motion studies that were believed to have been influential in obtaining the passage by Congress of the Bankhead-Jones Farm Tenancy Act. Other questions which we addressed at subsequent meetings included the race problem, the poll tax and matters having to do with Dixie industry and politics. There were also policy committees in the various states, and I was a member of the Virginia committee. We sought to deal with state-wide issues, notably the poll tax. But we could never get either modification or repeal. The tax was finally eliminated in the 1960s by federal action.

I was wont to refer jokingly to the policy committees as "self-appointed saviors of civilization." If we didn't save civilization, and we certainly didn't, we did manage to stir things up and to obtain action here and there. I wrote that "these conclaves have influenced many of the participants in subtle ways, have brought leaders in various Southern fields into ideological rapport, and have set in motion trains of thought which are having their impact in unexpected places." Since the South had been termed "the nation's Economic Problem Number One," which it undoubtedly was, the time had come for somebody to seek solutions for that problem.

Another agency involved in that endeavor was the Southern Conference for Human Welfare. Organized in 1938 at a meeting in Birmingham attended by prominent Southerners in all walks of life, it was participated in by Communists. I was supposed to attend and serve as chairman of one of the committees, but I became suspicious that Communists were pulling the strings and didn't go. Many were hoodwinked into attending, to their later embarrassment. Those who called the conference were dissatisfied with our Southern Policy Committee, as being too moderate and conservative.

Frank P. Graham, president of the University of North Carolina, always quick to aid any effort that he felt would meet human needs, was not disturbed by the fact that the Southern Conference for Human Welfare included Communists. He wrote me twice after the Birmingham meeting, urging me to become affiliated with the conference, which, he felt, was filling an essential role. I declined and tried to say as diplomatically as I could that I did not care to be associated with the Reds. He remained unconvinced. Frank Graham was so completely honest and guileless himself that he found it almost impossible to realize that there are people in the world who mouth high-sounding slogans while operating on a very different level. The Southern Conference for Human Welfare's principal accomplishment was the infliction of great damage on the Southern Policy Committee.

We Dabneys rejoiced over the arrival of our second child, Lucy Davis Dabney, named for my sister who had died in 1911. Our bungalow at 6005 Howard Road soon became too small for our growing family, and we began looking for another house. We found and bought a suitable lot, three fourths of an acre in extent, with many trees, on Tapoan Road, between the University of Richmond and the Country Club of Virginia. "Tapoan" sounds Indian, but is, in fact, a combination of the names Taylor, Powers and Anderson, the three earlier owners of property in that area. On the lot we built a comfortable clapboard house, and into it we moved in August 1939.

We had hardly gotten settled when we were awakened early on the morning of September 1 by the cry of "Extra! Extra!" Hitler had sent his panzers and dive bombers roaring into Poland, and World War II was on. I wondered whether I had lost my mind in loading myself up at such a time with what for me was a sizable mortgage. However, it turned out to be perhaps the best investment we ever made. The house and lot today will bring several times their cost.

When our infant daughter Lucy was a few years older, I told her a story every evening after supper about an extremely bad little girl named Geraldine. I refused to utter a word until Lucy had given me a big hug and kiss, but once that was bestowed, I was off and running. Flagrant misbehavior on the part of the *enfant terrible*, Geraldine, was the burden of my informal narrative, which most of the time I made up as I went along. It taxed my imagination to think up a new form of devilment every night, but somehow I kept this up for several years. It would not do, of course, for Geraldine to get away with her shocking misdeeds, so I emphasized that she was spanked or otherwise chastised with great regularity. This, I stressed to Lucy, was the inevitable consequence of sinful behavior.

When her younger brother, Heath, was three or four years old, I began a story with him about a disobedient little monster named Herman Hickenlooper, and kept it up for quite a while. But Herman somehow never quite generated the charisma that radiated from Geraldine. It could well have been my fault. My ingenuity in thinking up new escapades finally was exhausted.

The idea of producing a story each evening had not occurred to me when Douglas, our first child, was young. She was quite precocious, and I recorded her early words of wisdom in a book. In Europe at age four or five she picked up the German language more quickly than her parents. She sang songs and said her prayers in German, coached by Fraülein Clarenbach, and conversed easily with her little German playmates in the parks.

I became involved in the mid-1930s in the nation-wide hullabaloo over the so-called Edith Maxwell slipper slaying, which had to do with the killing of Edith's father, a blacksmith, in the small mountain town of Pound in southwest Virginia. The Hearst papers, news services and syndicates were chiefly responsible for stirring up a coast-to-coast furor over this case, and for depicting it as growing out of Edith's father's fury because she came home from college wearing "store-boughtened clothes" and refusing to obey the "mountain code" and the "mountain curfew, which shrills its warning across the hills three hours after sundown," notifying all women to be indoors. There wasn't any mountain code or curfew, as Edith Maxwell herself finally declared, but the Hearst trained seals and sob sisters didn't let that bother them. They kept on writing just as though Edith had never repudiated these weird allegations.

I did an article for the *New Republic* in which I stated that "few cases have been buried under a thicker coating of journalistic horsefeathers, baloney and banana oil than this Maxwell case." The editor of the weekly paper in the county where the killing occurred expressed the view that "most of the stories have been written in hotel rooms with a bottle of 'corn' in one hand and 'The Trail of the Lonesome Pine' in the other." James Thurber chimed in with a reasonably comprehensive and altogether objective piece in *The New Yorker*. In all fairness, the blame for the distortions did not rest solely with the Hearst organization, since the United Press distributed some of the worst nonsense, and the Washington *Post* kept a staff correspondent at the scene for weeks who parroted the hokum concerning the nonexistent mountain code. The case was described over and over in the press as the "slipper slaying," since Edith Maxwell said she struck her father with a slipper when he tried to beat her for staying out late, and that he fell and hit his head, inflicting fatal injuries. The jury didn't believe this, and after being out only thirty minutes gave Edith twenty-five years on the theory that she hit her father in the head with a blunt instrument as he lay in bed. Edith's college roommate testified that she had heard Miss Maxwell threaten "dozens of times" to kill her father.

A new trial was granted by the Virginia Supreme Court of Appeals, and this time Edith got twenty years. Governor James H. Price granted her a conditional pardon after she had served five of those years. Thus ended the Maxwell case, which afforded an almost perfect example of journalistic irresponsibility and lack of scruple. The *Times-Dispatch* helped to counteract the almost unbelievable absurdities broadcast by out-of-state newspapers, and aided in keeping the facts in perspective.

The paper also played a useful role in preventing participants in a strike at the Industrial Rayon Corporation of Covington, Virginia, from having to serve long prison terms under the Virginia antilynching statute. It was not until the *Times-Dispatch* sent a staff correspondent, LaMotte Blakely, to the scene, two hundred miles from Richmond near the West Virginia line, that this perversion of the antilynching law became known. We denounced the procedure editorially, and the local authorities had to back away from their plan to make mild disorder at the mill gate a felony instead of a misdemeanor. The Virginia General Assembly amended the antilynching statute at its next session, thus preventing future distortions of the law's intent.

Another area in which the *Times-Dispatch* sought to play a constructive role was that of intersectional amity. Antagonism between the North and the South was aroused from time to time as late as the 1930s by surviving veterans of the Civil War. These old men, in their eighties and nineties, erupted on both sides of the Mason and Dixon line with irrational outbursts.

Plans were announced for a monument at Appomattox to mark the place where the Civil War ended. The shaft was completely nonpartisan in character, it was designed by a Richmond architect and the bill providing for its erection by the national government was introduced in the U. S. Senate and House by Virginia members. The inscription was as follows: "North–South; Peace, Unity. Appomattox, the Site of the Termination of the War Between the States, 1861–1865."

Despite its totally impartial character, the plan was promptly denounced by various Confederate organizations, one of which termed it "an insult to General Lee and every southern soldier who fought and died for the Confederate cause." Not only Confederate veterans but sons and daughters of veterans echoed these absurd attacks on the entire concept. It was finally decided to abandon the plan, in view of the uproar.

The attitude of those Southerners who issued tirades in opposition to the proposed monument was in glaring contrast to that manifested by various posts of the United Confederate Veterans in the late nineteenth century. They welcomed several posts of the Grand Army of the Republic to Richmond in the 1880s and entertained them lavishly. Some members of both the UCV and the GAR were actually in tears when they parted. But with the passage of half a century a few of the veterans on both sides began trying to fight the war over again.

I wrote a letter in 1935 to the adjutant and chief of staff of the UCV in Nashville, suggesting that a last reunion of the Blue and the Gray be held in Washington. The old gentleman promptly gave my letter to the press, without any reply to me, declaring that since the GAR had insisted that no Confederate flags could be flown at any joint reunion, he would not consider the proposal for an instant.

Nevertheless, talk began not long thereafter concerning a possible gathering of the northern and southern veterans at Gettysburg before they had all passed to their reward. First the GAR convention said the Johnny Rebs could carry their flags, but then the GAR's commander in chief proclaimed to all and sundry that such a thing would never be permitted. Things went back and forth in this fashion, and it appeared that a reunion was out of the question. Whereupon, all of a sudden, both sides stopped bickering. The reunion took place in 1938 at Gettysburg, with 1,800 veterans in attendance, and all expenses paid by the federal government. The whole affair went off smoothly, the only serious problem being that a mere five cases of whiskey were made available at the outset, and these were consumed in short order, thanks chiefly to the elbow-bending prowess of the southern contingent. "That ain't even a good sniff, much less a drink" was the scornful comment of one former wearer of the Gray when he saw that each man was being given a small cup containing about a teaspoon of whiskey. Those in charge got the hint, and twenty-two more cases were hurriedly sent for. The result was that the well-lubricated vets forgot all their erstwhile animosity and swapped yarns under the trees while the bands played "Dixie" and "Yankee Doodle" and the United States and Confederate flags floated above. As the eight-day gathering neared its close, it was found that the whiskey was giving out again, and fifteen more cases were requisitioned. When adjournment came, the reunion was pronounced a roaring success by all concerned.

Perhaps this gratifying outcome mellowed the UCV chief of staff in Nashville who had given my letter to the press three years before, and scornfully rejected my suggestion for a last reunion. At all events, I got a letter from him inviting me to accept appointment as "historian-general of the United Confederate Veterans with the rank of brigadier-general." I thanked him most sincerely, but did not feel able to accept this awesome responsibility.

Our editorials during this period were by no means confined to such serious subjects as intersectional animosity, the rights of strikers or the threat of Hitlerism. I tried to have comment in lighter vein on the page every day. It wasn't always possible, but it seemed desirable, and we usually had such an editorial, generally written by me.

We had jocose comment over a five-year period concerning the relative merits of the two capitals of the Confederacy, Montgomery, Alabama, and Richmond. This pillow fight was carried on spasmodically between Grover C. Hall, editor of the Montgomery *Advertiser*, and myself on our respective editorial pages. It was the *Times-Dispatch's* contention, of course, that Richmond was "the only capital of the Confederacy that anybody ever heard of"; that, contrary to Montgomery's bumptious claims to the first streetcar, Richmond had the first streetcar system in the world, "even though its excellently appointed speed wagons had to be assisted by mules, on occasion"; and that a Montgomery firm had the impertinence to ship beaten biscuits for sale in Richmond, when everybody knew that Richmond's historic biscuits, munched by kings and queens, probably including Queen Victoria, were far superior, and so on. The *Advertiser* retorted in kind, and the Associated Press thought the controversy so amusing that it put a two-column feature story on the wire.

In order to give recognition to Virginians who were making valuable contributions in various spheres of endeavor, I inaugurated an annual *Times-Dispatch* honor roll in 1937. At the end of that year and for six years thereafter we chose about a dozen citizens annually, always including one black, and published their photographs, with sketches of their careers. The selection of the list and the writing of the profiles involved a great deal of work, and as the nation got more deeply involved in the war, and I had less and less help, it became almost impossible to continue this feature. We discontinued it after publication of the honor roll for 1943.

I accepted an invitation to lecture on "The New South" at Princeton University during the second semester of the 1939–40 session. Dr. Thomas J. Wertenbaker, the eminent colonial historian, was having a sabbatical, and I was one of those invited to substitute for him. At first I declined, owing to the great amount of work and travel involved, but finally concluded that I couldn't afford to refuse.

I had to work hard for six months in my spare time preparing the Princeton lectures. They began February 7, 1940, and ended May 9, with a one-hour lecture and one-hour seminar on two days of each week during that period. I caught the night sleeper for Philadelphia every Tuesday, changing trains twice en route, and the afternoon train back on Thursday. I was tired when I got there, as I couldn't sleep on the so-called sleeper, and almost exhausted when I got back to Richmond. The strain of trying to keep the editorial page going with only one assistant editorial writer, and of giving these lectures and seminars, was terrific. For example, I dictated one editorial over the phone from the railroad station just before leaving on the night train. I also had to write some of my weekly New York *Times* pieces from Princeton.

Since this whole experience was new to me, I confess that I was nervous before I went to Princeton and after my arrival. Under the system, the boys could enroll for the course and, after a lecture or two, could drop out if they found it boring. I waited apprehensively, and was relieved that nobody dropped, whereas several more enrolled, making a total of seventy-seven. My nervousness disappeared.

Among those in the class were John L. Lewis, Jr., son of the president of the United Mine Workers, and Philip H. Willkie, son of Wendell Willkie. I somehow never got to know Lewis, but saw a great deal of Willkie. At my request, he persuaded his father to give a guest lecture to the class on the Tennessee Valley Authority (TVA). Although Wendell Willkie had been head of the private power company which had to sell out to the federal government, thus paving the way for the TVA, he was remarkably objective in his discussion of the controversial issue. I tried to get David Lilienthal, head of the TVA, to give his side to the class, but was unsuccessful.

Wendell Willkie was being fervently boomed that spring for the Republican presidential nomination, since it was almost the eve of the national convention. Phil Willkie was enormously excited over this, and spent much time—too much, in fact—at his father's headquarters in New York. Phil had been voted the Princeton senior most likely to succeed, but he forgot, in the excitement, to study for some of his final examinations. The result was that although he passed my course easily, he failed something else and had to return the next year to get his degree.

Allen Tate, the poet, was lecturing at Princeton when I was there. Since he was one of the leading "Nashville Agrarians" who had published the book *I'll Take My Stand*, I asked him to give a guest lecture on the agrarian theme to my class. I was having a mild feud with the Nashville group, and was anxious to patch things up. Tate accepted my invitation and the lecture went off well. He seemed to harbor no ill feelings.

I never did understand exactly what the agrarians were driving at, but gathered that they were against too much industrialization of the South and in favor of retaining the old culture and values to the extent that this was possible. I shared some of these feelings myself. However, Donald Davidson, a member of the group for whom I had deep respect, became offended over something that I had written on this subject. It may have been my expression of a belief that some of the agrarians "even object to modern plumbing, and prefer candles to electric lights." I doubt now that this statement was true, and I shouldn't have written it. Anyway, Davidson was upset. When he was in Richmond for a convention, I called him on the phone and asked him to have lunch with me. He said he would let me know later; when he did so, he said he couldn't, and gave no reason. Still desirous of smoothing things over, I invited him to contribute an article on the agrarians to the Old South Issue of the *Saturday Review of Literature*, of which I was co-editor with Howard Odum, the University of North Carolina sociologist. He did so, under the title "The 'Mystery' of the Agarians." I suppose my gesture smoothed his ruffled sensibilities somewhat, although our correspondence was strictly on the formal side. After he sent in the manuscript, he decided that he wanted to change a phrase. He wrote me that if we couldn't make the change, the whole article would have to be killed. Such was his deadly earnestness on this subject. A colleague of his at Vanderbilt University said Davidson "would probably go to the stake, if necessary" for his agrarian beliefs.

The agrarians served a useful purpose by emphasizing that the South ought not to be turned into a vast sea of blast furnaces. I think this was one of their principal contentions, although Davidson's *Saturday Review* article still left me uncertain as to their precise philosophy and objectives. He spoke there of "numerous misrepresentations" of the agrarian point of view, but without identifying them.

For years it had seemed inevitable that the *Times-Dispatch* and *News Leader* would ultimately have to merge. This was the trend throughout the United States, since the basic economic facts made it impossible for two competing papers to realize reasonable profits in a city the size of Richmond, or, for that matter, a much larger one. Managements of both papers were unhappy over this necessity, for they agreed with their readers that competition was highly desirable. However, the papers had suffered during the Depression and by 1940 were ready to join forces. The *Times-Dispatch* abandoned its one-time horse stable on South Seventh Street and moved in with the *News Leader* on North Fourth. The building contained surplus space and there was remodeling.

John Stewart Bryan, publisher of the *News Leader*, became publisher of the combined operation, with John Dana Wise as vice-president and general manager. Douglas Freeman remained as editor of the afternoon paper and I of the morning.

It was deemed desirable that a competitive situation be maintained to the maximum degree possible, despite the unified management. Hence it was felt to be important for the two editorial pages to retain their individualities, with contrasting policies on some issues, where the editors sincerely held divergent views. Mr. Bryan agreed that he would hold to a minimum his participation in the formulation of *Times-Dispatch* editorial policy, and such formulation was left almost entirely to me. The two news departments continued their hot competition, with each making every effort to scoop the other.

Mr. Bryan was careful to live up to the foregoing arrangement. A gregarious and attractive man, with a fund of anecdotes, he would drop by my office frequently to chat. Occasionally he would disagree amiably with something that I had written, or would advance an argument concerning this or that public policy. But it was understood that I could disregard his views. I cannot recall that he took issue sharply with any of my editorial pronouncements.

In the case of such an important editorial stand as endorsement of a presidential candidate, he liked to be told what we were doing, and to offer his ideas. We endorsed Franklin D. Roosevelt all four times that he ran, but with diminishing enthusiasm each time. In 1944, when Mr. Bryan was in failing health, he asked me to bring my editorial, with its lukewarm endorsement, to him at his home, Laburnum, prior to publication. I did so, and he approved it, while making one or two helpful suggestions. We were willing to recommend Roosevelt's re-election for a fourth term on the ground that the war was yet to be won, and he was a more experienced leader than Thomas E. Dewey, the Republican nominee. We were not aware, of course, that the President was almost a dying man. Had we known this, the endorsement would not have been forthcoming.

The sell-out of Czechoslovakia to Hitler in 1938 had caused many Americans to adopt a relatively isolationist posture, at least temporarily. I was one of them. But as time passed, and most of Western Europe fell to the onrushing Nazi legions, while England was subjected to an almost pulverizing bombing attack and to the sinking of hundreds of her ships by German submarines, opinion in this country began to shift. I came to feel, with many others, that although the abandonment of the Czechs by Britain and France could not be condoned, it was essential that Hitler be stopped before he became invincible.

Our change of front was announced on December 1, 1940, in an editorial entitled "The Hour Strikes for America." In it we urged that the United States make it plain that we would not let Great Britain fall, and that we step up our aid to that country in munitions, supplies and money. The *Times-Dispatch* also suggested that consideration be given to letting Britain have fifty more destroyers, in addition to the fifty already sent, in order to strengthen her convoys against U-boat attacks.

A visitor to Richmond at about this time was the famous photographer Alfred Eisenstaedt, who was taking pictures for *Life* magazine of Richmond sights and personalities. Word came to the Tredegar Company that he wanted to take some photographs at the plant of that famous manufacturer of arms and armaments during the Civil War and both world wars. Tredegar officials accordingly arranged various exhibits in anticipation of his visit. Soon after he had entered the factory gate Eisenstaedt's eye fell upon a large pile of scrap metal, a mere collection of junk. He stopped in his tracks, took out his camera and snapped a picture of it. Whereupon he turned on his heel and started for the gate. Edward H. Trigg, the company executive who was steering him around, was much taken aback and pointed out that there were more interesting things at the Tredegar to photograph. They did not interest Eisenstaedt. He had what he wanted and departed.

An invitation came to me later in that year, 1940, from Appleton-Century to write a sequel to *Liberalism in the South.* John L. B. Williams, one of the firm's editors and a Princeton graduate, had learned of my lectures at his alma mater earlier in the year. I accepted, and *Below the Potomac* was the result.

Some of the material for the book was gathered on a vacation trip that my wife and I took through the Deep South, visiting Mobile, New Orleans, Vicksburg, Natchez and Jackson. We made a special pilgrimage from Jackson to what was left of Burleigh, the ante-bellum plantation of Thomas Dabney near

Raymond, Mississippi. It was hard to find. A small pile of bricks was all that remained of the large house, which had once been surrounded by gardens, a deer park, slave quarters and other out-buildings. The house had burned in the 1890s when inhabited by former slaves. We found one lone cabin, and in it an aged former Burleigh house slave, "Aunt Alice" Simmons, who was baking an ash cake over a fire. "Lawzy, is you a Dabney?" she exclaimed. "My white folks done come home!" and she threw her arms around me. Aunt Alice was apparently in her nineties, and since this was 1940, she would have been a teen-ager during the Civil War. I gave her a piece of folding money, and after viewing the desolate scene we took our departure.

I wrote *Below the Potomac* at nights and on weekends, when I would normally be assumed to be extremely tired, especially during so hectic as period. Yet I was never tired even once while writing it. To this day I can think of no explanation. The book appeared in the spring of 1942, a few months after this country's formal entry into the war—the worst conceivable time for publication of a volume about the South. People's minds were on the problem of coping with all-conquering Germany and Japan, and on the nation's survival. Reviews of *Below the Potomac* were good, but sales were terrible.

This period was enlivened by the birth of our son, Richard Heath II. The thrill occasioned by his arrival has been touched upon in Chapter Two. Heath's birthday was October 27, 1941, and his mother and I had planned a vacation in New York City for December. All arrangements were made and we expected to take off in a few days when the phone rang at about 2:30 on Sunday afternoon, December 7. It was our long-time friend Alexander W. Parker, whose brother, John C. Parker, had married my sister.

"The Japs have bombed Pearl Harbor! It just came over the radio," Alex said in an excited tone.

"What! They must be crazy!" was my more or less inane reply.

But they weren't crazy. They had wrecked our Pacific fleet in one of history's most devastating surprise attacks. True, the long-term effect of Japan's action was that they would ultimately lose the war, but the United States would have to fight its way back over a long and bloody trail.

The Pearl Harbor attack did have the effect of instantly unifying this country. Squabbling between interventionists and America Firsters ended at once, recruits began lining up for enlistment within a few hours and the whole nation began mobilizing for action. I saluted the occasion with an editorial that filled the entire space and was entitled "Japan Strikes and America Answers." In it I declared that "This country will back President Roosevelt as one man today when he asks Congress for a declaration of war."

Our New York vacation went by the board. I got no holiday that year, and the same was true for one other year during the war. It didn't really matter. With thousands entering the armed services, and the nation fighting for its life, the least I could do was to forgo a vacation or two. I resigned from the Country Club of Virginia, in order to have more money available for the purchase of War Bonds and more time for a victory garden. Tennis was out for the duration.

Needless to say I wondered whether I should enlist. I was forty years old, and without military experience, except for the "squads right" and "squads left" that I had done decades before at Episcopal High and the university during World War I. Some of my closest friends, such as Lewis Powell and Harvie Wilkinson, were going in, but most of them were in their early or middle thirties. Yet Alex Parker, a couple of years older than I, left his law practice, enlisted in the Navy, won a commission and was in some of the Pacific's hottest battles.

My fear was that if I went in I would be put into some branch of public relations and assigned to a desk in Washington, where I would shuffle papers endlessly. Given my newspaper background and lack of military experience, it seemed fairly probable that such would be my fate. Having been on the sidelines during the First World War, it troubled me considerably that I was now in the same uninspiring posture.

It troubled me so much that I finally wrote for advice to Major General James E. Edmonds, commanding general at Camp Lee, for whom I had acquired considerable admiration. His reply, in part, follows:

"As the responsible editor of an important newspaper, you can render a greater service to the armed effort than you possibly could render, at your age, in such branches of the army as you would undoubtedly be assigned to. More important still, your continuance as editor during the war will enable you to render an even more effective service in the even more difficult period of accomplishing a just peace and fixing for the future the role of this nation among the others of the world. . . .

"I stepped out of active editorship for three years during the old World War. It has been a matter of grave doubt to me during the years since, as to whether I pursued the right course—even though my age in 1916 was less than yours now."

General Edmonds' letter confirmed my own view that I would accomplish little or nothing by getting myself assigned to a desk somewhere in the armed services. I remained on the *Times-Dispatch*.

7

The Second World War

As soon as Japan struck at Pearl Harbor, the whole American nation began mobilizing for war. Many members of the *Times-Dispatch* staff left for training camps. Events were occurring in rapid succession, both in Europe and the Pacific, and my job of trying to comment on them was a demanding one. It was also exhilarating.

Associate editor Meacham and I carried the burden until he resigned in the fall of 1942 to become first chairman of the State Parole Board. He had served as first chairman of the Richmond Housing Authority, along with his editorial duties, and had gotten the program off to a fine start. His *Times-Dispatch* editorials laid the foundation, and Gilpin Court, the city's first "project," which cleared the worst slums in old Jackson Ward, was practically complete when he left the paper.

Bill Meacham was succeeded by Cowl Rider, who served later on the editorial staffs of *The Wall Street Journal* and the Charleston, South Carolina, papers. In 1944 Osburn Zuber, formerly of the Montgomery *Advertiser* and a Nieman fellow at Harvard, succeeded Rider. He was living in Washington when he came with us, and left his family there. This necessitated commuting to them each weekend on cinder-bestrewn trains, jammed with servicemen and others, and usually hours late. How he stood it is beyond me, but he kept it up for nearly two years.

Throughout the war we never had more than two full-time editorial writers, including myself, and occasionally I was the only one. A few editorials were contributed by free lances. My faithful and highly competent secretary for more than a third of a century, Mrs. Edward S. McCarthy, was a great help to me in those arduous times.

I organized the first War Bond parade in Richmond. I did not march, but functioned behind the scenes. When it ended I was utterly exhausted.

In fact, I was tired a good part of the time during these years, in contrast to the period immediately preceding, when I somehow managed to write a book without any exceptional strain. Since there now was war on a global scale, epochal events could occur at any hour of the day or night. I always listened at home to Elmer Davis when, in his dry, Indiana twang, he broadcast on the radio for five minutes each night at nine o'clock.

And speaking of broadcasts, we in Richmond tuned in for every one of Winston Churchill's magnificent orations. They went around the world by radio in the war's darkest hours, and nerved the Allied nations for their death struggle with the Axis. It is difficult to believe that Demosthenes or Cicero could have surpassed the rolling thunder of Churchill's defiance to Hitler, when Britain was reeling and London was in flames: "We shall fight in the landing grounds, we shall fight in the fields and in the streets, we shall fight in the hills, we shall never surrender!" And who can forget his tribute to the gallant youths of the Royal Air Force who turned back Goering's supposedly invincible airmen and saved England: "Never in the field of human conflict was so much owed by so many to so few." Truly it was, in Churchill's words, Great Britain's "finest hour."

I went to Washington from time to time during the war in order to get off the record information as to the true situation. By talking with such friends in the government as Edward R. Stettinius and Jonathan Daniels, and with such newspapermen as Arthur Krock, Raymond Clapper, Richard L. Strout and Ben McKelway, I was able to learn of events and situations that were highly useful for background but could not be mentioned in print.

I attended a number of White House press conferences, and was able to see President Roosevelt in action as he fenced with the newspapermen, his cigarette holder at a jaunty angle. In those early war years he seemed to be in perfect health, with powerful shoulders and neck, his face well filled out. He was always seated behind his desk, and was careful not to let himself be seen or photographed in a manner to show his paralyzed legs.

I had met Mr. Roosevelt in 1931 at the University of Virginia Institute of Public Affairs, when he was a principal speaker and I was a *Times-Dispatch* reporter. From 1928 to 1933 I covered the institute each summer, spending a week or so with my parents at the university. My wife and child accompanied me. Norman Thomas, the brilliant and perennial Socialist candidate for President, was almost always a featured speaker, and there were other celebrities on the program. Roosevelt's address at the 1931 institute was widely regarded as the opening gun in his campaign for the presidential nomination the following year. It dealt with the somewhat uninspiring topic of states' rights.

I attended several of FDR's White House press conferences prior to our entry into the war. One was shortly after I had attacked editorially his plan to pack the Supreme Court by appointing additional justices. It was our first big breach with Roosevelt, whom we had usually supported prior to that time. He probably was not aware of our change of front, for when I shook hands with him after the conference he asked pleasantly, "How's everything down on the old *Times-Dispatch?*" Since he was reputed to have an extra long memory for grudges, my guess is that he did not know of our backsliding.

At a White House press conference not long before Pearl Harbor, I was especially interested when J. Fred Essary of the Baltimore *Sun* was quizzing the President as to whether we had fortified or were fortifying the island of Guam. Roosevelt kept side-stepping Essary and the latter kept boring in. Meanwhile the Japanese correspondent for one of the principal Tokyo newspapers was taking down the entire exchange. I don't think the President ever answered Essary's question, perhaps because the Nipponese was present. It was an impressive example of how in an open society, such as ours, a sensitive issue such as the fortification of an important island can be introduced in the presence of a corre-spondent from a power with whom we may shortly be at war.

In the spring of 1940, when the German *Blitzkrieg* was roaring through northern France toward Paris, I stopped off in Washing-ton en route from one of my Princeton lectures and went to the White House press conference. Roosevelt was trying to prepare the American public for sacrifices that were to come, but he did not wish to alarm the country unduly. He told the assembled newspapermen to assure their readers that whereas certain steps would have to be taken, "Nobody will be discomboomerated" and "the ladies can still have their lipsticks and ice-cream sodas."

Many had been "discomboomerated" years later when I saw President Roosevelt at a press conference for the last time. It was the summer of 1944, at the height of the war, and shortly before the Democratic National Convention. The correspondents were trying to dig something out of him concerning his plans for nam-ing a vice-president to run with him. Henry A. Wallace was under fire from many directions, and the press wanted to know if Roosevelt would name Wallace again for the second spot on the ticket. He was extremely cagey in his replies, and nobody could tell what he had in mind. Later that day I was discussing this problem with Jonathan Daniels, who was on the inside of things, since he was administrative assistant to the President. "What's the matter with Harry Truman?" he said. It was the tip-off that Truman was to be the man.

I was surprised to find that I could get in to see Secretary of State Cordell Hull during these years. I had never met Mr. Hull and did not expect to do so. I wrote his secretary requesting to see someone in the State Department who could give me the facts concerning a problem that was puzzling me. He wrote back that I should come to a certain room at a certain hour. When I arrived, I was ushered into Secretary Hull's office. He not only discussed the question I had in mind but a number of others, and I was there for about an hour. I tried to leave several times, but he in-sisted that I remain. This was the first of a number of calls that I paid on the gentleman from Tennessee.

Cordell Hull had been born in a log cabin, the son of a feudin' moonshiner, but he looked like a patrician. His speech exhibited some of the characteristics of his early environment. For example, he said "ever'body" and "Ay-rabs." Then, too, he whistled audibly through his plates. He served as Secretary of State for eleven years, and gave the impression of great honesty and sincerity. He looked you in the eye and seemed to be telling you exactly what he thought on any subject that he discussed. In our talks he was occasionally profane, especially when referring to Undersecretary Sumner Welles, whom President Roosevelt consulted frequently without telling Secretary Hull.

Hull resigned as Secretary of State in the fall of 1944. Several months previously I dropped in at the office of Edward R. Stettinius, then Undersecretary of State. He had served ably since 1941 as head of the Lend-Lease system under which this country supplied its Allies with weapons and matériel of various kinds in huge quantities. "I need your advice," my old college-mate said. "Secretary Hull is resigning shortly, and President Roosevelt wants to appoint me to succeed him. How can I get out of it?"

Stettinius was not trying to shirk a duty; he was convinced, I am sure, that he was unqualified for the post of Secretary of State. His principal training had been with General Motors and U. S. Steel, and he was without diplomatic experience. He did well as head of Lend-Lease, but he did not feel up to the secretaryship. I told him that I could think of no reasonable way by which he could refuse to serve the commander in chief in wartime. He evidently couldn't either, for he accepted the appointment a few months thereafter, and did his level best with it. Roosevelt was, to all intents and purposes, his own Secretary of State, so less responsibility devolved on Stettinius than would otherwise have been the case.

Ed Stettinius was my most valuable news source in Washington during the war. He was in intimate touch with events on the various battle fronts. I could visit him in his office, and he would call up one or two people in key positions and tell me the true situation on this or that front, or which cities or rail lines had been bombed the night before by the Germans or the Japanese, and the approximate damage. What he said was off the record, of course. He was especially conscious of the sinkings of Lend-Lease cargoes shipped under his direction to Europe or the Pacific. I recall his acute dismay over the torpedoing of several shiploads of vital supplies destined for our Allies in the Far East, which had been assembled in the face of almost insuperable difficulties. They were within a few miles of port when enemy submarines found them, and sent them to the bottom.

Ed told me of his astonishment, if not bewilderment, at the amount of drinking done at the height of the war by the highest British officials. He described lunching in London with these men, and of being plied with cocktails or highballs before the meal, wines during the meal, and brandy and liqueurs afterward. He said that he was in danger of falling into a virtual stupor, but that his hosts appeared able to "carry on." The same was true when he spent a weekend in the country with Winston Churchill. The Prime Minister was handed a morning highball while still in bed, and he kept on drinking throughout the day and into the night. "He was still going strong at two o'clock in the morning," said the amazed Stettinius, who was completely unable to keep up with Churchill's pace, and didn't try. He marveled that "the Prime" was not drunk.

Stettinius was a handsome and attractive man, with almost snow-white hair when in his forties, and a deep voice that was peculiarly resonant. He spoke to me once of having to be careful about his health, since both his father, a Morgan partner, and his brother had died when relatively young of circulatory or coronary ailments. He himself appeared to have high blood pressure, and the strains of wartime must have intensified this condition. Walter Winchell, the gossip columnist and radio broadcaster, put something on the air to the effect that Stettinius was in poor health. Ed happened to be listening and had a heart attack, I was told. He lived only a few years thereafter.

The Office of Price Administration (OPA) offered me a job early in the war. This was the federal agency that was given the task of controlling prices. I was asked to take charge of the Southeastern Division, and travel over that region seeking to create citizen co-operation, even enthusiasm, for the objectives of OPA.

This was "war work" on the civilian front, and I gave earnest thought to the question whether I should leave the paper and accept the position. One thing that bothered me especially was the fact that the OPA job carried a somewhat smaller salary than I was getting, and I did not wish to be in the position of refusing to render service simply because it would cost me a few dollars. I finally turned down the offer, after Mr. Bryan told me what I suspected, namely, that I was not the type to be an effective promoter, of OPA or anything else.

Citizens were urged by the federal authorities to plant victory gardens, in order to supplement the food supply on the home front, since vast amounts were being shipped overseas. We made valiant efforts to have such a garden at 14 Tapoan Road, but to little or no avail. We dug up a small square in the back yard, fertilized it and planted tomatoes, lettuce, carrots and radishes. But I was totally unschooled in the art and mystery of raising vegetables and there was little sun on the plot. Trees on every side caused it to be shaded for all but two or three hours of each day. The result was that the garden produced scarcely anything that was edible. A few dishes of excellent lettuce were about all that we had to show for our labors.

There was real fear that the Germans and Japanese might somehow manage to bomb certain areas of the United States, especially those near the East and West coasts. Richmond was an important rail junction for shipments of munitions and matériel to Hampton Roads and thence to Europe. An air-raid defense system was set up, and I was a "block leader." We were all given instructions about what to do in blackouts and fire drills. I also took part in War Bond rallies.

My wife had the care of our three children, one of whom was quite young, but she found time to serve as a Red Cross Gray Lady at the Army Air Force Hospital, and later at the newly erected McGuire Hospital.

There was rationing of essential foods, automobiles, tires, gasoline and other things. I made it a point not to ask for special consideration because of my newspaper work. I could have gotten more gasoline, for example, than the average citizen, but I did not request it. Since I was counseling others in editorials, and urging them to be as sparing as possible in the use of essential foods and other commodities, it seemed only proper that I should take my own advice.

In order to conserve fuel oil we closed several rooms in our house, and got a large coal stove which we placed in the living room. The stove, which we christened "Gertie," stood well out in the room and gave off tremendous heat. The warm air percolated out into the hall and other rooms, thus achieving our objective of saving oil, but the stove was a staggering eyesore. It was a relief after the war when we could say good-bye once and for all to Gertie. Incidentally, as part of our conservation program we shut off the radiators in the dining room. On a cold night they froze and burst, squirting water over the ceiling and ruining the wallpaper.

Such hours of relaxation as could be had in those strenuous times were often spent with our friends and neighbors Ralph and Dorothy Begien. Ralph was an important executive of the Chesapeake & Ohio Railway, in direct charge of the enormous shipments of weapons and supplies, some of them highly secret, to Newport News, en route to the battle fronts. He and I and our wives frequently got together on weekends, except when Ralph or I had to be at the office because of some emergency. Rum drinks were the order of the day, since whiskey was unobtainable. The salubrious product of the Caribbean was a lifesaver to many harried souls on the home front who were trying to find surcease from care.

In the early 1940s I was doing considerable book reviewing for the New York *Times*, New York *Herald Tribune* and *Saturday Review*. A critique that I did for the *Herald Tribune* of W. J. Cash's book *The Mind of the South* had a surprising aftermath. My review was preponderantly favorable, but it did contain a few criticisms. These got under Cash's skin, for I received a tart letter from him in which he, in effect, accused me of criticizing his book because I had written about the South and didn't want any competition. I had scarcely digested this disturbing communiqué when another came, apologizing and asking me please to forget that he had written the first one. Apparently he was greatly overwrought. His tragic, much-to-be-regretted suicide a few months later could have resulted from an intensification of this condition.

I confess that I have never felt Cash's *The Mind of the South* to be quite the classic that many take it to be. This may well be, and probably is, my fault. One can hardly read a magazine article in any serious journal about the South, or a book that deals with the region, which doesn't quote Cash. His analysis has its excellencies, and is stylistically superior; yet I do not feel that it stands far above all other modern works that deal with the region. And I wish someone would explain, in intelligible English, what Cash means by the phrase "the proto-Dorian front," to which he is greatly wedded. I read one explanation, but it seemed as obscure as the phrase that it purported to elucidate.

Racial tensions were mounting during the war, and wild rumors were circulating. One that was prevalent in the Richmond area, as well as in many others, was to the effect that the blacks were buying up all the switchblades and ice picks with a view to carrying out a wholesale massacre of the whites under cover of darkness. The National Association for the Advancement of Colored People was demanding that every form of segregation be abolished, and that the Negro be placed on a plane of "complete political and social equality." Many blacks were quite naturally discontented because of their subordinate role in the armed services. A. Philip Randolph, prominent Negro leader, was threatening to lead a march on Washington, "and we don't give a damn what happens." All this caused southern Negrophobes to respond with threats, and there were three lynchings in Mississippi in a single week.

This highly disturbing situation caused me to write an article for the *Atlantic* with the title "Nearer and Nearer the Precipice." The article warned that unless both sides calmed down, we might have "the worst internal clashes since Reconstruction," and the war effort might be greatly hampered. This warning turned out to be at least partially well based, since within a few months the terrible Detroit and Harlem race riots occurred. However, I was too pessimistic as to the length of time I thought it would take for the white South to accept calmly contests between blacks and whites for political office. I believed it would be generations, but that was soon found to be quite wrong. I also declared that the entire segregation system could not and should not be abolished at once, as demanded by the NAACP, and I ended the article as follows:

"If the disturbing elements on both sides of the color line can somehow be muzzled for the duration, and if the slow but certain processes of evolutionary progress can function, then better interracial relations and accelerated Negro advancement will go hand-in-hand—and we shall be able to get on with the war." For expressing these sentiments I was loudly denounced by the NAACP and kindred bodies.

Prominent southern blacks had met in Durham, North Carolina, in 1942 with a view to providing helpful leadership and bringing the best thought of the South to bear on the region's increasingly tense racial situation. They issued a manifesto in which they firmly but politely urged the white South to provide some tangible evidence that greater fairness to the blacks and wider opportunities for them would be forthcoming in the not distant future. No demand was made for an end to segregation.

A group of southern whites, of whom I was one, met in Atlanta in the spring of 1943, and responded favorably to the Durham statement. Another meeting in Richmond followed, at which both whites and blacks were present. Dr. Gordon B. Hancock, a Negro leader from Richmond, sounded the keynote, and sought therein to impress on the white South the necessity for reasonable concessions, to the end that southern blacks might continue to speak for their race below Mason and Dixon's Line. "It makes a world of difference to the cause of race relations," said Dr. Hancock, "whether the capital of the Negro race is in New York City or Atlanta." His fear was that if whites in Dixie failed to provide tangible evidences of greater Negro opportunity, northern Negro radicals would move in with drastic solutions that might well lead to untold friction and even violence.

A few months later another biracial meeting was held in Atlanta, and plans were laid for the establishment of a Southern Regional Council. Its purpose was to carry forward the objectives enunciated by the black leaders at Durham the year before. The council began functioning in 1944, with headquarters in Atlanta. It sought to persuade white southern leaders that unless they could produce something more impressive than pious sentiments, southern blacks would lose control and Harlem would take over. Unfortunately, the council was never able to convince any substantial number of white leaders of the South to go along with this program. The average Southerner apparently took the view that the organization was merely "stirring up trouble." The business community, in particular, was unco-operative. Almost all officers and members of the council were educators, clergymen, labor leaders or journalists.

In an effort to provide specific evidence of black progress, I proposed editorially on November 13, 1943, that the segregation system be abolished on Virginia's streetcars and buses. I followed this about a week later with a more comprehensive editorial, outlining the background of the proposal and stressing the necessity for the south to forestall a takeover by northern blacks. I also suggested that black policemen be appointed for the Negro sections of cities, and that the Piedmont Sanatorium for tubercular Negroes at Burkeville, Virginia, be given an all-Negro staff. Copies of this second editorial were mailed to all the leading southern newspapers. A small journal in Kinston, North Carolina backed us up, but elsewhere in the South, except from a couple of black papers, there was thunderous silence. In the North there was much favorable editorial comment from both white and black publications. (My comprehensive editorial on the race situation appears in the Appendix.)

Times-Dispatch readers reacted in almost unprecedented numbers. Letters poured in, and to my astonishment those from whites were at least three to one in favor of our proposals. Blacks were virtually unanimous. However, it was impossible to obtain any backing from the state's political leadership, and nothing was done at the 1944 session of the General Assembly toward implementing the program. Six years later, Armistead L. Boothe, member of the House of Delegates from Alexandria, introduced bills providing for abolition of segregation on intrastate and interstate transportation lines and establishing a state commission on race relations. The *Times-Dispatch* supported this legislation, but it got nowhere.

Our espousal of the plan to repeal segregation laws on streetcars and buses caused *Time* magazine to publish a column and a half about me, with a photograph that looked as if I hadn't washed my face for weeks. The piece was complimentary in some respects, and especially so to my wife, but I was greatly annoyed by the following two sentences: "His editorials, ground out with painful slowness, are almost pedantically occupied with both sides of the question. They are invariably prosaic and humorless."

I had never heard before that my editorials were "ground out with painful slowness." Given the amount of stuff that I had to produce, they couldn't have been. As for my "invariably prosaic and humorless" commentaries, I wonder how many of them *Time* had read. True, during the war, when so many important and serious subjects had to be dealt with, there was little time or inclination for humorous material. But Mark Ethridge, no mean judge, had complimented my light editorials when he was our publisher, as had others. And I would devote more attention to this type of persiflage when the war was over. *Time* had sent my friend William S. Howland to Richmond for the purpose of gathering material for the article and writing it. But the final version was not Bill Howland's. As usual, *Time*'s editors were playing God and massaging the facts to suit their purposes. Samples of my "prosaic and humorless" editorials appear in the Appendix.

At about this time I became involved in an acrimonious controversy with John D. Wise, vice-president and general manager of the *Times-Dispatch*, who was second only to John Stewart Bryan in the management hierarchy. To some extent, it grew out of differences of opinion concerning the Westbrook Pegler column, which the paper carried and which I detested. Wise was a great Pegler fan. He accused me of not believing in freedom of speech because I wanted to toss out Pegler's abusive and ill-mannered attacks on everybody to the left of Calvin Coolidge. Wise seemed to think that freedom of speech implied that a newspaper was obligated to *buy* a column that it considered both objectionable and worthless. We finally dropped Pegler, but there was such an uproar from his admirers that Mr. Bryan put him back.

Jack Wise and I had enjoyed a pleasant relationship for the first few years that he was on the paper, but he grew increasingly conservative, if not reactionary, and we disagreed sharply on various issues. In an exchange of letters between us he termed me guilty of "notorious intolerance" and "puritanical intolerance." He also said I was "dragging the *Times-Dispatch* down to oblivion." I wonder now at my temerity in replying as follows:

"I confess myself baffled when a person who has been cynical, bitter and supercritical of practically everything that has happened in Washington over a long period of years begins lauding the virtues of 'tolerance.' When, in recent years, did you exhibit that characteristic in your comments on public affairs?"

He accused me of attacking his "personal characteristics" in the above observation, whereas, he said, he had merely attacked my editorial views, not my personal characteristics. It should be noted that my criticism of him had to do entirely with his "comments on public affairs." I stated that "the editorials in the *Times-Dispatch* are written by me or approved by me. They express my philosophy toward current events. It would be impossible for me to be intolerant and puerile as an editor, and not be so as an individual."

Wise did make one valid point in our intramural correspondence. He said I had approved a couple of pieces of legislation without reading them, i.e., the full text. This was true, and I should have read the complete texts before putting our editorial imprimatur on these measures.

I am convinced that Wise was trying to force me to leave the paper without actually trying to get Mr. Bryan to fire me. He wanted to make things so unpleasant that I would depart of my own volition. Our relations were strained until he retired in 1957.

The above-mentioned correspondence between us is in my papers at the University of Virginia's Alderman Library.

Speaking of the University of Virginia, the student newspaper there, *College Topics*, and its successor, the *Cavalier Daily*, conceived of me for at least a decade as perhaps the institution's prime enemy. All this began, as best I can make out, when the student editors concluded that I was responsible for the news policy of the *Times-Dispatch*, which had published some unfavorable accounts of student misbehavior. (Almost every institution of higher learning has the feeling, at one time or another, that the press is unwarrantably hostile, and not giving adequate publicity to its worthwhile achievements, while overplaying its derelictions.) At all events, I seem to have been blamed by the college paper for news articles concerning the university with which I had absolutely nothing to do.

I did write an editorial commending the university administration for screening out some of the "young wastrels," mainly from the North, who had been attending the institution. In addition to calling them "wastrels" I referred to this group of big spenders and sometime hell-raisers as "the Buick and bankroll set." Those phrases stuck in the craw of *College Topics* and the *Cavalier Daily* from year to year and almost from generation to generation. Each editor apparently would indoctrinate his successor with the conviction that Dabney was an enemy of all that was good at Jefferson's university. The paper got out a spoof sheet every spring, and I was the central figure in the 1949 issue, which was called the *Virginius Dispatchus*. The boys cudgeled their brains to come up with the headline best calculated to scare the pants off of the student body, and consequently placed the following in black type across the top of the front page: VIRGINIUS DABNEY APPOINTED NEW RECTOR. Of course I was described in the text as "frequent editorial critic of University social activities," and reference was made to my "repeated criticism of existing conditions at the University," against which I had "crusaded long and earnestly." This was poppycock, although I had indeed argued from time to time that a greater degree of discipline at the institution would be salutary in the extreme. My statements on the subject were milder than those made by others.

However, the youths had worked themselves into a tantrum over my supposed unfairness, and a firm belief in my incurable biases was nothing less than gospel to all *Cavalier Daily* editors. As a matter of fact, I had praised the university much more frequently than I had criticized it.

Finally, when the *Cavalier Daily* published for the umpteenth time that I was "one of the University's most active critics," I wrote asking them please to define the term "active critic," and I added:

"It might be helpful to you in formulating your definition if I mention that during the past year we have had editorials praising President Darden, praising President-Elect Shannon and also President Shannon, praising the University library and the new hospital, praising the undergraduate, graduate and professional schools, praising the beauty of the Grounds and warning against anything that might damage them, and commending the stricter rules governing student-owned automobiles."

No definition of an "active critic" was forthcoming, of course. The paper published my letter without comment. But it may be that my communication, only part of which is quoted here, finally convinced the editors of the student organ that their *bête noire* did not have horns and a tail. At least they referred to me no more as an "arch-foe," "enemy" or "critic" of the university.

Miss Ellen Glasgow, then at the height of her fame, was willing to help me in my early struggles to become a writer. I did an article about her for the New York *Herald Tribune Magazine* in 1929, and she expressed herself as pleased with it. James Branch Cabell had been asked by the New York paper to do the article, but he had declined and recommended me. This was a piece of good luck for me, as I gained an *entrée* with the *Herald Tribune*, and wrote for it from time to time thereafter.

Miss Glasgow read part of my manuscript for *Liberalism in the South* and offered helpful criticism. When the book appeared, she

provided me with a laudatory sentence or two for use in advertising.

Her love of dogs led her to serve for twenty years as president of
the Richmond branch of the Society for the Prevention of Cruelty to Animals. The organization was moribund when she took
over, and she proceeded to put it on the map.

The death of her dog Jeremy in 1929 was a traumatic experience from which she never recovered. Jeremy had been given her
by her one-time fiancé Henry W. Anderson, the nationally prominent Richmond lawyer. Whether this fact played a major role in
her grief I do not know. Certainly she was as deeply devoted to
the little Sealyham as to any member of her family, perhaps more
so.

When Jeremy died, Miss Anne Virginia Bennett, Miss Ellen's
long-time companion, called me on the telephone to announce the
dog's demise and to ask if I would write the obituary. It was an
unusual request, but I went to the hushed house at One West
Main Street to get the facts. Miss Glasgow was too prostrasted by
grief to see me, so I talked to Miss Bennett. She gave me such
data as she was able to assemble, plus a snapshot of the deceased,
and I repaired to my typewriter. Many obituaries were assigned to
me during my eleven years as a reporter, but this was by far the
most difficult of them all. I wrestled with it for a couple of hours,
and it appeared next day, September 8, 1929, with the snapshot of
Jeremy.

The account occupied about a column of space. "Miss Glasgow
rushed back to Richmond from Maine in order to be with Jeremy
in his last hours," I wrote. "The internationally famous novelist
was on the verge of collapse from worry over Jeremy, when she
left for the North a month ago, and it was only because of fear of
a nervous breakdown that she was persuaded to go. Jeremy had
been ill for many months.

"Billy, Miss Glasgow's French poodle, wanders about the house
distracted," the obituary went on. "Billy was the only dog Jeremy
ever had any use for."

Jeremy was buried in the garden behind Miss Glasgow's house.
When Billy died, he too was buried there. And upon the death of

their mistress, the little dogs were exhumed, in accordance with specific directions in her will, and placed in the coffin beside her.

Miss Bennett informed me that Miss Glasgow was much pleased with the obituary that I had written for her beloved pet. I was greatly relieved, since I knew how sensitive she was on the subject. Nearly forty-seven years later my account of the diminutive Sealyham's life, work and death was republished in the *Ellen Glasgow News Letter* (March 1976). Dr. Edgar E. MacDonald, the editor, described it as "a command performance consummately executed." (The full text of the obituary appears in the Appendix.)

Jeremy had been operated on in his last illness by Dr. Stuart McGuire, Richmond's most eminent surgeon. When he rendered his bill marked "Services for dog," Miss Glasgow was indignant. It should have read "Services for Mr. Jeremy Glasgow," she said, her eyes flashing.

My inability to see more of Ellen Glasgow in her declining years was highly regrettable, but World War II was on, and it was next to impossible for me to call on her. I had hardly any gasoline. I often got a ride into town in the morning in a car pool generously made possible by my neighbor W. Frank Powers, and I came home on the streetcar at night. It was so late when I left the office that calling on anybody was out of the question. Weekends were usually taken up with various chores.

During this period we attended a small cocktail party at James Branch Cabell's, at which Miss Glasgow was present. She and Cabell were discussing what the critics were saying about their books, and Cabell remarked, "I'm sick and tired of having them describe me as 'an embittered romantic.'" "Well," rejoined Miss Glasgow, "I'm tired of being called 'a repressed virgin.' I'm *not* a repressed virgin, am I James?" "I don't know, I don't know," said her rather flustered host.

Ellen Glasgow invited my wife and me to some of her attractive entertainments for visiting celebrities, one of whom was Gertrude Stein. Miss Stein, a short, stocky figure wearing strange masculine clothes and a masculine haircut, was accompanied by her lesbian lover, weird-looking Alice B. Toklas. Miss Stein had done a bit of traveling through Virginia, and had been interviewed by the *Times-Dispatch*. She made the remarkable observation that Virginia impressed her as being "uninhabited." Still more remarkable was the inscription she put in my copy of *The Autobiography of Alice B. Toklas:*

"To Mrs and Mr Virginius Dabney in memory of a pleasant meeting, in memory of a pleasant Richmond Times-Dispatch in memory of a charming Virginia and in memory of a charming visit to Virginia." Her signature beneath was wholly unreadable, whereas that of Miss Toklas was quite clear.

Sherwood Anderson was another guest at the Glasgow home. He mentioned having told Ellen that hers was just the kind of house that he liked—"old and homelike, comfortable and dirty. . . ." He professed to be surprised that she was not pleased by this dubious tribute.

After a long period of failing health, Miss Glasgow died. I was a pallbearer, and attendance at the service at One West Main was by invitation. Henry W. Anderson, her erstwhile fiancé, was not invited but he came anyway. I did not see him at Hollywood Cemetery, where the burial took place. At that time I was wholly unaware of their long-dead romance.

Publication of Ellen Glasgow's autobiographical work, *The Woman Within*, several years after her death caused a lively stir in Richmond and elsewhere, not only because of the revelations it contained concerning the author, but also because it infuriated Cabell. He was understandably angry because she dredged up, quite gratuitously, some long-forgotten and completely discredited scandalous rumors concerning him. So he devoted a chapter of his *As I Remember It* to deliciously pungent observations concerning the lady who had done him this disfavor. Some of Cabell's most delightful writing and most devastating irony is in this chapter, but most Richmonders are unaware of the fact, since the book, Cabell's last, sold hardly at all. In it he refers to *The Woman Within* as "Ellen Glasgow's autobiography, that beautiful and wise volume, which contains a large deal of her very best fiction." Apropos of her romance with a married man and her several betrothals, as revealed posthumously in *The Woman Within*, he wrote that "she implied her girlhood and her past in general to have been a constant entanglement, or say, a true tropical, torrid jungle, of love-affairs which, at the moment, she was unwilling to discuss."

I found these two books to be absolutely astonishing. The first, by Miss Glasgow, revolutionized my concept of its author, whom I had taken to be a maiden lady with a conventional past. The second book, by Cabell, spoke of things concerning this distinguished woman that she herself had not revealed, most of them not to her credit. She once remarked to me that she thought southern authors should begin rolling a few logs for one another, since the New Englanders had been doing that for many years, but I never heard her viciously criticize rival novelists, especially women, as Cabell said she was fond of doing.

Miss Glasgow was not troubled by one problem that plagued Cabell, namely the widespread mispronunciation of his last name. Every Virginian knew the proper pronunciation in view of the Cabell family's prominence, but elsewhere there was, and still is, a tendency to say *Cabell*. These frequent mispronunciations led Cabell to compose the following couplet:

> *Go tell the dirty rabble*
> *My name is James Branch Cabell.*

At about the time of Ellen Glasgow's death, Cabell's following began shrinking and sales of his books declined alarmingly. When the great prose stylist and master ironist died, my wife and I went to his funeral at Emmanuel Episcopal Church, Brook Hill, and were shocked to see it so sparsely attended. He was buried in the churchyard there, but his widow removed his body later to Hollywood. The handsome new library at Virginia Commonwealth University is named for him, and contains a collection of rare Cabelliana, donated by Mrs. Cabell.

We have been carried beyond the end of World War II by my discussion of Ellen Glasgow and James Branch Cabell. Miss Glasgow died November 21, 1945, a few months after the end of hostilities, while Mr. Cabell lived until 1958.

We on the home front in Richmond during the war underwent inconveniences but no severe suffering, except for those whose sons, husbands or brothers were in one of the danger zones. There were chiselers, present in all wars, who refused to obey the rules and hoarded food and other things rather than deny themselves for the benefit of those on the fighting fronts. I made a regular written report to Washington on morale, black markets and related matters in the Richmond area. R. Keith Kane, John Stewart Bryan's son-in-law, happened to be the individual to whom I sent my analyses.

Rationing of foods, gasoline, clothing and so on was introduced in 1942. At first, costs of these commodities soared, but prices were brought under a measure of control by the Office of Price Administration. Former Mayor J. Fulmer Bright of Richmond was OPA chairman for Virginia. Such things as scrap rubber and tin were collected in drives and put to use in the war. We were asked to send warm clothing to the Russians. My wife patriotically contributed her VMI sweater, symbol of her conquests at the institute, after removing the monogram. I donated a sweater that had less glamorous associations.

During the spring of 1944, when the Russians were "tearing the guts" out of the German Army, in Winston Churchill's graphic phrase, all eyes in America were fixed on the huge invasion force assembled in England for an assault on Hitler's "Fortress Europe." There were several false alarms, but the suspense ended on June 6 with the terse announcement from General Eisenhower's headquarters that the Allies had begun landing forces "on the northern coast of France." When this bulletin arrived at the *Times-Dispatch* there was relief coupled with apprehension lest the Americans and British find themselves unable to hold the narrow strip of coast that they had seized. Richmonders and other Virginians were in the first wave on Omaha Beach, one of the most desperately defended sectors. They held on grimly and refused to be driven into the sea.

First public notice of the invasion came in Richmond when the chimes of St. James Episcopal Church rang at three o'clock in the morning, heralding the Allied landings. Then came newspaper extras. Richmonders flocked to the churches that night in prayer for the success of the enterprise. The schools also held appropriate observances. There was no frivolity anywhere, since all recognized that a crucial turning point in the war had come.

Months of heavy fighting on the beaches and in the hedgerows of Normandy followed. All of us watched anxiously and wondered if the most massive invasion in world history had been halted in its tracks. But the Allies finally ended the bloody stalemate, freed Paris and began the headlong rush across the frontiers of tottering Germany.

Almost another year would pass before the fanatic and deranged Hitler was finally overthrown. That objective had almost been reached when the nation and the world were shocked on April 12, 1945, by news of President Franklin D. Roosevelt's sudden death at Warm Springs, Georgia. Ralph Begien, Jr., our neighbor who had charge of vital shipments over the Chesapeake & Ohio Railway en route to the fighting fronts, had seen President Roosevelt not long before. He reported to us confidentially that Roosevelt looked emaciated, with his shirt collar a size or two too big and his complexion a ghastly gray. So we were aware that the President's health had declined drastically. Nevertheless, we were not ready for the news from Warm Springs.

Osburn Zuber, our associate editor at that time, was one of Roosevelt's most worshipful admirers, and he wanted to write the editorial on the latter's passing. I agreed that he should do so. When the finished product arrived on my desk it was so completely overboard that I had to eliminate several paragraphs. Zuber practically had the whole nation in tears and the solar system draped in black. Even after the deletions, the editorial, when read today, seems to go too far in unrestrained praise, although FDR's achievements were, of course, memorable and his death brought grief to millions.

There had been numerous rumors during the spring that Germany was about to surrender, and on April 28 there was an incorrect report of an armistice. Then on May 7 came V-E Day, with the official announcement that the Germans had surrendered at Rheims. An estimated 35,000 persons flocked to Richmond churches for services of thanksgiving. But I wrote in an editorial, "Not until the Japanese also give in unconditionally can we really let ourselves go and celebrate victory with unbounded joy." Everyone was aware that the war in the Pacific was yet to be won.

There was a thrilling interlude the following month when General Eisenhower returned to the United States for a wildly enthusiastic welcome. I went to Washington to witness the stirring events, heard "Ike" address Congress and then attended his press conference.

Immediately following his arrival by plane from Europe, the commander of the Allied armies in the West headed a parade through downtown Washington. A more attractive and dynamic personality I never encountered. He was glowing with health and deeply tanned, and his famous smile seemed almost as wide as Pennsylvania Avenue. When he flashed that grin and raised his arms in a wide gesture to the cheering crowds, the effect was electric. The parade was an unbroken ovation.

Eisenhower's address to Congress was adequate but somewhat anticlimactic, since it was not too well delivered, but his subsequent off-the-cuff conference with the press was a complete success. His fast ripostes to queries from the newspapermen drew loud and sympathetic laughs. For example, when asked if he was ever worried about the outcome of the Battle of the Bulge, Hitler's last desperate effort the previous December and January to crash through to the coast, Ike shot back, "You bet! Three weeks later, when we got the American newspapers." He added, "We captured their general orders the first day, you know. We never had the slightest notion that von Rundstedt would reach Antwerp." He was unrestrained in his praise of the officers and men under his command, and gave them full credit for the victories that had been achieved.

My wife and I managed to get away, with the Begiens, for a week's vacation in July, while realizing that if Japan, by some freak of fate, should collapse, we would have to rush back to Richmond. Our vacation spot was Banner Elk, North Carolina, a lovely site in the North Carolina mountains where Lees-McRae College operated a small summer hotel. It was wonderfully peaceful and restful to breathe the clear, cool air and consume the excellent food.

Soon after our return, the first atomic bombs in history were dropped on Hiroshima and Nagasaki, and it was obvious that Japan would have to give in or be pulverized.

The surrender occurred on August 14. We were just finishing our Sunday night supper when President Truman came on the radio at seven o'clock and announced "full acceptance of the Potsdam Declaration which specifies the unconditional surrender of Japan." In almost no time, the *Times-Dispatch* was out with an extra carrying in gargantuan type the potent line "JAPS QUIT."

V-J Day was fixed officially for September 2. It was then that General Douglas MacArthur accepted the surrender of the Japanese on board the battleship *Missouri* in Tokyo Bay. We listened to every word of these climactic proceedings, as we had listened to so many other broadcasts throughout the war.

8

Buzzards Over Berchtesgaden

WITH THE END of the war, life on Tapoan Road was soon back to normal. Douglas and I rejoined the country club and I took up tennis again, usually playing twice a week. I also resumed rewriting *Dry Messiah*. Bishop Cannon had died the previous year, and it was now possible to publish a biography of him without risking an automatic libel suit, irrespective of whether libel was committed.

In March 1946, Winston Churchill, at the height of his fame, came to Richmond and addressed the General Assembly. He gave his well-known "V" salute to the crowd as the procession he headed moved through the rain to the Capitol. In his much-applauded address Churchill said he had had many invitations to speak in this country, and he had chosen to do so in "Richmond, the historic capital of world-famous Virginia." I was in the gallery and was much excited to see and hear this man who could almost be said to have carried the British people through the Battle of Britain on his powerful shoulders. There was an added bonus on this occasion when General Dwight D. Eisenhower, who accompanied Churchill as his aide, was called on insistently by the audience to speak, and finally responded. His sincere and graceful words were as enthusiastically received as those of the dauntless leader who had led Britain through the darkest hours of the German blitz.

Former Governor Colgate W. Darden, Jr., asked Churchill if he would be interested in seeing Jamestown.

"What's that, some sort of naval base?" the Englishman asked. He must have misunderstood Darden, or his mind was on something else, for Churchill shows complete awareness of Jamestown in his *History of the English-Speaking Peoples*.

It is astonishing, however, that so many persons on both sides of the Atlantic know nothing of Jamestown or its personalities. This was borne out some two decades later when my wife and I were in London and desirous of seeing the grave of Captain John Smith, without whose leadership the Jamestown settlement probably would not have survived. We had forgotten the name of the church where he lies buried, so we went to the English-Speaking Union's headquarters, confident that almost anybody there could give us the answer. But we asked one person after another concerning the whereabouts of Smith's tomb, and got only blank stares. Finally, after we had visited several offices, one lady spoke up brightly, "Was he in the Air Force?" Nobody could be found who had ever heard of Captain John Smith, so I rummaged through a pile of tourist literature and learned that his grave is in St. Sepulchre's Church.

Not long after Winston Churchill addressed the Virginia General Assembly, the University of Richmond conferred honorary degrees on General Eisenhower and Admiral Chester W. Nimitz. Dr. Douglas S. Freeman, rector of the university, entertained them at a large buffet luncheon at his home. Mint juleps were served, and photographs of the two principal guests grasping juleps appeared next day in the press. The University of Richmond is closely related to the Baptist Church and Freeman was a leading Baptist layman. Some of the clergy and deacons of that denomination were considerably upset over what they regarded as a display of moral depravity. Freeman came in for criticism, and Eisenhower remarked when I told him about it, "I got various letters from the Bible Belt giving me hell for setting such an example for the youth of the land." He added, "Hereafter when I have my picture taken, if I have a drink in my hand, or even a package of cigarettes, I'm putting it down until the picture is made."

A source of much merriment in these early postwar years was "Senator Beauregard Claghorn," a radio character who burlesqued southern politicians. Claghorn, a professional Southerner, appeared on the Fred Allen Sunday night program, and his accent and mannerisms were highly amusing. A typical utterance was, "In college Ah was voted the member of the senior class most likely to secede and Ah was graduated magnolia cum laude." Also: "When in New York Ah only dance at the Cotton Club. The only dance Ah do is the Virginia Reel. The only train Ah ride is the Chattanooga Choo-Choo. When Ah pass Grant's tomb Ah shut both eyes. Ah never go to the Yankee Stadium! Ah won't even go to the Polo Grounds unless a southpaw's pitchin'."

Part of an editorial I wrote entitled "Claghorn, the Dixie Foghorn," was placed in the *Congressional Record* by Representative Henry D. Larcade, Jr., of Louisiana. This truncated version omitted our references to Claghorn's highly diverting aspects, and created the impression that we regarded all southern congressmen as "nitwits and foghorns like Senator Claghorn."

PM, the New York newspaper, published an article based on the incomplete version in the *Congressional Record*, and the *Times-Dispatch* began getting letters from all parts of the United States. These correspondents were under the grave misapprehension that we couldn't take a joke and that we didn't think Claghorn was funny.

The uproar went on for weeks. We reprinted editorials on the subject from various widely scattered newspapers. I was kept busy explaining that I thought Senator Claghorn was one of the most entertaining characters of modern times.

He passed from the scene not many months afterward, apparently because his gag writer ran out of gags. But they were excruciating while they lasted, and the actor who played the role of Claghorn on the radio was superlatively comical. He also made Southerners look at themselves and wonder just how much truth there was in the caricature. (The text of my first editorial on Claghorn appears in the Appendix.)

The *Times-Dispatch* acquired an associate editor in 1946 who had had a varied experience in journalism. He was K. V. Hoffman, editor of the Bennington, Vermont, *Banner* for the preceding five years, and previously city editor of the Juneau, Alaska, *Daily Capital*. Hoffman was a Yale graduate, and while at Old Eli had played on the championship water polo team. He was more conservative than I on nearly all public issues. Upon the death of Thomas Lomax Hunter, Hoffman took over his column under the name of "Ross Valentine."

With the return of peacetime and a greater measure of prosperity, I was permitted to employ an additional editorial writer. I found him in Parke Rouse, Jr., who was back from the Navy, and who revealed a special talent for editorial commentary. Two years later he was made Sunday editor and I lost him.

Overton Jones, who also had served in the Navy, and who had been reporting City Hall for some years, succeeded Rouse. Jones was especially well informed on municipal affairs, and since I wasn't, he was a valuable acquisition. He also knew a great deal about traffic problems and highway safety, and was appointed first chairman of the Virginia Highway Safety Commission. Jones joined the editorial staff in 1949 and became associate editor in 1956, a position which at this writing he still holds. Another editorial writer, Will Harrison, came aboard in 1949 after serving in a public relations capacity with the armed forces in Germany. He left a year or two later and joined the editorial staff of the Toledo, Ohio, *Blade*.

Rabbi Edward N. Calisch, who took his Ph.D. under my father, and was a good friend of mine, came down to my office in the heat of a July day during World War II and invited me to join the Ember Club, a small discussion group. There were about a dozen members, most of whom were prominent in business or the professions. They met at one another's homes once a month. A guest or two might be invited to attend, and perhaps to speak informally. A subject for discussion was arranged for each meeting. This went on for several years, but as members died, the club dwindled and finally went out of existence.

The War Department was inviting representatives of the media, in the years immediately following World War II, to visit the wrecked cities of Germany and to study political and social conditions in that defeated country. A brief side trip to Italy and Austria also was included. An invitation came to me in December 1946 from Secretary of War Robert P. Patterson for such a visit to Europe in early 1947. I accepted.

Before our take-off on January 15 the ten newspaper and radio men in the party had lunch at the Pentagon with General Eisenhower and other brass hats. I sat next to Ike for a most fascinating hour and three quarters, during which he talked in the freest way about many things.

He had had a month's fishing vacation in Florida after his return from Europe. "I enjoyed that thirty days of loafing more than I have everything else put together in the past ten years!" said he. Bone fishing occupied much of his time. "I'll be damned," said the general, "if when one of those things hits your line you don't think lightning has struck you!"

En route to Florida he tried to stay out of sight and avoid being recognized. He wore old clothes and sat on the back seat of a somewhat battered Chevrolet. Yet two of his former soldiers penetrated his disguise and rushed up and greeted him. He thought that would be the end of it, but they telephoned ahead to the town where he was going fishing.

"It looked as if every seven-year-old kid within fifty miles was standing on the wharf when we pulled in," said he, laughing. He had to provide autographs for most of them.

Eisenhower revealed that he had an arthritic condition in both forearms, and the doctors had told him that if he didn't use them actively they would atrophy. So he took golfing lessons from the professional Joe Kirkwood, and said that "as soon as the weather opens up it'll be nine holes a day, or at least twice a week." When he became President several years later, he was still playing golf as often as he could get away from his duties. Many of the correspondents and commentators delighted to jeer at him for spending so much time on the links. In view of the condition affecting his forearms, of which few persons seem to have been aware, it is hard to see how he could have done anything else.

General Eisenhower revealed a comprehensive knowledge of the various American Presidents and their records—much more so than one might expect from an army chief of staff. I mentioned that seven generals had become President and he named six at once. Somebody else chimed in with Benjamin Harrison. Professor Arthur M. Schlesinger, Sr., of Harvard had sent out a questionnaire to sixty persons throughout the country, of whom I was one, asking them to rank the Presidents in five groups, based on performance in the White House and nothing else. The results had been sent to us, but had not yet been published in *Life* magazine. I mentioned to Ike that all sixty of us put two Presidents in the fifth, or lowest, group. He said at once, "They must have been Grant and Harding." This was correct, but most of those whom I asked afterward to name the two have failed to come up with the right ones. Informed that only one President was put in the first group by all sixty, the general said, "It must have been either Washington or Lincoln." This was correct, but he guessed Washington and the answer was Lincoln—at which he expressed surprise. When I mentioned that James K. Polk ranked high in the second group, Ike said immediately, "He's the one who was elected on the slogan 'Fifty-four Forty or Fight!'" He discussed the Battle of Gettysburg in great detail, saying it was undoubtedly Lee's poorest tactical performance.

Secretary of War Patterson spoke to us briefly and informally at the close of the luncheon. He made it plain, as did others, that we were not expected to express the official point of view in what we wrote, and that we should feel free to ask to see anything that seemed of interest in the occupied zones.

With us on the army transport plane to Europe was Signor de Gasperi, Prime Minister of Italy, and his party, who were in a separate compartment. He had spent nine days in the United States, and he granted us an interview when we came down in the Azores. De Gasperi was the first of various European officials we encountered who had served time in prison for their political or personal views. He spent four years behind bars because of opposition to Mussolini, and showed the effects of his incarceration.

Arriving in Paris at around midnight, we spent two and a half hours in a hotel and then took off for Rome. We understood that we were held over in Paris so that the plane would arrive in the

Italian capital at 9 A.M., thus making it possible for adequate crowds and a brass band to greet Signor de Gasperi.

The unbelievably beautiful sunrise over the Alps as we crossed the Riviera and the Mediterranean made the wait altogether worthwhile. The sun was almost over the horizon as we neared Marseilles, and as it rose it illuminated one of the most gorgeous scenes it has ever been my privilege to witness. Below us was the Mediterranean shore line, with the Riviera stretching away to the left, the waves breaking over its curving beaches, while behind it rose the snow-capped peaks of the Alps-Maritimes. Ahead was rugged Corsica, silhouetted against the rising sun. That island was 150 to 175 miles in front of us, but it appeared to be only twenty-five to fifty miles away, the atmosphere was so crystalline. As we neared Corsica we looked back at the rose-tinted sunlight on the peaks of the Alps and down at the mountainous and picturesque island beneath us. It was unforgettable.

An audience with Pope Pius XII was the highlight of our stay in Rome. We asked him questions about the political situation in Europe, the inroads of communism and so on. He replied graciously but largely in general terms. The morning sun was shining straight into the eyes of several of our group, and His Holiness expressed concern. He got up from his chair, walked over to the window and pulled down the shade. Since he could have called on any member of his staff to perform this office, we were impressed. Some months later, after our return to the States, I read that the Pope had done exactly the same thing when another group had an audience, and the morning sun was bothering one or two of them.

Coleman Harwell, executive editor of the Nashville *Tennessean* and a member of our party, had a letter of introduction to Monsignor Carroll, who was on the staff of the Vatican secretariat of state. The monsignor invited him to lunch, and told him he could bring a friend. I was the fortunate one, and we enjoyed a meal of staggering proportions, lasting no less than two hours, at the Villa Anastasia, habitat of Monsignor Carroll and other American monsignors. The repast included several courses, and was preceded by cocktails, accompanied by wines and topped off with cognac. In addition to providing us with this Lucullan repast our hosts put us in touch with a Signor Raspati, who served as an admirable shopping guide.

We boarded a luxurious train for the trip to Trieste, our next stop. Germany was the principal objective of our journeyings, but we took a hasty look en route at war's aftermath in Italy and Austria. The train was the conveyance of General John C. H. ("Courthouse") Lee, and each of us had a private stateroom with bed and wash basin. There was a club car, with bar, and also a diner. General Lee got behind the bar and genially mixed and dispensed drinks. The liquid and solid refreshments were superb, but the train's road bed was extremely rough, and the ride reminiscent of travel aboard a bucking bronco. En route I was impressed by the evidences of Allied precision bombing. The railroad stations were destroyed, but damage in the immediately adjacent areas was at a minimum. The rusty skeletons of the wrecked stations were still there.

An elaborate dinner was given us in Trieste at the Hotel Grande by General Bryant E. Moore, commanding the 88th Division. A needless extravagance, one of a number during the trip, was the presentation to each correspondent of from two to four sizable cakes, each inscribed in icing with the name of the recipient's paper or radio station. At the dinner in Rome at the Hotel Excelsior a few evenings before I had remarked to General Lee that the wine was very good. Whereupon he summoned a waiter and said, "See that Mr. Dabney gets a case of this wine." I protested loudly, but finally accepted the wine, after it had been brought to me, lest I be thought rude. I divided it with the other members of the group. Another embarrassing extravagance was the action of army public relations officers who seemed to be trying to outdo one another in plying us with fifths of liquor. Of course, all this largesse was at the expense of the American taxpayer.

Trieste had been the principal port of the old Austro-Hungarian Empire, but was now a bone of contention and was about to be taken over temporarily by an international commission. We toured the harbor in a motorboat, and saw the effects of wartime bombing along the docks and among the warehouses. Several ships, including the great Italian liner *Rex*, were upside down or on their sides in the water.

We went thence by train through the mountains to Gorizia, with its ancient fortress in the center of town, used as a lookout point for watching the movements of the Yugoslav soldiers across the nearby border. En route were numerous stunning views. One was of the rushing Izonzo River, crossed by a beautifully arching bridge which had escaped the bombing. Another was of Castle Miramar, overlooking the Adriatic, where Emperor Maximilian lived, and where his widow, Carlotta, died insane, after his execution in Mexico. In Gorizia, we wholly unmilitary newspaper and radio men joined General Moore in "reviewing" a smart-looking contingent of the general's division in the city square. I felt a bit silly.

[handwritten marginal note: SHE DIED 60 YEARS LATER IN A BELGIAN CHATEAU]

That night we took the train for Vienna. I awoke at 7 A.M., and looking through the window of my stateroom saw mountains covered with snow and white flakes floating steadily down. This was the Semmering area of Austria, and we were approaching Semmering, the well-known resort, which was on the dividing line between the British and Russian zones. We assumed that the Russians would allow us to enter their zone after a perfunctory examination of our papers, but this was far from correct. Hours went by, and we sat on the track while those in charge of our expedition tried to prevail on the Russians to let us through. Finally our army authorities managed to telephone Red Army headquarters in Vienna, and to explain what this strange-looking group of visiting firemen was up to. All this took exactly seven hours, during which we sat in our train. Fairness compels the admission that the mix-up was the fault of the Americans, who should have given the Russians proper advance notice that this expedition was on the way.

On our arrival in snow-covered Vienna, we noted colossal destruction on every hand. Along the Ringstrasse there was heavy damage to the Opera House, the Burgtheater and the Kunsthistorisches Museum. St. Stephen's Cathedral was also terribly smashed. We were taken to luxury suites in the Bristol Hotel, only a couple of blocks from Russian headquarters at the Imperial.

That night we were given a fine dinner at the hotel by General Geoffrey Keyes. I sat between him and Chancellor Figl of Austria. The chancellor had spent six years in German concentration camps because of his opposition to the Austrian Nazis. He knew about as much English as I did German, and we carried on a fairly successful conversation in the two languages. I was happy to note that General Keyes said there would be no speaking at the dinner. I had been spokesman for the group at the dinner in Rome.

We were entertained with songs by two opera stars, and also by music from the Hotel Bristol orchestra, which played during the meal. The half-starved and impoverished Viennese musicians probably regarded it as a godsend to be able to make some extra cash playing for the Americans. The lady opera singer was lovely, but she looked as though she hadn't had a square meal for months, and was so pale and thin that her skin seemed almost transparent. The ration for urban Austrians had just been raised to a meager 1,550 calories per day from 1,200. After dinner an excellent floor show was provided for our sole benefit in the Bristol's night club—another example of unnecessary extravagance. We were just a group of newspaper and radio men, but one would have thought from the deference paid us by generals and other dignitaries, and the brass bands that saluted us, that we were visiting heads of state.

U. S. Minister John G. Erhardt gave the group a luncheon on the following day. I sat next to Buergermeister (Mayor) Theodor Koerner, a saintly looking old man who had served a year in jail on orders of Chancellor Dollfuss because of his militantly Socialist views. (The guide who showed us the wreckage of St. Stephen's Cathedral had been locked up for seven years in the German concentration camp of Mauthausen because he protested the Nazis' public abuse of Cardinal Innitzer.) Erhardt told me at the conclusion of the luncheon that he would say a few words and asked me to respond, which I did. I had this responsibility on other occasions when we reached Germany.

In Vienna we had our first of many briefings by U.S. generals or other officials, sometimes interspersed with statements from representatives of the occupied country. These usually lasted for hours, and we were sometimes groggy by the time they ended, but they were quite informative.

Cigarettes were being used for currency both in Austria and Germany, and were much sought after by the natives, who could buy food and other necessities with them. A cigarette was valued at about fifty cents. We gave the guide at St. Stephen's two cigarettes, which was altogether adequate and pleased him very much. On the advice of the U. S. War Department we had brought several cartons with us from this country for such purposes.

We left Austria on our fancy train, which now included cars that had been used by big-shot Nazis, Goering and Himmler among them. Train operations and all arrangements for our comfort were efficiently supervised by Colonel Ray J. Laux, who was strictly business and did not attend any of the functions in which we participated in the various cities. Colonel George S. Eyster, who occupied the Goering coach with Mrs. Eyster, accompanied us to the functions in question. The Goering coach had a bathtub, built into the floor, large enough to accommodate a hippopotamus—approximately the dimensions of Herr Goering.

The question as to which two correspondents would enjoy Himmler's luxurious quarters was settled by a rolling of the bones. Erik Oberg, representing the industrial press, and I were the winners. I wondered if I would have nightmares traveling in quarters that had been occupied by one of the archcriminals of all time.

It was much colder in Germany than in Austria; in fact the winter in the former country was said to be the coldest in fifty years, with temperatures well below freezing nearly all the time, and thirteen below zero in the Rhineland. The ground was covered with snow throughout the trip, and the rivers were frozen over. I broke out my long flannel underwear.

There was nothing to drink on board the train except coffee and whiskey. Prior to making the trip I had not been able to indulge in a cup of coffee after noon of any day, or I would stay awake that night. But for about three weeks in the cars there was no alternative to drinking coffee at all meals. Strangely enough, I was soon cured of my sleeping problem, and ever since have been able to take coffee at any hour.

Although whiskey was always available on the train, there was little excessive bibulosity. One or two of the boys got plastered after we had been listening to briefings most of the day, but nothing of the sort occurred during business hours.

We were warm and comfortable in those fancy coaches, and pathetically shivering Germans, many of them in thin, shabby and badly worn garments, looked at us balefully from station platforms as we passed. I couldn't help feeling sorry for them, for many had been unsympathetic to Hitler, as we had found out in 1934, and they were now having to suffer for his frightful misdeeds.

Much destruction from bombing was in evidence all across Germany before we reached Berlin, but the devastation in the German capital had to be seen to be believed. For two and a half miles in every direction from the Brandenburg Gate, at the head of Unter den Linden, the city was 95 per cent destroyed, according to our U. S. Army informants. It was more like 100 per cent, as far as we could tell, for there was nothing remotely resembling an intact building in the heart of Berlin.

I telephoned Dr. Georg Kartzke, who had shown us many courtesies in 1934 as chief representative of the Oberlaender Trust in the German-speaking countries, and told him that I wanted to pay him a visit. He expressed a desire to see me, so I commandeered the army car, with chauffeur, that was always at our disposal. We drove through the center of the city to East Berlin, and the eerie landscape was like the mountains of the moon. Destruction so colossal I had never imagined. The once beautiful Tiergarten was a desert, with only a few scrubby trees remaining, and the Column of Victory still standing ironically in the center. The only thing left unsmashed, except for the aforesaid column and a few forlorn statues of Prussian kings, was the large Russian monument to the Red Army, guarded night and day by soldiers from that army. In the Potsdamer Platz, once the Times Square of Berlin, and as far as the eye could see during miles of driving through that part of the city, there was nothing whatever but gutted buildings. The seared and blasted façades, with holes that once were windows, were like eyeless skulls. There was practically no sign of life in any of these thousands upon thousands of deserted stores, shops, public buildings and dwellings. People were walking in the streets, and seemed to be going about some sort of business, but it was difficult to tell what that business might be. There was no retail trade in that section of Berlin except for a very rare shop set up in the fragment of a building. Nor did I discern a single thing that might be termed the dwelling place of a family. I found that a great many Berliners were living like moles—beneath the rubble in the still-intact cellars of their gutted homes—a mode of life that appeared almost inconceivable for a civilized people.

Finally we arrived at 54 Am Treptower Park, the same address that the Kartzkes had had thirteen years before, but it was sadly changed. The handsome apartment house had been bombed, and the whole front caved in. I finally managed to get in through a side entrance which had on it a shiny brass plate bearing the words "Herr Professor Dr. Georg Kartzke." The Russians had been impressed with this plate and the Kartzkes had been careful to keep it shined. A *Herr Professor* was entitled to an extra ration of coal.

I rang the bell and a young German maid answered. She took me through the cold corridors, absolutely without heat in that icy weather, to one small room, which had a stove. Dr. Kartzke looked a good deal older, but he greeted me warmly. He had never been a Nazi or a Nazi sympathizer, and now he was having to suffer for the Fuehrer's crimes. The once comfortable apartment with its grand piano and book-lined library was a shambles. Furthermore, early in the war he had taken the family heirlooms, the portraits and the silver, to a castle in East Prussia, "out of the danger zone." But that castle was one of the first burned by the invading Russians, so the Kartzkes' treasures were consumed in the flames.

Despite these calamities, Dr. Kartzke was remarkably cheerful. He was teaching a course in democracy under U.S. auspices, and was getting $55 a month, after taxes. This he described, with a straight face, as "a fine salary." He was too proud to admit that he was suffering. I had brought him and Mrs. Kartzke six chocolate bars from the United States and a similar number of cakes of soap. He accepted the chocolate reluctantly, since I told him I had carried it across the ocean for him; he all but refused the soap, although he admitted that the so-called soap he was getting was of the poorest grade. At last he said he would take it if I was going to throw it away. His son was there in the apartment with him, having just escaped from a British prison camp, and he seemed less reluctant to accept the small gifts. Mrs. Kartzke came in as I was leaving, and was most appreciative.

Her husband's description of the Russians' entry into Berlin was a harrowing one. The two of them had been spending the nights in the basement air-raid shelter, "sleeping on chairs." When Berlin fell, the Red Army entered the city from the east, passing in front of their bombed-out living quarters. The Red Army actually brought along many camels, which Kartzke said he would not have believed, had he not seen them. The animals apparently had come all the way from Mongolia as part of the Russian transport system.

That night the Kartzkes learned that the Russian troops were raping women on a wholesale scale, so with some thirty others they went to the apartment house basement and sat there in total darkness. After a time they heard the sound of heavy boots on the stairs, and Russian soldiers entered the basement, with flashlights. They located most of the women and dragged them out to be raped. By a freak of fate, they overlooked Mrs. Kartzke, but for days and nights she and her husband lived in terror. He told me that if he had had access to poison, both of them would have taken it. Finally, a semblance of order was restored.

I took my leave after an hour with the Kartzkes, and drove back to our lodgings in West Berlin. It was dark, and I had been warned not to remain in the Russian sector after nightfall.

Next day it was windy, cold and snowing, and we visited the wreckage of Hitler's gigantic chancellery. Its façade on the street was unpretentious and apparently was intended to create the illusion that the Fuehrer was a modest and unassuming man. But there was nothing unpretentious about the once imperial magnificence of the interior. One moved from the great courtyard to a mosaic-lined hall reminiscent of the Egyptian temples. Then there was another huge hall, and from it one entered Hitler's office, almost as big as a tennis court, with a large fireplace. The office looked out on a sort of esplanade which was raised above an extensive garden in which Hitler liked to walk. All this was in ruins, of course, scarred and blasted by bombs and shells, but the proportions were obvious. The Roman emperors seldom achieved anything more sumptuous. Yet the U. S. Army captain who served as our guide said this was merely the temporary chancellery, and that a still more splendid one had been planned for the vicinity of the old Reichstag building.

We went down into Hitler's bunker, forty feet underground, where he and Eva Braun committed suicide as Berlin was falling to the Russians. All fixtures and furnishings had been removed, and flashlights were necessary as we moved through the maze of small rooms. One was Hitler's bedroom, another was Eva's, a third was the scene of their suicide and a fourth was where Goebbels, his wife and their six children took, or were given, poison. When we returned to the surface, most of the group was photographed standing on the spot near the entrance to the bunker where the bodies of Hitler and Eva were burned, after being soaked with gasoline.

Traveling thence along the Wilhelmstrasse we noted the indescribable wreckage of all the imposing public buildings which were to have been the heart and soul of the "Thousand-Year Reich." Then down Unter den Linden, where everything from Kranzler's once famous cafe to the *Schloss* of the Kaiser was in ruins. However, the statue of Frederick the Great in the middle of the street and the memorial to Kaiser Wilhelm I seemed entirely or relatively intact.

The official Barter Market was our next stop. Operated by the U.S. authorities, it gave the hard-pressed and often hungry Germans an opportunity to swap silver and other possessions for cigarettes, which, in turn, could be bartered for necessities. I obtained eleven silver objects in this way—a silver cigarette case, trays, tongs, spoon, dish, etc. For them I paid ten cartons of cigarettes. When I returned to Richmond a Jewish friend of mine was genuinely shocked when I told her about these transactions. She felt that it was highly improper for an American to take advantage of the suffering Germans in this way. I told her that it was done through an official U.S. agency, and that however unhappy it must have made the Teutons to part with their silver, they evidently wanted to trade it for cigarettes with which to buy food or other necessities. She was not in the least convinced, and was obviously much more compassionate than I. In view of the holocaust visited upon the Jews by the Nazis, I regarded my friend's high-mindedness as beyond all praise.

Nuremberg, once the finest surviving large medieval city in Europe, was our next destination. On arrival we found once more that terrible destruction had been wrought by Allied bombing. Late in the war, when the German cause was hopeless, members of the fanatical S.S. who were defending the city refused to surrender. The bombing followed.

We went directly to the Department of Justice, where twenty-three German doctors were on trial for fiendish medical experiments on Russians, Poles and Jews. Four U.S. judges were sitting. It was the courtroom where Goering and the other Nazi potentates had been tried some months previously, ten of whom were hanged. We sat in front-row seats, reserved for VIPs. There was a good deal of joking among us concerning this VIP thing, as none of us took it seriously.

The doctors were charged with brutal experiments involving freezing, sterilization, bone and nerve operations and other inhuman procedures, from which many died. Since the thorough Germans left photographs showing the victims at various stages, and also minutes of the conferences with verbatim statements, the doctors were hard put to it to defend themselves. They said they were not accurately quoted in the minutes or that they personally had nothing to do with the experiments, all of which was unconvincing. Counsel for Dr. Handloser, chief of medical services for the Wehrmacht, was making his opening arguments when we arrived. The principal defendant was Dr. Karl Brandt, Hitler's personal physician, youthful and rather insolent-looking. On the whole, the group was not as revolting in appearance as I expected. A number were wearing the uniform of the infamous S.S.

At luncheon we were able to talk with one of the American judges. He said that Goering was believed by nearly everybody who heard it to have "made a monkey" of U. S. Supreme Court Justice Robert Jackson when Jackson cross-examined him at the first Nuremberg trials.

We were taken on a tour of the cells where those on trial for war crimes were held, and where the "Big Seven," who weren't hanged after the first trial, were incarcerated, pending completion of repairs at Spandau Prison, Berlin. One of the Nuremberg cells that we visited was number five, where Goering escaped the noose by taking poison. I saw Rudolf Hess in his cell, striding up and down in hobnailed boots, making quite a clatter, and Admiral Karl Doenitz, a typical Prussian in appearance, who gave me a venomous stare as he sat on his cold bunk. In the courtyard the next group of defendants was exercising. These were judges of the People's Court, the Nazi tribunal that sentenced accused persons to death with hardly a chance to defend themselves. The "judges" were walking about the courtyard looking as if they were considerably preoccupied. They were not allowed to talk to one another, to stop walking or to pick up anything from the ground.

Nearby was the gymnasium, scene of the hangings of ten of the topflight Nazis. It was smaller than I expected. Bodies of those executed were cremated secretly, but the newspapermen reporting the event were completely fooled as to the destination of the remains when empty coffins were loaded on a truck and carried out through one of the exits. The reporters rushed after these empty caskets, while the ashes of the dead were being smuggled out through another door.

The thought occurred at Nuremberg, as it has often to me and many others in subsequent years, that these hangings set a precedent that may well rise to plague us if, God forbid, we should be so unfortunate as to be defeated in a future war. True, those executed were guilty, directly or indirectly, of unspeakable crimes against civilization. Yet the fact remains that the Nuremberg trials may be used by some possible future conqueror as a precedent for executing our leaders.

In Nuremberg we were given further exposure to the excruciatingly bad taste exhibited in German residential construction dating from the late nineteenth and early twentieth centuries. The prime example was the *Schloss* built by the Faber family of Eberhard Faber pencils fame. A castle from the eighteenth century formed the nucleus of the structure, but it had been vastly enlarged, apparently in the early 1900s. It offers an example of modern German taste at its unutterable worst. The monstrosity is said to have cost $3 million, and it probably did, for the stairs are of solid Italian marble, various rooms are heavily paneled, other walls are hideously frescoed, the ceilings are adorned with frightful flower designs and the rooms are huge. Of all the atrocious taste I have ever seen exhibited in a residence, mansion or castle, this Faber creation is the prize example. Yet there were almost equally horrendous houses in the swank residential areas of Berlin before World War II. We saw them in 1934. Destruction of many of these in the bombing might be regarded—at least from an architectural standpoint—as one of the few blessings to come out of the conflict of 1939–45. It occurred to me that when Europeans begin commenting on the low level of American culture and taste, their attention might be directed to houses in the best residential districts of Berlin before World War II.

From Nuremberg our train carried us through the snow-covered countryside to Munich, where the destruction once again was staggering. Our quarters were in what was left of the swank Hotel Vier Jahreszeiten, the city's finest. It had been badly hit, and had little heat; all the clerks in the lobby wore overcoats. We took our meals in Hitler's House of German Art, since the hotel had not been re-equipped with dining facilities.

A trip a few miles outside Munich to the notorious concentration camp at Dachau was a memorable and shattering experience. The murder apparatus had been kept intact by the Bavarian Government as a memorial to "the 238,000 persons who died in Dachau," and as a warning to future generations. Over the entrance were the words *Arbeit Macht Frei* or "Freedom Through

Work." This mocking slogan appeared over the entrance to various Nazi concentration camps. Dachau was on a smaller scale than some of the other murder factories, such as Auschwitz, but the techniques for torturing and killing were almost identical.

I assumed that the gas chamber at Dachau had been used for wholesale slaughter, but when my wife and I visited this place of horror and death in 1962, we found that such was not the case. A pamphlet we purchased there said that because of repeated sabotage of the gas chamber by inmates of the camp while the chamber was being built, it could never be got into operation. The thirty-three-page pamphlet was written by Nico Rost of Amsterdam, a former prisoner in the camp, and was published by the Comité International de Dachau, Brussels.

Since the gas chamber never became operative, tens of thousands of Jews, Russians and Poles at Dachau were shot in the back of the neck, hanged, beaten to death, starved to death, worked to death or allowed to die of typhus and other diseases. Dachau played a significant role in Hitler's plan for the extermination of Polish intellectuals. In 1947, U.S. military men pointed out to us trees from which they said prisoners were hanged naked by their arms, while enormous hungry dogs were set upon them to tear them to pieces. Our attention was also called to bunkers at which thousands were shot in the back of the neck. The S.S. guards got so tired of cleaning up the blood that an underground catch basin was constructed to save them the trouble. Then, too, the gallows was in constant operation.

When American forces liberated Dachau in April 1945, they found a tremendous pile of bodies in a room next to the crematorium. The bloodstains on the wall were clearly visible to us in 1947, and extended to the ceiling, where bits of human hair could still be seen. These grisly reminders had been removed when my wife, Douglas, and I returned fifteen years later, but the crematorium and the other essential elements of the camp were there for all to see.

In the carefully maintained museum are numerous incriminating documents. There is, for example, the official directive for getting gold teeth from corpses and collecting hair from dead women. Also on view is the official Nazi calculation of the pecuniary profit derived by the regime from working the prisoners in slave labor for "an average life span of nine months." Adding in the gold teeth, "valuables" and "money" taken from the deceased, and deducting the cost of cremation (fifty cents) there was an average "total profit" of 1,631 marks, or slightly over $400 per inmate.

The S.S. even operated a racket with the ashes of the dead. It shipped cheap urns of ashes—any old ashes—to grieving relatives, informing them that these were the ashes of their loved one. The charge was $25.

Did the inhabitants of the nearby town of Dachau know what was going on in the camp? They were aware, of course, that it was a concentration camp for "enemies" of the Nazi regime, but they may not have known of the unspeakable atrocities committed there. The pamphlet quoted above addresses this question and states that the town of Dachau "bears no responsibility." It goes on to say:

"During these twelve years a gulf existed between a part of the population and the S.S. . . . The young girls of Dachau, for instance, refused to dance with the S.S., and there were regular fights between the young men of Dachau and its neighborhood, particularly during traditional festivals. Brave men and women secretly handed the odd cigarette or piece of bread to camp inmates when they were led through the town. In many other ways they tried to ease the lot of prisoners, although they themselves risked incarceration in the camp for doing this."

The visit to Dachau in 1947 was, for me, the most unforgettable part of my German tour. The incredible brutalities of the Nazi regime seemed all to be epitomized in this authentic chamber of horrors only a few miles from the lovely old Bavarian city of Munich. The dungeons of the Middle Ages, with their thumbscrews and racks, their drawings and quarterings and breakings on the wheel were no whit worse than the almost unbelievable barbarities deliberately carried out in the middle of the twentieth century by followers of the hooked cross. To have seen with my own eyes where all this occurred—the barracks, the barbed wire and the incriminating documents, the furnaces and the mass graves—was one of the moving experiences of my life.

From Munich our train took us to the charming Alpine village of Berchtesgaden, Hitler's favorite retreat, which was deep in snow and looked like a Christmas card. The village had suffered no visible bomb damage.

On arriving there I was reminded of something that was said during the war concerning a lachrymose ballad widely sung both in Great Britain and the United States. It forecast that when peace at last returned there would once more be

> *"Bluebirds over*
> *The white cliffs of Dover . . ."*

This brought forth the sardonic comment "To hell with the bluebirds! I want to see buzzards and a deathlike silence over Berchtesgaden."

Buzzards were nowhere to be seen, but there was indeed a deathlike silence over Hitler's luxurious mountain villa, high above the town, when we drove to the site in jeeps. The whole area was in ruins. The villa itself was a mere shell, and nearby was the wreck of the Platterhof, the swank hotel built by the Nazis for the entertainment of party bigwigs and visiting celebrities. Not far away was what was left of the elaborate residences of Hermann Goering and Martin Bormann. There were still a few fragments lying around on the floor of Hitler's blasted villa, and I picked up a piece of thick glass beneath the picture window of the living room and brought it back as a souvenir. Through the gaping hole that was once the window we had an incomparable view of the great mountain opposite, the Untersberg, and the snow-covered mountains and valleys beyond.

On the return to Berchtesgaden I rang the bell at Pension Hohe Warte, where we had stayed thirteen years before. Nobody answered. The Frommel sisters, who had operated it, could well have died in the interim. The place was obviously down at heel, and no wonder; there hadn't been any tourists in the town, except Germans, since 1939 when war broke out. But at least the building was still standing, whereas bombs had left no trace of our 1934 pensions in Berlin and Munich.

In Stuttgart, our next stop, we were again in contact with General Lucius D. Clay, deputy military governor and U.S. representative on the Co-ordinating Committee for Germany. We had attended one of his briefings in Berlin and been greatly impressed by his keen grasp of a multitude of facts and problems. Indeed, he seemed to be more on the ball with respect to details concerning matters assigned to some thirty-five members of his staff than the staff members who had the immediate responsibility. Once more in Stuttgart we marveled at General Clay's brilliance. We were told that he had trouble getting people to serve under him because they were so often embarrassed at not knowing as much about their own specialties as he did.

An awkward aspect of the denazification process came to light in Stuttgart. It appeared that whereas sincere and strenuous efforts were being made in the U. S. Zone to keep former Nazis out of key positions in government and education, no such effort was being made in the French and Russian zones, and in the British Zone co-operation in this matter was less than 100 per cent. In the first two zones just about anybody who seemed qualified was being employed. For example, seventy-six faculty members were fired from Heidelberg University in the U. S. Zone for pro-Nazi activities or sympathies. Many of them were promptly hired by a university the French opened in Mainz.

At Wiesbaden we partook of a typical 640-calorie midday meal, on which the Germans were supposed to subsist, unless they could somehow scrounge additional food, as many did. This, for the natives, was the largest repast of the day, since the total daily allowance in Germany, as in Austria, was 1,550 calories—raised shortly before from 1,200. My appreciation of the woes being suffered by the Germans was greatly heightened after I had tried to consume this meal, which, while sufficient to keep body and soul together, was a dismal affair. There was an edible potato and some beans, as well as an acceptable apple, but the black bread was accompanied by a bit of oleo the size of one's thumbnail, which made most of the bread unappetizing, while the coffee was unspeakable. It was a ghastly brew of acorns, horse chestnuts and burnt grain.

A greatly contrasting and altogether delightful luncheon was given me by a fellow Virginian, General Withers A. ("Pinkie") Burress, with headquarters in the handsome, gigantic and unbombed I. G. Farben Building in Frankfurt. Those present included General and Mrs. Carter Magruder (General Magruder, from Albemarle County, said I had eliminated him from a tennis tournament back in 1915), Colonel George Eyster, Captain Edloe Donnan, Jr., of Richmond, and General and Mrs. Burress and their daughter Cynthia.

There was much mirth over a stupid mistake I made en route to the luncheon. The elevators in the I. G. Farben Building were unlike any that I had ever seen. They resembled perpendicular escalators, for they never stopped, but kept moving at a slow pace, and the passenger was supposed to get in and out while they were in motion. I walked up to one of them without noticing that it was moving, and also without reading the sign immediately adjacent to the button, which said "Do Not Press Except in Case of Emergency!" I pressed the button, as I was in the habit of doing with all other elevators, and instantly the entire mechanism was brought to a halt. A fellow on board was caught between floors. "Hey, what the hell's the matter?" he yelled. "How am I going to get out of here?" I realized at once what I had done, and fled ignominiously to another part of the building. Presumably the engineers were summoned and the apparatus was gotten back into operation.

We stopped over in Paris for a few days on our way home. I took advantage of the opportunity to call on Uncle Tom's widow, Vergy, his former pupil whom he married some years after our visit in 1912, and whom we had met at Sèvres in 1927 after her husband's death. She did not remember ever having seen me before, but was genuinely appreciative of my call. I brought her half a dozen cakes of soap and eighteen chocolate bars, for which she was grateful. Such things were hard to come by in Paris during the years immediately following the war.

We flew back via the Azores, but had a long wait in those islands while repairs were being made to a leaky gas tank. It had been cold in Paris when we left, and I had on my long flannels. In the balmy Azores the heavy underwear was extremely uncomfortable, and I spent much of my time scratching. I couldn't change, since the baggage was inaccessible. After many hours, we took off for Bermuda. Soon we ran into forty-eight-mile-an-hour headwinds which bounced us around and brought several of us, including me, to the verge of active nausea. The headwinds fell later to ten miles an hour. Finally we were told that we would be in Bermuda in twenty minutes. But at the end of that time there was no sign of Bermuda. Another forty minutes went by, but no land was in sight. Ditto for sixty more minutes. We were all silent —and worried. I looked down at that angry sea and wondered anxiously whether we could make it to our destination. Inquiry revealed that our navigator admitted having been guilty of a large error in calculating our position. The thing that made it particularly frightening was the fact that we had been told in the Azores that the gas tanks on the plane did not hold enough fuel for us to make Bermuda against headwinds—and that was exactly what we had. At last, to our intense relief, Bermuda hove into view. None of us quite realized how alarmed all the others had been until the plane taxied across the field, and we exchanged glances denoting our intense relief. Dwight Young, of the Dayton, Ohio, *Journal-Herald*, an aviation enthusiast, summed up the feeling of the group when he said with deep emotion, "It was hell!"

I got out of my flannel underwear and into a clean shirt. After a brief stopover we headed for Washington, arriving twenty-four hours late, thanks to the long delay in the Azores. Doug, who had been waiting in Washington since the preceding day, met me at the airport and it was wonderful to see her. We had left on January 15 and it was now February 17.

Next day the group met at the Pentagon with Secretary of War Patterson, General Eisenhower and others. We discussed the trip for about an hour, giving our impressions of what we had seen and our conclusions as to the type of itinerary provided. We felt that the tour had been too lavish, but hesitated to criticize those who had arranged it and made available such expensive food, drink and accommodations, all of which we had accepted. Toward the close of the interview, I put in the suggestion that there had been too much formal briefing and too little free time. I expressed the view that it would subject the War Department to less criticism if the next group were permitted more opportunities to make their own investigations. General Eisenhower said at once, "I'll see that it's done." As a matter of fact, I had made a list of ten persons whom I wanted to talk with in Berlin, but I saw only one, Dr. Kartzke.

En route to Washington we journalists had agreed that on future tours of this nature, it would be well if the persons invited or their papers paid a substantial part of the cost, if not all of it. Several of us also were united in saying that we would not hesitate to criticize the War Department hereafter in our papers for any public position it might take. The *Times-Dispatch* did criticize the department thereafter from time to time.

I had been back in Richmond only a few months when I was invited in June 1947 by Secretary of War Patterson to go on a thirty-day tour of Japan and Korea, leaving July 8. "Full opportunity will be provided for observing problems of occupation as well as matters of personal interest," his telegram said. It was simply impossible to get away from my desk for another such trip within a period of some seven months, and I declined. I have never had another chance to see the Far East.

9

Truman, Mencken, Marshall, Churchill and Perón

ON THE AFTERNOON of May 3, 1948, the telephone rang on my office desk and Frank Fuller, Associated Press chief for Virginia, said, "Hey, V, did you know that you won the Pulitzer Prize for editorial writing?" It was the first I had heard of it. A couple of minutes later Bill Howland, in charge of the Atlanta Bureau for *Time* and *Life*, called long distance to offer congratulations. An hour or so after that a telegram came from Columbia University with the official word.

The award was for editorials written during the year 1947, with no editorial or series specifically mentioned. I had not submitted anything for the committee's consideration, although I had done so on several previous occasions with no results.

There was this interesting circumstance: one night in the week preceding the announcement of the prizes I received a telephone call from New York. It came from Arthur Krock, head of the New York *Times* Bureau in Washington, who asked me to look up a couple of my most recent editorials on the race problem and send them to him by telegraph, "to be on my desk [at Columbia University] tomorrow morning." I agreed, went to the office, found the editorials and wired them, as requested. I knew Krock was on the Pulitzer Prize Advisory Board, which was then in session, and couldn't help wondering if there was some connection. However, he was asking for editorials published during 1948, and the prize was for work done during the previous year. Hence I was considerably confused as to the meaning of his call.

Arthur Krock never explained to me just why the board wished to see my most recent editorials on the race question. Apparently they wanted to be certain that my attitude on this important public issue was acceptable.

When John Hohenberg's book *The Pulitzer Prizes* was published many years later, I learned that the noted Frank R. Kent of the Baltimore *Sun* "opposed the selection of Virginius Dabney for the editorial writing prize on the horrendous ground that the editor of the Richmond *Times-Dispatch* was an enemy of Harry Flood Byrd." However, "the board did not regard this as a disqualification by any means and voted Dabney the 1948 award, over Kent's objections." Hohenberg says Kent later found out that he was mistaken as to my attitude toward Byrd.

Because of this award, the Richmond Inter-Club Council gave me a dinner at the John Marshall Hotel. Jonathan Daniels, editor of the Raleigh, North Carolina, *News & Observer*, my friend for many years, came to Richmond and made the address. He adorned my brow with bay leaves much beyond my deserts. I had known him since our college days, he at Chapel Hill and I at Virginia. During that era we attended house parties at Upperville, in Virginia's horse-raising and julep-drinking belt. I was at the party of Mary Custis Lee and Anne Carter Lee, granddaughters of General Robert E. Lee. My invitation came because of my friendship with Hunter DeButts, fellow student at Episcopal High and the University of Virginia, who was courting Mary Lee and afterward married her. Jonathan was a guest at the Oxnard house party nearby, where his virtuosity as a crap shooter was demonstrated on the Oxnard's veranda. There were many dances at these handsome country estates lasting pretty much all night, and there was also a tennis tournament.

At about the time when the Pulitzer award was announced, the *Times-Dispatch* became embroiled with the Virginia General Assembly. The paper found much to criticize in various doings of the lawmakers during the session of 1948, including most particularly a proposed bill whereby the State Democratic Committee or the State Democratic Convention would have been empowered to cast Virginia's electoral votes for somebody other than Harry Truman in the presidential contest of that year, irrespective of whether Truman carried the state. The *Times-Dispatch* was not advocating Truman's election, but it recognized that the legislation in question was nothing short of a monstrosity. It was also evidence that the Byrd machine was overstepping its prerogatives.

Our attacks on the General Assembly of 1948 got under the skins of the members to such an extent that the House of Delegates instructed the State Corporation Commission to "investigate" Richmond Newspapers Inc. This, in turn, led me to write a defiant editorial entitled "We Will Not Be Intimidated," which said in part:

"The *Times-Dispatch* does not intend to be silenced by any such political skulduggery. This newspaper has spoken its mind freely during the recent session of the State Legislature, and it will continue to speak its mind. No threats from any section of the State, or from any branch of the General Assembly, nor yet from the Democratic machine, will influence its course. . . ."

There was no investigation. The gentlemen had gone off half cocked.

I submitted the above-quoted editorial, along with a number that had preceded it, for the 1948 national editorial award of the Society of Professional Journalists, Sigma Delta Chi. The series won the award, and the editorial quoted here was given special mention in the citation. (The full text of this editorial appears in the Appendix.)

Lord and Lady Dorchester and Lady Radcliffe, their close relative, came to Richmond for a visit soon after World War II, and we were asked to entertain them. Lord Dorchester arrived in this country with exactly one pair of pants, the ones he was wearing. Some friend in Charleston, South Carolina, bought him several additional pairs on his arrival there a short time after leaving Richmond. The Dorchesters' two fine houses in England had either been destroyed or badly damaged in the bombing. They were strapped for funds for their trip, as extremely strict rules covered the amount of money that any citizen could take out of Great Britain. Lord Dorchester could have brought out a much bigger sum if he had been willing to give a spurious reason for his journey, such as a desire "to study the cattle situation in Canada," for example. He scorned to do this.

The expressions of gratitude from our guests for the little attention we showed them were touching. We gave them some clothes that our children had outgrown, and which were just right for their grandchildren. They enjoyed hugely the buffet dinner at the Country Club of Virginia to which we took them. So lavish a meal had not been seen in England for a long time. We had several cordial letters from them.

During the war we had enjoyed entertaining Captain Williams of the British cruiser *Birmingham* for a weekend. The warship had been badly hit, and was being repaired at one of the Hampton Roads shipyards. Later, we had lunch on board, at the invitation of the captain. After H.M.S. *Birmingham* was repaired, she returned to England just in time for the Christmas holidays. Captain Williams was looking forward eagerly to being with his family again, after so long an absence. But as soon as his ship reached port, she was ordered to the Far East, and his long-awaited reunion with his wife and children had to be postponed indefinitely.

Captain Williams and Lord and Lady Dorchester took in stride the calamities that they experienced during the war. The British have an ability to stand adversity and to fight on against seemingly overwhelming odds that has won admiration around the globe. May they triumph over the extremely serious ordeals that have afflicted them of late!

Our seven-year-old son, Heath, had an almost fatal illness in 1948. A galloping infection suddenly developed behind his left eye, and in a few hours the eye was horribly swollen and protruding over his cheek. Dr. Paul Howle, our family physician, saw at once that this was a grave emergency. He rushed the boy to the Medical College of Virginia Hospital and called in Dr. E. W. Perkins, an eye specialist. I was in the hospital at the time for a brief stay, as my good friend Dr. Peter N. Pastore had just done a "window operation" on my left antrum which, it turned out, cured my sinus trouble completely. I vacated my private room for Heath and moved in with three other patients.

A number of doctors began working on the youngster. It was realized that the time was short, for unless the infection were checked, it would soon go to the brain, with fatal consequences, permanent brain damage or the loss of the eye. Heath was in terrible pain, and neither a sulfa drug nor penicillin was having any effect on the rampaging infection. As a last resort, when only a few hours remained before it would be too late, another of the new antibiotics, streptomycin, was tried. The result was almost miraculous.

A turn for the better came at once. I left the hospital, since I was over my slight disability, and Doug and I were at home when the telephone rang. It was Heath's nurse, who said Heath wanted to speak to us! His mother talked with him and then I followed. His voice was strong and sounded normal. When I asked how he was, he said, "I'm fine." When he hung up the phone, his mother and I wept in each other's arms. We knew then that our son would get well, thanks to streptomycin. "Ten years ago the little boy probably would have been gone," Dr. Howle told us later.

Some time afterward, Heath assembled an awesome collection on his dresser. It consisted of his tonsils and adenoids in one bottle, his older sister's appendix in another and two bottles of pickled snakes.

When the time came to explain to him the facts of life, it seemed that he knew practically nothing about this subject, even less than I did at his age. When I sought to elucidate where babies come from, his response was, "That's too complicated. I don't think I'd be interested."

During these years I got into a prolonged, yet amicable editorial feud with the Louisville *Courier-Journal* over the origins of the mint julep and the proper method of mixing and consuming that delectable drink. The Louisville paper claimed priority for Kentucky in the invention of the celebrated tipple—something that I did not feel Virginia could take lying down. I pointed editorially to the words of a well-known historian who declared that many Virginians in the colonial era were wont to have "a julep before breakfast." In that era Kentucky was a part of Virginia. This failed to convince the mulish Louisvillians, who seemed to assume that Kentucky was entitled *ipso facto* to all priorities involving Bourbon whiskey, the basic ingredient of every authentic mint julep. We agreed with the *Courier-Journal* that calamitous concoctions called juleps which included such things as rum and grenadine, plus slices of pineapple, lemon and orange, would make the shade of "Marse Henry" Watterson, the paper's famous editor of an earlier era, tear his mustachios with rage. I wrote a letter to *Life* magazine, loudly deploring their julep recipe, published the week before, which not only included several of the foregoing ingredients but called for their consumption through a straw. The magazine published my letter and a retraction, accompanied by a charming sketch of a southern colonel in a rocking chair, gazing balefully at a drink that contained slices of fruit and had two straws protruding from the cup.

The notion that a julep should be drunk through a straw was one of the heterodoxies of which the *Courier-Journal* was guilty. The paper admitted that Colonel Henry Watterson's recipe did not call for straws, but went ahead nonetheless and defended their use. The argument against straws is that one delectable element of drinking a julep resides in the fact that in doing so one's nose comes into contact with the aromatic mint. Also, "the lips should meet the rim of the frosted cup with a caress as gentle as your sweetheart's first kiss," as one commentator has expressed it.

This learned discussion came to the attention of the New York *Herald Tribune*, which devoted editorial space to it. The New York *Times* thereupon asked me to write a brief summation for its Sunday magazine, which I did. The controversy went on for several years, with other newspapers getting into the act. Finally it faded from the public prints. Neither side had convinced the other.

When Vice-President Harry S Truman was catapulted into the presidency by the death of President Franklin D. Roosevelt in the spring of 1945, I joined millions of other Americans in wishing him well. He seemed at first to be handling the job with reasonable effectiveness, considering that Roosevelt had told him absolutely nothing concerning inside happenings in the international field.

Mr. Truman's background as an officeholder in Missouri under the notorious Pendergast machine did cause me to view him with some skepticism, but I was willing to give him the benefit of the doubt, unless and until he showed that he did not deserve it. However, his letter to the music critic who panned his daughter Margaret's singing was a classic of vulgarity and bad taste, and as time went on, I came to feel, in the early years of his term, that he was not up to his job. I inclined strongly to that opinion when he made other blunders, and somebody coined the *bon mot* "To err is Truman." Then J. William Fulbright of Arkansas had the almost unparalleled audacity, for a freshman Democrat in the Senate, to say publicly that Truman had shown such ineptitude in the presidency that he ought to resign.

So when HST got the nomination for another term at the Democratic convention in Philadelphia, I shared the prevailing view that he had no chance of election.

A few months before, I had witnessed the change in Truman's speaking style that he would use to great advantage throughout his campaign for the presidency. It was at the annual convention of the American Society of Newspaper Editors (ASNE) in Washington, and the President had read a dull, wooden speech on price control. When he finished and the perfunctory applause had died down, he turned around and said, "Is that thing turned off?" meaning the radio. It was. Whereupon HST proceeded to deliver a pungent, lively off-the-cuff speech on foreign affairs. His political advisers had put him up to this with a view to seeing how it would work. It worked so well that from then on he usually spoke without a manuscript, especially on his whistle-stop "Give 'em hell, Harry" election swing by train from coast to coast. It was undoubtedly one of the principal factors that led to his election in November, in the face of unanimous predictions from the pollsters and other "experts" that he didn't have a chance.

The *Times-Dispatch* was caught offside in its early editions on election night, as were most of the other papers. I had to stay at the office into the early morning hours rewriting completely the editorial in which I saluted "President-Elect Thomas E. Dewey." Fred Seibel's cartoon, showing Dewey riding the GOP elephant into the White House, had to be yanked.

I met President Truman at several conventions of the American Society of Newspaper Editors. He was an extremely likable man, whether one agreed with him or not. In fact, I told his press secretary, "Joe" Short, that it was "almost impossible to dislike him."

The press had been highly critical of him for years, and the great majority of newspapers had not supported him in his 1948 campaign, with the result that he was understandably without enthusiasm for the Fourth Estate. I was program chairman for the ASNE convention of 1949, and we expected that Mr. Truman would receive us at the White House, as usual. Yet repeated efforts to find out whether he would do so got only evasive replies. I was at my wit's end, trying to decide what to do with several hundred delegates and their spouses, for until an hour before the White House reception was supposed to take place, we had had no definite word. At last the President decided that he had tortured us enough, and I got a message that we were to come over at once. We went, and President Truman was his affable self. But he had evidently enjoyed playing cat and mouse with us.

As a matter of fact, I applauded several of his major policies editorially, including the epoch-making Marshall Plan and the Berlin airlift. These were spectacularly successful, but they did not become so until after his election in 1948. On the other hand, I opposed the so-called Truman Doctrine, whereby $400 million was appropriated to bolster the defense of Greece and Turkey against Communist intrusions. This too turned out well, but only because Tito of Yugoslavia closed his border to Greece, thus depriving the Greek Communists of their sanctuary.

As for Truman's initiation of what he termed the Korean "police action," I thought he was right to intervene, and I was thrilled by the support of the United Nations. As time went on, however, the role of the UN was revealed as a nominal one, with the United States carrying practically the entire burden of the war. It dragged on for years, without our achieving victory, and the whole thing turned out to be a rather dismal chapter, second only to the later debacle in Vietnam.

Harry Truman deserved praise for firing General Douglas Mac-Arthur. We applauded his courageous action editorially on the ground that the general had been flagrantly insubordinate in Korea and had repeatedly disobeyed the President, his commander in chief, and the Joint Chiefs of Staff.

After he was relieved of his command, MacArthur returned to the United States for one of the most triumphal popular welcomes in American history. It was stated to me by an eyewitness that a hard-boiled newspaper photographer at the Washington airport was so overcome by the presence of the great man that he dropped his camera when the general hove into view. Other cameramen were "quaking with emotion."

The annual editors' convention was in progress when MacArthur arrived to address Congress. I was much impressed by his handsome, patrician face under the familiar gold-braided cap, and his masterful manner. Many editors, myself among them, heard his address to Congress over the radio. At his famous climax, "Old soldiers never die, they just fade away," listeners were sniffling and dabbing at their eyes. I was not moved, except by the drama of the occasion.

The general was supposed to make a talk to the editors that afternoon, following his congressional address and a brief appearance before the Daughters of the American Revolution. Through some mistake, he never showed up at our meeting, but went to his room at the Statler for a nap. Our entire convention, together with many nonmembers of our society, waited for a couple of hours in the Statler ballroom for him to appear. I happened to be presiding, and I kept hoping that he would show up. At one point, David Lawrence, the columnist, told me that the general would be there in five minutes. I announced this, but nothing happened. Lawrence came back and said he would be there in half an hour. Again, no general. We finally adjourned at 5:40.

General MacArthur woke up at about six, and was said to have registered annoyance over not having been reminded of his engagement with us. He sent a message that he and Mrs. MacArthur would shake hands with any and all members of ASNE in the Congressional Room at 7 P.M. About 150 showed up. The MacArthurs were most gracious, and seemed to lean over backward to atone for the blunder of the afternoon. I was too tired and hungry by that time to stand in line, so I did not grasp the general's hand.

To return to President Truman: a particularly inexcusable performance was his denial that he had ever tried to persuade Eisenhower to run for President on the Democratic ticket. I sat next to President Eisenhower at the ASNE luncheon of 1958, and we talked of various things. He took occasion to comment on Truman's denial, and stated that when he was writing *Crusade in Europe* he asked Truman if he had any objection to inclusion in the book of the fact that HST had told him in Berlin that he would like to support him for the presidency. Ike declared that Truman not only agreed readily, but added, "Why don't you mention the other time that I said the same thing to you?" Eisenhower replied that he merely wanted to mention the one episode, and that is what he did. "I suppose Truman just persuades himself that things never happened if he doesn't want them to have happened," President Eisenhower added, without bitterness.

In view of the foregoing, and of other similar performances, I have been somewhat astonished to note that in recent years there has been a well-orchestrated effort to depict Harry Truman as a man who never equivocated, who spoke the truth under all circumstances and who did not play politics. The series of interviews with him, published posthumously under the title *Plain Speaking*, has contributed notably to the creation of this myth. In those interviews he discussed every controversy from his point of view, giving only his side, and not infrequently embellishing his contentions with statements which, I am informed, are far from factual. It could be that he erred honestly in presenting an erroneous picture of certain events or circumstances. Suffice it to say that those who accept *Plain Speaking* as an accurate picture of what occurred during Truman's career in the White House will, in my view, be walking on extremely thin ice.

For example, one would never learn from reading this volume that Truman's second term was shot through with corruption, especially in the Bureau of Internal Revenue. Yet the President refused for years to admit that anything was wrong, as one high federal official after another went to the penitentiary. I could never forgive Harry Truman for this. He was not personally involved in any of the crookedness, but he was much too slow in acknowledging that it existed.

Someone has said, quite aptly, that "Harry Truman gagged on the gnats and swallowed the lions." On the big decisions, in other words, he was generally right, whereas he erred badly on some of the lesser ones. I would rank him among the first ten Presidents, despite his crudities and his petty political acts of one sort or another. The "busted haberdasher" acted like one, at times, but he also rose to great heights.

The time had come for me to complete *Dry Messiah*, my biography of Bishop James Cannon, Jr., the devious prohibitionist leader. I had been working on it spasmodically, rewriting it from beginning to end. H. L. Mencken had helped me to get a contract with Alfred A. Knopf for its publication, and I went to Baltimore to see Mencken after I had completed the writing. I sent him in advance the chapters dealing with the bishop's flour hoarding, bucket-shop dealing and adventures with the ladies.

"These chapters are first-rate," HLM told me when I met him at the offices of the Baltimore *Sun*. "I think I know good writing and competent workmanship. I wouldn't change them in any respect." He argued against reducing the length of the book, whereas Alfred Knopf wanted me to shorten it. (Since Mr. Knopf was the publisher, I accepted his advice and eliminated some 16,000 words.)

After Mencken had made such comments as he cared to on my manuscript he began discussing public affairs, expressing himself vigorously and profanely concerning various persons and events. The phrases and words that occurred most frequently were "hound," "bastard," "son of a bitch" and "louse." He was vehement in his excoriation of Franklin D. Roosevelt, especially on the ground that he deemed FDR a hypocrite in his attitude toward prohibition. Although Roosevelt had been politically, but not personally, dry until shortly before the Democratic National Convention of 1932, he shouted to the assembled delegates, "We want beer!" "The goddamned hound!" Mencken exclaimed with evident disgust.

Mencken's complexion was florid, and it became more so as he blasted Roosevelt and others whom he detested. He appeared to have high blood pressure. My suspicion seemed to be confirmed when he suffered a severe stroke a few months later and was never himself again. This man who had read avidly all his life could not now read, and his mental processes were affected. He was a tragic semi-invalid for the rest of his days. Along with his iconoclasm and his prevailingly negative attitude, he set fire to many a stuffed shirt and was, as Bernard Shaw said, "an amusing dog and a valuable critic." He also helped many struggling young writers, as I can testify personally. Mencken has not been forgotten, and is quoted frequently today.

Dry Messiah had an astonishing critical reception when it appeared in 1949. It was widely and favorably reviewed in all parts of the United States, there were prominent and complimentary critiques in the leading New York newspapers, the New York *Daily News* devoted its entire editorial space to it, Walter Winchell applauded it in his syndicated column, it was reviewed in both *Time* and *Newsweek* and my picture adorned almost the entire front cover of the *Saturday Review*. Yet the first printing of five thousand copies was by no means sold out, and the book was remaindered, i.e., many copies were put on sale for a small fraction of the original price. I know of no better illustration of the fact that favorable reviews in the principal media are not enough to sell a book, if there is no real public interest in the subject. Cannon was dead and practically forgotten when *Dry Messiah* appeared, prohibition was but a fetid memory and it seems clear that few people wanted to read about it or him.

Winston Churchill was in the United States for about a week in March and April 1949. A telegram came to me from Bernard M. Baruch, counselor to several Presidents of the United States and long-time friend of Churchill, inviting me to attend a "small stag dinner" in Churchill's honor at Louis Sherry's in New York on the evening of March 30. I lost no time in accepting.

Mr. Baruch and I had corresponded, and I was one of his admirers, but I had never met him. His telegram said the dinner was for "a few friends," but I was not surprised when the number turned out to be sixty.

At the cocktail party which preceded the dinner the guests were introduced individually to Mr. Churchill by the host. When I was presented, Churchill had a scotch and soda in one hand and an hors d'oeuvre in the other. He made a deprecatory gesture, but soon disposed of the hors d'oeuvre and shook hands. Whereas he was reputed to drink more than anybody else, such did not seem to be the case in this particular instance. He appeared to be taking only about as much in the way of alcoholic refreshment as the rest of us.

The dinner was at a large U-shaped table, with Churchill and Baruch seated at the curve of the U, and guests in alphabetical order from the guest of honor's right. Jack Alexander of the *Saturday Evening Post* was next to him, with Joseph Alsop, the columnist, flanking Alexander, and so on down the line. I was some distance away, between Colonel Frank Clarke, an old friend of Churchill, and Elmer Davis, the author and broadcaster. Others on hand included the editors of New York and Washington papers, Edward R. Murrow, the broadcaster, important columnists and numerous men eminent in journalism and radio.

The meal was absolutely superlative, with each guest served a whole lobster, plus filet mignon and unlimited champagne. About halfway through the banquet Alexander was replaced at Churchill's right by someone I didn't know. When the time came for dessert, this man got up and came to where I was sitting. He tapped me on the shoulder and said I was to take his place at Churchill's right. I was completely dumfounded, but I went at once.

Winston Churchill and I chatted about various things. He was seventy-four at the time and extremely alert mentally, but his eyes seemed to be those of an old man. He said he had seen eastern Virginia, but had never been to the Shenandoah Valley, and he wanted to go there. The campaigns of Stonewall Jackson were his principal interest.

I expressed the hope that he would allow his numerous admirers in the United States to create a fund in tribute to him with which young Britons would be sent to study at our universities, a proposal I had made editorially in 1947, and which the English-Speaking Union wished to carry out, if Churchill agreed. But in our conversation he demurred to the proposal, saying he had been in touch with the E-SU that day, and had told them he would have to think it over. "It seems better for a thing of that kind to be done after you're dead," he told me.

At the end of the dinner he made a ten-minute off-the-record talk. I was still sitting next to him. Huge cigars, the size that he preferred, had been passed around, and he puffed on one of these between sentences. It went out a couple of times while he was speaking, and he paused to grab a candle and relight it.

Churchill was saving his principal ammunition for his address the following night at the Massachusetts Institute of Technology. While he was his usual engaging and witty self in his remarks to us, he said nothing momentous. In the question period he was asked to give his opinion of the Yalta Agreements. His reply was that they should be considered in light of the situation existing at the time—which seemed to mean that he didn't think they were too bad.

We rose from the table at about 10:30. The guest of honor departed soon thereafter and took the train for Boston.

As soon as I got back to Richmond I wrote President Francis P. Gaines of Washington & Lee University, in the Shenandoah Valley, that here was a golden opportunity to get Winston Churchill for an address on that campus, with a visit thereafter to the haunts of Stonewall Jackson. He made the effort, but could never perfect arrangements for an address at W & L by Churchill. The latter found it impossible to make such a commitment months in advance.

The campaign in 1949 for governor of Virginia pitted Francis P. Miller, my associate on the Southern and Virginia Policy committees, against State Senator John S. Battle of Charlottesville. Miller was greatly disappointed when the *Times-Dispatch* supported Battle, since he had assumed that he would have our support. U. S. Senator Harry F. Byrd was backing Battle, and to my considerable annoyance Miller insinuated that this was why I was supporting the same man. I had to adapt myself to "the Byrd policy line," as he put it.

The fact is that I preferred Battle. He was a member of the moderate wing of the Byrd organization, an experienced and forward-looking legislator who could, and did, get things done. He had the support of large majorities in both branches of the General Assembly, in which he had served with distinction for twenty years. If Francis Miller had been elected—and he very nearly was —he would almost certainly have had a frustrating four years in the governorship, similar to that of James H. Price a few years before. The machine-dominated General Assembly had cut antimachine Jim Price's throat from ear to ear, and it is altogether likely that the same thing would have happened to Miller. Battle, on the other hand, had a successful administration which was especially constructive in providing large additional financial aid for the public schools.

It may be argued, as Miller did, that it would have been beneficial to the Commonwealth, over the long pull, to have unhorsed the Byrd organization for the second time in a dozen years. Although I recognized that the Byrd organization had its shortcomings, and that Byrd used unfair tactics at times in fighting Miller, it seemed to me that John Battle's qualifications for the job of governor outweighed his opponent's, and that he deserved our backing. This despite my realization of Francis Miller's great ability and his experience in many capacities around the globe.

Miller ran against Byrd for the U. S. Senate in 1952 and lost by a wide margin. Again, we supported Byrd. We felt that he was serving as an invaluable check on wild spending programs in Congress, had great seniority and set an impressive example of integrity in public life. Then, too, I was becoming more conservative.

Senator Joseph McCarthy of Wisconsin swam into my ken in the spring of 1950 when I heard him speak to the American Society of Newspaper Editors. He impressed me as sinister in the extreme.

A couple of months before, he had made his notorious speech in Wheeling, West Virginia, which included wild charges concerning large-scale communism in the State Department. At Wheeling he caused a nation-wide furor by saying, "I have here in my hand a list of 205 persons that were known to the Secretary of State as being members of the Communist Party, and are still working and shaping the policy of the State Department." Soon thereafter the number 205 was magically metamorphosed by McCarthy into 57. The fact was that the rabble-rouser was thrashing about in the hope of finding an issue with which to startle the public and win publicity for himself. He had no hard facts to support either figure, and never showed anybody the "list" that he held "in his hand."

Swarthy, heavy-set McCarthy impressed a good many of the editors favorably when he appeared before ASNE, among them Roy Howard, head of the Scripps-Howard chain. That group of newspapers promptly began whooping it up for the fearless patriot from Wisconsin. He already had the backing of the Hearst papers and the Chicago *Tribune*. It must be conceded that McCarthy's platform manner was forceful, his English fluent and his voice powerful. (He described it as a "hawg-calling" voice.) Furthermore, his poise was complete, he was not thrown off stride by any of the questions fired at him and he took ribbing good-naturedly. He seemed a type who would be a tough opponent on the hustings or the Senate floor.

In McCarthy's favor was the fact that there was, and doubtless always will be, a certain amount of foreign espionage in the State

Department, and McCarthy was shrewd enough to capitalize on this. By means of blunderbuss charges and outright lies, he was able to hoodwink millions of Americans into believing that the department and the government as a whole were riddled with "treason," as he put it.

His address to ASNE dealt with this theme. Waving the "Communist threat" before his audience, he succeeded in convincing many that he was on the trail of genuine spies. Of course he never produced any, but he managed to stir up a nation-wide storm. He was described as "a potential Huey Long," and, like Long he harbored presidential ambitions and seemed destined to go far.

I saw McCarthy a couple of years later in Richmond. He delivered an address which I did not hear, but I was invited to meet him afterward. I remarked routinely that I was sorry Mrs. McCarthy had sprained her ankle and could not come with him to Richmond. This "ankle injury" had been given by him publicly as the reason for her nonattendance. "She didn't sprain her ankle," he laughed, "she just wanted to do some Christmas shopping." When I mentioned that I had heard him speak to ASNE in 1950, he said, with an ominous look, "And I haven't been invited back."

While I viewed McCarthy as a disgrace to American civilization, I also felt that his importance was being magnified out of all proportion by many persons, especially speakers and editorial writers, who seemed obsessed with the subject. Commencement orators, particularly in the Ivy League colleges, appeared unable for years to think of anything to talk about except "McCarthyism." At least that was the impression given by accounts of their orations in the press. Newspaper reporters and headline writers had the same obsession, and the merest reference to McCarthy in a speech was pulled out of context and made to seem the major theme.

One of the things that I held against John F. and Robert F. Kennedy was their close association with McCarthy in the early years of that demagogue's un-American series of assaults on American citizens. Those who are interested will find the facts in Arthur Krock's *Memoirs* (pp. 342–43).

I always thought Jack Kennedy was far more attractive than Bob, but I had only a bare speaking acquaintance with both of them. The last time I saw President Kennedy he was welcoming newspaper editors to one of the ASNE receptions at the White House. In contrast to Lyndon Johnson, who was boorish to editors like myself who had not been supporting him, Kennedy was pleasant and polite to all. I'm sure he kept up just as closely as Johnson with the attitudes of the various newspapers toward his administration, and we had not been backing him at all regularly. But when my wife and I came down the receiving line, he was not only courteous in greeting us but also directed our attention to the fine portrait of Thomas Jefferson that Paul Mellon had given the White House shortly before.

I have never understood the adulation of the Kennedys by millions of Americans and Europeans, even Communists. Jack, to be sure, was an attractive and witty fellow, but he was not in the presidency long enough before his tragic assassination to build a really significant record. His trysts in the White House and in hotels with a woman agent of the Mafia, and his notorious affairs with other women, are brushed off as inconsequential. He went to Berlin and uttered four words of German, *Ich bin ein Berliner*, after practicing assiduously, and the Germans almost swooned in ecstasy. If anybody else had done the same thing, little attention would have been paid.

Despite Chappaquiddick and his string of transparently phony explanations and alibis in connection with that shocking affair, Senator Edward Kennedy regularly leads all polls among possible Democratic presidential nominees. I can only say that I think a large number of the American people need to have their heads examined.

An idea of the hold that the Kennedys have on the admiration and affection of European Communists may be had from an episode described to me by a card-carrying professor at the University of Leningrad with whom I dined a few years ago. He stated that his son, a student in the university, came to him one morning and said that whereas he was supposed to take an important examination that day, it would be completely impossible. "Why?" inquired his father. "Because Robert Kennedy has just been assassinated, and I am so crushed that I can't think of anything else," replied the student. "If I take the examination, I will get zero, for my mind can focus on nothing but Robert Kennedy." "Very well," said his father, "you need not take it."

In June 1950 I accepted an invitation from Juan Trippe, president of Pan-American Airways, to be one of about thirty newspaper publishers and editors, plus a couple of magazine editors, on an inaugural flight to South America. Pan-Am would be launching one-stop service to Rio, via Trinidad, and would also fly us to Montevideo and Buenos Aires. In accepting I stated in my telegram, as pleasantly as I knew how, that I would have to feel free in the future to criticize Pan-American Airways editorially, if the occasion should arise.

Pan-American is so important to South America that such a flight was treated as a great event by the various governments there. We were entertained lavishly at cocktail parties, receptions and elaborate dinners. I have never been plied with so much whiskey, gin, wine and brandy. Our only worry was caused by the outbreak of the Korean War a few days before our take-off from New York on June 29. Since we would be back in the United States on July 6, nearly everybody was able to go. One or two did feel it necessary to cancel at the last minute.

Ben McKelway, the much-admired editor of the Washington *Star*, a member of the party, was disturbed throughout the journey by the outbreak of war in Korea. His sons had gone through World War II a few years before, and he was fearful that they would be called up again.

After a couple of hours' stopover in Trinidad we continued to Rio, whose harbor is easily the most spectacular that I have ever seen. It is not only beautiful but incredible—scores of rocky peaks jut out of the water and along its edge, while others rise to great heights inside the city.

There was a particularly unforgettable view of Rio and its harbor one night from the roof of the Press Club. Lights glowed from thousands of windows in the great new skyscrapers, the Southern Cross hung in the heavens, the moon shone with lambent brilliance over the burnished water, leaving a golden trail, and Sugar Loaf was silhouetted against the velvet Brazilian sky.

A memorable episode at the dinner tendered us by the Rio Chamber of Commerce was the howler committed by Amon Carter, the well-known publisher of the Fort Worth *Star-Telegram*. Rising to speak for the journalistic contingent, he began by apologizing for making his remarks in English, "since I am pretty rusty on my Spanish." The fact that Brazil is a Portuguese-speaking country seemed to get by him completely.

In Buenos Aires we were entertained at luncheon by the Jockey Club, the most famous club in Latin America. The place card next to mine bore the name of Peter Grimm, which I recognized at once as that of the proprietor of Pension Grimm in Budapest, where we had stopped in 1934. Grimm and his whole family had fled when the Hungarian capital was fought over by the Germans and the Russians. The Grimms came to this country and took U.S. citizenship. He obtained a position with Pan-American Airways.

Phil Graham, publisher of the Washington *Post*, invited me to go with him to the offices of *La Nacion*, one of the foremost newspapers below the Rio Grande. With *La Prensa*, Buenos Aires' even more famous paper, *La Nacion*, was being put in a squeeze by Argentine dictator Juan Perón that threatened its extinction.

Señor LaFarrere, editor of *La Nacion*, to whom Graham had a letter of introduction, came out and talked with us in an anteroom. He was obviously alarmed by the increasingly restrictive policies of Perón. LaFarrere spoke no English and we spoke no Spanish. So LaFarrere and I conversed in French, and I translated for Phil. The courageous Argentine editor besought us not to let up in our criticism of Perón; if we did, he said, the cause of press freedom in the Argentine would be lost. He emphasized that we probably were not aware of the weight that American press opinion carried in his country. We assured him that as far as we were concerned, there would be no letup, and that we didn't think any other papers in the United States would soften their attacks. As we left, I said, "À *bas*, Perón!" as emphatically as I knew how, although not in a loud voice, for I feared we were being spied on. I didn't want to send LaFarrere to jail or get myself thrown out of the country.

We returned to our hotel and made ready to attend a press conference with this same President Perón at the Casa Rosada, or Red House, his official residence. *El Presidente* greeted us there in a large ornate room. A virile-looking man, he came in smiling broadly and shook hands all around, bowing stiffly from the waist. U. S. Ambassador Stanton Griffis introduced him and said Perón would be glad to answer questions.

William R. Hearst, Jr., and I were sitting next to one another, and were wondering whether if we offered a query as to press freedom in Argentina it would embarrass Juan Trippe, our host for the flight. Trippe had told the group to go ahead and ask whatever we felt like asking, but we knew he was anxious to promote better business for Pan-American Airways, and we hesitated. Hearst finally took the plunge and queried Perón as to the state of press freedom in his country. The reply was ridiculous. Perón said he believed in nothing so strongly as freedom of the press, that the Argentine system insisted absolutely upon it and, indeed, forbade no criticism of any kind "except criticism of freedom." In other words, "Hail to *la libertad!*" Further questions followed. Perón said *La Prensa* and *La Nacion* had increased their circulations greatly since he took office, and that he was in the same position as President Truman, who won election despite newspaper opposition. He actually had the gall to say, "If there was not an opposition press in Argentina I would create one." The fact is that he was intimidating the opposition press in many ways. Newsprint, on which papers are published, was being strictly rationed, and reserve supplies had been confiscated. *La Prensa* and *La Nacion* had only enough for five days, and were constantly afraid that the supply would be shut off entirely.

I asked Perón if he had ever put anybody in jail for criticizing his regime, and he denied loudly that he had done so. Technically, he probably had a case, since hostile editors were being jailed on specious charges, such as "violation of sanitary regulations." The very next day an editor from the provinces was arrested when he alighted from the train in Buenos Aires. He had been critical of Perón.

While we were talking with the dictator, his equally famous and influential wife, Eva, arrived. She came in street clothes, attractively dressed, a good-looking blonde, demure and not at all loud or flashy. This was a surprise. It turned out to be another act, like the whole press conference. Eva sat next to Juan, who said he would "now take a back seat," but she insisted, with what was supposed to be extreme modesty, that she was merely trying to help her husband and "build a bridge between him and the people of Argentina." Neither of them spoke English, so an interpreter translated all statements by them as well as our questions and their answers. The Peróns discussed their housing program, saying that 250 separate projects were under way, with at least 200 units in each. They described these and other measures as necessary to combat communism.

The whole group of newspapermen felt that this was a synthetic performance from beginning to end; many of the answers to questions were outright lies or half-truths. We knew that whereas Eva pretended to be very much the retiring and devoted wife, she was actually terrifically powerful politically in her own right, and fully aware of the fact. She was making countless public appearances and rousing her followers, called "the shirtless ones," with fiery oratory. "Without fanaticism one cannot accomplish anything," she frequently declared. Peter Grimm said as we broke up that the whole thing reminded him of Hitler's program in the early days of the Nazi dictatorship.

Our plane was christened "The Friendship" by Eva Perón at the airport, and we were invited to attend the christening. Most of us didn't. Children lined the route, dressed in white and waving pennants with "Evita" on them. Next day we were told that we would have the rare opportunity of visiting some of Eva's "favorite charities." We had to be ready at 8 A.M. for the expedition, and I was not that anxious. Those who went said it was a phony performance. In fact, a member of the expedition told me later that he got definite evidence on the point. The party was being taken through a so-called orphanage, and small children were on the premises, waving the usual pennants bearing the word "Evita." These boys and girls were represented as living in the building. My informant said he was determined to find out whether they were or not, so he lagged behind the group, pulling open drawers in the "bedrooms." They were completely empty. The "orphanage" was a Potemkin-like deception, designed to impress visitors with Evita's wide-ranging sympathy for the "shirt-less ones."

Before we flew back to Washington from Buenos Aires there was an elaborate luncheon at the airport. The Minister of Finance presented each of us with a photograph of Juan Perón, personally inscribed by him with the words *"con gran afecto."* I deliberately left mine on the plane when I got off. The indefatigable representatives of Pan-American wrapped it carefully and mailed it to me in Richmond.

General George C. Marshall was guest of honor at the Virginia Military Institute on May 14–15, 1951, when the Marshall Arch was dedicated there. My wife and I were in Lexington for the two days. I had an opportunity to talk with the general and also to attend the wonderfully impressive New Market Day ceremonies, held each year in memory of the VMI cadets who died at the Battle of New Market in the Civil War.

General Marshall had just been undergoing approximately one week of grueling cross-examination at the hands of joint U. S. Senate committees probing into the recall of General MacArthur from Korea. Yet he looked fresh and relaxed. I asked him how he did it, and he replied, "I never take these things home with me." He went on to say that somebody in his office had recently given him ponderous documents to take home with him every night, "but I never looked at any of them."

The general said he had been cross-questioned by twenty-three senators, some of whom were quite hostile. He spoke somewhat jokingly of how difficult it was to answer each of them promptly and courteously and at the same time not get oneself tripped up. Some of the senators, he went on, are past masters at cross-examination, and the first questions may seem entirely harmless and irrelevant, "but you never know what they might lead to." Also, a friendly senator attempted to ask him a helpful question, "and it was the most embarrassing question of all."

General Marshall's quiet, modest demeanor and his uniform courtesy were notable. He seemed to be enjoying himself in an atmosphere where everybody tried to make him feel at ease. He impressed me as a man of immense moral force, strength of character and patriotic dedication.

He was said to be austere, and was regarded by some as humorless. Yet while he did not sparkle or effervesce, he was kindly and gently humorous and graciously polite to all. His mind was machinelike in its precision, as had been demonstrated in his appearances before ASNE in Washington during the Second World War.

Bernard M. Baruch was the speaker at the dedication of the Marshall Arch. At eighty-one years of age he delivered an immensely virile and eloquent tribute to General Marshall. His deep voice boomed out like that of a man half his age. I was reminded of the similarly vibrant tones of elderly Secretary of the Army Henry L. Stimson when he addressed ASNE in 1943.

James S. Easley, prominent Halifax attorney and, like Marshall, a VMI graduate, told me that in 1936 he was on a committee that was looking for a superintendent of the institute. He called General MacArthur to see if he would consider taking the post. MacArthur said that ordinarily he would be glad to, but that he was committed to leave shortly for the Philippines. Easley asked if he had any suggestions for filling the superintendency and the general mentioned "Colonel George C. Marshall, the most brilliant officer in the Army; he'll be chief of staff someday."

Jim Easley had another interesting quotation. He said General Richard J. Marshall, MacArthur's chief of staff, told him that when General George Marshall came to the Pacific theater in World War II, MacArthur went to another island rather than greet him. "MacArthur cannot bear to have anybody around who outranks him," said his chief of staff, who was in many ways MacArthur's admirer.

General Lewis B. ("Chesty") Puller, the most decorated of all U. S. Marines, with five Navy Crosses and countless other medals and citations, was caustic in his comments on General MacArthur's actions and utterances upon the latter's return from Korea. "President Truman should have sent him off to Australia and told him to keep his mouth shut," said he.

The great combat marine, a native of West Point, Virginia, and resident of nearby Saluda, was back from Korea in June 1951 and a guest, with Mrs. Puller, at a cocktail party in Richmond given by Mrs. Victor Williams and a dinner given by Mr. and Mrs. Lewis C. Williams. My wife and I were among the guests at both events.

I was much impressed by General Puller's square-jawed, square-shouldered determination and poise. A modest, quiet man, he was said to dislike the nickname "Chesty," which indeed did not seem especially appropriate. He was not chesty, but his voice was deep and had a tone of authority. His nose seemed to have collided with a truck or a brick wall, for it had obviously been broken, perhaps more than once. Puller's absolute fearlessness was proverbial, and he thought nothing of exposing himself in battle with utter recklessness, leading his men when bullets were whizzing around him and shells were plowing up the ground. He had been wounded numerous times. In the desperate action on Guadalcanal, one of the critical battles in the Pacific, he was hit by a shell fragment or bullet and ordered back to a first-aid station. He refused to go, and fought on. It is easy to understand why he was idolized by his men.

I asked him what had been his closest call among the hundreds that he had had in Latin American jungles (where he was known to his enemies as *El Tigre*), in battling his way from island to island in the Pacific in World War II or in Korea. He said it was in the retreat of his marines through arctic North Korean weather from the Chosin Reservoir, out of the trap set by the Red Chinese. Although vastly outnumbered by the Chinese forces,

Puller's marines fought their way back in November and December through howling blizzards and at temperatures far below zero.

Puller, then a colonel, gave his hard-pressed regiment the following tongue-in-cheek reassurance: "The enemy is in front of us, behind us, to the left of us and to the right of us. They can't escape us *this* time!"

Ten years later, General Puller was in my office at the *Times-Dispatch* for well over an hour talking about his experiences as a marine. He would remain seated for perhaps two or three minutes, and then would get up and begin walking around the room. He was on his feet almost throughout our conversation. "You must think I'm a nervous man," he remarked, "but I formed the habit during all my military life of staying on my feet, even when in my own office, to keep my legs hard for marching." No wonder he could outmarch men half his age. He was indeed a combat marine and front-line fighter with few peers in our history—the idol of the noncoms and privates in the corps.

When Dwight D. Eisenhower and Adlai Stevenson ran for the presidency in 1952, the *Times-Dispatch* supported Eisenhower enthusiastically. It was the first time in more than a century that we had backed a Republican for President. The editorial in which we took our stand won for me a second Sigma Delta Chi national editorial award. "The time has come," I wrote in that editorial, "for a change from top to bottom in Washington, with a new party in control and, if possible, Republican majorities in both branches of Congress. . . . Governor Stevenson . . . is the strongest man they [the Democrats] could have chosen, a man of integrity, genuine intellectual stature and extraordinary oratorical attainments. Yet despite this, Mr. Stevenson is in a large sense the prisoner of his party, and it would be impossible for him, as President, to do much more than provide window-dressing for what would be, basically, the same crowd that has disgraced the republic, brought to the Federal government unparalleled waste, bureaucracy, centralization and corruption, and caused millions to cry out for a change. . . ."

This last was pretty strong stuff, and I must say that today it strikes me as an exaggeration. On the other hand, it serves to buttress my contention that Harry Truman's years in the White House were not exactly one long uninterrupted idyll, reflecting single-minded devotion to the public weal. Since Adlai Stevenson, the Democratic candidate, referred openly during the campaign to the "mess in Washington" under Truman, things in the nation's capital must have sunk to a rather low ebb.

Stevenson spoke in Richmond during the 1952 canvass to a large and appreciative audience that jammed the Mosque. He had been given a Cleveland–Stevenson badge from the presidential campaign of 1892—when Adlai Stevenson, his grandfather, was the vice-presidential nominee. The badge was on his lapel as he addressed the gathering, and he made the characteristically witty comment, "If Grandfather looked like that, I feel better about myself."

Dwight Eisenhower was incapable of such drollery, but I have never met a public man who exuded so great a measure of sincerity and warmth. I am impressed, furthermore, with the thought that his two terms in the White House were marked by peace and prosperity, a low rate of inflation and city streets that were generally safe for citizens, both before and after dark. The contrast between the foregoing and what came after is a glaring one. Ike wasn't the most brilliant man in American history—although by no means the inept fumbler that many journalists sought to depict—but he came close to being the most beloved, both in this country and around the world. He probably could have been elected to a third term if the Constitution had not forbidden it.

10

"Massive Resistance" and Cambridge Adventure

AN EARTH-SHAKING CONTROVERSY over the manner in which restaurants in the Deep South force grits on customers, whether they want them or not, erupted in the press during the early 1950s. The uproar grew out of an editorial I wrote on my return from Atlanta, where a waitress had brought breakfast with grits on the plate, although I had not ordered the dish. I didn't want the grits, and didn't see why people should be plied, willy-nilly, with this dubious culinary item in restaurants. So I wrote, in part:

"Grits aren't too bad, taken once in a while and in small doses. . . . But the manner in which they are tossed at you every single morning of the year in the Cotton States, and in a special built-in compartment on your plate . . . is nothing less than an outrage."

That did it. The "dead cats," mainly tongue-in-cheek, began raining down from various corners of the former Confederacy. It was strongly hinted that being from Virginia, I was geographically almost a Yankee anyway, and that having shown my true colors with my heretical views concerning grits, it could be seen that I was probably a first cousin of General William Tecumseh Sherman. One Virginia editor espoused the cause of the Deep South and remarked, Brutus-like, that "Dabney speaks only for himself." However, I was comforted by a volley from the Shreveport, Louisiana, *Times*, which contrasted the zestful aromatic dishes of New Orleans with grits and other "greasy decoctions" reminiscent of "the discarded contents of a crankcase." A New Yorker who lacked enthusiasm for the Far South's favorite cereal wrote, "I don't like the damned stuff either."

Newsweek got into the act with an amusing report on the fracas. It quoted blasts, all of them more or less good-humored, from various parts of the South. And the Southern Newspaper Publishers Association *Bulletin* reprinted a follow-up editorial of ours, in which I had written:

"Some of our critics missed the point of our pronouncement. The Savannah *Morning News*, for example, seemed to think that the *Times-Dispatch* was objecting to the fondness of denizens of the Far South for grits. Pointing out that Africans love grasshoppers and ants, that Mexicans gobble up food 'that would scorch the inside of a blast furnace,' and that Chinese dote on whole frogs, the *News* asked what sense there is in anybody's poking a derisive digit at these people because he doesn't fancy their menus.

"If the *News* wants to compare grits to grasshoppers, ants and frogs," our editorial went on, "that's all right with us, but it was never our purpose to quibble over the culinary preferences of Africans or Georgians. If either or both cherish a yen for grasshoppers or even ants, far be it from us to protest. All we can say is this: When we go into a restaurant in Savannah, we don't want a dish of ants poked at us, in a special built-in compartment on our plate. That's what happens in the case of grits."

All this furor erupted long before President Jimmy Carter entered the White House. By the time he leaves the presidential office, grits, for all we know, may have been adopted as the national dish.

While the foregoing controversy over the South's dietary preferences was going forward, the region was sitting figuratively on the edge of its chair, awaiting the United States Supreme Court's epoch-making decision on segregation in the public schools.

In an article I wrote for the *Saturday Evening Post* in late 1952,

I predicted that the court probably would not outlaw segregation. Two liberal journalist friends of mine who had pipe lines of a sort to the court told me they were confident that the tribunal was not ready to rule out "separate but equal" for the white and black races. Their prediction was probably correct at the time they made it, but the appointment of Earl Warren as Chief Justice in 1953 and his influence over the court evidently caused a reversal on the part of several justices. This resulted in the court's unanimous finding in 1954 that segregation in the schools was unconstitutional.

I stated in the magazine article referred to that "throughout much of the South it is conceded that segregation cannot be maintained forever," and I was one of those who held this view. But I was convinced that complete and immediate abolition of all segregation in the schools would be premature, unwise and productive of much trouble, even violence. The violence was not long in coming. It has been widespread and may continue indefinitely.

Despite my apprehensions as to the results that might be expected to flow from the Supreme Court's ruling, I was hopeful that the decision could be implemented with a minimum of antagonism and a maximum of good will. Virginia's Governor Thomas B. Stanley reacted calmly at first, and said "views of both races will be invited." But Senator Harry F. Byrd was not interested in such an approach, and it seems safe to say that his preferences were conveyed to the governor. The latter accordingly "invited the views of blacks" by calling in several of their leaders and requesting them to ignore the court's decision and acquiesce in a continuation of segregation! They, of course, refused.

Governor Stanley then appointed an all-white commission to study the situation and devise "legal means" whereby the court's ruling could be circumvented and integration prevented. This body had a preponderance of members from the ultraconservative regions of the state that are heavily populated with blacks. Nevertheless, it came up with recommendations that local option be allowed, i.e., every political subdivision would be free to decide whether to integrate or not. There were other provisions, but this was the overridingly important one, and I was hopeful that the relatively enlightened approach would be approved by Senator Byrd. But this was not to be. The senator let it be known that he had no intention of accepting any such solution, and came up with the doctrine of "massive resistance." Local option was shelved, and legislation was rammed through the General Assembly requiring the closing of any public school that integrated its pupils.

The *Times-Dispatch* attacked Governor Stanley and the Byrd organization's legislative leaders in several editorials for going back on their assurances that there would be local option. We termed it "a breach of faith" and a "cynical piece of business." They went ahead anyway. This was the last time that I was able to assail the machine leadership editorially for its manhandling of the school situation.

Publisher D. Tennant Bryan and Vice-President and General Manager John D. Wise were sincerely in favor of "massive resistance," as was Alan S. Donnahoe, who succeeded Wise after his retirement. They apparently believed that it could be made to stick, at least temporarily. I believed just the opposite, and was convinced, furthermore, that the policy was potentially disastrous. The closing of schools seemed definitely counterproductive to me and, carried to its ultimate conclusion, appeared likely to turn Virginia into an educational slum.

I recognized that the owner of a newspaper has the final say as to policy, and that on critical issues he determines the paper's editorial stand. This is the view of so liberal a publisher as Barry Bingham of the Louisville *Courier-Journal*, for example. Bingham said that those who wrote editorials for the *Courier-Journal* had to conform, in general, to his philosophy. Similarly, Robert Lasch, chief editorial writer for the equally liberal St. Louis *Post-Dispatch*, said, before his retirement, "No matter how many [editorial] writers there may be, the publisher on critical issues casts a majority vote. There is no getting away from that. He does bear the final responsibility for the newspaper's policy."

The Richmond *News Leader*, under the same management as the *Times-Dispatch*, and edited by James J. Kilpatrick, carried the ball, as it were, for massive resistance. The *Times-Dispatch*, under my editorship, did not attack massive resistance, although I would have liked to have done so. Neither did we espouse it actively, except perhaps in two or three editorials written by Alan Donnahoe. Most of the time we simply acquiesced in it silently, without making overt gestures in its behalf.

Kilpatrick came up with a militant crusade in support of the long-forgotten doctrine of "interposition." Under it, the state was supposed to be able to "interpose" its sovereign authority between itself and the federal government. David J. Mays, a leading Richmond legal scholar and historian, told me that interposition was "neither legally nor historically sound," and Lewis F. Powell, Jr., who later went on the bench of the U. S. Supreme Court, said the same thing. None of this deterred the supporters of this theory, which had not been seriously invoked since the Civil War. The Richmond newspapers published a pamphlet containing Kilpatrick's well-written editorials, and sent it to key officials throughout the South. The result was that several southern states passed "resolutions of interposition." Virginia Attorney General J. Lindsay Almond ruled after the passage of the Virginia resolution that it was not a legislative enactment having the force and effect of law, and that it could not be asserted as a defense in court. The *Times-Dispatch* did not join the *News Leader* in its flaming crusade on behalf of this long-outmoded theory. I could not conscientiously do that, and Messrs. Bryan and Donnahoe, to their credit, did not insist that I do so. I merely expressed approval of the resolution as a gesture, and with the express proviso that it must not call for any form of nullification.

The excitement generated by the controversy over school integration and the proper approach to it bordered on hysteria at times. One finds it hard to realize today how intense was the ferment and how bitter were the feelings on the part of some of those concerned. One thinks back to the controversy over slavery on the eve of the Civil War, and the Supreme Court's Dred Scott decision, which declared, among other things, that the Negro "had no rights that the white man was bound to respect." We have come a long way since that judicial finding was handed down. Horace Greeley, the famous editor of the New York *Trib-*

une, said it carried no more weight than if it had emanated from some Washington barroom. Other Republican editors called it "infamous" and "a judicial lie." A century later, there were similar editorial expressions concerning the Supreme Court's holding that segregation in the schools was unconstitutional.

At the height of the crisis over massive resistance, *Life* magazine asked me to write an article explaining Virginia's position and the attitude of most Virginians on the race issue. This appeared in the issue of September 22, 1958, and was reprinted immediately in *U.S. News & World Report* and *Reader's Digest.* Nothing I ever wrote received such wide publicity. The volume of mail was likewise unprecedented, and most of it was favorable.

Entitled "Virginia's 'Peaceable, Honorable Stand,'" the article did not express my own views in all respects, since I had been asked to give those of the state's political leadership and the majority of its citizens.

I pointed out that New York City had experienced "a wave of rapes, knifings and beatings in the schools" the previous winter "without a parallel in American history." One school principal committed suicide and seven schools had to be patrolled inside and out by police. Virginians were alarmed by these happenings.

I called attention to the fact that in Chicago, special police details had been patrolling the Trumbull Park housing project night and day for five years, after the first blacks moved in. At one point, 1,200 police were called out to protect a single black family from the fury of white mobs.

New York City had passed a housing law intended to prevent discrimination, and I found it amusing that the New York *Times,* which was attacking the South regularly for its "bigotry," was arguing aginst the measure on exactly the ground that Virginia and the South were opposing the Supreme Court's integration order. "We do not think the people of New York have been adequately prepared for the passage of this bill," said the *Times.* "Progress must be a matter of education and spiritual growth rather than a consequence of legislation." My comment on this was that "the white South could not have put more perfectly the case against the 1954 Supreme Court decision."

Objectors to the decision felt, furthermore, that the court had sought improperly in its ruling on the schools to legislate by judicial decree, and had misconstrued the Fourteenth Amendment.

Of course, my article did not influence the course of events, but it helped to get across to the country the reasons why Virginia was resisting the court's decision by all legal means.

Messrs. Bryan and Donnahoe were pleased with the article. They were more conservative than I on the race question and various other questions, despite the fact that I myself had grown more conservative. I wrote and published editorials on a variety of subjects with which they did not agree, but I refrained at times from expressing my editorial opinion on a few other matters, in deference to their wishes. The whole situation made me unhappy over a period of years, and I seriously considered resigning and going to some other paper. But in trying to decide where to apply, I could think of no other daily with whose major policies I was in complete agreement. Even if I had found such a publication, the very real question had to be faced whether there would be an opening for me on its editorial staff.

I was greatly relieved, in the fall of 1958, when Messrs. Bryan and Donnahoe came to the conclusion that massive resistance could not be upheld much longer, and that it was time to announce a shift in the position of the *Times-Dispatch* and *News Leader* on the issue. They felt that it would be the courteous thing to inform Harry Byrd personally of our impending change of front, since we had been friendly with him over the years, and they did not wish to take him by surprise on anything as close to his heart as this. So we drove up to Berryville in Tennant Bryan's car to apprise the senator of our intentions. In the party were Bryan, Donnahoe, Jack Kilpatrick, editor of the *News Leader*, columnist K. V. Hoffman of the *Times-Dispatch* and myself.

Senator Byrd was courteous but far from happy over our plan. He was by no means ready to throw in the towel, and he didn't think "the people of Virginia" were either. However, he put up only a modest amount of argument against our proposed course—seeing, no doubt, that argument would be futile. Harry Byrd, Jr., then a member of the Virginia Senate, was in on the conversation, but said little. Soon after our return to Richmond both papers began veering away from massive resistance. We were confident that the courts would outlaw it in the near future, which they did. The papers bowed to the courts, and backed Governor J. Lindsay Almond's plan for "freedom of choice" or local option. Had the *Times-Dispatch* not done so, I would have felt impelled to resign as editor. I had managed to go along with the policy of resistance, so long as it was legal, and so long as I was not involved in writing such editorials as had graced the columns of the *News Leader*. But a policy of defiance and obstruction, after the courts had spoken, would have been too much. Fortunately, the paper's management decided on a policy that I could accept.

It was the end of a difficult period for me. I was somewhat comforted by the thought that no editor can be altogether free to write whatever he wishes on every conceivable subject, unless he owns the paper. Even when he is the owner, he must occasionally, for one reason or another, not write *exactly* what he thinks. So a few compromises are inevitable here, as in all other aspects of life.

The *pace* at which change in fundamental social mores should be brought about seems to me to be of crucial importance. It is altogether obvious that the integration that took place peaceably in Virginia in 1959 would not have been remotely possible five years before, immediately following the Supreme Court's ruling against segregation in the public schools. Whatever one may think of the legal maneuvers resorted to by state and local authorities to avoid integration in the years 1954–59—and I greatly preferred token integration under local option to the course that was followed— those maneuvers at least bought time. And when all legal devices were exhausted, and the state and federal courts held the school closings to be unlawful, Virginia and its localities obeyed the judicial edicts without question. My views on the rate at which fundamental social change should take place are more fully set forth in "The Pace Is Important," *Virginia Quarterly Review*, Spring 1965.

In that article I also discussed the question whether full-scale integration would lead, in the long run, to wholesale intermarriage. I quoted from Allan Nevins, the eminent American historian, and Arnold Toynbee, the equally eminent British historian, in support of the view that it would. Nevins said that intermarriage "will proceed with increasing rapidity," and that he "could cite a dozen analogies from history to prove that such a process is inexorable, irresistible." Toynbee declared that "what is an accomplished fact in Mexico today will come to pass tomorrow in the Old South of the United States." Commenting on the foregoing in the magazine, I wrote:

"The principal question here is whether the two races concerned ought to strive to maintain their racial identities and cultural heritages, or whether they should determine to merge. If the latter course is decided upon and carried through to fruition, we shall have a very different United States of America in a century or two. Some will consider it superior to what we have today, some will consider it inferior. All will doubtless agree that the face of the nation will have been transformed."

It seemed to me then, and it still does, that Americans, whether white or black, should take pride in the achievements of their race, and should wish to retain that race's individuality. There is nothing here of Nazi-like bigotry or racial chauvinism, but rather a feeling of satisfaction in the accomplishments of one's ethnic group. Unfortunately, the trend in this country is steadily in the direction of ultimate racial amalgamation.

President Eisenhower stated in private conversation at an American Society of Newspaper Editors luncheon in 1958 that he tried to prevent the Supreme Court from handing down its decision outlawing segregation in the public schools. "I went as far as I could," he said to me, "but was unsuccessful." He did not mention Chief Justice Warren, but was reliably reported soon thereafter to have told others that he greatly regretted having named Warren to the court. It was "the biggest damfool mistake I ever made," William Manchester quotes him in his book *The Glory and the Dream* as having remarked.

Eisenhower told me on this same occasion that he felt obligated to send troops to Little Rock, Arkansas, when determined efforts were made there to prevent blacks from entering all-white

Central High School, "My brother who is a lawyer, says I had no business doing that, but I felt that I had to back up the courts," he said. The paratroopers with fixed bayonets whom he ordered into Little Rock were deeply resented throughout much of the South. Ike was convinced that segregation would and should come to an end eventually, but said "if you try to go too far too fast, you are making a mistake."

Dwight Eisenhower was a man of basically fine instincts, whose essential humanity was manifest. An episode at another ASNE convention which he addressed was evidence of this. The dinner was nearing its close, when there was a thunderous crash behind the President's chair. It sounded as if the roof had fallen in. Everybody jumped, including the Secret Service men. A waiter had dropped an entire tray of dishes a few feet from Mr. Eisenhower and stood disconsolate amid the debris, looking as if the end of the world had come. Ike reached into his pocket, took out a couple of bills and pressed them into the waiter's hand. Nobody saw him do it except Mrs. Earl Warren, who was seated next to him. She told later of the President's generous gesture.

I confess that I was amazed when a speaker before the annual convention of the American Historical Association in 1961 revealed some astonishing facts concerning the means by which the Supreme Court had been induced to outlaw segregation in the schools. The speaker was Professor Alfred H. Kelly of Wayne State University.

He told his fellow historians that in 1953 he was requested by Thurgood Marshall, then general counsel of the Legal Defense and Educational Fund of the National Association for the Advancement of Colored People, to produce an interpretation of historical events during the years immediately following the Civil War that would make it possible for Marshall and his associates to "get by those boys down there," meaning the Supreme Court. Kelly spoke, in part, as follows (*U.S. News & World Report*, February 5, 1962):

"The problem we faced was not the historian's discovery of truth, the whole truth and nothing but the truth; the problem, instead, was the formulation of an adequate gloss on the fateful events of 1866 sufficient to convince the court that we had something of a historical case. . . .

"It is not that we were engaged in formulating lies; there was nothing as crude and naïve as that. But we were using facts, emphasizing facts, bearing down on facts, sliding off of facts, quietly ignoring facts, and above all, interpreting facts. . . .

"I am convinced now that this interpretation, which we hammered out with anything but historical truth as our objective, nonetheless contains an essential measure of historical truth.

"History is art, as well as fact; everyone in this room knows that the facts do not automatically arrange themselves without the historian's creative leap, which occurs in our craft, as well as in the exact sciences. . . ."

Kelly said his partner in hammering out "anything but historical truth" in order to "get by" the Supreme Court was Yale law professor John Frank. The court evidently accepted the version they presented. Kelly added that Thurgood Marshall "wrote some of us letters of thanks, assuring us that enlisting the history profession on his side had been the NAACP's smartest move in the complicated case."

It was indeed a smart move, but just what the "history profession" thought of these bland admissions has not been revealed. I left no doubt, in editorial comment, as to my own opinion. It struck me as the sort of thing that a historian would be loath to admit, much less to proclaim.

In the spring of 1954 I received an invitation to lecture at the third annual Fulbright Conference on American Studies at Cambridge University, England. The program was to last for five weeks, and it seemed virtually impossible for me to get away for that length of time. I had about decided to decline when John C. Parker, a much-admired Franklin, Virginia, attorney who had married my sister Alice a couple of decades before, and to whom I have always been deeply devoted, said, "V, why don't you do it?" That made me give it further thought, and I began looking into the question whether it would be acceptable for me to attend for three weeks instead of five. It was, and I went. It counted as my vacation for that year.

I was greatly disappointed when I found at the last minute that Douglas and our daughter Lucy could not accompany me. Mr. Chelf, my father-in-law, then ninety-three, was ill and my wife, conscientious as usual, did not feel that she could leave him. Mrs. Chelf was also an invalid. So I went alone, which made the whole experience far less enjoyable.

The Fulbright conferences, which lasted only a couple of years after 1954, were financed with appropriations from the U. S. Congress and Rockefeller funds. They were attended by professors and graduate students in British universities who were teaching or studying subjects having to do with the United States. Fifty-six of these men and women, most of them professors, were enrolled for the first session in 1954, which lasted for three weeks. The second session of two weeks was for British schoolteachers. I had to leave just as it was beginning.

American professors had done all the lecturing at the two previous Fulbright conferences, held at Cambridge in 1952 and Oxford in 1953, but in 1954 it was decided to include one newspaper editor, one author, one foundation director and one city manager among the eleven lecturers. The author was Eudora Welty, and among the professor-lecturers were John Hope Franklin, the Negro historian, then on the Howard University faculty; Arthur M. Mizener of Cornell, author of *The Far Side of Paradise*; and C. Lowell Harriss, professor of economics at Columbia University and David Truman, professor of political science at the same institution.

Each of us gave three lectures, and we also held an indeterminate number of seminars. We were available, furthermore, for conferences with those enrolled in the course. It was a strenuous routine, especially for someone like myself, who had not been lecturing previously on the subjects that he was presenting, whereas most of the others had been giving courses in their specialties for years.

Peterhouse College, oldest and smallest of the Cambridge col-

240

leges, was the scene of our conference. The weather was abnormally chilly for summer, and I was grateful that I was lodged in Fen Court, a new building which had electric heating. Peterhouse was reputed to serve the best meals of any of the colleges, and they were altogether adequate, although the British cuisine was never notable for imagination or variety. Voltaire's observation that "the English have twenty religions and only one sauce" is still not without merit.

The business of lecturing to a group of university professors, especially British professors, was, for me, rather staggering, accustomed as I was to being on the receiving end of lectures from professors. I was sufficiently reckless to choose what were perhaps the three most controversial subjects then extant: "The Negro Question in America," "Joseph McCarthy" and "Anglo-American Relations."

My three lectures went over better than I had expected. No doubt the fact that the subjects were of peculiar interest at the time helped to give them acceptability. The British even laughed at my jokes, and pounded with the flats of their hands on the desks in front of them—the British method of showing approval of something said by a speaker.

I was able to slip off a couple of times to London, and to get into the press gallery at the House of Commons. Prime Minister Churchill was there, looking extremely old and white-haired, but he answered questions from the Laborites well and showed considerable verve in his replies.

The astounding thing to me was the amount of noise in the House and the rowdy behavior of the supposedly staid and dignified British. There is nothing remotely like it in our American Congress. Roars, hoots, jeers and cheers are almost routine in the Commons, and the decibel content of a debate there must be several times as high as that for a comparable discussion in our Senate or House of Representatives. Members of the august British Parliament not only greet statements which they like with cries of "Hear! Hear!" cheers and the waving of papers, but when the Opposition disagrees, as it usually does, insults are hurled right and left and rude imprecations fill the air. "Sit down!" "Shut up!" "Belt up!" "Get stuffed!" "Resign!" "Nonsense!" "Scandalous!" "He's drunk!" "Knock off!" "Disgraceful!" and "Put a sock in it!" are among the choice epithets tossed about with utter abandon. This has been going on for a long time. When Benjamin Disraeli rose to make his maiden speech in the Commons back in the 1830s, every sentence was received with "yells, hoots, cat-calls and hyena laughter," Hesketh Pearson states in *The Lives of the Wits*.

Another custom of ancient vintage, which I witnessed with astonishment, is for the leader of the Opposition to sit practically on the back of his neck with his feet almost in the face of the Prime Minister when the latter is speaking—a gesture of disdain if not contempt. Former Prime Minister Clement Attlee sat with his feet almost under Prime Minister Churchill's nose, as I looked down from the gallery. Since Churchill had once called Attlee "a sheep in sheep's clothing," the contempt was obviously mutual. The House of Commons was bombed out in World War II, but it had been handsomely restored when I was there, with perfect acoustics, attractive carved woodwork and bluish-green leather seats.

I also took occasion to look in on the beautiful red and gold chamber of the House of Lords. The members were sedate gray-haired gentlemen, apparently in their seventies or older, and the unseemly din which often pervades the Commons was nowhere to be seen or heard. The Lords have lost nearly all their power, and there is even talk of abolishing that chamber entirely. It may never happen, but given the leveling process that is going forward in Britain and so much of the rest of the world, it is a possibility.

Bomb damage was obvious in certain parts of London, even in 1954, especially in the City, the oldest section. There were gaps where rebuilding had not begun; purple and yellow flowers grew in the ruins.

When in London I enjoyed the hospitality of John M. ("Jack") Patterson, author and former star reporter on the *Times-Dispatch*, and his wife Hope. I spent a couple of nights with them, and took them to *Pal Joey,* which was having a run in London. The Pattersons were renting the house of Alistair Buchan, Washington correspondent of the London *Observer.*

Other pleasant interludes occurred when Arthur Mizener and I played tennis with the Cambridge boys, one of whom was a member of the championship doubles team of Peterhouse. Since it was summer, his partner and many other students were not in school, and we played against various doubles combinations. There were six matches, and Arthur and I won them all. The Cantabrigians were considerably bewildered and discouraged by this. Actually, they were not very good, which explains our success.

Professor W. R. Brock of the Cambridge faculty was in charge of the Fulbright Conference, assisted by Michael Newton, an able and attractive recent graduate. Brock entertained us in his home, as did Newton. The latter's family lived at nearby Bishop's Stortford, and several of us drove over for dinner one evening. It was the beginning of a lasting friendship between the Dabneys and "Mike's" parents, Ursula and Karl Newton. Karl was a banking executive, since retired. The Newtons and Brocks have since been our guests in Richmond. Michael Newton is now an American citizen and the full-time head of the American Council for the Arts in New York City.

I wrote one brief article for the *Times-Dispatch* from Cambridge. In it I expressed the view that reports of a widening breach between Britain and the United States were greatly exaggerated. When I got back to Richmond, I expanded on this theme in the New York *Herald Tribune Magazine.* My analysis also appeared in the Manchester, England, *Guardian.*

Near the end of my sojourn at Cambridge I was greatly saddened to receive the news that my wife's uncle, our beloved Dr. Paul Howle, had died. It was not really surprising, for he was ill with cancer when I told him good-bye a few weeks before. Our family's debt to him is beyond reckoning, for he not only presided over the births of our three children, but was on call at any hour of the day or night for everything from a sore throat to removal of an appendix. He never sent us a bill, and all we could do was give him a few presents—completely inadequate tokens of our gratitude and appreciation. Uncle Paul was one of the vanishing breed of old-fashioned family doctors who treated every sort of problem —medical, surgical or personal—and was withal a trusted friend and confidant.

Nancy, Lady Astor, the first woman to serve in the British House of Commons, was an occasional visitor to Richmond during these years. She was a distant relative of mine, and usually rang me up when she came to town. I would drop in to see her and discuss matters of mutual interest.

She was an able, attractive and vivacious lady, who could be extremely charming when such was her desire. She could also be quite the opposite when the mood was upon her.

On one occasion, when I made a talk at the Hotel Jefferson to a women's group, she was in the audience. After the meeting we were standing in the auditorium, chatting about nothing in particular. A woman of seemingly rather humble background began hovering around us, evidently anxious to speak to Lady Astor. Finally, she moved up to us and said, quite respectfully, "Lady Astor, I've always wanted so much to meet you." "Don't you see that I am talking to Mr. Dabney?" replied the British M.P. in her haughtiest manner. The distraught woman walked away, and I was greatly embarrassed.

A meeting of a couple of hours with John L. Lewis, the beetle-browed czar of the United Mine Workers, was an interesting experience of the year 1954. He was the guest of Cyrus Eaton, board chairman of the Chesapeake & Ohio Railway, on a special train from Williamsburg to Charlottesville (with Monticello as the objective), operated under the auspices of the Institute of Early American History and Culture. Eaton's son-in-law, Lyman Butterfield, was the director of the institute; hence the special train. I had been a member of the institute's board of directors, and my wife and I were invited to go along.

Eaton asked us to join him and Lewis for luncheon in his private car, along with the Kenneth Chorleys and the Butterfields. Ken Chorley was president of Colonial Williamsburg.

Lewis entertained the group with stories and anecdotes. The grim boss of the miners, who had shut down the productive machinery of much of the nation several times with strikes, even in wartime, was an altogether different person when taking part in a social gathering such as this. An excellent mimic, he was especially amusing when imitating Calvin Coolidge's nasal intonations. Lewis chuckled a lot while telling his stories. On a more serious note, he predicted correctly that President Eisenhower would run for election in 1956. He also spoke of Herbert Hoover, saying that Hoover wrote his own speeches and that he had "broadened very much in recent years."

Quite a while thereafter I saw Lewis in the lobby of a Washington hotel, so I thought I would say hello. I walked up to him and said, "How are you, Mr. Lewis? I had the pleasure of meeting you some time ago when you and Mr. Cyrus Eaton were traveling on his private car from Williamsburg to Charlottesville." "I believe so, sir," said John L., as he turned on his heel and walked away. I don't know what caused his complete change of attitude. I had always denounced him editorially for his arrogant behavior in calling strikes, contrary to the public interest. On the train he had shown no resentment, but he may not have connected me with the editorial attacks. When I saw him again in Washington, he apparently had awakened to the fact that I had been assailing him editorially for years. I can think of no other explanation for his 180-degree turn.

With his beetle brows, John L. Lewis was a cartoonist's dream. Any such prominent facial characteristic—Richard Nixon's ski nose, or Jimmy Carter's teeth—is seized upon by the pen and ink artists and exploited, to the delight and amusement of the public.

Fred O. Seibel, the *Times-Dispatch*'s nationally known cartoonist, who contributed to the paper's editorial page for forty-two years, loved to draw the Lewis eyebrows. Seibel was a genuine artist, and masterful in his ability to caricature public figures. Franklin D. Roosevelt with his cigarette holder at a jaunty angle, Hitler with his forelock and toothbrush mustache and numerous others were grist for Fred's mill. For many years his work was reprinted as frequently in the press of this country as that of any cartoonist. The old *Literary Digest* had him in practically every issue, as did the Sunday New York *Times*. Fred Seibel was the most modest of men, and he refused over and over to submit his drawings for the Pulitzer Prize. This doubtless accounts for the fact that he never got it.

Thousands of his originals are in the Alderman Library at the University of Virginia—all, in fact, except the hundreds that he donated to persons who asked for them. U. S. Senator Harry F. Byrd requested and got more than two hundred dealing with himself, but these are now in the Alderman Library. Fred hated parties or crowds, and was almost petrified when he attended the ceremony at the University of Virginia celebrating the acquisition of his huge cartoon collection. He told me that he was much surprised and pleased to find that the library officials and professors who came were normal human beings who made him feel at ease.

Born in upstate New York, Seibel was on the Albany *Knickerbocker-Press* in 1926 when he answered a *Times-Dispatch* advertisement for a cartoonist and came to Richmond. He found the city to his liking, and turned into a red-hot Southerner and Confederate sympathizer. Many Northerners who move south to live seem to become more "southern" than the natives, and Fred was no exception. Almost as soon as he got to town he entered into the spirit of the place, and expressed the Dixie point of view, both personally and in his cartoons.

He took particular pains to put a dash of humor into practically everything he drew. Not for him the meat-ax assault of a Herblock or the bludgeoning attack of a Fitzpatrick. Seibel used the rapier when he wished to be critical of a public figure, but he wielded it with a light twist that made even the victim laugh.

Although an artist and a person of taste in most of his judgments, Fred made a remark to me on one occasion that has always mystified me, it seemed so unlike him. He had been on a vacation in Canada, and I asked him if he had enjoyed the trip.

"I liked part of it," said Fred, "but I didn't enjoy Quebec. People were walking around there in funny clothes; they looked like

Europeans or foreigners. I left and went to Toronto. That's a real town."

"Moses Crow," the little bird that appeared regularly in one corner of Seibel's cartoons, was an important part of the design and an integral part of the message. Such a bird or animal was often a cartoonist's cachet, so to speak, and Fred called Moses a "dingbat." Moses Crow was a favorite with Seibel's public, and if Fred forgot to put him in, he heard from Moses' admirers immediately. Moses entered into the spirit of every cartoon in which he appeared. He would register joy, terror or profound gloom, depending on the mood of that particular drawing. Fred had had a real crow for a pet in New York State, and he carried a snapshot of the bird in his wallet for many years after he came to Richmond. Originally named "Jimmy Crow" by Seibel, he realized the inappropriateness of the appellation and rechristened the bird "Moses." Many saw a striking facial and bodily resemblance between Moses Crow and Fred Seibel. Both had long noses and wore glasses, and both were small and skinny.

Seibel was a loner. He had no close friends, and was ill at ease in any gathering. After his wife died, my wife and I invited him for Thanksgiving dinner. We probably knew him as well as anyone, but he seemed so tense and unhappy that we never invited him back. I took him on a couple of day-long fishing trips, but he didn't really relax.

The excellence of Seibel's cartoons was due to his own genius, and I made little or no contribution. If I wanted him to do something to accompany an editorial, I would tell him well in advance, and he always co-operated fully. But the decision as to how the idea would be expressed in pictorial terms was invariably his. He always brought the daily cartoon to me after he had completed it, but never showed it to me before he had put the finishing touches on it and had brushed any dust or other debris from it with a wild turkey feather—an invariable ritual. Sometimes the lettering was imperfect or a word was misspelled, and I made the correction. Other than that, I made no contribution. When Fred came to my office with the completed drawing, we usually chatted for ten minutes or so about the state of the world. He seemed more relaxed then than at any other time.

During the century's middle years I made the acquaintance of Carl Sandburg and Robert Frost. Both were great poets and memorable personalities.

My wife and I were guests at a small dinner for Sandburg at the Hotel Jefferson, following his appearance that afternoon at a Children's Book Week observance. He had spoken and plunked his guitar for an hour and a half, without so much as mentioning children's books, but his audience was fascinated.

He didn't bring his guitar to the dinner that evening, but put on a great show, reading unpublished poems on such unconventional subjects as "A Fly, A Flea and A Flip-Flop" and "Two Maggots." When he wasn't reading poems he was talking, nonstop.

His conversation ranged from the race question to presidential politics. He was a decided liberal in both areas, of course, for he had been reared in the Socialist tradition of Eugene V. Debs. Sandburg revealed that he had been asked by Henry Wallace to run with him for Vice-President on the Progressive ticket in 1948, but he was not interested.

At this point in the conversation, he astonished everyone by making derogatory remarks concerning Wallace's frequent use of the phrase "the common man." For some strange reason the author of *The People, Yes,* and other works glorifying the average citizen, was greatly annoyed by the term "the common man," and he grimaced every time he said it. Sandburg stated specifically that he had not used it in *The People, Yes.*

He was also caustic in his references to Senator Harry F. Byrd, which wasn't surprising, given Sandburg's liberal views. He declared that Byrd's statements on economic and political topics "remind me of a lobster in a window which moves its flippers or claws aimlessly in this direction or that."

Admiral Richard E. Byrd, brother of the senator, also came in for criticism. It seemed that Sandburg and Byrd had been on the same platform in New York in 1941, and in that critical period just before the United States entered World War II, Byrd exhorted his hearers in such mild terms as "We should do our utmost" and "We should strive earnestly." Sandburg felt that Byrd should have spoken with much more vehemence and passion, and said, "He should have shouted 'For Christ's sake, the world is on fire!'"

Sandburg, then seventy-two, had arrived at the Jefferson Hotel from the home of Dr. Douglas S. Freeman with a woolen scarf wrapped tightly around his throat. He said he had slept in a draft coming to Richmond on the train from his home near Flat Rock, North Carolina, and had both a sore throat and a "crick" in his neck.

After dinner we listened to the poet laureate of Chicago and biographer of Abraham Lincoln read his poems and chat. He was sitting next to a fifth of 100-proof Old Fitzgerald. Ever and anon he would partake, putting a bit of the Bourbon into a glass with a piece of ice. It served wonderfully to keep his flow of conversation going. Toward the end of the evening, he proclaimed that his throat was cured and also his neck.

Sandburg was supposed to depart for Dr. Freeman's home at 9 P.M., but he was still going strong at 11 P.M. He finally decided to tell us good-bye at 11:30. We could only surmise what the Freemans had been thinking during all those hours.

Carl Sandburg resembled his contemporary Robert Frost in various ways, although their verse contrasted sharply. Both had strong, rough-hewn faces that almost seemed to have been carved out of native rock. Both were witty and amusing in conversation and on the platform.

I first met Frost at the Richmond home of the late Dr. and Mrs. William Branch Porter, where the New England poet addressed the Virginia Writers' Club. He read from his works and commented on them with frequent flashes of off-the-cuff humor.

A couple of years later Frost was a speaker at the Miller & Rhoads Book and Author Dinner, and was easily the hit of the occasion. His remarks were filled with humor, feeling and pathos.

Frost was approximately seventy-five at the time, but the years had not diminished the sharpness of his mind or the acuteness of his perceptions. He didn't read his poems, he recited them, and usually without hesitating.

At one point he did temporarily forget his own lines. The audience was beginning to squirm, as he stood there on the platform groping for the words. Suddenly he relieved the tension by saying, "You're more embarrassed than I am," and there was a great laugh. Immediately thereafter he went on with the recital.

He gave the delightful poem *Departmental*, saying, "It's about an ant I met in Key West."

Frost attached prime importance to his poem *The Gift Outright*, which he had read before the Phi Beta Kappa Society of the College of William & Mary in 1941. He urged his audience to ponder the words carefully. The poem opens as follows:

> *The land was ours before we were the land's*
> *She was our land more than a hundred years*
> *Before we were her people. She was ours*
> *In Massachusetts, in Virginia . . .*

Robert Frost and Carl Sandburg are gone, but both left imperishable legacies to the American people. Frost seemed to embody the simplicity and conservatism of rural New England, about which he wrote with such feeling and grace. Sandburg spoke for the more proletarian Middle West; for Galesburg, Illinois, where he was born, and for Chicago, *City of the Big Shoulders*. Each man was unique in his own sphere, and each was a great personality around whom many stories are woven, many anecdotes told.

I was shocked in December 1956 to be informed by my longtime friend Branch Spalding, headmaster of Christchurch School for boys, Christchurch, Virginia, that he was apparently about to be forced out of that position. Our son Heath had been a student at the school for several years, and I admired greatly Spalding's remarkable achievement in taking over in 1949 a second-rate, money-losing institution, which was not accredited by the State Department of Education, and turning it in a few years into a first-rate, fully accredited, profitable enterprise. I couldn't believe that the Episcopal diocese of Virginia, under whose auspices

Christchurch was operated, would allow the man who had done these admirable things to be forced out. Yet it soon developed that the chairman of the school's local board, for reasons best known to himself, was determined to oust Spalding, and that he probably would succeed unless something was done.

I joined with four other patrons of the school, whose sons were enrolled there, in an effort to prevent what we regarded as an outrage. The others were William McL. Ferguson, Newport News attorney and president of the Christchurch Patrons Association; Edgar R. Lafferty, Jr., Richmond businessman; Dr. James Asa Shield, Richmond psychiatrist; and the late Webster S. Rhoads, Jr., department-store head.

Incredibly, the local board of the school was demanding that Spalding leave his position on ten days' notice, effective January 1, 1957. Yet no remotely convincing reasons for this demand were brought forward. We five patrons sought to have him retained as headmaster, if at all possible, and if not, to obtain for him reasonable severance terms.

We attended various hearings, at not one of which was a single charge made that reflected in any way on Branch Spalding's integrity, or proved in the slightest degree that he was unqualified to continue as headmaster. Despite the rumors that had been circulated against his character and capacity, the general board of the diocese ended by asking him to remain as head of Christchurch. This, in the words of William Ferguson, president of the Patrons Association, "was a truly rare vote of confidence in a man who has been so viciously attacked." But Spalding, quite naturally, was unwilling to remain, since he would have had to serve under the very same local board that had caused all the trouble.

So he was deposed, despite his accomplishments, despite the backing that he had from the vast majority of students, faculty and patrons of the school. One bit of evidence of the place that he held in the boys' admiration and affection was their presentation of his portrait to the school after his departure.

It was officially stated from diocesan school headquarters in Richmond that "there have been *no* charges or suggestions involving the moral character of Branch Spalding," and that "the Local

Board and the Executive Committee have often expressed their deep gratitude to Branch Spalding for his magnificent work in the development of the Christchurch School." The sole criticism mentioned by diocesan headquarters was that Spalding had "certain weaknesses in general administration and in his dealings with board and faculty members." No one is perfect, and if he had had no weaknesses at all, he would not have been human. But these "weaknesses," whatever they were—and we five patrons could never find that they existed—were as dust in the balances when placed beside his tremendous accomplishments and his services to the diocese.

The Richmond *News Leader* carried an editorial on January 9, 1957, which said, in part.

"Under Mr. Spalding's superlative and enthusiastic leadership, this small school has come back from near bankruptcy in 1949 to a high place among Virginia's crack private institutions. As scholar, teacher and counsellor of young men, Mr. Spalding has done an outstanding job. It is a pity that in a choice between dismissal of the local board and dismissal of the headmaster, it is Mr. Spalding who goes and the board which remains."

We five patrons did succeed in getting for Spalding much better severance pay and allowances for moving expenses than he would otherwise have received. And at the last, although the special committee appointed by the diocese to study the whole controversy did not question the sincerity or motives of the local board, it declared that the board had "lost the confidence of a great number of patrons of the school," and that it should be "reconstituted."

Yet that same board, with Branch Spalding's bitter enemy at its head, had been allowed to have its way. Just what sense any of this made for the cause of justice or that of education is something that I shall never understand.

11

Journalistic Responsibilities and Trip to Russia

QUEEN ELIZABETH II of Great Britain, a direct descendant of Colonel Augustine Warner (1611–74) of Warner Hall, Gloucester County, Virginia, was in the Old Dominion in 1957, when the 350th anniversary of the Jamestown settlement was being celebrated. She was the guest of Colonial Williamsburg, and my wife and I were presented to her briefly in the Palace Garden there. Our principal impression was that she is far better looking than her photographs, especially because of her beautiful "peaches and cream" English complexion and her lovely blue eyes. Her manner is quite gracious, and her handshake firm. We did not meet Prince Philip, her husband.

Queen Elizabeth's mother, the wife of King George VI, was the daughter of Claude Bowes-Lyon, fourteenth Earl of Strathmore, who came down in a direct line from Augustine Warner of Warner Hall, and through John Smith of Purton, Gloucester County, Virginia; the Reverend Robert Porteus of Bedford County, England, and the Reverend Robert Hodgson, Dean of Carlisle. The Warner family has still another distinction: Mildred Warner of Warner Hall was the grandmother of George Washington.

The year 1957 was also the year when the American Society of Newspaper Editors met in San Francisco instead of Washington. Douglas and I had never been to the Pacific Coast, and this was a rare opportunity to do so. We took our fifteen-year-old son Heath with us.

We had our introduction to buffalo meat in a Chicago restaurant, en route to the West, and boarded the Burlington Vistadome. Such railroad trains are no longer operating, sad to say. Our passage through the Rocky Mountains just beyond Denver was somewhat anticlimactic, since the Rockies do not rise as far above the surrounding high plateau as one might suppose. Denver is a mile above sea level, so that the nearby mountain range, unlike the High Sierras farther to the west, or the Canadian Rockies, seems relatively low. California's Feather River Canyon, through which we passed on the following day, was indescribably beautiful.

At the ASNE convention, I was elected president, as successor to my friend Jenkin Lloyd Jones of the Tulsa *Tribune*. In order to discharge the duties of the office, I had to resign from various boards and positions, including the chairmanship of the Southern Educating Reporting Service of Nashville, Tennessee, financed by the Ford Foundation. This agency was set up to furnish authoritative reports of interracial happenings in the seventeen southern and border states following the Supreme Court's decision outlawing segregation in the public schools. We signed up topflight correspondents in each state to give objective reports on events. The published results are valuable to students, researchers and other scholars.

San Francisco was delightful, of course; the views of the Bay were charming, the cable cars were unlike anything else in the United States and young Heath was fascinated by looking down at Alcatraz prison from the heights above. ASNE was entertained by the local newspapers at the Tao Lee Yon Chinese restaurant. There were ten courses, among them barbecued squab, sauté lobster, broiled boneless duck, fish ball stuffed, shrimp fried rice, chicken filet, roast pork mince, and chunk pork tenderloin. We were hardly able to walk after this gastronomic orgy.

With a rented car we drove eastward to Lake Tahoe, nestled like a shimmering sheet of jade amid the surrounding mountains. After two nights there, we were off to Tioga Pass, the eastern entrance to Yosemite Park. Tioga Pass has since been made safer and less alarming to travelers, but in 1957 the drive along those narrow, curving roads through the rugged Sierra Nevada, often past sheer drops of thousands of feet, and no railing, was terrifying. My wife was at the wheel, which was fortunate, since she is a much better driver than I, but both of us had nightmares after we arrived at the Ahwahnee Hotel in Yosemite Park.

During our brief stay there we reveled in the beauty and majesty of the Yosemite, and then drove to exquisite Monterey and Carmel on the California coast, high above the sea, with waves breaking on the cliffs below.

The Southern Pacific took us to Seattle, where we were able to see our friends John Ambler and Dave Jarvis. Then on to Victoria by steamer, and thence to Vancouver. Our next stop, Lake Louise, was the high point of our Canadian journey, although Banff was also spectacular. The view from Chateau Lake Louise of the lake's emerald waters, against the backdrop of snow-covered, jagged Mount Lefroy and the Victoria Glacier, is one of the unforgettable sights on the globe.

It deserves to rank with the stunning view of the Jungfrau from Interlaken, the Grand Canyon of the Colorado, the harbor of Rio de Janeiro, Yosemite Falls and El Capitan, the Blue Ridge Parkway in the Virginia and North Carolina mountains, Feather River Canyon, Mont Blanc and the surrounding snow-covered peaks, viewed from the air, the Koenigsee near Berchtesgaden seen from the Malerwinkel and Italy's Amalfi Drive.

Our journey by rail took us from Banff to St. Paul, Minnesota, and thence for many miles along the picturesque upper Mississippi River and ultimately to Chicago. We entrained there for Richmond.

We had enjoyed a magnificent opportunity to view the glorious panorama that is America—its rolling prairies and craggy coastline, its lush green valleys and mountains white with snow, its pulsating expressways and winding lanes, its monuments and shrines, its quiet graves with the dust of heroes.

My duties as president of ASNE occupied much of my spare time, following our return to Richmond, but I did not travel over

the United States addressing groups of editors and other such audiences. I accepted the position with the understanding that I
would not be able to do this, since my staff at the *Times-Dispatch*
was so small that my responsibilities there required my almost
constant attention. The great majority of my predecessors had
traveled widely and spoken to many state associations of editors.
One, in fact, told me that he had covered about 100,000 miles. A
few others had done only a limited amount of traveling and
speaking, and I probably did less than any.

Preparation for the Washington convention in April 1958 was a
major responsibility. The International Press Institute (IPI),
which included editors from all over the globe, would be meeting
simultaneously with ASNE, and some of our sessions were to be
held jointly. We were anxious to have President Eisenhower address a joint luncheon. I went to Washington to extend the invitation, accompanied by several other editors.

The President had just been pronounced "completely recovered" from his slight stroke of a few months before. He was jovial and relaxed. I informed him that we were hoping that he
would address ASNE and IPI on some phase of foreign affairs.
The idea seemed to appeal to him, although he did say, "At my
age I've got to conserve my strength."

President Eisenhower expressed himself as anxious to promote
better relations and greater understanding between the peoples of
the U.S.A. and the U.S.S.R., and said he was considering urging
that ten thousand Russian students be admitted to American colleges and universities. However, he had serious doubts as to the
plan's feasibility, and burst out, "Damn it! I don't know how we'd
pay for those ten thousand Russian students."

Pursuing the subject of foreign affairs, I remarked that Aneurin
Bevan, the British Laborite leader, seemed to have improved
somewhat in his attitude toward us. "Oh, hell, no!" Ike exclaimed
with a gesture of disgust. When I mentioned that I understood a
summit conference with the Russians was about to be urged by
their ambassador to the United States, Eisenhower replied, "I
wish somebody would tell me what those fellows are up to!"

About a week after the interview I was notified that the President would address the luncheon. When he did so, there was an attendance of more than one thousand, and I pointed out in my opening remarks that it was "the first time in history" that so large a meeting of European, Asian and American journalists had been held. In his speech Mr. Eisenhower did not confine himself to foreign affairs, but touched at length on the military strength of this country. Widespread publicity was given to his statement that there would be in America "no single chief of staff, no Prussian staff, no czar, no 40-billion-dollar blank check, no swallowing up of the traditional services, no undermining of the constitutional powers of Congress."

The President and I chatted at some length during the meal. He looked well and showed no sign of his stroke, either in his appearance or his fluency of speech. The gist of our conversation with respect to the Supreme Court's segregation decision, and Harry Truman's denial that he had asked him to run for the presidency, was touched upon in the previous chapter.

Lyndon B. Johnson, then majority leader in the U. S. Senate, was the speaker at the ASNE dinner on the final night of the convention. During our conversation at table before the speech, I expressed the hope that he would be a candidate for President in 1960.

"I won't do it under any conditions," said he. "In the first place, I've had a severe heart attack, and I don't think anybody who has had such an attack should run for President. In the second place, I couldn't get the nomination, because no Southerner can get it under existing conditions. The northern and western liberals in the Democratic party hate us; they simply hate us, there is no other word for it. They will never allow a Southerner to be nominated.

"I won't go to the convention, and I won't let the Texas delegation nominate me. I probably won't go so far as to make a 'General Sherman statement' [refusing to run, if nominated], but I'm going to do just about everything else to make certain that my name is not brought forward."

Needless to say, Lyndon Johnson changed his mind completely well before the Democratic National Convention of 1960, and made a determined effort to get the nomination there. He was thwarted by Senator John F. Kennedy, of course, and went on the ticket with Kennedy as the nominee for Vice-President. Everyone has a right to change his mind, but I have seldom seen such a complete switch within a period of a little more than one year.

Johnson also reversed his position on various major issues. He had been a rather typical Southerner in his stand on most questions until he began running for the presidency, whereupon he charged off in the opposite direction on half a dozen issues. He was running for re-election to the Senate in 1960 at the same time that he was a candidate for Vice-President, and the two platforms on which he ran were diametrically opposed to one another on seven different important questions then before the public.

When Johnson succeeded to the presidency, following John F. Kennedy's assassination, he continued to espouse the very causes that he had fought against a few years before. It was the major reason why the *Times-Dispatch* endorsed Senator Barry Goldwater for President in 1964. We did not trust Johnson.

Walter Lippmann once wrote that he regarded Lyndon Johnson as the most unpleasant man who had ever occupied the presidency. Whereas I had had good relations with Johnson until he became President, the *Times-Dispatch* then began criticizing him, and he became rude. Members of ASNE were received at the White House more than once during his incumbency, and he and Mrs. Johnson stood in line, shaking hands with us as we came in. LBJ was effusive in greeting those who had been supporting him, but all I got was a grunt. Mrs. Johnson, by contrast, was always extremely polite.

We had hoped to get Winston Churchill for the ASNE program in 1958, and I had been in touch with Bernard M. Baruch, who agreed to help. We were hopeful that Churchill would appear at our gathering and deliver a final message to the American people. "Come on out for the last round, champ!" Baruch told him over the transatlantic telephone to the French Riviera. Sir Winston said he would do it, but then he got pneumonia and the whole thing had to be called off.

Baruch rang me up from his plantation near Kingstree, South

Carolina, to give me the bad news. In the course of our conversation he imparted the surprising information that Churchill was always quite nervous before making an important speech.

"Winston always insists that I go with him whenever he makes a significant address, if I am anywhere near," said his long-time friend. "You always make me feel better if you are in the audience, Bernie," Baruch quoted Churchill as telling him. "I know you're deaf as a post and can't hear a damned word I say, but I feel more secure when you're sitting out there."

Baruch described an appearance of Churchill before the National Press Club in Washington several years previously.

"He made me go with him, as usual," said the famous financier and adviser to half a dozen Presidents. "He was pacing up and down before the speech. 'I'm nervous, Bernie,' said Churchill, 'Give me another scotch.' I gave him one, and he felt better. 'I'm still nervous, Bernie,' he went on. 'Oh, pull yourself together,' I replied. 'But suppose they ask me about McCarthy,' Churchill said, referring to the senator from Wisconsin who was then a storm center. 'What shall I say?' 'Oh, tell them that you don't stick your nose into other people's domestic affairs,' I replied. 'Splendid!' said he. 'I'll do it.' He did, and the speech went off without a hitch."

It was distressing that we were not able to have Sir Winston as the principal attraction for the ASNE convention of 1958. His last words to the American people would doubtless have been somewhat different from those elicited by U.S. newspapermen on an earlier visit. When asked for a message to the citizens of America, the great Englishman rumbled, "Gentlemen, your newspapers are too thick and your toilet paper is too thin."

My ten-day coast-to-coast visit to military and naval installations, on invitation of the Department of Defense, was a memorable experience of the year 1960. It was the first Joint Civilian Orientation Conference that included so large a group of installations. There were seventy civilians, representing steel, aluminum, machine tools, utilities, banking, education, law, advertising and journalism.

The group was divided into four "flights," and each elected its "flight leader." I was in the "gold flight," which was identified with the infantry, and was chosen its leader. Few responsibilities were involved, except that I and the other three flight leaders each made a talk at one of four dinners tendered us. The dinner at which I spoke was at Fort Benning, Georgia, near the end of the trip, and happened to be much the largest, with some three hundred persons present, including much army brass.

The tour began at San Diego, and I had an infuriating experience with my luggage, a not unprecedented occurrence in air travel. I had flown from Richmond to Los Angeles, where I changed planes, but when I arrived at the San Diego airport my bags were nowhere to be seen. The premises were ransacked, but the suitcases could not be found. Since the opening dinner that evening was black tie, I was considerably embarrassed. I called the Los Angeles airport and was assured that they would look for my luggage. They called back later and said it had been located, with my name on it, but the next Los Angeles plane would not arrive in San Diego until 10 P.M., much too late. I hung up the phone, and was fuming over this bad luck when there was a knock at my hotel-room door. It was a bellboy with my bags! I have never had the remotest idea how this could have happened.

We spent the next night on board the aircraft carrier *Kearsarge*, off San Diego, and since it was the date of the first fateful presidential campaign debate between John F. Kennedy and Richard M. Nixon, we watched it on board the vessel. While I did not think Nixon had a clear advantage, I thought he held his own, and was not aware at the time that Kennedy had demonstrated superiority in the minds of most onlookers.

We witnessed antisubmarine warfare from the deck of the *Kearsarge* fifty miles at sea, and later visited the great San Diego naval base and the U. S. Marines' Camp Pendleton. Vandenberg Air Force Base on the California coast was reached by air, after which we flew northward to the two adjacent naval bases at Point Arguello and Point Mugu. After viewing Atlas, Titan and Samos missiles on their launching pads, and the elaborate installations surrounding them, we enplaned for the North American Air Defense Command (NORAD) at Colorado Springs. There the U.S. and Canadian governments conduct a far-flung operation involving radar and other devices to warn this continent of any oncoming missile or bombing attack.

Thence to headquarters of the Strategic Air Command (SAC) near Omaha, Nebraska, where we saw an amazing complex of world-wide controls covering bombing planes armed with thermonuclear bombs, and intercontinental missiles with nuclear warheads, all poised and ready to strike, if word should come from NORAD or elsewhere that an attack against the United States was on the way. Release of our nuclear bombs had to be cleared by the Joint Chiefs of Staff in Washington and the President, an arrangement that presumably is still in effect.

Each of us was given an opportunity to ride in an Air Force T-33 training jet, with one of the Air Force pilots. At that time, riding in a jet was a novel experience, and I confess that I was a bit nervous as I climbed into the cockpit. I didn't think the pilot was going to do any stunts, but wasn't sure. He didn't, and it was merely a pleasant cruise over Omaha and the surrounding area. We civilians were photographed in our flying gear and given a large photo to show to posterity, or to luncheon clubs when we addressed them on our return to home base. This was one of the unnecessary expenses that have been criticized in connection with these Joint Civilian Orientation Conferences. However, it may be arguable that the relatively low cost of the trip was justified, if it helped to give civilians a better concept of the armed services—as it certainly did.

Fort Benning, Georgia, the immensely impressive infantry training school, was our final stop before flying to Washington for a conference with Defense Secretary Thomas S. Gates and the Joint Chiefs. We found at Benning that today's infantry is a far cry from the footsloggers of World War I, for it is highly mobile and mechanized. We also learned of the intensive training given the Rangers, which included three weeks in Florida swamps and three more in the Georgia mountains, with most operations at night. The men go into the wilderness with practically no rations, and are ordered to subsist on what they can find. Tasty delicacies include rattlesnakes, alligators, acorns and wood fungus.

At Benning we were given an amazing demonstration of sharp-shooting by infantrymen, and each member of our civilian group took a shot, while lying prone, with an M-14 rifle at a simulated man four hundred yards away. I astounded everybody, including myself, by hitting the fellow in the heart. Since I have never been in the service or used firearms at all, this was pure beginner's luck.

At the dinner, where I spoke for our flight, I took as my tongue-in-cheek theme "The South Will Rise Again." Major General Hugh P. Harris, commanding officer at Benning and our host, was a Southerner, as were several other important officers and men we had encountered that day in stellar roles. I arranged with the conductor of the band to play a few bars of "Dixie," pianissimo, immediately after I told a joke involving a Confederate veteran. It was in the days before the great Confederate song, so admired by Abraham Lincoln, had been put on the *index expurgatorious*, and the novelty was well received.

On my return to Richmond I wrote a series of five articles for the *Times-Dispatch*, published later in the *Congressional Record*, in which I stated that every man in the group of seventy had been "vastly encouraged" by what he had seen. "The personnel of our armed forces from the top ranks to the lowest is extremely good," I wrote. "The expertness with which officers and men handle modern weapons of great complexity is reassuring. Every American would profit from such a trip."

Many of us were skeptical when we began the journey, but everyone ended it with the feeling that our defenses, as of 1960, were in good hands. Among the seventy were experts in the manufacture of military hardware who were not likely to be fooled.

Everybody paid his expenses to San Diego and from Washington back to his home base. The government took over for the intervening ten days, but it was emphasized that we witnessed normal training operations, and that these would have had to be staged in any event. True, it obviously cost money to carry us around in planes, to provide us with food and, for example, to give each of us a set of slides showing scenes from our trip. On balance, however, the outlay impressed me as justified, in view of the interest in and understanding of our defense establishment created by the program. Such trips were operated at six-month intervals. Ours, the thirty-first and the most extensive up to that time, enabled our group to visit elements of our defense establishment that half of all U.S. generals and admirals had never seen. At least, so we were told.

One of the real dividends of the trip was flying the length of the two-hundred-mile-long, mile-deep Grand Canyon of the Colorado. It was a rare privilege to view this wonder of the world from the air, to look down upon that enormous gorge, formed by erosion over millions of years, with the beautifully shifting colors in the cliffs at its sides, and the ribbon of water flowing far below.

A trip to Russia was the great event of 1961. Publisher Tennant Bryan felt that it was important for both of his editors to see the country. My wife and I took off in April for London, where we stopped briefly en route. A highlight there was a visit to St. George's Church, Gravesend, where Pocahontas was buried in 1617. No one knows whether she lies "in the chancel," as the vestry book says, or in the churchyard, but certainly her dust reposes in one of these two places. There is a statue of her in the yard, a copy of the one at Jamestown, while a tablet in the church relates that "she was the friend of the earliest struggling English colonists whom she nobly rescued, protected and helped." Two memorial windows in her honor were placed in St. George's by the Colonial Dames. We thought of Pocahontas' brief life, and her early death en route back to her native Virginia, as we walked among the graves.

On our flight to Moscow by way of Copenhagen, we arrived in the Soviet capital, via Scandinavian Airlines, a few days before the great annual celebration on May 1. Our rooms at the National Hotel overlooked Red Square and the tomb of Lenin, a most fortunate circumstance. Since no tourist was told in advance which hotel he would be assigned to, we might well have been dumped down in some Muscovite fleabag miles from the center of things.

The National Hotel was said at that time to be the best in

Moscow, with the best food. Actually, the food was mediocre, and the accommodations were about on a level with an 1890 hotel in the United States. Furnishings were redolent of that era—tasseled lamp shades, overstuffed furniture, bathtub with claw feet, etc. In accord with apparently unvarying custom, there were no stoppers in the wash basin or the tub, but having been forewarned, we had brought our own. It was a luxurious suite of its type, with bedroom, bath and huge living room, which harbored a grand piano and a large desk. The ceilings were about fourteen feet high. Our reservation had been made in advance through Intourist, and we booked the top level of accommodations. Anything less than first class in the U.S.S.R. would have been altogether too risky.

We were slightly tense on the flight and on our arrival at the hotel, and wondered if our quarters were bugged. The *Time-Life* Bureau was immediately underneath, and our assumption was that it undoubtedly was being subjected to electronic surveillance. We were careful not to say anything in our suite that might get us into trouble. The hotel staff was extraordinarily accommodating and anxious to please, but one never knew what the Soviet espionage apparatus might be up to.

Our Intourist guide, who accompanied us daily on our visits to the sights of Moscow, was the pretty and attractive wife of a doctor. She was one of the few good-looking women we saw during our ten days in the Soviet Union. The great majority looked weather-beaten and wore shawls over their heads. The lovely young women in various ballets were notable exceptions.

While many of the Russians with whom we came into contact in our hotels in Moscow and Leningrad were pleasant and cheerful, one seldom saw smiles or heard laughter on the streets. The Slavs were living up to their reputation for being melancholy and sad.

And Moscow was hardly less than an architectural eyesore, except for Red Square, the Kremlin, the Bolshoi Theater and a few churches. The hundreds, if not thousands, of new, boxlike, shoddily constructed apartment houses were of uniform drabness, and all exactly alike. The enormous Moscow University building, costing $750 million, and containing 1,900 laboratories, 15,000 rooms and 113 elevators, the tallest structure in Europe except the Eiffel Tower, was a perfect example of what was derisively known as "Stalin Gothic." Someone called it "a cross between the Woolworth Building and a wedding cake." The university has intramural athletics, but no intercollegiate sports. Hence there are no alumni howling for winning teams at old Moscow U.

Swan Lake at the Bolshoi was one of the memorable events in our lives. To begin with, the theater is easily the most beautiful in the world, as far as our knowledge goes. We haven't seen them all, of course, but those in Washington, New York, London, Paris, Berlin, Rome, Munich and Vienna are not in the same class, handsome as those are. Magnificent in its proportions, the Bolshoi—built by the czars, of course—is being perfectly preserved and maintained by the Communists. A huge crystal chandelier hangs in the center of the auditorium, and smaller bronze chandeliers, with electric candles, adorn the tiers of seats, which extend to the ceiling far above. No fewer than six of these tiers rise from the main floor. The whole interior, described by one observer as "prerevolutionary gilt-and-red-velvet splendor," is done in exquisite taste, except for a fairly obscure portrait of Lenin at the top of the curtain and the faint hammer and sickle design worked into it and some other areas of the decor.

The dancing in this presentation of *Swan Lake* was superlative, by far the finest ballet we have seen anywhere. Maya Pliseteskaya, the renowned prima ballerina, was in a class by herself, and the supporting cast was brilliant. The sets were dazzling and the orchestra complemented the dancers perfectly.

When the ballet ended, Pliseteskaya received a stupendous ovation. Bouquets of flowers began pouring down on the stage from several directions, including seats far up in the fifth or sixth tier. The ballerina stood amid this mountain of floral tributes, bowing repeatedly. She finally left the stage, and the flowers were collected. Whereupon thunderous applause began again, she came out and once more the bouquets came raining down, until another large floral mound rose in front of her. The supposedly unemotional Slavs were extremely emotional on this occasion, as wave after wave of hand clapping, punctured by cheers and bravos, swept through the hall.

May Day was another unforgettable experience. Moscow was spectacularly decorated with huge red banners and enormous electric signs. On Gorky Street, near our hotel, there was a gigantic electric display, comparable to those in Times Square. It exhibited the chief Soviet heroes, among them Major Gagarin, the first man in space, who was shown hurtling through the sky, as well as a machine moving across a field of wheat, and a handsome, illuminated map of the Soviet Union, plus various Communist slogans. Billboards around the city were adorned with the heads of Lenin Peace Prize winners, among whom I noted one American, Cyrus Eaton, the railroad magnate.

Literally millions of people were walking about the streets the night before the ceremonies, gawking at the signs and the blazing red banners that flared on every hand. Many wore heavy overcoats, although the weather on the last day of April was not particularly cold. Russians, for some reason, seem to like to wrap themselves up during mild weather—all except the boys, who seem reluctant to wear warm clothing, even in bitter temperatures. In this respect, they are carbon copies of boys in the United States.

On the morning of May 1, loudspeakers began blaring at seven o'clock from a cluster of horns on the nearby Moscow Hotel. Under our window in the square, military units were parked in serried array—motorized equipment, small rockets and foot soldiers.

We had been told not to open our windows on May Day, but I was so eager to photograph the military hardware that was only about fifty yards from us that I, most foolishly, disobeyed instructions. I opened the window, took a couple of snapshots and closed it as quickly as possible. In no time there was a rap on our door, and we were told in no uncertain terms not to do that again. About an hour later there was another rap, and the rapper demanded to know if our window was open. We showed that it was not. After two more hours, when the parade was still passing, there was another knock, and we were informed, this time in

French, "Someone has telephoned from the square that your window is open again." This was genuinely alarming, and we demonstrated once more that all our windows were shut. By this time I was wondering if I had lost my mind in trying to get those snapshots, when the most casual observer in the square could see at once what I was doing. And now my single transgression was being represented by someone as having been repeated. And when somebody telephones from Red Square, I said to myself, his version may well be accepted as gospel, no matter how absurd the accusation. I had visions of a cold cell in Lubyanka Prison, the notorious Soviet Bastille in Moscow. Fortunately, nothing else happened, but I have often tried to understand, in subsequent years, how I could have been so utterly reckless and stupid as to have disobeyed official instructions, when it was virtually certain that I would be caught.

The instructions, furthermore, were not unreasonable. What the Soviets were afraid of, I learned later, was not picture taking, but the possibility that some sharpshooter might pick off Khrushchev or other Soviet bigwigs atop the mausoleum. We could see them rather clearly from our windows, although they were perhaps a quarter of a mile away.

The May Day parade began at 10 A.M. sharp with a ten-minute march-past of new Soviet weapons, including a seven-hundred-mile rocket and an ominous-looking atomic cannon. The brevity of the entire military demonstration was surprising. Then began the well-nigh endless procession, which lasted until 1:45 P.M. It included trade unions, farm co-operatives, colorfully dressed youth organizations, etc. etc. Most of them carried red banners, others bore pictures of Soviet potentates and the great majority also had artificial flowers and greenery. The over-all effect was immensely impressive, but it had some of the frightening quality of the Nazi demonstrations staged by Hitler and Goebbels.

Five minutes after the formal celebration ended the street-cleaning brigade was at work tidying up Manege Square under our windows and adjacent Red Square. Considerable litter had been left in both areas. This was attacked by the usual squadron of frumpy-looking middle-aged women, wielding brooms made of twigs, and by modern trucks with equipment for hosing the streets. Within fifteen minutes Manege Square was as neat as the proverbial pin.

That night fireworks exploded in the darkness over the Kremlin, as the full moon shone down on the battlements of that citadel of the Middle Ages, its towers topped with dark red stars, which glittered vividly.

The striking architectural qualities of the Kremlin are perhaps not fully appreciated abroad. It is far more than just a grim fortress. Not only are its powerful thick walls, built nearly five hundred years ago, ruggedly impressive, but within those walls are three of the most picturesque cathedrals to be found anywhere. They are no longer used for worship, of course, since the regime is aggressively antireligious.

Within is also an extraordinary museum of jewels, coaches and gold plate once owned by the czars, and rich objects looted from churches and monasteries. All this serves as perfect propaganda with much of the Russian proletariat, since it is presented as evidence of the extravagance, callousness and corruption of the old regime.

The restaurants we patronized in the U.S.S.R. were all bad, by American standards. The tablecloths were often spotted, and so were the waiters' jackets. There was great monotony in the menus and the service was terrible. Two hours, or more, was always required for dinner. A standard menu in five languages—French, German, Russian, Chinese and English—was used in our hotels in Moscow and Leningrad. Each was badly soiled and had fingerprints all over it. Some ten pages long, it listed a most tempting array of game, fish, meat, salads, soups, vegetables, desserts and wines. Unfortunately, 95 per cent of these delectable items were never to be had. "We are out of that just now" was the almost invariable reply. We ended by eating the same humdrum dishes over and over, since little else was available. We got the same dessert six or eight times. It was called "Plombiere Intourist," and consisted of ice cream perched on a piece of meringue, with cookies stuck in the sides. These last must have come down from the time of Peter the Great, for they were always so stale as to be absolutely inedible. We ordered chicken several times, and invariably the bird had been chopped up with some instrument that must have resembled an ax, with total disregard for the joints. It was full of bone splinters, and one found it extremely difficult to tell which part of the chicken one was consuming.

Russian ice cream is good, and the same is true of the vodka and caviar. The best Russian vodka is smooth, mellow and expensive, much superior to that made in the United States. We drank it frequently. In the Soviet Union it is taken chilled and neat, in a small glass about the size of our liqueur glass. This vodka was not obtainable in the United States until recent years.

The Moscow subway is, of course, in a class by itself. Each station is a veritable museum piece, decorated with marble, crystal and bronze, and sometimes with sculpture. Although the subway is perhaps a hundred feet underground, reached by fast escalators, it is perfectly ventilated, and so spotlessly clean that one can almost literally eat off of the floor. Millions of passengers use it daily, and the trains are frequent and on time.

In another area of Soviet civilization, religion, the church is fighting for its life. A few houses of worship remain open, but the government knows that the religious people, who are nearly all elderly, will die off in time. It expects the younger generation to follow the Communist line and grow up as atheists. We attended services in a Russian Orthodox church in Moscow and in the famous monastery at Zagorsk, forty-five miles from the city. The congregations in both were perhaps 95 per cent middle-aged or older, with a preponderance of sad-eyed, shabby women in peasant dress. The services were picturesque and impressive, with much swinging of incense, and the music was gorgeous. I recall particularly the organlike tones of a basso profundo in the choir of the church in Moscow. The Russians seem to have the finest bass voices in the world.

We saw the bodies of both Lenin and Stalin in the Red Square mausoleum, lying waxlike in the dim light. (Stalin hadn't been moved in 1961.) Both were in business suits; Lenin wore no decorations but Stalin wore his. The possibility exists that both "bodies" are fakes, but if so they are just about the most perfect fakes in existence. For example, I could clearly see gray hairs on the back of Lenin's neck. Possibly these were spurious, but I rather think not. Russians stand in lines half a mile long, winter and summer, to enter the tomb. Foreigners are put at or near the head of the line, so we did not have to wait for more than a few minutes.

The Soviets are rightly proud of the manner in which they have almost banished illiteracy from their country. In 1917 the illiteracy rate was about 65 per cent. Today's educational system impresses the visitor as much more rigorous than ours, with more work demanded of the pupils and far stricter discipline. We visited an English class in one of the schools, and heard the recitation, which was well done. The class was reading *Uncle Tom's Cabin*—of course. Yet in our Leningrad hotel one night the orchestra was playing "Way Down Upon the Swanee River," with its nostalgic yearning for a southern slave plantation. The U.S.S.R. is full of surprises.

Only about 20 per cent of high school graduates are admitted to the Russian universities, and they have to pass a tough entrance examination. About 15 per cent of those who gain entrance flunk out later—at least such were the percentages when we were there.

The schedule of daily work in a Soviet institution of higher learning is much harder than that in the average American institution. There are no tuition fees; on the contrary, most students are compensated by the state. If a student's grades fall sharply, his stipend ceases until he pulls them up. No cutting of classes is permitted, and excuses for failure to turn in written assignments on time are not accepted. After graduation the student must work for the state for three years in return for his education, but he is paid for this. I am assuming that rules and regulations approximately the same as the foregoing are still in effect.

Leningrad is far more beautiful than Moscow, and its citizens have long regarded Moscow's inhabitants as brutish and uncultivated. Founded by Peter the Great on the banks of the Neva River, and originally named St. Petersburg in his honor, it is truly an imperial city. Its streets and squares, its churches and monuments have an elegance about them that is rarely seen in Moscow. Some of its principal buildings were designed by Italian, French, German and Dutch architects. If Leningrad has no theater or opera house quite up to the Bolshoi, or any ballet troupe in the same superlative category, it has the oldest ballet school in Russia, in which many of the Bolshoi's renowned ballerinas are trained.

The collection of paintings at the Hermitage, part of which recently toured the United States, is obviously greatly superior to anything of the kind in the Soviet capital, and worthy to rank with those in the Louvre, the Uffizi and Pitti, the Vatican and the Prado. Like the Prado, the Hermitage is wretchedly lighted, but the collection is amazingly broad. It was impossible for us to be in the museum for more than three or four hours, which was hardly enough to get a general idea, much less to savor and appreciate its almost incredible richness. Many of the old masters were acquired by Catherine the Great. We had to forgo the wonderful collection of French Impressionists, for lack of time.

The Winter Palace, in which the Hermitage is located, is a prime example of the unbelievable extravagance of the czars. It has 1,400 rooms, many decorated with costly rock-crystal chandeliers, Carrara marble columns, bronze of the heaviest and most expensive type, lapis lazuli, malachite, jasper and so on. Just as Louis XIV and his Palace of Versailles helped to bring on the French Revolution, so Catherine and her successors were instrumental in bringing on the Russian Revolution. The absurd extravagance represented in the Hermitage and in other palaces, such as Tsarskoe Seloe and Peterhof, could scarcely have had any other ultimate result. We saw Tsarskoe Seloe, now known as Pushkin, in the process of its scrupulously accurate restoration. Genuine gold leaf was being carefully applied in one handsome room with a brush made from a squirrel's tail. The palace was set afire and blown up by the Germans when they finally had to lift the nine-hundred-day siege of Leningrad.

The heroic resistance of the city during that period is one of the great sagas in the annals of war. Natasha, our guide in Leningrad, said that her mother, a surgeon, was evacuated across Lake Ladoga on the ice during the siege, under the bombs and artillery fire of the Germans. It was the last remaining exit to the outside world. Natasha's father was killed at the front. Over 600,000 citizens of Leningrad died rather than surrender. Most of them starved to death.

All this horror seemed long in the past when we strolled about the Nevsky Prospekt, renowned in Russian literature, or viewed the splendid statues and public buildings that adorn the country's one-time capital. Leningrad had been completely restored, as far as we could see, despite the prolonged heavy bombing and shelling by the Germans. There were visible reminders in the form of tablets and monuments that this was where the Russian Revolution began, with Lenin at its head, but that was to be expected. The city, by and large, retained much of its antique charm.

Our hotel in Leningrad, the Europa, was not as commodious or comfortable as the National in Moscow. Our bedroom was hardly less than fantastic, for it contained eight chairs, four tables, a sofa and a large desk, a dressing table, with mirror, and twin beds, but not one single drawer in which to put anything. We had to leave our clothes in our suitcases, or hang them in the wardrobe-type facility that graced the anteroom just inside the door. Furthermore, the running water in the tub was muddy and not very hot. The hotter it got, the muddier it became. We were so thirsty that we took our lives in our hands and drank some of it once. We didn't do it again, and there were no serious consequences.

We traveled to and from Leningrad on the Red Arrow, an overnight rail trip in both directions. The Russians boasted that the Red Arrow was always on time. Actually, it was thirty minutes late going and forty minutes late coming.

I was in the upper berth, which was not more than eighteen inches wide with no railing or rim of any kind. A lurch by the train, and I would have landed six feet below, on my head or some other portion of my anatomy. Hence I couldn't sleep. I got up at around 4 A.M. and looked out of the window for some four hours at the flat, dull countryside, consisting mainly of forests of birch and fir, and fields extending to the horizon, interspersed with occasional villages and towns. The sun came up at 4:30 out of the woods and bogs, at which time a few muzhiks were stirring. Smoke was issuing from their squalid huts. The scenery along the railroad between Moscow and Leningrad is far from exhilarating.

We flew from Moscow to East Berlin on an East German plane. Half a dozen Red Army generals were on board, one of whom paced up and down the aisle throughout the flight. He seemed extremely nervous.

As we approached the unimpressive little East Berlin airport, the plane began pitching and tossing crazily, and a black squall line appeared ominously on our right. We managed to land safely, although the wind of almost hurricane force seemed to come within a hairsbreadth of turning the plane over as it touched the ground. We were immensely relieved at not cracking up, and admired the skill of the pilot.

Nobody could leave the aircraft until the Red Army generals were photographed getting off in the face of the junior tornado. As we emerged behind them, the wind hit us broadside, and along with it a downpour such as I have seldom seen. The force of the cyclonic gale almost knocked us down, and we found it impossible to get our coats on. We staggered through the deluge, and reached the airport drenched to the skin. Fortunately the temperature was mild.

This was a few months before the erection of the Berlin Wall, and we were able to board a bus for West Berlin. We had an appointment for that afternoon with West Berlin's mayor, Willy Brandt, and I intended to keep it, wet clothes and all. Douglas said she simply couldn't go, under the circumstances.

As we passed through East Berlin, the immense devastation was still quite visible, although the war had ended sixteen years before. There was no problem about getting to bustling, completely rebuilt West Berlin. We left the bus at the Ostbahnhof, and took a taxi to the Hotel Kempinski.

Fräulein Gretel Spitzer, of NBC's Berlin Bureau, had made the appointment with Mayor Brandt, and she picked me up in her car at the hotel and took me to the Schöneberg Town Hall, then serving as the West Berlin Rathaus. It was the first of many kindnesses she performed for us during our stay.

The interview with Mayor Brandt went off well. He discussed the mounting crisis over Berlin, occasioned by the fact that some five hundred East Germans a day, most of them relatively young and including many able professional people, were departing for West Germany. They were doing this although they risked arrest, and usually had to leave all their possessions behind. On every holiday, about one thousand of them were "voting with their feet" for freedom. Chairman Khrushchev of the U.S.S.R. had called the headlong exodus "a bone in the throat," and was threatening to do something about it.

I returned to our hotel, and changed to dry clothes. We took Fräulein Spitzer to dinner at an attractive Swabian restaurant. Her account of her experiences in Berlin during the wartime bombings and after the city's fall to the Russians was hair-raising.

During the orgy of rape that followed the capture of Berlin, a Russian officer tried to grab her. She had on heavy ski boots, and kicked him in the groin so hard that he was temporarily paralyzed. She fled and hid under a blanket on the floor, lying there motionless for three days. The Russians never found her. Thousands of other women were less fortunate. The thirteen-year-old daughter of a minister was raped a hundred times.

Gretel Spitzer saw long-haired Mongolian troops bivouacking in the area that had been the Berlin Zoo. They sat around campfires, cooking chunks of meat, their ponies tied nearby. In command was a high-ranking Mongolian Red Army general with a parrot chained to his shoulder.

She related an episode that highlighted the gloomy atmosphere of East Berlin after the war. It seems that while she was chatting with an Englishman on a street corner there, he let out a loud guffaw. Such unseemingly and well-nigh unprecedented behavior caused various officials and others to come running to see what was wrong.

We returned to the hotel, and I awoke late that night with a fever. My soaking at the East Berlin airport, and the wet clothes that I wore for several hours thereafter, apparently accounted for my coming down with some form of influenza. I was in bed for three days. The hotel's doctor scorned the antibiotics that I had brought with me, exclaiming, "*Ach! Das ist eine Kanone* [That's a cannon]"—in other words, "much too powerful." He prescribed something milder, and I recovered. Neither German nor Austrian physicians believe in prescribing antibiotics unless one is seriously ill. I had a similar experience some years later in Vienna, where the doctor used almost identical language in rejecting my tet-ramycin.

The management and staff of the Hotel Kempinski were astonishingly solicitous for my well-being during my indisposition. The assistant manager accompanied the hotel physician on his visits to my room. The manager sent up a basket of fruit and cookies with his compliments, and after I recovered asked us to meet him in the lobby for a chat. We talked with him there for about fifteen minutes. The maids and bellboys were similarly thoughtful. The following year, when we were back at the Kempinski, one of the bellboys recognized me and recalled at once that I had been sick on my previous visit.

The Germans are a great puzzle to me. In ordinary times, they are the most warmhearted, kind and courteous people imaginable, but let them get into a war and many of them go absolutely berserk, committing atrocities worthy of Attila or Genghis Khan.

Consider, furthermore, the following extract from correspondence between a well-known German drug firm and the commandant of the infamous Auschwitz concentration camp:

"We should be grateful if you would supply 150 women for experiments with a new sleeping drug," the company official wrote. When the reply came back that the women would cost 200 marks each (about $40), the official complained that the price seemed excessive, and offered 170 marks. The women were sent, and the firm's spokesman wrote later, "We have received the consignment of 150 women. . . . The experiments have been carried out. All the test cases have died. We shall contact you shortly re another supply."

How could important elements of a people that often appears highly civilized have behaved in so barbarous a manner?

The ever-obliging Miss Spitzer took us in her car to Marienfelde, on the edge of town, to see the refugee center for the accommodation of the East Germans, who were fleeing in droves to the West. The center was almost bursting at the seams with a thousand refugees from the previous day—a holiday—and five hundred more during the succeeding twenty-four hours. We attended a screening session at which the newcomers were being closely questioned, lest there be Red spies among them.

Our stay in Berlin was at an end, and we flew to Copenhagen for a week. It was a delightful and relaxing interlude. The pleasant and hospitable Danes, with their delectable viands and uninhibited *joie de vivre,* charmed us completely. The widely circulated postcard that shows Danish policemen holding back a smiling crowd while a duck and her ducklings cross the street appeared to typify the friendly inhabitants of that country. And most of all, there was Tivoli, the amusement park in the center of Copenhagen, with its pantomimes and parades, its variety shows and musical events, and its evocation of the spirit of Hans Christian Andersen, "like horns from elfland, faintly blowing." Tivoli expresses the spirit of the Danish people in much the same way that Munich's Oktoberfest, with its foaming steins, its brass bands and its well-upholstered burghers bellowing *"Ein Prosit!"* seems to express the ultimate essence of Bavaria.

It was during these years, the fifties and sixties, that our three children were married. To our great joy, all of them settled in Richmond.

Douglas, the eldest, married James S. Watkinson in 1953. Jim is the son of English parents who emigrated to California. His father, John Watkinson, enlisted in the Canadian Black Watch as soon as the fighting broke out in World War I, and was in the first gas attack of the war, launched by the Germans at Ypres in 1915. Jim was in the U. S. Army in the early 1950s, and met our daughter on a weekend trip to Richmond. He rose in a few years to the presidency of Morton G. Thalhimer, Inc., Virginia's lead-

Douglas G. Dabney, second from left, with three Jewish playmates in the Vienna Volksgarten in 1934. Four years later Hitler seized Austria, and the fate of these Jewish children is unknown.

ABOVE, Douglas G. Dabney
just before her wedding to
James S. Watkinson in 1953.
Her sister, Lucy Davis Dabney,
now Mrs. Alexander P. Leverty II,
who was maid of honor at the
wedding, is putting a sixpence
into the bride's shoe
for good luck.
(Wendell B. Powell)

RIGHT, Richard Heath Dabney II,
son of Virginius
and Douglas Dabney,
an officer of the
Richmond Federal Savings
and Loan Association.

...nily group at the V. Dabney home in Richmond. Left to right: John C. Parker and Alice ...ney Parker, his wife; Douglas C. Dabney and V. Dabney, her husband, and Lily Heth ...ney, mother of Alice and V. Dabney, five days before her ninety-fifth birthday. *(Carl Lynn)*

Part of a group of ten newspaper, radio and magazine men who visited the wrecked cities of Germany in the winter of 1947 at the invitation of the U.S. War Department. They are standing on the spot outside the Hitler bunker in Berlin where the bodies of Hitler and Eva Braun were doused with gasoline and burned. Left to right: Coleman Harwell, Nashville *Tennessean*; E. F. Tompkins, New York *Journal-American*; Dwight Young, Dayton *Journal-Herald*; Victor O. Jones, Boston *Globe*; John H. Martin, International News Service; V. Dabney, Richmond *Times-Dispatch*; Frazier Hunt, Mutual Broadcasting System, and Erik Oberg, Industrial Press. *(U.S. Army Signal Corps)*

resident Dwight D. Eisenhower and V. Dabney ex-
hange pleasantries before the American Society of
ewspaper Editors' luncheon in April 1958 at which
abney, president of ASNE, presided. Eisenhower was
e speaker at the luncheon, which was held jointly with
e International Press Institute and was attended by
litors from all over the world, the largest meeting of such
urnalists held anywhere up to that time. (*Associated
ress photo*)

Ceremony at the unveiling of tablet at Jamestown, Virginia, commemorating the coming of the English common law to these shores in the first charter granted the
Jamestown settlers in 1606. The tablet was placed by the
Virginia State Bar after the need for such a marker was
pointed out by Virginius Dabney in a *Times-Dispatch*
editorial. He is shown on the left, behind the tablet, and
Miss Ellen M. Bagby, long-time head of the Jamestown
committee of the Association for the Preservation of Virginia Antiquities, is on the right. (*Thomas L. Williams*)

V. Dabney, aged seventy-six, on the tennis courts in 1977. Tennis was for him a lifelong hobby, and since his retirement in 1969 he has played regularly three times a week—only doubles in recent years. He terms tennis "the greatest relaxer known to man." (*David R. White*)

Caricature of V. Dabney by Fred O. Seibel, Richmond *Times-Dispatch* cartoonist, drawn for the *Bulletin* of the American Society of Newspaper Editors.

Douglas and V. Dabney are shown in front of St. Basil's Cathedral in Red Square, Moscow, on their trip to the Soviet Union in the spring of 1961. *(Associated Press photo)*

Premier Salazar of Portugal, left, poses on the porch of his official residence in Lisbon following the audience he granted Douglas and V. Dabney in 1965. They felt that his private personality was about as unlike that of a díctator as could well be imagined. In the published interview, however, Salazar was stern, and said he had no intention of letting the United Nations tell him what to do with the African provinces of Angola and Mozambique.

ing real estate firm. He and Doug have four children—James Dabney, Kathleen Douglas, Sarah Drew and Robert Fielding Watkinson.

Lucy was wed five years later to Dr. Alexander P. Leverty II, a leading young pediatrician, son of the late William G. Leverty, for many years my colleague on the *Times-Dispatch* and long-time member of the Washington & Lee University journalism faculty. Alex's mother, the former Sarah Maude ("Sally") Taylor, is a University of Alabama Phi Beta Kappa. Alex and Lucy have three children—Lucy Harrison, William Gordon II and Alexander Taylor Leverty.

Heath was married in 1963 to Ann Hardy Blake, the beautiful daughter of Alfred L. Blake, Jr., one of the city's leading realtors, and his wife, Ann Hardy Blake. Heath was in the U. S. Army, stationed at Fort Bliss, El Paso, Texas, and he and Ann preferred to have their wedding in El Paso rather than in Richmond. So both families flew down for the ceremony. It was performed by the Reverend Robert T. Gibson in the chapel of the Episcopal Church of St. Clement. Heath was transferred later to the Pentagon, where he was assigned to extremely important intelligence operations until his discharge. He is making a fine record with the Richmond Federal Savings and Loan Association. Ann and Heath have three children—Richard Heath III, Virginius Beauford and Sarah Blake Dabney.

That makes ten grandchildren in all. I could brag at some length concerning the talents and good looks of our children and grandchildren, but I shall forbear. Since they are all based in Richmond, we see them at frequent intervals. We have volunteered repeatedly to serve as baby-sitters for the grandchildren as they were growing up, but their considerate parents apparently didn't quite believe that we loved to do this. The result is that we have baby-sat only sparingly.

Our eldest grandchild, "Jay" Watkinson, now in Germany with the U. S. Army, was married late in 1976 to Deborah Raykes, a charming girl, who is with him overseas. Several other grandchildren are away at college, or about to be. Our greatest pleasure each year is to have all the children and their spouses, and the grandchildren, at our home for dinner on Christms Eve. Needless to say, we would never think of leaving Richmond at Christmas under any conditions.

When Heath was married in El Paso in 1963, it was a not-to-be-missed opportunity for his mother and me to visit Mexico, which we had never done. Consequently we flew to Mexico City for a week, with a side trip to Taxco, via Cuernavaca.

Glowing, colorful, flower-garlanded Mexico captivated us. It was the week before Christmas, and we have never seen any metropolis so beautifully decorated as Mexico City. Lights festooned the streets for miles. In one park, tall trees were draped with lights from bottom to top, while hawkers with festively painted balloons plied their trade. The University of Mexico's extremely picturesque campus, with its unique library of colored mosaics and its eighty thousand students, impressed us immensely. The nearby pyramids of Teotihuacan, possibly contemporaneous with the Egyptian pyramids, carried us back thousands of years to the time when their pre-Mexican builders worshiped the sun and moon. And the Ballet Folklorico de Mexico was as thrilling a folk ballet as one could imagine.

12

"The Wall," Budapest, Bullfights, Salazar and Kekkonen

AN INVITATION CAME to me to visit West Germany for two weeks in 1962 as the guest of the West German Government, and I accepted. Since I was in sympathy with the over-all objectives of that government, I did not feel that I would be putting myself in a seriously compromising position by benefiting from its hospitality. I was clear in my own mind that I would criticize West German policies editorially in the future, if the occasion arose. My hosts told me specifically to write "both the good and the bad." I advised them that I would be bringing my wife, at our expense, and they found this entirely acceptable.

We landed at the Cologne–Bonn airport, after flying via Lufthansa from New York. Tastefully adorned with beds of flowers in the greatest profusion, Cologne–Bonn was the most attractive airport I ever saw. We were met by Udo Grobba, a pleasant young man who had made various appointments for me with government officials in Bonn.

During our six months' sojourn in Germany and Austria in 1934, we had spent two enjoyable weeks in Bonn, with a side trip to the politically tempestuous Saar. The old university town on the Rhine was now the country's capital, and its population had almost trebled. Traffic was heavy and the city was badly overcrowded. The opinion prevailed that Bonn would not remain the capital indefinitely.

From our room in the Hotel Koenigshof near the Rhine we could watch the enormous river traffic on that stream, with an almost unbroken succession of barges and other vessels in both directions. Since the Rhine traverses the Ruhr, the pulsating heart of German industry, it carried then, and probably still carries, the greatest tonnage of any river on the globe.

Grobba took me to several appointments with German officials. The question whether they should frankly tell German youth all about the Nazi atrocities was discussed. An official pointed out that if they did inform the younger generation, they would get into arguments with its members as to how and why such things were allowed to happen; if, on the other hand, they did not inform them they would be accused of suppressing vitally important information. Grobba said he could testify personally that there were many problems and difficulties involving the two generations. His father had been German minister to Baghdad under Hitler, and had "gone along" with the Nazi regime.

On a visit to the Ruhr a few days later, the president of the Federation of German Industry granted me an interview in his Cologne office. He confirmed the correctness of the figures I brought with me, showing that Britons, Frenchmen and Italians were at that time working more hours per year than Germans. He also said that the Italian Fiat plant was the most modern automobile factory in the world.

At Oberhausen I talked with the press chief for the huge Gutehoffnungshuette, producer of steel and machinery. He mentioned that in Germany's coal and steel industries, half of the directors for a given company were from the unions. Furthermore, these directors chose one person from management who was given access to all the company's books. The plan had proved successful, he felt, and the attitude of the working-class directors was co-operative. Strikes had been rare in the Ruhr.

Contamination of the atmosphere in this heavily industrialized region was a serious problem. The official said that when he parked his car in Oberhausen for just a couple of hours, it was covered with dust and dirt spewed out by the mills. The air, furthermore, was polluted by fumes. It was surprising, therefore, to find the Ruhr River beautifully clear and the river valley verdant. The stream from which the entire region takes its name had somehow escaped contamination.

We decided to travel by train to West Berlin, through Communist-held East Germany. Several persons whom we consulted thought we were out of our minds to do this instead of flying. It was an eleven-hour train trip, whereas by air it was something like one hour. But one sees little from a plane, and we wanted to see as much as possible of what was going on behind the iron curtain.

The journey from Bonn to the East German border was uneventful. It was the remaining third, about 110 miles, that we were waiting for. As soon as we crossed the line into the domain of the Reds, the contrast with West Germany was apparent. For example, the railway station at Brunswick, the last large West German city through which we passed, was new and handsome, and the flowers in large braziers on the platform added a strikingly beautiful touch. But the station in Communist-held Marienborn, the first stop beyond the barrier, was beat up in appearance and suffered from a third-rate paint job.

Just before we reached the station, we passed the border, where a watchtower stood on each side of the tracks. At least one armed guard was in each tower, and the area had been cleared, so that there was a field of fire in every direction.

The station platform at Marienborn was swarming with Communist police and guards when our train arrived. Their headquarters was in a house adjacent to the station. Several women in uniform were also in and around the train.

Two male and two female police or ticket takers came into our compartment in succession, checking our passports, taking up our tickets, collecting from us a fee for the "transit visa" required for passage from West into East Germany, etc. These Communist functionaries were not at all unpleasant in manner, although the men carried pistols, and we felt that if we got out of line in any way, we would be in trouble. We were told later that the Commies were making a special point of treating tourists politely, in an effort to convince the world that they are not complete ruffians.

As we left the station, we saw two more watchtowers, on opposite sides of the tracks, each with two gunmen. We were clearly entering one of the "people's democracies," where they are so "democratic" that they shoot anybody on sight who tries to leave.

The rural scene along the railroad tracks from Marienborn to Berlin was remarkable chiefly for the fact that practically no motor vehicles were visible on the highways. One felt that these vistas could easily have dated from the year 1920 or even 1900. A good many fields seemed well cultivated, but hardly any farm machinery was in evidence. As a matter of fact, the farm situation in the so-called German Democratic Republic was in a frightful mess. There were acute shortages of meat, milk and butter, commodities that were plentiful and readily available in most countries of Western Europe.

The biggest city of East Germany on the Marienborn–Berlin railroad line is Magdeburg—slightly larger than Richmond. The train stopped there for ten or fifteen minutes. Nobody was allowed to get out, but as we looked from our window it was astonishing to note that not a single automobile was parked near the station. Any comparable station in West Germany would have been surrounded by a sea of cars, both moving and parked. Yet here the scene was weirdly lacking in any dynamic quality whatever. The station itself was in need of paint. The German love of flowers was apparent here, as elsewhere, but there was nothing else to lighten the gloom.

Magdeburg is on the Elbe River. When we crossed that stream, immediately after leaving the station, we noted two barges lying motionless in the river. No other vessels were visible. The lack of water-borne traffic was partly accounted for by the fact that West Germany controls the mouth of the Elbe. But there was an almost equal dearth of automobile traffic in the city, as far as we could observe.

We arrived at the Zoo railroad station in West Berlin without mishap, and were met by a youngish man named Karl Krätschmer, representing the West German Government. He was attractive and outgoing, and looked after our every need. With him was a good-looking woman, a German model whom he was evidently wooing.

After we had gotten into a taxi, en route to the Hotel Kempinski Krätschmer told us that the station platform that we had just left was under control of the East German authorities, and that various persons had been kidnaped there by East German police and had simply vanished. A few hours later, Udo Grobba, our guide and mentor in Bonn, called our hotel from that city to see if we had arrived safely. He was evidently uneasy.

Krätschmer met us next day with a car, and we drove to "The Wall." This monstrosity had been erected since our visit of the preceding year in order to stanch the hemorrhaging of East Germany's lifeblood to the West, as thousands of its youngest and best fled to freedom.

The barrier, of concrete, cinder blocks and barbed wire, which slashed the face of Berlin like a livid scar, had to be seen to be believed. Police with guns were not only manning watchtowers on the East German side, but were slinking behind the ruins of gutted buildings and firing through slits in the masonry at anyone who tried to escape. An estimated 13,000 married couples were forcibly separated by the wall.

There were memorials, with many floral tributes, along the barrier where various men and women had been killed trying to reach the West. The largest and most impressive was to a youth named Peter Fechter, who was hit while climbing over the wall, and who lay there moaning for an hour until he died. A large wrecked building immediately behind the barrier in East Berlin was the hiding place from which the gunman fired the fatal shot. A U.S. lieutenant was nearby at the time, and some felt that he should have gone to the aid of the dying Fechter. But this young officer was, in fact, powerless without instructions from higher up, since our delicate relations with Russia were involved.

Another touching memorial was inscribed "*Dem Unbekannten Flüchtling* [To the Unknown Escapee]," who swam the Spree to get away, but was shot as he reached the farther shore. A picture of him in his coffin was at the base of the cross erected near the spot, and looped around the cross was a length of barbed wire. He had not been identified, despite the wide publicity.

Four more memorials lined the Bernauerstrasse, which forms the boundary between the East and West sectors of Berlin for a considerable distance. These were dedicated to persons fatally injured when jumping from windows, an elderly woman among them. And slightly back from the Bernauer, on a side street, a white-haired woman was staring out of a window toward West Berlin, "looking for her son," we were told. She stood or sat near that window nearly all the time. But even if she had caught sight of her son, she was forbidden so much as to wave to him, or she would have been arrested. A tall screen of fiberboard, higher than the wall of masonry, had been erected at various points to prevent East Berliners from seeing into West Berlin and waving to their loved ones.

All sorts of ingenious schemes were devised by those wishing to escape. One of the cleverest was that conceived by East Berliners who made headdresses of stuffed swans, and swam the canal successfully, with only the "Swans" visible on the surface. When the Communists realized what a trick had been played on them, they began slaughtering swans right and left on the waterways, until an estimated fifty to sixty of the beautiful birds had been shot.

Should the United States have tried to prevent erection of the wall by forcible action? Some Germans argued that we should have sent in bulldozers on the night of August 13, 1961, and knocked down the first bits of masonry. The Communists would have retreated and stopped building the barrier, they contended. But suppose the Communists had begun shooting and the confrontation had touched off thermonuclear war? This last seems improbable, but it does appear fairly likely that if we had smashed the building blocks on the border, the Reds would have pulled back a couple of hundred yards to territory into which we were forbidden by international law to intrude and erected the wall there. All in all, it appears that our authorities were right in not risking war to stop the construction.

Of course, the entire border between the East and West zones of Germany, some 830 miles long, was, and is, lined with almost every conceivable type of obstacle to prevent anyone from escaping. Electrified wire, mine fields, several rows of barbed wire with antipersonnel mines on the fence posts, and a wide, cleared "death strip," with gunmen in watchtowers constantly on duty, are among the obstructions. Homes or other buildings that got in the way were ruthlessly torn down.

Yet the Reds had put on a masterful campaign to convince the world that stories of walls and death strips were simply a lot of "capitalist propaganda." Krätschmer said that, a short time before, he had piloted along the wall seven correspondents of Indian newspapers stationed in London, who had come at the invitation of the West German Government. Six of them were found to be amazingly pro-Soviet. The six asked the following question:

"Are the West Germans fleeing through the wall to East Germany, or are the East Germans fleeing to the West?"

Also the following:

"Why don't the Americans, the French and the British pull their troops out of West Berlin so that West Berlin and East Berlin can unite, and be free of domination by anybody? If these three powers would just get out of Berlin, everybody would be happy."

A West German official who was present became so furious that he left the room, rather than risk an explosive insult to the visitors.

These topflight Indian correspondents had had access to full and accurate accounts in the British press of what was happening in Germany and Berlin. Yet six of them had swallowed the Communist line.

And that wasn't all. The Minister of Communications and Transport from Nepal was in Berlin at about the same time, and when he saw the wall remarked:

"Well, I declare! I see there really is a wall here. I had read about it, but to tell the truth I thought it was just a lot of propaganda."

That from a minister of *communications!*

In an effort to counteract Soviet Russia's highly successful misrepresentations throughout much of the world, three separate broadcasting operations were being conducted in Germany under American auspices.

I visited the offices of RIAS (Radio in American Sector), the station that was broadcasting daily to East Berlin, with what appeared to be excellent results. Robert Lochner, son of Louis Lochner, Berlin correspondent of the Associated Press for many years, was in charge of RIAS. He impressed me as able and articulate. The trapped inhabitants of East Berlin were evidently listening to his station, for they were sending in about eight hundred letters a month, despite censorship and terrorism. Furthermore, RIAS was denounced regularly by the Communist radio, which evidenced Red concern over its success.

RIAS got its funds from the U. S. Treasury, whereas Radio Free Europe, with headquarters in Munich, was financed by the CIA and private contributions. The CIA's role did not become public until years later. RFE's broadcasts were, and are, beamed exclusively to the five satellite countries of Eastern Europe—Poland, Czechoslovakia, Hungary, Romania and Bulgaria.

Radio Free Europe was keeping the eighty million inhabitants of the Soviet satellite bloc informed concerning events in the West. A striking example of the number who listen to its broadcasts had occurred in 1959 when Richard Nixon visited Poland. The Communist radio did not give the time of his arrival or his route. Yet an estimated 250,000 cheering Poles lined the streets when he passed.

We were anxious to visit our friends the Kartzkes, in East Berlin, but were advised against it by various functionaries of both the American and German governments. They feared not only that we would get into some sort of trouble but that we would also cause trouble for the Kartzkes with the Communist regime if we visited them. We had about decided not to go when I discussed the matter with Robert Lochner of RIAS. He said we should by all means make the trip, and pointed out that he didn't hesitate to visit friends behind the wall. "I've done it numerous times, and have never gotten into trouble myself or embarrassed the friends I was visiting," he said. "And I'm at the top of East Berlin's s.o.b. list. If I can go, you certainly can; you'll be foolish not to."

So we went. It was impossible to telephone across the wall, but it was still permitted to send a telegram via Munich, of all things. Thus we wired the Kartzkes that we would be there the following afternoon at about three o'clock. We bought two half-pound bags of the best coffee and some cream, and took off in a car with an Iraqi student as driver. He knew his way around, for, as we found out later, he had been frisked from head to foot three days before at Checkpoint Charlie, compelled to undress completely and held for an hour on suspicion of smuggling currency. This time nothing of the sort occurred, and after routine checking of our passports and money, and looking into the car's trunk and its glove compartment, the guards told us to proceed.

East Berlin was not as deserted or as drab as it had been the year before when we passed through from the East Berlin airport en route to West Berlin. There had been a bit of tidying up and reconstruction during the year, and the wall had been built. This last meant that some 300,000 persons who had been working and shopping in West Berlin were now cooped up behind the wall. Hence these people were having to find such work as they could in East Berlin and they also had to do their buying there. Since there were far fewer shops for them to patronize, those shops were now fairly well filled with patrons, although the quality of goods offered was decidedly inferior. Krätschmer said he had visited the principal shoe store in East Berlin with a view to buying a pair of shoes. The only two salespeople were women who knew nothing about shoes. The store's stock of footwear was piled in the middle of the floor, and one of the ladies became almost hysterical trying to find his size in the pile. He was in the store for an hour and a half, but was never able to get any shoes.

We found the Kartzke apartment at 54 Am Treptower Park without difficulty. It had been rebuilt since the winter of 1947 when I had visited the family briefly as they huddled in the ruins, with heat in only one room. Dr. and Mrs. Kartzke, now looking a good deal older, greeted us warmly, and were happy to get the coffee, which was far better than anything obtainable in East

Berlin. They also were convinced that our visit would not cause them embarrassment, and apparently it did not.

The next day was their fiftieth wedding anniversary, and they had somehow managed to get permission for their two sons, three grandchildren and other relatives, a dozen in all, to come through the wall for the occasion. The coffee was therefore doubly welcome.

We chatted with them for about half an hour. They were resigned to remaining in East Berlin permanently, for if they left, they would be permitted to take hardly any of their possessions with them. Nor did they wish to live with one of their sons in West Germany. To our amazement, they told us that they had never seen the wall, which had been erected six weeks before, and was about a mile from their apartment. Dr. Kartzke, who was seventy-nine, seemed somewhat feeble and not in good health. When his usually merry and ebullient wife told us good-bye, her eyes were filled with tears. She apparently felt that her husband had not long to live. The following month, after we had returned to Richmond, we received a black-bordered announcement in German that Dr. Kartzke had died. He was a charming man, handsome and patrician, courteous and cultivated, representing the best citizenship of the old Germany.

After leaving the Kartzke apartment, we drove around Treptower Park, beautiful with its flowers, grass and trees, and visited the enormous Soviet War Memorial, erected over the bodies of thousands of Russians who fell in the fight for Berlin. This monument is a perpetual thorn in the side of the Germans, and will probably be the first casualty, if the Soviets are ever ousted.

We in the United States can have only a remote conception of what most Europeans have gone through in this century. Two world wars and other upheavals, such as the Russian Revolution and the Nazi regime in Germany, have toppled dynasties, wrecked economies, taken the lives of tens of millions and enslaved other millions. Certain portions of the American South during and after the Civil War endured comparable ordeals and hardships, but Americans of the twentieth century can scarcely imagine how horribly vast numbers of Europeans have suffered since 1914.

Consider, as one example, the tragedies that overwhelmed the family of Karl Krätschmer, our guide in Berlin. He told us that he grew up in the Sudetenland, the German-populated fringe on the northern edge of Czechoslovakia which Hitler demanded be returned to the Reich. Karl was thirteen years old when Hitler took the Sudetenland in 1938. The Russians overran it in 1945, and Krätschmer's entire family were expelled "with only two suitcases." Some of them settled in East Prussia, from which they were again expelled by the Russians, and again they lost everything. When the Russians took over Czechoslovakia, his sister, who had had a baby shortly before, was raped by four Russian soldiers who held his father and compelled him to watch. The sister never got over it and died some years later. The husband of another sister went through the entire war without being wounded. After the war, when he had been back in Czechoslovakia for only two months, a Czech who was driving a tank ordered him to do something, and he didn't act quickly enough. The Czech ran over him with the tank and killed him. Krätschmer was able to discuss this succession of calamities with a relative lack of bitterness and a degree of fortitude that I feel sure I could not have mustered under the circumstances.

Munich was our next stop. The city was crowded because of the *Oktoberfest*, and we could not get a room at the Regina Palast Hotel. We were routed to the Ambassador, not nearly so centrally located, but within a few hundred yards of the Theresienwiese, where the famous beer-drinking festival was being held. We had dinner at the hotel with Fräulein Greta Schüssler, who had met us at the plane as representative of the Bavarian State Government, a pretty and accomplished girl who was a great help to us.

We then walked over to the *Oktoberfest*, which was in full blast. Seven huge smoke-filled wooden pavilions, erected by Munich's seven famous breweries, were each jammed to capacity with some five thousand beer-hoisting revelers. Brass bands wearing Lederhosen were giving forth from a raised platform in each pavilion with plenteous and resounding oompahs. The carousers were locking arms, grasping steins, jumping up and down in time to the music and roaring ditties such as *"Ist Das Nicht Ein Schnitzel-*

bank?" No festival could be more typical of its country's history and traditions.

In addition to the seven crowded pavilions, countless other activities were well patronized. These included merry-go-rounds, scenic railways, ferris wheels, shooting galleries and so on. Oxen were roasting on spits, chickens likewise, fish were frying over coals and countless varieties of *Wurst* (sausage) were being consumed, along with candy and soft drinks, including American ones.

We got a liter of beer apiece, which is the minimum quantity sold, and watched the high jinks. A liter (slightly more than a quart) was then fifty cents, but a decade later the price had doubled, and it probably has gone still higher today. A total of three million liters were drunk during the two weeks of the 1962 festival.

We saw only one individual who obviously had been imbibing too freely, but we left early and there may well have been many more. A special tent provided a haven for such overenthusiastic celebrants, and was equipped with nurses to soothe fevered brows and administer medicaments. Each brewery also furnished a chauffeur to drive inebriated customers home, if need be. With typical German thoroughness, all pertinent statistics are compiled at the end of the fest. These include the number of liters consumed and the number of drunks arrested, as well as the number of persons who dropped dead of heart attacks or who had attacks of gallstones.

Although we were practically next door to the *Oktoberfest*, we went only once, as we had other things on our agenda. These included a visit to nearby Dachau, with its notorious death camp still preserved as a warning to future generations. It was my second visit, and I found it as shattering an experience as the first. Miss Schüssler, who went with us, said she and many other Germans knew that *something* was going on in the concentration camps, but she seemed entirely sincere in saying that she did not suspect the lengths to which the Nazis had gone until the dreadful facts were revealed at the end of the war. She was only eight or ten years old during the conflict, and seemed typical of the younger generation of Germans who were shocked beyond measure when they grew up and discovered what had been happening. The pamphlet by a former inmate that I bought at Dachau, with its remarkable revelations concerning the sabotage of the gas chamber and the efforts of the town's citzens to aid the prisoners, was described in Chapter 8 of this book.

Next day we visited Radio Free Europe headquarters on the edge of the English Garden. I was convinced by what I saw and heard that RFE was exceptionally effective in checkmating Communist propaganda in the East European satellite countries.

Istvan Bede, former Hungarian ambassador to London, a charming gentleman in exile from his native land, was in charge of the Hungarian Broadcasting Department of RFE. He said that most people in Hungary were badly disillusioned by the failure of the West to come to their aid in the revolution of 1956 against the Soviets, and no longer trusted the West. They didn't trust the Communists either, he added. Somehow the Hungarians had gotten the impression that if they revolted against the Reds, help would be forthcoming at once from the free world. None was given, of course, and the revolt was crushed in blood, with the loss of 30,000 Hungarian lives and the flight into exile of 200,000 other citizens. Many more were in prison, he said, although nobody knew how many.

I asked Mr. Bede what the West could have done in 1956 that would have been at all effective. He said it should have sent Dag Hammerskjold, secretary general of the United Nations, to Budapest at once, with directions to recognize the independence of Hungary. Bede expressed confidence that this would have worked. I must say that I strongly doubt it. A power such as the U.S.S.R., which sent massed tanks and mowed down Hungarians in the streets by the thousands, would hardly have been stopped by a proclamation from the UN.

Of course, there was the highly distracting Suez crisis, with the involvement of Britain, France, Egypt and Israel, which occurred almost simultaneously, and our Eisenhower–Stevenson presidential election, which took place at that time. These two events made it more than ordinarily difficult for the West to act in any decisive way to aid the brave Hungarians.

Our next visit was to Geretsreid, a city of some 8,500 population near Munich that the indefatigable Germans created out of practically nothing after World War II. From the ruins of their economy and the rubble of practically all their centers of population, they somehow built about a dozen cities, of which Geretsreid is one. Millions of refugees from Prussia, Poland, Silesia and the Sudetenland were flooding into wrecked Germany with hardly anything but the clothes on their backs. These people had to be cared for somehow, and the newly created cities were a partial answer.

We were amazed at the attractive appearance of Geretsreid, fashioned, in part, from what was left of a bombed ammunition factory. Many altogether new homes were also constructed, as well as churches and schools. The handsome public square, complete with city hall and shops, was created from the ground up.

This little town had been in existence for only about a decade, but it was shipping products from its scores of small factories to eighty countries around the globe. Such things as chemicals, metal objects, musical instruments and articles made of wood from the nearby forest were being manufactured. Among the last-named were toys, chess men, dice and Moslem rosaries. Business was booming to such an extent that Greeks and Italians had to be brought in to fill out the work force. A better example of the ingenuity and drive of the Germans would be hard to find.

Our two weeks as guests of the West German Government were at an end, and we went on our own to Vienna and Budapest. After a brief stay at the Hotel Sacher in Vienna, our favorite hotel in what is probably our favorite city, we rode on the Orient Express to Budapest. The contrast between the Budapest of 1962 and that of 1934 was depressing. From a glamorous and beautiful city, architecturally distinctive and pulsating with life, it had declined to a rather dingy metropolis in which hardly anybody seemed to be having a good time. Public buildings were unpainted, and the people were glum. Twenty-eight years earlier the clean streets had been thronged with stylishly dressed men and women—the best-looking and best-dressed women I have ever seen. But they were no longer stylish or attractive. The clammy hand of communism had reduced the city and its population to a dead level of mediocrity.

Budapest had been fought over by the Germans and Russians in World War II, and some of the shell and bullet marks were still visible. It had been a place of horror in those days. The Germans were first to take possession, and they mined all the bridges over the Danube. One of the biggest blew up, apparently by accident, on a Saturday afternoon when it was crowded with streetcars and automobiles. All of them fell into the river, and countless persons were killed or drowned.

During World War II the Nazis began sending hundreds of thousands of Hungarian Jews to the gas chambers at Auschwitz. Mrs. Valentine deBalla, sister of Henry M. Cowardin of Richmond, was living in Budapest, married to a prominent Hungarian. She told me that she and her husband were on a streetcar when they saw a long line of Jewish women being marched away under guard. It was dusk and raining, and one of the women fell down an embankment, without being noticed by any of the Nazi soldiers. The deBallas got off the streetcar, hid the woman behind their umbrella, tore from her clothing the yellow label that proclaimed her a Jew and got her to a place of safety. They had never seen the woman before, and were risking death when they did this courageous thing.

Later, in the winter of 1944–45, when the Germans and Russians were fighting for Budapest, which was finally taken by the Russians, many bodies were left lying in the streets and the wrecked buildings. Destruction was such that virtual chaos reigned, and in the icy weather corpses remained where they fell until spring, at which time the stench was terrible. During the entire winter the nude body of a woman lay in the window of a bombed apartment not far from that of the deBallas', while a dead man lay in a nearby street during the same period. He had been hit by a shell just as he was getting into his car. The utter *sang-froid* with which Mrs. deBalla related these harrowing and frightening experiences enlisted my complete admiration.

Like Magdeburg on the Elbe, Budapest on the Danube had an extremely limited river traffic. The contrast with the Rhine was startling. The first day we were in the Hungarian capital we saw absolutely no movement on the river in either direction. The only excitement was when a man caught a fish near the Liberty Bridge. Later we did see a few barges going to and fro, but they were as nothing compared to those on the Rhine. Since the Danube had been a major commercial artery of southeastern Europe for centuries, this was an extraordinary phenomenon. True, the iron curtain descends upon the river at the Austro-Hungarian border, whereas in former days the stream was open from its source to its mouth. This inevitably makes for a substantial reduction in traffic.

The Red masters of Hungary were trying to make the people forget the bloodbath of 1956 and their ruthless crushing of the Hungarians' temporarily effective revolt. When we were there, Communist police were nowhere to be seen, nor were there any statues or publicly displayed pictures of Soviet leaders. Red banners and Communist slogans in the streets were conspicuous by their absence, although the eighth annual convention of the Hungarian Communist Party was in session. There were, however billboards advertising a "Chinese Circus," while "Chinese Tea" and "Peking Ink" were seen in store windows.

The apartment houses that were going up in many places in Budapest were a considerable cut above the dismal packing crates that are seen everywhere in Moscow. In Hungary there was somewhat less uniformity in the structures, and pastel shades were employed.

There is always a chance in the Communist countries that one will suddenly be surprised by something totally unexpected. Just as the orchestra in our Leningrad hotel astonished us by playing "Way Down Upon the Swanee River," the musicians in our Budapest hotel, the Gellert, startled us with the dulcet strains of "I Wonder Who's Kissing Her Now," a hit in the United States about the year 1910. In a restaurant the next night the orchestra played "The Glow Worm." In contrast to 1934, we heard no gypsy music, in earlier days so typical of the land of the Magyars. The food and service at the Gellert Hotel were excellent, in glaring contrast to that in Moscow and Leningrad, and the Tokay wine delightful.

Hungarian women were not wearing lipstick in 1962. It was apparently unobtainable. The lady who kept the hotel newsstand, where only Communist newspapers were available, leaned over to my wife and asked in a whisper, with eager anticipation, if she had a lipstick that she could spare. We went to our room, found a slightly used one and Doug gave it to her. She was one of the homeliest women I ever saw, and it was impossible to believe that lipstick would do much for her, but her gratitude was touching. One would have thought that we had presented her with a brand-new Moskvich automobile.

For the three nights that we were in Budapest the full moon hung like a lantern above the Danube outside our window. More than a quarter of a century had passed since we had walked along the river's magic strand, in the fragrance of May, past the crowded, brightly lit cafes with their gypsy violins and lovely women, and felt the intoxication of that enchanted evening. But now this once lighthearted metropolis had been turned into a place for workers and peasants, and looked the part.

Meanwhile, during the early and middle sixties Virginia and Richmond were integrating their schools, not willingly but peaceably. Virginia was the only state on the Atlantic seaboard from Massachusetts to Florida in which the National Guard did not have to be called out to quiet racial strife. It was a fact in which I took much pride.

Governor J. Lindsay Almond had stood in the breach when the going was toughest, and had managed by the slimmest of legislative margins to lead Virginia away from massive resistance and into an era where freedom of choice prevailed. The *Times-Dispatch* supported him in this vitally important battle. In Richmond the personal qualities of two men, H. I. Willett, city school superintendent, and Lewis F. Powell, Jr., school board chairman, made possible one of the smoothest transitions in the nation. They received significant aid from Booker T. Bradshaw, black vice-chairman of the board. I sought to back these men and their policies both personally and editorially, but what they achieved was due to their own courageous and public-spirited efforts.

In an article I wrote for the *Saturday Review* (February 24, 1964), entitled "Richmond's Quiet Revolution," I endeavored to put Richmond's remarkable accomplishments in perspective and call them to the attention of the magazine's readership. Both Arthur Krock and Holmes Alexander dealt with the article in their nationally syndicated columns. Krock pronounced Richmond, as I described it, "a model for every town, city and county in the United States." Alexander pointed out that as a result of the civilized behavior of both races in Richmond, the city had been "spared the violence and hatred that have visited other communities."

Some Richmonders felt that I had presented the situation in the city in a bit too roseate terms. I see now that they had a point, and that I should have included a paragraph or two stressing more than I did that there was much tension at times beneath the surface. While the facts that I cited with respect to the peaceable integration of schools, libraries, fire and police departments, theaters, restaurants and so on were correct, I created the impression, at least in some minds, that all this happened rather more smoothly than was actually the case. I certainly did not intend to mislead anyone.

The liberal Washington *Post* had published a prominently displayed feature article captioned "Richmond Quietly Leads Way in Race Relations," which was pretty good evidence that the city was handling its problems well. I said, correctly, in my magazine analysis that while Richmond's white leaders were "strongly opposed to wholesale integration . . . they have come to realize that certain changes are overdue," and I added that the city's black citizens, "using only legal methods and quiet pressure, have, in a few short years, gained many of their objectives."

The steady advance of integration in Virginia and other states, and the accompanying interracial trauma, led to efforts on the part of the almost defunct Ku Klux Klan to revive its moribund racket. The Klan had never made much headway in Virginia, and when it began trying once more to get a foothold in the Com-

monwealth, I wrote a number of editorials blasting the organization. Cross burning was a felony under Virginia law, except on
private property with permission of the owner, so the Kleagles and
Kludds were reduced to meeting in cow pastures and other such
places of rendezvous. Governor Mills E. Godwin, Jr., offered
$1,000 reward for the arrest and conviction of any Klansman who
violated these prohibitions. I backed the governor enthusiastically
in editorials, and my telephone began ringing after midnight and
into the early morning hours. Most of these anonymous heroes
would simply hang up when I sleepily took the receiver from the
hook, but there were occasional threats, such as "If you write any
more of those editorials, we will not be responsible for your
safety." I hope it is unnecessary to state that the editorials kept on
appearing. One of them, entitled "KKK Karpetbaggers," is published in full in the Appendix. It opened as follows:

"Virginia has been completely free for many years from the
affliction of the Ku Klux Klan, but this aggregation of krackpots,
klowns and kooks is apparently trying to get a foothold in the Old
Dominion, with a North Carolina karpetbagger leading the effort."

We were able during these years, and practically every year
thereafter, to take a brief trip outside the United States, usually to
Europe. In 1965 we visited Spain and Portugal for the first time.

Before our departure I was able to form a connection with the
North American Newspaper Alliance (NANA), and this enabled
me to obtain interviews then and later which otherwise I could
not have had. NANA had about 150 member newspapers, and the
possibility of reaching so large an audience appealed much more
strongly to a European statesman than an interview with a representative of one medium-sized paper, the *Times-Dispatch*.

Generalissimo Francisco Franco of Spain seemed a good prospect for an interview when I wrote our embassy at Madrid about it
some weeks in advance. The embassy replied that there seemed to
be no problem. But when I arrived Franco was otherwise occupied, and I never could get through to him.

However, we found much to interest us in Madrid and other
areas of Spain. Aside from the Prado Museum, the thing that

stood out above all others in or near Madrid was the Valley of the Fallen—in my opinion, the most moving war memorial in the world.

A five-hundred-foot-high cross stands on a rocky height in the geographical center of Spain, in tribute to the one million men and women who died on both sides in the bitter civil war of 1936–39. The rock that supports the cross also has a height of five hundred feet, so that the memorial is a thousand feet over-all, and is visible from great distances across the barren and stony countryside.

The simplicity and grandeur of this monument is overwhelming. It seems to blend with the austerity of the surrounding terrain, and to symbolize Spain's three-year agony. The cross and rock are so perfectly proportioned that we found it almost impossible to realize that their dimensions are so gigantic.

A huge basilica, the largest ever built, was constructed underground, beneath the monument and every bit of it had to be excavated, much of it through rock. Total length of the crypt, from the entrance to the transept, is an incredible 286 yards. The maximum height of the ceiling is about 43 yards. The crypt is simply yet forcefully designed and gives an impression of strength. The altar, hewn from a monolith of polished granite, is severe and unadorned, and upon it rests a wonderful crucifix, carved in ebony. The ensemble, both inside and out, is almost indescribable. Mere words are inadequate, and it must be seen to be fully appreciated. Every traveler to Spain should visit the Valley of the Fallen.

I have always found little to admire in Francisco Franco, but he must be credited with conceiving and executing this marvelous memorial to *all* who fell in the civil war. It had the effect of helping to bind up the dreadful wounds opened by that sanguinary confrontation, in which he commanded the victorious Fascist armies. It may well be, as has been charged, that Franco expected to be buried there himself. Certainly that is what happened when he died in 1975.

From Madrid we journeyed to Lisbon by bus, stopping overnight en route. Upon reaching our destination, I was able to obtain an interview with the Portuguese dictator, Prime Minister

Antonio Salazar. It was one of the few interviews that he had granted to a foreign journalist. The time was late October.

Salazar received my wife and me at his official residence, situated in the heart of Lisbon on nearly five acres of ground, the former home of a wealthy banker. It was a large and handsome structure, whose graveled walks wound past beds of bougainvillaea, geraniums, nasturtiums and chrysanthemums, with here and there a pool or fountain.

The Premier seemed vigorous for his seventy-six years, and responded alertly and promptly to my questions, through an interpreter. I daresay there never was a dictator who looked less like one than Salazar. A former professor at Coimbra University, he appeared not to have changed outwardly since leaving that lovely institution's cloistered halls many years before. He chuckled occasionally during our conversation, and throughout it had the manner of a genial grandfather. Conservatively dressed in a somewhat scruffy dark suit, he wore high black laced shoes, the contours of which proclaimed the presence of large bunions.

But if Premier Salazar looked unlike any despot that I had ever imagined, he was altogether firm in stating his position on public questions, notably with respect to Angola and Mozambique. Those African provinces were considered by him to be "a part of the mother country," and in no sense colonies. Consequently he regarded the term "colonialism" as completely inappropriate, insofar as Portugal's relation to these provinces was concerned.

Salazar also declared that he had no intention of letting the United Nations dictate Portuguese policy with respect to Angola and Mozambique. "The UN can pass all the resolutions it wishes to," said he. "It will have no effect whatever."

I asked him when we might expect him to grant freedom of the press in Portugal. "That's what the newspapers here want to know," he said, laughing. Of course he had no intention of doing so.

After the interview, which was officially termed an "audience," Dr. Salazar willingly posed for a couple of snapshots. Then he strolled with us in the beautiful sunny garden, amid the tinkling of fountains and the quacking of ducks.

We took our departure, and went to the Associated Press office to use a typewriter and produce my story. We then did some sight-seeing. On our return to our hotel, the Ritz—it was the only time in our lives that we felt sufficiently affluent, or reckless, to stay at a Ritz hotel—we found that Dr. Salazar had left two visiting cards for us. Whether he appeared at the hotel in person, or sent the cards by messenger as a courteous gesture, we never knew. In all likelihood, it was the latter. At Christmastime, about two months later, we again received two of his visiting cards, on one of which he sent "all good wishes" for the season, and added, "Thank you very much for your article." I had apparently quoted him accurately.

We saw our first bullfight in Madrid and another, of a different character, in Lisbon. It was a worthwhile experience in both places, but the orthodox Spanish bull-ring encounter was much too gory for us. The brutality with which the animal is tortured and then fatally stabbed made us never want to see another such event. One doesn't have to be a charter member of the Society for the Prevention of Cruelty to Animals to be revolted by this bloody spectacle.

In Portugal, on the other hand, the bull is not stabbed and mutilated, and he is never killed in the ring. In fact, he has a sporting chance to win, and sometimes does. We greatly preferred the Portuguese bullfight, with its skillful capework, its superb horsemanship and the truly remarkable example of raw courage on the part of eight youths who wrestled the charging animal with their bare hands.

This species of bullfight is considered completely unacceptable in Spain. The bull's horns are taped or sawed off in Portugal, so that he is much less likely to gore somebody to death than is the bull who snorts around the Spanish arena. In Spain, furthermore, the demise of the bull within twenty minutes, after the animal has been goaded to fury with stabs in his back and *banderillas* with fishhook barbs in his neck, is considered an absolutely essential part of the ritual. A Spanish matador who botches the job badly in failing to dispatch the beast within the prescribed time is subject to a fine, and even a jail term. By contrast, a Portuguese *espada* who kills the bull can be fined. Unfortunately, there is rising sentiment in Portugal for patterning its bullfights on those of Spain.

It cannot be gainsaid that a Spanish bullfight is in some ways a thrilling spectacle, especially if you enjoy seeing the sand stained with blood. Spine-tingling trumpets herald the various events, the crowd's excitement is contagious and the bravery of the cape-wielding matadors is admirable. They are frequently gored and sometimes killed. But there is also much about such bullfights that is far from pleasing. Indeed, some Spaniards are less than enchanted by these brutal spectacles, although for the vast majority they are part of the national mystique. One citizen of Madrid who did not care for them was our charming guide, Luisa Maria de Cuesta, who had served for a time as a teacher of Spanish language at Woodberry Forest School in Virginia. She took us to our one and only Spanish bullfight, but told us that she did not relish this particular variety of polite butchery.

On our return to the United States I wrote a magazine article in which I expressed a preference for the Portuguese bullfight over that of Spain. I explained my preference in much the same terms that have been outlined here. Immediately I was the recipient of indignant communiques from various parts of the country and the globe. It was deemed almost sacrilegious to cast aspersions on Spain's time-honored *corrida*. My article was termed "unfounded, slanderous and disgusting." One correspondent hinted darkly that he was acquainted with a Chicago disc jockey, and that I would know what to expect. Perhaps I missed something, but that was the last I heard of the disc jockey.

Sometimes a "fighting bull" in the ring at Madrid or Seville turns out to be another "Ferdinand," who isn't mad at anybody and merely wants to "smell the flowers," like the legendary animal in the tale. When on rare occasions such a bull appears in the *corrida*, right-thinking Spaniards regard his behavior as almost contrary to Holy Writ, and he is loudly hooted and jeered. I read about one such beast who, after much pulling and hauling, was finally gotten out of the ring with the aid of friendly cows. They were brought in and moved out through an exit. "Ferdinand" trotted off obediently behind them.

On one of our visits to France, we made a special pilgrimage to Omaha Beach on the coast of Normandy, where the first wave of the Allied invasion in June 1944 smashed through Hitler's supposedly invincible Atlantic Wall. Virginia units were in that wave, and sustained heavy casualties.

As we stood on the heights above the beach, where the Germans had been entrenched, the gentle swells of the English Channel beyond the narrow strip of sand gave no hint of the fury and thunder that had rained down from those heights more than two decades before. The Americans' landing craft had to pass through thickly planted mine fields and underwater obstructions offshore, in addition to the curtain of fire laid down from above. And the landings had to be made under almost point-blank range from German cannon, rockets and machine guns fired from concrete bunkers and other emplacements along the ridge. Many Americans were drowned; others were blown to pieces and disappeared. For some hours it was not known whether the invading force could maintain the precarious foothold it had managed to win.

On the plain above Omaha Beach one sees today the beautiful and vast American cemetery. My wife and I walked among the 9,385 graves, each with its white cross or Star of David in Carrara marble. Names of the more than 1,300 men whose bodies were never found are inscribed on a curving marble wall, flanking a lovely rose garden. At that end of the cemetery are also a colonnade and flower-bordered reflecting pool, with a bronze figure of heroic size representing the spirit of idealism and sacrifice of the American soldier. At the central axis of the cemetery is a small, tastefully designed chapel.

The assault on Hitler's Fortress Europe became more vivid when we visited the museum some miles up the beach at Arromanches, where the British invaded. It includes a diorama, as well as motion pictures of the actual event. The diorama is complete with sound, light and motion. It shows ships moving to shore, parachutists dropping at each end of the invasion belt, cannon booming and bombs exploding. The motion picture, taken by cameramen who risked their lives, shows the Allies hitting the beach, and some of them falling. All this made the assault extremely graphic for us.

Offshore, the massive concrete breakwaters, built under heavy fire, were still clearly visible. These were a part of the Mulberry installations, the artificial harbors which were a vital element in the assault. An idea of what these Mulberry projects involved can be glimpsed from the fact that 600,000 tons of concrete went into two of them, one off Arromanches and the other off Omaha Beach. All this and much more had to be towed across the English Channel at about four miles an hour before the invasion could take place. I shall never understand how so massive an operation could have been successfully completed, despite the supposed vigilance of the Germans.

Every American who has the opportunity should visit Omaha Beach as well as nearby St. Laurence Cemetery, with its acres of white crosses, and the Arromanches Museum. The ensemble produces an unforgettable emotional impact.

The following year in France we were made aware that members of the Resistance, or Underground, in World War II are more widely honored and memorialized than the nation's soldiers and airmen who participated in that conflict. This is hardly surprising, in view of the collapse of the military forces in the face of the German onslaught.

On the streets of Paris and other cities and towns one sees small tablets on walls, sometimes with faded flowers beneath. "*Ici tombé* . . . [Here fell . . .]" is the usual inscription, followed by the name, some words of tribute and the date when the person in question was shot by the Nazis.

We were greatly moved by these memorials, especially by one in Chartres to Jean Moulin, who organized the Resistance in that entire area, and was caught by the Gestapo and tortured to death. A large fist in stone, grasping a broken sword and standing amid ashes brought from the Nazi death camps, recalls the courage and sacrifice of this "Hero and Martyr."

Most striking of all these memorials to the daring men and

303

women of the Resistance, and others deported to the murder camps—two hundred thousand in all—is to be found well behind Notre Dame Cathedral on the Île de la Cité. We would never have known of this stunning tribute, if my sister Alice had not told us of it. Few visitors to Paris appear to realize that it exists, for the guide books either leave it out or fail to stress it, and the organized tours seldom include it.

One must walk down a flight of steps to see the memorial, situated as it is below ground, at the very edge of the island behind the cathedral. Hauntingly beautiful inscriptions by such writers as Saint-Exupéry, Sartre and Aragon give this monument a rare inspirational quality, and evoke in somber yet powerful words the fate of the hundreds of thousands of men, women and children of France who were deported and exterminated. Especially stirring is the Tomb of the Unknown *Déporté*, a simple black sarcophagus, seen down a long, dim corridor, simulating the barracks of a concentration camp, with a single light at the far end. It creates an illusion that is overpowering.

An interview with President Urho Kekkonen of Finland, one of the few granted by him during these years, was an interesting event of 1967. I was anxious to see and talk with Finland's able leader on or near the fiftieth anniversary of his country's achievement of independence from Russia, and to write for the North American Newspaper Alliance an article reflecting the accomplishments in the preceding half century of that courageous little democracy.

Kekkonen's remarkable success in piloting Finland during the difficult postwar years, and remaining on cordial terms with neighboring Soviet Russia without being forced into the Communist mold, had interested me greatly. The fact that the U.S.S.R. had not absorbed Finland after defeating her in the Winter War of 1939–40 and World War II was in itself extraordinary. Latvia, Lithuania and Estonia, the three nearby Baltic states, had been far less fortunate. I could only conclude that the Finns' heroic resistance to Russia, especially in the Winter War, had given the Soviets such respect for that recklessly brave people, that the

U.S.S.R. was reluctant to try and absorb or completely dominate them. Such an effort could well have brought more grief to the Russians than it was worth. A highly significant fact was that the Communist Finns battled the Red Army just as desperately as, if not more so than, anybody else in the Finnish fighting forces.

Kekkonen is a typical Finn in appearance, with high cheekbones and slightly slanted eyes. Tall, vigorous and well knit, he was accustomed at age sixty-seven, when I saw him in 1967, to run from three to five miles before breakfast, and to go on skiing marathons through Lapland, covering hundreds of miles. "That's the way a man ought to live," he told me. He had been national high-jumping champion in his youth, during the era when the great Paavo Nurmi was winning races in the Olympic Games.

Our interview took place at the presidential residence on a lake near the edge of Helsinki. I was dismayed at the outset when Mr. Kekkonen said that I could not quote him directly on anything. He was apparently uneasy for fear that I would misquote and embarrass him. Since he had never seen me before, this was understandable. However, after we had talked for fifteen or twenty minutes, I decided to try and persuade him to change his mind. I protested that an interview with no direct quotations at all would be almost unreadable, and posed certain questions that I felt he would like to answer concerning his relations with Russia. By that time I had apparently won his confidence, and he gave me permission to quote him as saying, for example, "The Communists have kept the agreement on which our government was formed," and "We can't see anything in the future that could cause any difficulties in Russo–Finnish relations." He also declared that world politics in the 1960s was at a stage where you can't judge all issues as black or white, all Communists as "bad guys" and all anti-Communists as "good guys."

I found during the conversation that Mr. Kekkonen had a sense of humor. For example, he laughed heartily when I mentioned that his critics sometimes referred to Finland as "Kekkoslovakia."

The interview did not produce any earth-shaking statements, but it helped greatly to fill out my article on the fiftieth anniversary of Finland's independence.

I have never been able to restrain my admiration for the Finnish Government and people. In addition to their incredibly brave resistance to Russia, at the cost of 85,000 lives, they paid every installment of their World War I debt to the United States—the only government that did so—and actually sent us one installment at the height of the Winter War.

With all this as background, it was a particularly memorable experience to visit Hietaniemi Cemetery in Helsinki, where roses were blooming on thousands of neatly trimmed graves of the young Finns who fell fighting the Russians from 1939 to 1945. Near the center, in an imposing tomb, lay the body of Marshal Carl Gustaf Mannerheim, who commanded the Finnish forces in those desperate encounters. Towering over all was a great cross, creating a panorama difficult to match anywhere.

A candle glowed on every soldier's grave on the night of December 6, 1967, in accordance with the poignant custom observed annually on Independence Day. Candles are also lighted there at Christmas, Easter and All Saints Day.

The quality that has made the Finns what they are is expressed in the Finnish word *sisu,* which in English may be roughly translated as "guts." The Finlanders have it in abundance.

13

Wherein I Retire But Stay Approximately As Busy As Ever

As I APPROACHED my sixty-fifth birthday, I began contemplating the prospect of retirement. Not that retirement would be compulsory at age sixty-five, for it would not, but the time had come for me to give thought to the problem of when I would leave the *Times-Dispatch,* and how I would occupy my time when I did so. It would necessarily be within a few years.

Inevitably, when I relinquished the editorial reins, I would continue to write, but what? Something in the nature of history or biography seemed indicated. The writing of fiction was and is an art and mystery of which I know absolutely nothing. A life of Richard Henry Lee, a highly significant but largely neglected figure in our revolutionary era, was a possibility. It would require much research in this country and England, and I was not at all sure that I could do such a book acceptably. I wondered if a biography of Harry F. Byrd would be a more suitable project.

Casting about for a subject, I sought advice from my friends John M. Jennings and William M. E. Rachal, the two extremely well-informed top executives at the Virginia Historical Society. Both declared that a one-volume history of Virginia was sorely needed, and recommended that I attempt it. Harper & Brothers had asked me to do such a book about a decade before, but it was impossible while I was editing the paper. Much earlier, when I was younger, I had been able to summon the energy to produce an occasional volume while performing my editorial duties—by working on weekends and at night—but I no longer possessed the stamina and drive to operate on so intensive a schedule.

The suggestion of John Jennings and Will Rachal that I write a history of the state was much on my mind when, by an extraordinary coincidence, a letter arrived from Doubleday & Company inviting me to do just that. Miss Sally Arteseros, a Doubleday editor, was the signer of the letter.

Her proposal tempted me greatly, but I did not see how, at my age, I could undertake a major piece of writing, such as this, along with my demanding editorial and other responsibilities. I suggested, therefore, that I would fix a definite date for retirement, three years in the future, do research on the Virginia history in my spare time during those years and begin the writing immediately upon resigning the editorship. Writing, for me, is far more exhausting than research. Miss Arteseros accepted this proposal, and the problem of when to retire and what to do after I did so had been solved. I signed a contract with Doubleday, and began reading and taking notes on the history of the Commonwealth.

I was also busy in other directions. The Current Events Class that Dr. Douglas S. Freeman had conducted for many years, until his death in 1953, had been continued under James J. Kilpatrick, editor of the *News Leader*, and myself. It was rechristened the Forum Club, and the membership was enlarged. Kilpatrick and I alternated in moderating the monthly programs and reviewing current happenings for the group. There was almost always another speaker, and it was up to us to make these arrangements for the meetings at which we presided. Kilpatrick discharged these functions until his resignation from the paper, and I stayed on until my retirement. Our editorial successors then took over.

Governor Mills E. Godwin, Jr., was moving effectively in 1966 to upgrade public education in Virginia, at the elementary, secondary and college levels. He decided to hold a state-wide conference in connection with his campaign, and asked me to aid in the arrangements and preside. I was only too happy to accept. Held on October 5, 1966, it was the largest such conference in Virginia history, and was regarded as highly successful. Governor Godwin inspired the audience, which filled the Mosque auditorium and spilled over into the mezzanine, with his address on behalf of better schools and colleges. Thomas C. Boushall, the nationally known banker, was responsible for a breakthrough that had far-reaching results. He urged that the state constitution be amended to permit the issuance of general obligation bonds for educational purposes. Inability to issue such bonds had hobbled the Commonwealth for decades, and Boushall's proposal, promptly endorsed by the governor, resulted ultimately in the desired constitutional amendment and much badly needed construction for educational and other objectives. The interest generated by this conference, which was attended by delegates from every part of Virginia, also had much to do with the subsequent enactment of a sales tax, which brought in hundreds of millions for education and other worthy causes. Thus the state's backwardness in such fields as welfare, health and schooling was substantially remedied, and its ranking drastically raised.

Creation of Virginia Commonwealth University (VCU) in Richmond was a related event. This combination of the Medical College of Virginia (MCV) and Richmond Professional Institute (RPI) was made a reality in 1968, pursuant to recommendations of a commission headed by Edward A. Wayne, president of Richmond's Federal Reserve Bank. It was universally assumed that Wayne would be VCU's first rector, or board chairman, but he declined to accept the position. I had been appointed a trustee of the university, and when Wayne said firmly that he could not take the rectorship under any conditions, I was asked to do so. I was carrying a considerable burden of work already in various directions, and would soon begin writing my Virginia history, in accordance with my contract. It was decidedly against my better judgment to become rector of VCU, but I consented.

In addition to the fact that, as rector, I had to preside over the merger of two totally contrasting institutions, the president of one of these accepted another post, and the president of the other suffered a physical breakdown. So we had to find an over-all president for the newly created university—with about 12,000 students —and at the same time appoint persons at both MCV and RPI to manage their respective affairs.

For the five months after my election as rector, and prior to my retirement as editor of the *Times-Dispatch*, I had a secretary—the same Mrs. McCarthy who had served in that post since 1934—and she was a great help in dealing with correspondence and all the other details that had to be taken care of. But when I cleaned out my desk at the newspaper in January 1969 and retired to my home on the edge of town, I lost the services of Helen McCarthy. People called me there on the telephone about every kind of problem—such as why little Willie wasn't admitted as a student, or why the elevators in the MCV hospital were so slow. Of course, I had no jurisdiction over any of this, since I was simply chairman of the trustees, and not charged with responsibility for administrative details. There was also considerable correspondence, and while I could call on the services of a secretary at the university downtown, it was six miles from my residence. This was a far cry from having secretarial assistance in the next room.

Although Edward A. Wayne had declined to accept the rectorship, he agreed to be a trustee and to serve as chairman of the search committee for a president of the newly created university. But at the height of this endeavor, he had a severe gall bladder attack and an operation. He was out for six weeks, and I had to take over the chairmanship of the search committee. The principal burden also fell on me to find persons to manage RPI and MCV.

By the late spring of 1969 all three positions had been filled, but I was in a state of near-collapse, and my digestive apparatus had sustained permanent damage. I told my colleagues on the board that I would have to go away at once for a complete rest before I cracked up, and that I could not possibly appear at the commencement exercises. Douglas and I accordingly drove to Hot Springs and put up at The Cascades. I slept for some twelve hours as a starter. For a day or two I was so tired that I scarcely felt like doing anything. Finally, when I was sufficiently rested, I got in some tennis, which was like a tonic. The combination of sleep and exercise enabled me to return to Richmond at the end of ten days.

But I was certain that the strain was such that I would have to resign as rector in the near future, and I so informed several trustees. Then, all of a sudden, a small group of black students at VCU issued a statement demanding that I be ousted, not only as rector but also from the board, as being "too conservative." No details were vouchsafed as to why I was thus categorized, but perhaps it had something to do with my having been editor of the *Times-Dispatch* during the era of massive resistance. At all events, the only black member of the VCU board, James E. Sheffield, now judge of the Richmond Circuit Court, came strongly to my defense in a statement to the press, and the student newspaper, the *Commonwealth Times*, did likewise. Governor Godwin espoused my cause. I had not the slightest intention of resigning *from the board* until my term was up, and said so.

However, my plan to step down *as rector* had to be delayed, as I did not wish to appear to be quitting that job under fire. A couple of months later I quietly relinquished the rectorship. Nothing further was heard of the ouster effort. Those were the days when undergraduates were acting up all over the United States, and one never knew what would happen next. We were constantly fearful that the riots and sit-downs that were breaking out in so many places would spread to the VCU campus, but they never did. I am still on the board, but when my current term expires in 1979, I shall be off it for good, under the rules, which require rotation. Service there has given me exceptional satisfaction.

In another area of education, a development of recent years has been the unionization of college professors and schoolteachers. The trend has been halted in Virginia, at least temporarily, but no one can say what the future holds. It is greatly to be hoped that the Old Dominion's professors and schoolteachers will not join unions, as they have done in various other areas. Teachers in some states have gone on strike for weeks and months, apparently heedless of the fact that educational opportunity was being curtailed for tens of thousands of children. The Virginia Education Association (VEA), which previously voted against having its members affiliate with organized labor, has recently reversed its stand by a two-to-one margin, and is doing its utmost to get the General Assembly to authorize unionization. When my long-time friend Dr. Robert F. Williams was the VEA's able executive secretary, he threw his great influence in opposition. Upon his retirement in 1973 a trend in the reverse direction set in, and the organization now endorses not only unionization but the right to strike. It is an alarming situation. Time was when schoolteachers and college professors were dedicated to their profession, almost like ministers of the gospel, and nothing would have been further from their thoughts than striking and leaving pupils without instruction for weeks and months. I can well imagine what my father, a professor for over half a century at low pay, would say on this subject if he were alive today.

The time had come in early 1969 for me to retire as editor of the *Times-Dispatch*, in accordance with the agreement I made with Doubleday, and to begin work in earnest on my Virginia history. My last day on the paper was January 4. A couple of weeks prior to that date three of my closest friends, Lewis F. Powell, Jr., J. Harvie Wilkinson, Jr., and George D. Gibson gave me a farewell dinner at the Commonwealth Club.

These three men had been my luncheon companions off and on for more than forty years. Among the ablest citizens of Virginia, their conversation was stimulating and their company agreeable. I always looked forward to those luncheons. For the past twenty or thirty years, two or three of us had met on an average of perhaps twice a month, and discussion of events of the day was invariably in order. Although Powell and Gibson were corporation lawyers and Wilkinson a bank president, they were by no means stereotyped in their thinking. Widely read in many fields, open-minded in their approach to public questions and often ahead of their contemporaries in their analyses of pressing problems, these three individuals were not only brilliant but provocative as well. The elevation of Lewis Powell to the United States Supreme Court—I wrote the first editorial anywhere urging that he be named to that tribunal—has, of course, deprived me of the pleasure of his company, except on rare occasions. I am happy that the other two are available, and we still lunch together fairly frequently.

Thirty-one persons attended the dinner they gave me, including Governor Godwin. George Gibson was toastmaster, and on such an occasion his quips and jests are original in the extreme. The governor spoke briefly, and in my response I expressed the hope that he could be kept in public life, since his record as the state's chief executive had been superlative. The dinner itself was truly superior, in keeping with the fact that one of the three wines was the memorable vintage Château Lafite Rothschild 1964. My warmest Richmond friends were there, as well as my son Heath, my two sons-in-law, Jim Watkinson and Alex Leverty, and my brother-in-law, Johnny Parker. It was for me an unforgettable occasion.

A number of my editorial colleagues in Virginia and the Carolinas commented on my retirement, Grover C. Hall, Jr., wrote a nationally syndicated column on the subject and I was interviewed at some length by the New York *Times*. While the comment was more favorable over-all than I deserved, a couple of editors viewed with concern the fact that I was no longer the "liberal" that I had been in earlier days. That was also the overriding thought in the *Times* interview. While I had undoubtedly become more conservative, when measured against the "liberals" of recent years, I never approved personally of massive resistance, as noted in a previous chapter.

It was pleasing to read Grover Hall's appraisal that I was "as Virginian as any Confederate statue along Richmond's magnificent Monument Avenue, for Virginians are more grossly a breed than citizens of any other state." That word "grossly" apparently was not intended to be complimentary, but the rest of Hall's piece was entirely too much so. And being typically "Virginian," if that is what I am, is something I am not ashamed of.

Richmond City Councilman Howard Carwile, an erratic individual who was then writing a column for the Richmond *Afro-American*, erupted there with an outburst captioned "A Gutless Reactionary," meaning me. Carwile was at that time in the good graces of the blacks, and had received their virtually solid support when he was elected to the council on what was approximately his tenth try. His tart reaction to my retirement contained the following typically Carwilian phraseology:

"Only a bumptious bootlicker or a fawning intellectual could pretend to see one consistent strand of honest liberalism in the life of Virginius Dabney, recently retired editor of the Richmond *Times-Dispatch*. His cringing, insipid, maulding [*sic*], shoddy editorials never failed to sicken my soul and agonize my brain. . . . Senile guts in the days of sunset have never been an inspiring substitute for a living backbone."

Not too long thereafter, the *Afro-American* tossed Carwile's column out of the paper, and he lost most of his black support. This was because he reversed his position on various issues dear to the hearts of the National Association for the Advancement of Colored People. This great "liberal" then proceeded to run against and defeat for re-election the first black elected to the Virginia House of Delegates since Reconstruction. But Carwile's political gyrations finally caught up with him, and he himself was defeated for re-election, with the aid of the black vote. Thus I, the "gutless reactionary," had the last laugh on this vociferous and pharisaical one-time champion of the Negro.

I had done enough research on my history of Virginia to begin writing the early chapters as soon as I retired from the paper. Heath's old room on the second floor of our house was fitted up as a place to do the work. Research was far from complete, but I was sufficiently well along to go full speed ahead with the writing. This I did daily between breakfast and luncheon, while doing reading and research in the evenings when nothing intervened. Three afternoons a week were set aside for tennis, and I made it a point to walk two miles on several of the other afternoons.

An invitation came at about this time to join a group of congenial spirits who met once a month for dinner, and then sat around until about ten o'clock discussing the nation and the world. There were nine of these elderly men, including myself, when I joined, and each was host once a year. We did not meet

in the summer. The others were J. Ambler Johnston, engineer and
Civil War authority; Carrington Williams, M.D., noted surgeon;
former Governor J. Lindsay Almond, who got Virginia out of the
massive resistance morass; Archibald G. Robertson, John T.
Wingo and Eppa Hunton IV, leading attorneys; Henry Taylor,
prominent retired contractor; and General Edwin Cox, nationally
known scientist and gentleman farmer.

Ambler Johnston died some years after I became affiliated with
the group. He had performed many services for the community,
and was much beloved. A unique contribution was his organization of a Prison Civil War Round Table at the Virginia State
Penitentiary. A group of inmates there, including some life-
termers, became deeply interested in the Civil War, and were genuine authorities on the subject. Ambler Johnston heard about
them. He accordingly organized a Civil War Round Table inside
the prison, similar to those composed of free citizens that he had
been addressing in many parts of the United States, and arranged
for speakers at periodic intervals. It gave the prisoners something
to look forward to, and study of the conflict helped to occupy
their time. One speaker wrote to ask when he should appear before the Prison Civil War Round Table. The reply was, "Come
any time; we'll be here."

The two youngest members of our supper group, those to
whom I was closest, died within a few months of each other.
Eppa Hunton IV, the immensely popular senior member of what
is perhaps the leading law firm in the Southeast, was killed in an
automobile accident in late 1976, and Edwin ("Pete") Cox, one
of the best-informed and best-liked men I ever knew, died of a
heart attack in early 1977. Their places in the group were taken by
retired Chief Justice Harold F. Snead of the Supreme Court of
Virginia and W. Moscoe Huntley, retired judge of the Richmond
Hustings Court.

Roland Banks, the fine Negro man who worked for my wife's
parents for a number of years until their deaths in 1956, and
then came with us, was much mystified by our supper group. He
couldn't understand a number of men getting together once a
month and not doing anything except talk.

315

"They don't do nothin', don't play poker or cards, just sits around and talks," said he. Banks shook his head sadly, unable to understand how anybody could spend time in so dull and fruitless a manner.

In the spring of 1968 my wife and I took a leisurely automobile trip through much of the Southeast, stopping at Charleston and Beaufort, South Carolina, Savannah, Athens and Gainesville, Georgia, and Winston-Salem, North Carolina. I had a speaking engagement at Brenau College, Gainesville, and this was the excuse for our journey.

It was April 4, and following my speech we moved from the auditorium to an adjacent parlor. At that point someone came up with the news that Martin Luther King, Jr., had been assassinated a few hours before in Memphis. We were all aghast, and the universal comment was that this was the worst thing that could have happened to race relations in the South and the nation. The dire results were not long in coming, for the blacks began rioting and setting fire to cities. Vast areas were reduced to cinders.

I have always had mixed emotions with respect to Martin Luther King, Jr. One can only admire a man who risked violent harm and even death to win long-denied rights for his race. But President Harry S. Truman, certainly a friend of the blacks, called him "a trouble-maker," and the similarly friendly Washington *Post* denounced him unsparingly for his utterly unfair attack on the United States concerning its policies in Vietnam.

Dr. King was also taken sharply to task by many black leaders, and the Associated Press declared, "Perhaps his greatest enemies were members of his own race, the black supremacists." Furthermore, his policy of nonviolence led frequently to violence. The Negro-owned newspaper the Norfolk *Journal & Guide* spoke with obvious irony of "the commotion that exploded in Chicago just last summer when Dr. King and his nonviolent corps moved in."

King was awarded the Nobel Peace Prize, and he gave his life in the cause of Negro progress. He was a courageous and eloquent spokesman for his people, and his fame will undoubtedly grow. Assassination does more than almost anything to achieve immortality for a public man. Already a new bridge in Richmond has been named for him, and there is a determined and rather ridiculous effort to make his birthday a state holiday, although he was not a Virginian, and neither Thomas Jefferson nor Patrick Henry has been accorded this honor. I confess that I have reservations concerning Dr. King's methods, but I am willing to concede that in making the ultimate sacrifice for his race's advancement, he deserves a large measure of renown.

The trip through the South in the balmy temperatures of late March and early April was delightfully relaxing. Unfortunately, the weather had been unduly chilly, and the blossoms were behind schedule. Hence the Middleton and Magnolia gardens near Charleston were not the gorgeous spectacles that had enthralled us in earlier years.

Whenever I am in Charleston I make it a point to visit the grave of James Louis Petigru in the churchyard of old St. Michael's. The epitaph on his grave is one of the treasures of our literature. Many inscriptions on tombs are preposterous in their verbosity and mawkishness, but that of Petigru is noble in its phrasing and unforgettable in its description of a man. Petigru, a prominent Charlestonian, was almost alone in that city, on the eve of the Civil War, in dissenting from the fiery secessionism of the hour. To fight against the frenzy that had gripped his fellow citizens took rare moral courage. But he stood firmly against the tide, and died at the height of the war, mourning the course that his beloved South had taken, but honored for the manner in which he stood by his convictions. Petigru's epitaph reads as follows:

JAMES LOUIS PETIGRU
Born at
Abbeville May 10th, 1789
Died at Charleston March 9th, 1863
JURIST, ORATOR, STATESMAN, PATRIOT
Future times will hardly know how great a life
This simple stone commemorates—
The tradition of his Eloquence, his
Wisdom and his Wit may fade:

But he lived for ends more durable than fame,
His Eloquence was the protection of the poor and wronged,
His Learning illuminated the principles of Law—
In the admiration of his Peers,
In the respect of his People,
In the affection of his Family
His was the highest place;
The just meed
Of his kindness and forbearance
His dignity and simplicity
His brilliant genius and unwearied industry
Unawed by Opinion
Unseduced by Flattery
Undismayed by Disaster,
He confronted Life with antique Courage
And Death with Christian Hope.

In the great Civil War
He withstood his People for his Country,
But his People did homage to the Man
Who held his conscience higher than their praise;
And his Country
Heaped honours on the grave of the Patriot
To whom, living,
His own righteous self-respect sufficed
Alike for Motive and Reward.

It is impossible to see how anyone could read those words without being inspired by them. They were written by William Henry Hurlburt, a Charleston native and friend of Petigru, who was a New York newspaperman and shared Petigru's views on slavery and secession. An exceptionally able journalist, some called him a genius, Hurlburt was editor of the New York *World* after the war. He wrote the electrifying final draft of the epitaph at the request of Petigru's daughter, Caroline Carson.

The sort of intellectual and moral integrity that led Petigru, in a highly charged emotional atmosphere, to stand alone for what he felt to be the honorable and patriotic course is rare in any age.

It is, of course, not necessary to agree with him to feel that, in strength of character, he set an example for us all.

When we reached Savannah, that city was a revelation, for the restoration of its downtown area was absolutely stunning. Savannah has shown the nation how to preserve its architectural heritage. Its "revolving fund" technique for promoting the acquisition and rehabilitation of dilapidated properties by private buyers has been widely copied. The twenty small squares in the center of town were subjected to this salutary treatment, with the astonishing result that downtown Savannah now is rivaling downtown Charleston as a nostalgia-provoking, flower-filled prototype of the Old South.

Involvement in matters historical, especially those relating to Virginia and the South, has always been one of my principal passions. Hence I have been more than pleased to serve for many years on the executive committee, or board of trustees, of the Virginia Historical Society, and as its president for three years (1969–72). I first became a member of the committee in 1942, but was under such pressure during World War II, with a limited editorial staff, that I resigned the following year. During that period the society was operating on an annual budget of around $12,000, and an endowment of $46,000. Its cramped offices were in the wartime home of Robert E. Lee at 707 East Franklin Street, and it was unable to do more than conduct a holding operation, serving as custodian for such manuscripts and other materials as came its way, while publishing the *Virginia Magazine of History and Biography*. I rejoined the executive committee in 1950, at which time the society was entering a new and much more prosperous era.

Mr. and Mrs. Alexander W. Weddell had been killed in a railroad wreck, and had left the society $950,000, along with Virginia House, the handsome sixteenth-century residence they had brought to this country from England and rebuilt in modified form in Windsor Farms. The Weddells' generous bequest made it possible for the society to move forward in many directions. It acquired Battle Abbey and built a commodious, fireproof annex to that classically designed structure on the Boulevard in Richmond's West End. With professionally trained, remarkably versatile John M. Jennings as director, the staff was enlarged, William M. E. Rachal was made editor of all publications, a series of scholarly books was issued under the society's imprint and the magazine came to be regarded as equal to any journal of its type in the United States.

Manuscripts flowed in from many directions, as old Virginia families found trunks of letters and other papers in their garrets, and it was also possible, at last, for the society to purchase such materials. The result has been that the organization has in its archives invaluable manuscripts from virtually all the great Virginians of the colonial, revolutionary and antebellum eras, and students and researchers from throughout this and other countries use its facilities constantly.

The Virginia Historical Society's collection of portraits is the largest assemblage of historical portraiture south of Washington. Its unrivaled assortment of bullet-torn battle flags, borne in practically all the major engagements of the Civil War, hang silently from its walls. I have found it intensely moving to gaze, for example, upon the banner of the First Virginia, most celebrated of all regiments of the Old Dominion, riddled with shot and shell in Pickett's immortal charge at the Battle of Gettysburg. Or to stand in the building's opposite wing before Hoffbauer's renowned murals, where one can almost hear the sound of bugles, the clatter of hoofs in one of Mosby's daring moonlight raids or the wild rebel yell of charging Confederates.

One of the strengths of the Virginia Historical Society lies in the fact that its executive committee is composed of both practicing historians and business and professional people who are deeply interested in history. In the former group might be mentioned Joseph C. Robert and James I. Robertson, Jr. In the latter category typical persons would be Langbourne M. Williams and the late Samuel M. Bemiss, B. Randolph Wellford, M.D., Eppa Hunton IV and Edwin Cox. And there is a third category—business or professional men who are, or were, also historians, such as Admiral Ernest M. Eller, C. Waller Barrett and the late Wyndham B. Blanton, M.D., David J. Mays and Lenoir Chambers.

Membership in the society is approximately 2,600, more than half of whom live outside of Virginia. This contrasts with the system followed by the Massachusetts Historical Society, for example, which has only a couple of hundred members, each of whom is carefully screened and elected as a particular honor.

It happens that I have a special bond with the Virginia society, since my great-grandfather, James E. Heath, was one of its founders in 1831, and its first recording secretary. Upon the death of my mother in 1973, I inherited an excellent portrait of Heath, which I presented to the society. It hangs in the portrait gallery there.

The White House of the Confederacy was sorely in need of substantial funds in the late 1960s, and Robert H. Kline, a Richmond advertising and public relations specialist, suggested the sale of fine bone china plates bearing color reproductions of Confederate personalities and scenes. I had agreed to serve as co-chairman of the drive, along with Bruce Catton, the Civil War historian, and I told Bob Kline that he needed to have his head examined. He believed a million dollars could be raised through the sale of these plates, but I was sure that nothing like so much could be realized. The campaign got under way in 1970. Robert H. Kline Inc. had become Morrison & Kline, with the addition of William Morrison, and this organization conducted the appeal. By 1973 one million dollars net had been realized from the sale of the plates. I was more than happy to dine on crow.

Approach of the nation's bicentennial led to the organization in 1972 of the U. S. Bicentennial Society, the brainchild of Morrison & Kline. I agreed to serve as chairman of its trustees. One of our principal objectives was to issue and sell, in limited editions, finely crafted reproductions of historic swords, pistols and other objects having a direct relationship to the bicentennial, as well as to other periods of our country's early years.

Some persons argued that the nation's two hundredth birthday should not be commercialized in any way, and one cannot quarrel with those who held this view. However, it seemed to me that there was nothing improper about making available to collectors and others exquisite reproductions of historic and artistic objects. There was a deluge of cheap, tawdry stuff during the bicentennial —ashtrays, bath towels, balloons—of no historic or aesthetic merit, and these were rightly condemned. By contrast, several commentators specifically complimented the U. S. Bicentennial Society on the high quality of its products—among them John Chamberlain, the syndicated columnist, who applauded this activity of the private sector. Replying to one of our critics, I issued a statement saying, in part, "We felt that there was a need for an organization sensitive to artistic and historic interests, which would issue objects of quality and sponsor events related to the bicentennial. It is true that the society is a private corporation, and we hope it will be profitable. Is this a sin? We should like to think that you would applaud the efforts of free enterprise to salute the nation's birthday in a spirit of patriotism, and in accord with the principles of a free economy."

George Washington's inaugural sword and his pair of handsome flintlock pistols were two of the objects reproduced by us for sale in limited editions. Wilkinson Sword of London made us their exclusive agents in this country. There was also the American Revolutionary Patriot Collection, twelve plates of the finest bone china, bearing color portraits of that number of revolutionary patriots. Also the Royal Copenhagen Colonial Coffee Service, with each piece commemorating a colonial patriot, and the Double Eagle Crystal Collection, bearing the striking double eagle created especially for the society. The original dueling pistols used in the Hamilton–Burr duel were also reproduced, with the concealed hair trigger that we discovered, and which was not previously known to exist. The sword worn by General Cornwallis at Yorktown is another object reproduced by us. In addition, there was the Young America Collection, six elegant bone china plates bearing reproductions in color of that number of Winslow Homer's greatest paintings. When President and Mrs. Richard Nixon toured the Middle East in 1974, they presented a set of these plates to their host in each of the five countries visited. They also gave one to Leonid Brezhnev of Russia. More recently, President Jimmy Carter gave sets of these plates to heads of state overseas.

A bicentennial volume, *The Patriots: The American Revolution Generation of Genius*, was edited by me and published by Atheneum under the society's imprint. A handsome book, it contained an exceptionally fine 20,000-word introductory essay by the internationally known historian Henry S. Commager, one of our trustees. There were full-page illustrations, many in color, of fifty revolutionary patriots, with brief sketches of each by such contributors as Samuel Eliot Morison, Bruce Catton, Alistair Cooke, Jenkin Lloyd Jones, James Thomas Flexner, Shelby Foote, Kingman Brewster, William F. Buckley, Jr., Michael DeBakey, Henry Cabot Lodge and Archie K. Davis. The *Atlantic Monthly* said that *The Patriots* "may well be the one Bicentennial book to have, if you're having only one."

The U. S. Bicentennial Society gave convincing proof that it was not interested solely in making a profit from the nation's two hundredth birthday when it donated $5,000 toward the underwriting of Morton Gould's composition created especially for the bicentennial entitled American Ballads.

Anticipating the decline of interest in the bicentennial after 1976, Robert H. Kline, president of our society (Morrison had left to accept a position in Washington), wisely decided to change the organization's name to U. S. Historical Society. It is continuing to reproduce the same kinds of objects that brought it an excellent reputation during the nation's birthday celebration.

Under the leadership of Erica Wilson, one of our trustees and a nationally recognized needlework authority, a quilting contest was organized in collaboration with *Good Housekeeping* magazine. Another significant activity was the society's important work in helping to raise one million dollars in this country for the restoration of Canterbury Cathedral. A poll of history department heads in a hundred United States colleges and universities, asking them to rank the Presidents of the United States in order of excellence, brought a large response and interesting results. They were carried nationally by United Press International, and analyzed by Dr. Henry S. Commager in a magazine article.

Publication of my *Virginia: The New Dominion* took place November 19, 1971, and the book turned out to be my first that remotely approached best-sellerdom. On the day that it went on sale at Miller & Rhoads in Richmond, five hundred copies were sold in the first few hours, which Doubleday's Virginia representative said was unprecedented hereabouts, as far as he knew. The first printing of 4,500 copies was sold out in a couple of weeks, and for two more weeks no copies were to be had. Finally, a second printing came through a week before Christmas, and this was snapped up. A third printing was ordered in February, and at this writing there have been seven printings, including paperback. The paperback has been, or is being, used in several Virginia institutions of higher learning as the basic text in Virginia history. A number of University of Virginia students who studied it have been good enough to tell me that they are enthusiastic over the book as a text.

With the five years of work on this volume at an end, I relaxed briefly, and then spent about three months writing a memoir of my father, for the children and grandchildren. It is something over one hundred typewritten pages, and is illustrated with photographs. Xeroxed copies were placed in the Alderman Library, the Virginia State Library and the Virginia Historical Society, and other copies were made for the family. I sought in this memoir to give a true picture of my father's remarkable personality and character. John Jennings of the Virginia Historical Society pronounced it the best thing I ever wrote.

When this task was completed, with the valuable advice and assistance of my wife and the John C. Parkers, I began researching my history of Richmond. Some of the material that I had uncovered during the Virginia project was more suitable for a book about the city, and I had accordingly filed it with this in view. But much the greater part of the Richmond story had to be researched from the beginning. As with the Virginia history, I wrote for three or four hours each morning six days a week, took an hour's nap after lunch, played tennis three afternoons, took a long walk most other afternoons and often did research in the evenings. Writing a book is for me a rigorous business, and I usually have to do each passage over at least three times.

The Richmond history was completed in three years, and appeared in the early fall of 1976. It had a second printing a couple of months after publication.

Six days on the Dalmatian coast of Yugoslavia were a highlight of our year in 1972. The sojourn was made doubly pleasant by our chance acquaintanceship with Dr. and Mrs. Samuel P. Hall of Oakland, California, who happened to be our agreeable fellow travelers. The cities of Split and Dubrovnik were especially fascinating. We stayed in Dubrovnik two extra days, the place was so exceptional, with its massive, medieval walls surrounding the old city. A week in Vienna was followed by four days in Salzburg at the Hotel Goldener Hirsch, as delightful a hostelry as we have ever enjoyed. The inn is several hundred years old, but altogether modern in its essential appurtenances, and the restaurant is superlative.

We went thence to Berchtesgaden to renew acquaintance with that Alpine town, and were shocked at the extent to which its quiet pastoral charm had been wrecked by the coming of "progress." Hotels and motels had gone up on every hand, and superhighways had been built through the region, with the result that thousands of tourists swarmed over the town and the adjacent countryside. The Watzmann, the most conspicuous Alpine peak in the vicinity, still towered over all, but we couldn't even find Berchtesgaden's attractive market square, with the quaint fountain in the middle, one of our favorite haunts in 1934.

I decided to mount the Kehlstein, Hitler's "Eagle's Nest." Doug does not like high places, so she went only halfway, whereas I took the bus to the top. It was October 20, and a blizzard descended. The magnificent view was completely obscured by the whirling snowflakes, and it seemed questionable whether we would be able to get down. After a couple of hours, the Germans finally got a snow plow and scraper into operation, and our path was cleared. Doug was about to be put out of the mountainside cafe where she was awaiting my return, for the place was closing. I arrived just in time to save her from being pushed out into the night.

It was noteworthy that whereas Hitler and the Nazis were to the forefront everywhere in Berchtesgaden in 1934, and the swastika was flying on all sides, there was an obvious and deliberate effort in 1972 to play down everything relating to Hitler. A diligent search resulted in the discovery of one lone postcard showing the wreck of his Alpine villa on the heights above. Otherwise it was as though the Nazi era had never existed.

I was fortunate to be chosen a delegate to the Society of the Cincinnati's Paris convention in 1974. Douglas and I flew over on Air France with the American delegation, at a special rate that was low enough to compensate for the expensive accommodations that we occupied at the Hotel Meurice, convention headquarters.

French Army officers had much to do with organizing the Society of the Cincinnati after the American Revolution, and their countrymen still regard the society as something special. We were entertained lavishly and escorted about Paris by motorcycle police, a novel experience, surely. A buffet luncheon at the Hotel de Ville, another at the French Senate, a tea, actually a cocktail party, at the residence of U. S. Ambassador Irwin, were highlights. One evening the delegates and their wives were entertained in the homes of French members. We were guests of the charming Baron and Baroness de Baulny in their apartment, along with Colonel and Mrs. A. Sidney Britt, Jr., of Savannah. There was a simple ceremony at the grave of Lafayette in Picpus Cemetery. The climactic event was dinner in the Galerie des Batailles in the Château de Versailles, while fountains played.

Many of the delegates went on a bus tour through Normandy and Brittany, and back to the city of Vendôme, where a new statue of General Rochambeau, of revolutionary fame, was placed on the pedestal from which the original had been carted off by the Germans in World War II. We had been to practically all the places on this itinerary, so we elected instead to spend a week on the island of Madeira. It was a wonderfully restful and pleasant time, especially since it was passed at Reid's Hotel. Reid's has been owned and operated by the same British family for generations, and has an atmosphere all its own. Most of the guests are Britons. We had a room with a balcony overlooking the sea from the cliff on which the hotel stands. Gardens lush with flowers the year-round girdle the hotel. It is one of the few caravanserais left in the world with distinctive characteristics and clientele. We returned from our stay there refreshed and rejuvenated.

Cruises marked the years 1973, 1975 and 1976. Our first was on board the *Royal Viking Sky* from Copenhagen along the coast of Norway all the way to the edge of the ice pack, only about six hundred miles from the North Pole. The ship was the finest we had ever been on, the accommodations and food superb. As on all cruises, I walked two miles a day around the deck, except when the weather made it impossible.

In 1975 we boarded the *Rotterdam* at Norfolk for our first Caribbean cruise. We liked it so well that we went to the Caribbean again the next year, on the *Statendam* out of Miami. All Caribbean jaunts seem to end with St. Thomas in the Virgin Islands, where $200 worth of duty-free goods can be brought to the United States, and where liquor prices are unusually low. Especially interesting on the second cruise was a visit to the Mayan ruins at Chichen Itza. The only way we could reach them was by means of a bus trip of 175 miles each way from the Mexican port of Playa del Carmen. These relics of a lost civilization were well worth the strain of the long bus ride. But we got no satisfactory answer to the riddle of how millions of Mayans, with a high level of civilization for that era, could have virtually disappeared in a short time. They seem to have been swallowed up hundreds of years ago in the dense jungles of Central America.

On our last day aboard the *Rotterdam* we were astonished to see several women passengers hugging and kissing Indonesian stewards good-bye in the dining room, in front of everyone. The stewards seemed considerably abashed by these fond adieus, and stood with their hands at their sides.

The following year on the *Statendam,* we saw no such wholesale osculation of Indonesian stewards, but our Indonesian dining-room waiter proceeded, to our amazement, to buss my wife lustily on the cheek when we told him good-bye. His farewell to me was altogether perfunctory.

During the summer of 1975 I was asked to take part in the oral history program being undertaken by Virginia Commonwealth University in collaboration with the University of North Carolina. This involved six sessions of two hours each in which I was asked questions by two VCU professors, with the entire series of conversations recorded on tape.

Daniel P. Jordan and William H. Turpin, of the history and journalism faculties, respectively, were my interlocutors. These bright young men had prepared themselves thoroughly, and few if any aspects of my career escaped their sharp-eyed scrutiny. They began their inquisition at a point well before I was born, and came down to the present day. The result was that they recorded what may well be a lot more than anybody will wish to know. When it was all over, and the transcript had been typed at Chapel Hill, Columbia University requested a copy for its files. The concept of oral history, recorded through interviews with living persons, originated at Columbia, with Allan Nevins as the prime mover.

Another event of 1975 in which I was involved was Charter Day at the College of William & Mary. As the bicentennial speaker of the occasion, I decided to attempt an answer to the derogatory allegations of Fawn Brodie and Gore Vidal concerning Thomas Jefferson and George Washington, respectively. Brodie's so-called intimate biography describes Jefferson as the father of a brood of mulatto children. Vidal's novel *Burr*, which the author terms "history, not invention," calls Washington incompetent, slow-witted, greedy and serpentine. Both volumes were choices of the Book-of-the-Month Club, which may go far to explain why so many people were deceived by them.

My speech on this subject was reprinted by the college and distributed widely. *Time* magazine devoted more than a column and a half to it, and the full text appeared in *Representative Ameri-*

can Speeches, 1974–1975, *Vital Speeches of the Day*, April 15, 1975, and the *Congressional Record*. I received a large volume of mail, nearly all of it favorable.

Fortunately, I was able to quote the three greatest living authorities on Jefferson—Dumas Malone, Julian P. Boyd and Merrill Peterson—as saying that Brodie's thesis was nonsense. Excellent reasons for this belief were cited, including admissions by two of Jefferson's nephews that they fathered the children in question. All of which failed to impress Mrs. Brodie, who blandly reiterated the whole charge in subsequent statements and articles, and even made the preposterous assertion, in commenting on the above-mentioned item in *Time*, that Jefferson's defenders were denying his "capacity for love."

A point belabored by Mrs. Brodie and her defenders was that her critics were "racists," since they denied that Jefferson fathered the mulattoes, but admitted that in his youth he tried to seduce the wife of his friend John Walker. I can testify with certainty concerning only myself, while morally sure that her charge is equally inapplicable to the other persons in question. The reason I conceded the correctness of the allegation as to Mrs. Walker was that, in the first place, Jefferson admitted it, and in the second, I wished to establish that we were not claiming that he was a plaster saint. What we were interested in were the facts, and facts establishing Jefferson's paternity of the children were nowhere to be found in Brodie's vulnerable thesis. Furthermore, Mrs. Brodie contended that in fathering them, Jefferson acquired a guilt complex which plagued him for the rest of his days, and this was "the unwritten and unadmitted tragedy of Jefferson's life." So, as described by her, his paternity of this brood of illegitimates affected his entire outlook thereafter. This spurious charge, and not "racism," explains why the leading Jeffersonians have been unwilling to accept her thesis. After studying the Master of Monticello throughout their careers, they have found no evidence that his life was shadowed by a guilt complex.

Comparatively little got into the public prints concerning Gore Vidal's caricature of George Washington, which he contended was based on Washington's own words and the observations of his contemporaries. Vidal's picture of the Father of His Country as devious, stupid and grasping may have impressed most intelligent persons as too ridiculous for serious discussion, but the book kept on selling. I was able to counter these absurd allegations with statements to the contrary from leading British and American historians. On both sides of the Atlantic they termed Washington the greatest man of the age.

Finally, in 1975 I began writing these reminiscences. They required less than two years for completion, since so much of the material was ready to hand in my scrapbooks, diaries, memoranda and clippings. Whereas much research had gone into my other books, this memoir called for relatively little, as so much of it came from the above-mentioned sources or from my recollection of events. Wherever possible I checked my remembrance against the written record.

14

The Press—
Yesterday, Today and
Tomorrow

CRITICISM OF THE PRESS during the past few years has exceeded anything in my experience. There were always those who said "You can't believe anything you read in the newspapers," but this sort of statement was heard only occasionally. Today there is an almost continuous barrage of such disparagement. Since I have devoted the greater part of my working years to journalism, this has caused me much concern. I shall list the criticisms and shortcomings of today's press at the outset, and then address myself to the positive side.

In using the term "the press" I include electronic journalism, of course. In fact, the adverse criticism is even more strident in the case of television than in that of the newspapers. And I also include leading elements of the periodical press.

However, in order to keep this problem in perspective, we must bear in mind that the press has been under fire for centuries, both in this country and abroad. Take, for example, the blistering lines of the English poet William Cowper (1782):

> *Thou fountain, at which drink the good and wise*
> *Thou ever-bubbling spring of endless lies . . .*

Or the somewhat ridiculous outburst by a character in one of Richard Brinsley Sheridan's plays at about the same time:

"The newspapers! Sir, they are the most villainous—licentious—abominable—infernal—not that I ever read them—no—I make it a rule never to look at a newspaper."

Thomas Jefferson, a militant advocate of a free press, wrote, nonetheless:

"A man who never looks into a newspaper is better informed than he who reads them, inasmuch as he who knows nothing is nearer the truth than he whose mind is filled with falsehoods and errors."

Other quotations could be cited to show that "scalawag newspapermen" and "ink-stained wretches" have been held in low esteem in certain quarters for a very long time.

It should be noted that newspapers are being criticized nowadays not only on charges of factual inaccuracy but on those of distorted emphasis, slanting of news and failure to be objectively fair. One seldom hears a defense of the press, except from those in its employ. I have been studying this phenomenon for the past decade, and the thing that stands out in my mind, after wading through a pile of books, articles and clippings on the subject, is that the profession has scarcely any defenders beyond its own ranks.

Since I have been out of active journalism for nine years, it is probable that statements critical of the press are more likely to be made in my presence now than when I was a reporter or editor. Certainly the amount of denunciation that has come to my ears in the recent past has far exceeded anything of the kind that I experienced previously.

I myself have become more critical of the press. This, I believe, is due to my realization that the public has more valid complaints than I was aware of, and also because the current mania for "investigative reporting" has led to obvious excesses. The Woodward–Bernstein ten-strike in the Watergate–Nixon scandal has raised up a horde of young reporters who seem to think that their mission in life is to expose some individual or organization.

I was the beneficiary of attentions from a couple of these hot-eyed young men a few years ago. They represented the now-defunct Richmond *Mercury*, an antiestablishment weekly, and they came at me as if I were some sort of miscreant who deserved to be unmasked before the world. Though my sins be as scarlet, there was in that instance nothing to warrant the suspicions of these callow inquisitors.

Or take the case of the book *The Final Days*, the Woodward–Bernstein sequel to *All the President's Men*. My grandson has quite properly termed this best-seller nothing less than "journalistic pornography," and many others have been revolted by the authors' brazen invasion of the Nixons' privacy and personal affairs. The "people's right to know," so often rightfully cited by the profession, does not extend to such areas as Mrs. Nixon's personal relationship with her husband, or to third-hand gossip concerning Richard Nixon's prayers to the Almighty or his supposed drinking habits. Direct quotations are put into the mouths of persons by Woodward and Bernstein without anything remotely resembling adequate authority, and the Nixon family is made to suffer needless humiliation and anguish. In fact, one wonders if this disgraceful performance was not a contributing cause of Mrs. Nixon's stroke.

But apparently anything goes with certain elements of the press where the Nixons are concerned. If the Washington newspaper corps had put one tenth the effort that it expended on the Nixon scandal into ferreting out the source of Lyndon Johnson's millions or exposing John F. Kennedy's extracurricular affairs with the ladies, the public would have been far better informed. Furthermore, Tom Wicker, the ultraliberal New York *Times* columnist, has written that what was done under Johnson and Kennedy to invade the civil liberties of dissident citizens was fully as inexcusable as anything done by Nixon's "White House plumbers."

Important elements of the periodical press are flagrantly guilty of sins against objectivity and fairness. This was brought forcefully and courageously to public notice by Harry Reasoner, the well-known TV commentator, at the height of the congressional inquiry into President Nixon's squalid misdeeds. Reasoner said over the ABC evening news on March 12, 1974, that he was far from being an admirer of Richard Nixon, but he went on:

"Having said that, I also have to say that I have had it with *Newsweek* and *Time* magazines and their unprofessional handling of the whole Watergate story. Week after week their lead stories on the subject have been more in the style of pejorative pamphleteering than objective journalism, and since they are highly visible and normally highly respected organs of our craft, they embarrass and discredit us all."

Referring to the issue of *Newsweek* then on the stands, Reasoner said, "I found more than thirty instances of phrases that any editor should automatically strike out. . . . Times change, but the principles of journalism should not."

This sort of slanted reporting of the Nixon administration was all too prevalent, and bothered me constantly. But President Nixon was not the only victim of this bias. President Gerald R. Ford, seeking re-election in 1976, suffered from some of the same treatment. For example, he was pictured over and over as a "stumble-bum" who banged his head on helicopter doors, fell down when getting off airplanes and so on—slip-ups that might happen to anybody. Furthermore, when he and Jimmy Carter debated on television, the questions from the reporters' panel were often flagrantly slanted against Ford. I was shocked by such partisanship.

"There was something very wrong with this campaign," Richard Reeves wrote in *New York* magazine, "and in the final analysis it was not them [the candidates] and it was not the American people; it was us, the press. . . . We were pompous and petty, overbearing and adolescent." Reeves also wrote, "I found out that antipress feeling was more intense than I had imagined—and I had started out thinking that it was probably pretty bad."

This lack of confidence in the printed media is shown in the polls. As long ago as 1939, radio was appraised in a *Fortune* magazine survey as far more believable than newspapers. More than one fourth of the readers queried felt that newspapers were either inaccurate or misleading. Current polls indicate that the public relies more heavily on television for news than on the papers, but both forms of communication are viewed with much skepticism. We have examined some of the reasons for this feeling on the part of the public. There are others.

Publication by certain journals of facts damaging to the national interest is one example. I was one of many startled and dismayed to find the names of the CIA's secret agents in various countries appearing in the public prints. This resulted in the assassination of one of them and the imperiling of numerous others. Yet one journalist indicated, in discussing this matter, that he didn't regard "the national interest" as of any importance, and said he would publish such names again, if opportunity offered.

The London *Daily Telegraph* took note of this attitude in an excellent editorial that said, "It's time America's friends spoke out with some nasty questions to . . . the press, sections of Congress, television commentators, comedians, university pundits and a lot of other people who think there is a dollar to be made out of denigrating their country's institutions and leaders."

George Gallup has been quoted as saying that he finds himself "at odds with most of the working journalists of today [who assume] that if it isn't bad news, it isn't news." Someone else pointed out that if a scientist somewhere issues an alarmist statement concerning the dangers of lethal accidents at nuclear power plants, this is given nation-wide coverage, but little interest is shown in publicizing the reassuring reply from perhaps a dozen or a hundred scientists. There is much truth in this.

Howard Flieger wrote recently in *U.S. News & World Report* that "people accuse journalists in all branches of communication of distorting, sensationalizing, personalizing the news, of concentrating on the trivial and ignoring the important in their eagerness for 'good copy.'" And Roscoe Drummond, the veteran columnist, wrote in 1974 apropos of failure on the part of the press to give adequate opportunity for the public to state its side of the case in the papers, "It seems to me nearly inevitable that the media will have the right to reply imposed upon them by law unless they voluntarily concede this right more equitably in practice." In fairness, it should be noted that the newspapers afford many more opportunities for reply than television, for on TV such opportunities are virtually nonexistent.

Many journalists are unaccountably prejudiced against the free enterprise system. "'Profit' is positively obscene," in the view of large numbers of them, according to John J. McGrath, a former newspaperman, now in public relations. Sixty-one per cent of college students polled by Louis Harris a few years ago thought the profit motive unnecessary. The printed and electronic media are regarded as responsible to a considerable degree for this attitude. The late Chet Huntley wrote in *The Wall Street Journal* after his retirement from broadcasting, "One general characteristic of the American press which seems inexplicable to me is the basic antipathy towards business and industry which I believe exists in our journalism." Walter Wriston, chairman of New York's Citibank, has accused the media of "incessantly accenting the negative that erodes optimism, one of the cornerstones of democracy."

It is incredible but true that certain reporters—a small minority —regard themselves as above the law, and advocate the use of illegal and dishonest means of getting news. At least one of a group of young western Massachusetts newsmen attending a conference concerning ethics and law in 1975 expressed the view that pretty much anything goes in digging out information. This man actually declared, "I would violate the law if the stakes were worthwhile."

"And what right do you have to do that?" asked Professor Charles Nesson of the Harvard law faculty. "Are you different from everybody else just because you're a reporter?"

"Yes," answered the newsman, "because I am the eyes and ears of the public."

"Who gave you the right to lie, steal and cheat to get a story?" asked Nesson.

"Sometimes it's necessary," said the reporter.

In the book *Investigative Reporting* by David Anderson and Peter Benjaminson (Indiana University Press, 1976), the authors flatly declare that "many fundamental techniques of investigative reporting involve actions some would label dishonest, fraudulent, immoral and perhaps even illegal." Berl Falbaum, a journalism teacher, has written that "all the reporters with whom I have discussed this book have expressed disgust, chagrin, embarrassment and, most importantly, complete disagreement." This is encouraging, but the fact that such doctrine appears in a volume on investigative reporting, written by such reporters, is dismaying in the extreme. It helps to explain the low regard for journalism in many quarters today.

I myself had a disillusioning experience with a reporter from one of the nation's leading newspapers who was interviewing me some years ago. He spent twenty or thirty minutes questioning me on a variety of matters. Finally he brought up the race question, saying that this was not what he was primarily interested in, but that he would like my views on certain aspects of it. We talked about that for a time, and I was left with the distinct impression that race would be mentioned only slightly, if at all, in the published interview. But when it appeared, no other subject was referred to throughout the entire article. This was exactly the opposite of what I had been led to expect.

One of the most frequently heard criticisms of the American press is that the news is slanted, instead of being handled objectively. Stories that are ostensibly fair all too often contain the subtly injected biases of the writer. "Interpretative reporting" has its uses, when clearly labeled as such, and the reader understands what it is, but many persons are not sufficiently sophisticated to make the distinction between news and opinion. It is, of course, right and proper for opinions to be expressed in editorials and signed columns, but the news side of the paper should be above suspicion.

Another justifiable complaint against the papers revolves about what appears at times to be their belief that the First Amendment guaranteeing freedom of the press supersedes all other sections of the U. S. Constitution. It doesn't, of course. There is, for example, the right of a defendant to a fair trial, free from unfair and prejudicial reporting. And some reporters appear to believe that there is no such thing as an individual's right of privacy. U. S. Supreme Court Justice Louis D. Brandeis once termed the "right to be let alone . . . the most comprehensive of rights and the right most valued by civilized man."

When reporters use improper methods in getting stories, or write inaccurate or slanted copy, there is too great a disposition on the part of their superiors on the paper to defend them. Standing up for one's employee is admirable, within limits, but this is often carried to extremes. There is a tendency on the part of city editors or managing editors to leap to the defense of the reporter, and to assume that the complaining party is in the wrong. Granted that persons interviewed often welsh on what they have said, and claim that they were misquoted when they weren't, there should be a more open-minded effort on the part of news executives to recognize the valid grievances expressed by the public.

Inability of much of the press to take criticism has been noted in various quarters. Former U. S. Senator J. W. Fulbright, who has enjoyed highly favorable treatment from the media for the greater part of his career, nevertheless declared not long ago that when editors are criticized they go "into transports of outraged excitement, bleeding like hemophiliacs."

The decline of the New York *Times* as a reliable publication, and its steady slide to the left, is one of the disturbing trends of our era. The paper had its shortcomings in the early years of this century, says Oswald Garrison Villard in his provocative book *Some Newspapers and Newspaper-Men*. But though dull, the *Times*, I believe, was more objective and fair in that era than it is today. Too much "investigative reporting" by writers with a strong bias is one of its problems. When the far more readable *Herald Tribune* was murdered by the labor unions—one of the grievous events of recent decades—it left the *Times* with no New York competition in its particular journalistic sphere, since the *Daily News* appeals to an entirely different clientele.

The *Times* sometimes lets its prejudices show in its news coverage. For example, its feud with Mayor John Lindsay in 1972 led to strange and wonderful accounts of events involving the mayor, who was seeking the Democratic nomination for the presidency. Nicholas Pileggi addressed himself to this state of things in an article for *New York* magazine. He wrote:

"Where Long Island's *Newsday* recently reported LINDSAY WOWS THEM, the *Times*' version of the same story said '1,500 students at the University of Buffalo greeted the mayoral message with almost sullen silence.' When the Tampa *Tribune* headline read, LINDSAY DRAWS TAMPA THRONGS, the *Times* reporter in Tampa wrote in his fourteenth paragraph, 'The crowds at the parade shopping center were slim, by New York standards.'

" 'That was outrageous,' a [New York] *Daily News* reporter later told the *Times* writer. 'How can you call a huge Tampa crowd slim, by comparing it with New York? That was just wrong.' "

This sort of thing, unfortunately, is not an isolated phenomenon in the columns of the *Times*. And the irrational positions taken by its editorial page are often simply bewildering. For example, at the height of New York City's recent financial crisis, the *Times* opined cheerily that there should be higher taxes on business in the city. Such levies would not only have come close to wrecking the paper, but with businesses moving in wholesale lots to Connecticut and other states to escape the already staggering tax burden in Gotham, it would have just about ended New York's hopes for recovery.

Since I was a *Times* Watchtower Correspondent for nineteen years (1929–48), writing signed dispatches on conditions and trends in my area, and a fairly frequent contributor to its *Book Review* and *Magazine*, it pains me to witness the paper's decline. It is still the best newspaper in the world, all things considered, but it could be better.

There have been two especially significant attempts by outside agencies in the past several decades to appraise the shortcomings of the United States press and advance constructive solutions.

The first was that of the Commission on Freedom of the Press, headed by Robert M. Hutchins, then chancellor of the University of Chicago. The study was financed by *Time, Inc.* and the *Encyclopaedia Britannica.* Members of the commission were chosen by Dr. Hutchins, and unfortunately there was not a newspaperman among them.

Their report, A *Free and Responsible Press,* published in 1947, listed numerous criticisms of the newspapers, many of them valid, and recommended among other things that a new and independent agency be established "to appraise and report annually upon the performance of the press."

It also made the highly questionable, if not dangerous, proposal that the federal government attempt to compensate for the short-comings of the press by entering the news business. The government, said the commission, "should state its own case . . . supplement private sources of information and . . . propose standards for private emulation." Such naïve faith in the beneficent effect of governmental intervention in this area is astonishing.

Recommendations of the commission were received with hostility by the overwhelming preponderance of the nation's press. Nothing was done toward establishing the independent agency that was proposed. I, for one, am not convinced that this recommendation was practical. On the other hand, the media should have been more open-minded with respect to some of the commission's other suggestions and criticisms.

A further comprehensive effort to cope with this problem came in the early 1970s under the auspices of the Twentieth Century Fund. It appointed a task force to study the press, the majority of whom were affiliated with the media. The final report, published in 1973, recommended the establishment of a National News Council, with limited jurisdiction. Great Britain's Press Council, which monitors all the media in the United Kingdom, was deemed impractical for the United States, with its vast size and great diversity. Hence the Twentieth Century Fund's task force report, entitled *A Free and Responsive Press*, proposed that the council have responsibility for only the nation-wide wire services, the national weekly news magazines, national newspaper syndicates, national daily newspapers (New York *Times*, Los Angeles *Times*, Washington *Post* and *Wall Street Journal*) and nation-wide commercial and noncommercial broadcast networks.

A major problem has been the refusal of important elements of the press to co-operate by responding to complaints concerning their news articles. They are convinced that the creation of the council was dangerous and tended toward ultimate government intervention. For this and other reasons, the council has yet to demonstrate that it can survive. However, the British Press Council encountered similar indifference and hostility when it was established more than two decades ago; yet it is widely accepted in the United Kingdom today, and apparently is playing a useful role.

Frequent as are public criticisms of the newspapers, they are not so continuous and vehement as the almost uninterrupted blasts against television. I agree with many of these strictures.

More Americans than ever are watching "the tube." The average set is said to be turned on daily for an almost unbelievable six hours and eighteen minutes. A University of Washington child psychiatrist estimates that the average American youngster has seen 18,000 murders on TV by the time he or she is graduated from high school. This is widely believed to be partly responsible for the nation's appalling crime rate. It is difficult to see how this constant depiction of criminal acts could fail to influence impressionable minds.

The networks are piling up huge earnings, and can undoubtedly afford to provide better programs. Over the past five years profits from television and radio increased 192 per cent, as compared with 89 per cent for all corporations in this country, according to estimates made in 1977 by *U.S. News & World Report.*

Television is "chewing gum for the eyes," said Fred Allen, the witty radio performer, by which he meant to say that TV is not nourishing. The fact is that its news is fragmented and often slanted, while its crime shows and soap operas generally are geared to fourteen-year-old mentalities.

It is so much easier to look at a thirty-minute evening news program, with its graphic pictures and brief bulletins, than to read a newspaper, that many persons have come to rely increasingly on television for their half-baked understanding of current events. It is one of the principal reasons why evening newspapers are having a hard time surviving in many cities.

I always try to watch the thirty-minute evening news, although it consists of only about twenty-two minutes of news matter, mostly brief bulletins, while the rest is taken up with commercials. (The news program is more comprehensive in New

York, but hardly anywhere else.) The bulletins are usually less than a minute in length, so only the bare facts can be included. It is impossible, under the circumstances, to give perspective to events. Yet in 1976 an Alfred I. DuPont–Columbia University survey showed that the three major networks, as well as public television, were reducing the news content of their programs, overall, despite promises by the network presidents to increase news coverage.

Walter Cronkite of CBS, generally considered the dean of American broadcasters, is highly critical of the manner in which television news is compressed into brief bulletins, and of what he terms the "show-biz" style that is altering the character of news programs. He and David Brinkley of NBC have said that it is necessary to read newspapers to be well informed, and that watching the TV programs is not enough.

The enormous power of television makes improvement imperative. TV has drastically affected the American home, since it absorbs more than one third of the waking hours of those in the average household. The standards, or lack of them, set by it necessarily have a tremendous impact on the people of this country, their mores and their thought processes.

The liberal bias of nearly all the leading TV commentators has frequently been noted. One of those who has done so publicly is Craig R. Smith, a University of Virginia professor of speech communication and CBS news consultant in the last two presidential campaigns. "Everybody I meet in broadcasting is a liberal," Smith declared. "How can viewers get an objective report from someone whose hair stands on end during an appearance by a candidate like Ronald Reagan?" He correctly termed television the most powerful institution in America.

It is their liberal bias that causes the networks to provide slanted documentaries concerning prominent public figures. For example, when Mao Tse-tung died, one would hardly have learned from television that this Chinese despot had murdered his fellow citizens by the millions. He was depicted as one of the great statesmen of the ages, a man who had accomplished marvels for his people and his country. Some of this last was true, but at what cost? This aspect of the matter was glossed over, if not ignored. Professor Richard L. Walker, who heads the University of South Carolina's Institute of International Relations, prepared a documented study for the Senate Internal Security Committee in which he estimated that Mao and his cohorts killed anywhere from 34 million to 64 million people. These figures may be too high, but the total of those slain was undoubtedly enormous. This aspect of Mao's blood-soaked career received scant notice in the newspapers and the periodical press.

The networks are prevailingly antibusiness; yet this antibusiness attitude is heavily underwritten, through advertising, by some of the nation's largest corporations. For example, the oil companies are leading TV advertisers, but they have been among the principal victims of misleading publicity on TV.

Lewis F. Powell, Jr., said, before he was appointed to the U. S. Supreme Court, "One of the bewildering paradoxes of our time is the extent to which the enterprise system tolerates, if not participates in, its own destruction."

The best defense that I have seen of electronic journalism was given by Eric Sevareid, the eminent CBS broadcaster, in the *Saturday Review* (October 2, 1976). He did not touch upon the leftward tilt of the networks, but made several telling points, among them the following:

Radio created an audience for music, including the best music, such as had never existed before, and television has increased book sales enormously. He also noted that TV is on the air from eighteen to twenty-four hours a day the year-round—something that no other medium of information or entertainment has ever attempted. "How many good new plays appear in the theaters of this country each year?" he asked. "How many fine new motion pictures? Add it all together and perhaps you could fill twenty evenings out of 365."

As an example of the cultural influence of television, Sevareid mentioned that after his first TV conversation with Eric Hoffer, "his books sold out in nearly every bookstore in America—the next day." Also, "at the end of a program with Hugo Black, we announced that if viewers wanted one of those little red copies of the Constitution, such as he had held in his hand, they had only to write us." There were 150,000 requests.

Sevareid conceded that there is excessive violence on TV, but he made the argument, "Don't lecture the networks . . . and then publish huge ads for the most violent motion pictures in town, ads for the most pornographic films and plays, as broadcasting does not."

Like Cronkite, Sevareid favors extending the evening news program to one hour in the country as a whole, but he adds, "It is not the supposedly huckster-minded monopolistic networks that prevent this; it is the local affiliates."

So much has been said earlier in this chapter concerning the shortcomings of the newspapers, and the shrill criticisms now being heard, that it is essential for us to consider the positive side. What's good about the papers, as they are operated today—there is much to be said here—and why should a young man or woman choose journalism as a career?

Let us remember that the press was recognized by the Founding Fathers as a pre-eminent guardian of our liberties. This is why they put into the First Amendment to the U. S. Constitution, "Congress shall make no law abridging the freedom of the press."

It is well known that when dictators seize power, one of their first steps is to muzzle the press. In the Virginia Declaration of Rights, the model for the Bill of Rights in the U. S. Constitution and those in the constitutions of all the states, George Mason wrote, "That the freedom of the press is one of the greatest bulwarks of liberty, and can never be restrained but by despotic governments." Thomas Jefferson, another pioneer in the field of civil liberties, declared, "Our liberty depends on freedom of the press, and that cannot be limited without being lost." Nikolai Lenin spoke for all despots when he said:

"Why should freedom of speech and freedom of the press be allowed? Why should a government which is doing what it believes to be right allow itself to be criticized? It would not allow opposition by lethal weapons. Ideas are much more fatal things than guns. Why should any man be allowed to buy a printing press and disseminate pernicious opinions calculated to embarrass the government?"

Such is the attitude of all enemies of democracy, as the men who founded the United States of America were well aware. And it cannot be emphasized too strongly that the Founding Fathers gave press freedom so high a priority because they knew that once it is abolished, other freedoms are almost certain to be eroded or crushed. Furthermore, they riveted this concept into the organic law *as a vitally important protection of the people and not of the newspapers.* Some of the statesmen who wrote our Constitution had been assailed unmercifully and outrageously in the press. They had no love for newspapers, as such, but they realized that an unfettered press was essential to the preservation of our dearly bought liberties.

There are manifest abuses of journalistic freedom in this country today, and they must not be ignored or glossed over. The public, furthermore, is doubtless tired of having the First Amendment thrown in its face on so many occasions, despite the lack of integrity shown by some newspapers and newspapermen. But with all its faults, the press is a bulwark of freedom, and an essential instrument for protecting "the people's right to know" what their government is doing.

Since it has been reliably estimated that at least five thousand separate facts are mentioned in the average modern newspaper, I sometimes wonder how the dailies manage to be as accurate as they are. The whole package has to be put together in a fairly short time, especially on afternoon papers, so that the opportunity for error in so monumental a deluge of facts is obviously great.

Let us take note of the many positive accomplishments of journalists. In his book *Newspaper Crusaders* (Whittlesley House, 1939), Silas Bent cites a great number of such achievements. In addition to numerous exposures of political corruption, he mentions "the fight against racial and religious intolerance, the integration of communities, the liberation of persons unjustly imprisoned, the rehabilitation of a city's reputation and fortune, the reduction of taxes and rates charged by public utilities, the improvement of working conditions . . . the reformation of state prisons and institutions for the insane." Incidentally, Bent states that during the 1930s, the Richmond *Times-Dispatch*, in its support of the Wagner–Van Nuys federal antilynching bill, "was the most active [of southern newspapers] and made itself most widely felt among Southerners."

A recent tragic example of the risks that newspapermen run in the course of their efforts to expose criminals and racketeers is seen in the fatal wounding of Don Bolles, reporter for the Arizona *Republic* of Phoenix. Bolles was horribly mangled by a bomb hidden in his automobile. He was investigating land fraud and its link with politicians and gangsters in Arizona. Other similar examples might be cited. Many editors and reporters have continued probing into the crooked doings of the underworld or of shady politicians, despite threats against their lives.

Consider the courage shown by the Anchorage, Alaska, *Daily News*, when this small paper, with less than 12,000 circulation, dug out the facts concerning the strangle hold of the teamsters union on the workers who were building the Alaska pipe line. Or the determination and ingenuity of the Des Moines *Register* in unmasking the bribery and corruption involved in the scandalous handling of this country's grain shipments abroad.

Scores of correspondents and cameramen have been killed or have disappeared on the battle fronts of the world while trying to bring to their papers or their broadcasting networks descriptions or pictures of actual conditions on the front lines. It requires even more courage for a civilian reporter or photographer to go where the bullets are whizzing and shells are bursting than for a soldier who is accustomed to being under fire.

Against the severe criticism leveled at newspaper coverage of the 1976 presidential election we have the contrasting opinion of James ("Scotty") Reston, the internationally known writer for the New York *Times*. He takes the view that reporting of that campaign was "better than any other since the last world war." I disagree. Reston also says that he regards today's newspaper reporting as distinctly superior to that which prevailed when he began his career several decades ago. "I believe we are looking at our communities with a much wider lens now, trying to get things in better perspective," he declares. Reston points out that when he began as a journalist, he reported what was on the police blotter, i.e., "what went on in the community the day before . . . largely the news of conflict and contention." This last impresses me as a fair and accurate appraisal.

John S. Knight, of the Knight–Ridder chain, one of the most intelligent and broad-minded of American newspaper publishers, refers to the superiority of today's papers over those of earlier generations. "Today's newspapers," he has written, "are infinitely superior in nearly all respects to the partisan, one-sided press of my father's time."

The glaring contrast between the U.S. press of the mid-nineteenth century and that of the late twentieth may be seen in the statement of Frank Luther Mott, the newspaper historian. Most papers in the earlier era were spokesmen for a political party, and there was "virtually no news of the opposition party," Mott says. And he goes on:

"A Jackson paper wouldn't print a speech by Henry Clay; not the text of it, not even a summary of it. . . . And the same thing can be said of the Clay papers."

Two examples of the kind of rank partisanship that characterized the party press in the late eighteenth and most of the nineteenth century will show the lengths to which those papers went. When George Washington completed his second term, the Philadelphia *Aurora*, the country's leading opposition paper, actually declared that the retiring President was "the cause of all the misfortunes of our country . . . every heart ought to beat high with exultation that the name of Washington from this day ceases to give currency to political iniquity and to legalize corruption."

Some sixty years later, when Abraham Lincoln and Stephen A. Douglas were holding their historic debates, Republican journals had Lincoln virtually destroying his opponent every time they met, whereas Democratic papers pictured Lincoln as "blanching under Douglas' onslaught," says Benjamin P. Thomas, one of Lincoln's biographers. "When Lincoln's friends carried him off the platform on their shoulders . . . opposition papers reported him too weak to walk."

When Adolph S. Ochs bought the bankrupt New York *Times* in 1896, he did much to lessen the prevailing one-sidedness of this country's press. Ochs decided to stress facts rather than opinions, and to eschew the blatant slanting of news that had characterized the papers for more than a century. The huge journalistic and financial success of the *Times* as a *news*paper necessarily had its impact, not only in New York but throughout the country.

I have found the career of Adolph Ochs fascinating. When I began as a reporter on the Richmond *News Leader* in 1922, I made it a point to read about him and the other great figures in journalism, both in New York and elsewhere. The elder James Gordon Bennett, who founded the New York *Herald* in 1835 and made it pre-eminent for that day in news-gathering, and Horace Greeley, who launched the *Tribune* six years later, were the foremost figures in Gotham's early journalistic annals. The historian Allan Nevins, a former newspaperman, said Bennett's "corps of correspondents, European and American, was unrivaled," while the *Tribune*, under Greeley, "set a new standard in American journalism by its combination of energy in news-gathering with good taste, high moral standards and intellectual appeal."

After the Civil War there were three other notable figures in New York who interested me especially. First came James Gordon Bennett, Jr., who took over where his father left off. He maintained the *Herald*'s reputation for superiority in getting the news by sending Henry M. Stanley to Africa in a successful search for David Livingston, and by performing other spectacular feats. Unfortunately, he ended by almost wrecking the paper with his endless succession of foibles and follies.

Next was Charles A. Dana of the New York *Sun*, who made that journal well written, bright and witty, though cynical and unpredictable, and caused it to be termed "the newspaperman's newspaper." Dana surrounded himself with a scintillating staff, and was a man of wide intellectual and aesthetic concerns. He would occasionally shock his admirers by supporting devious Tammany politicians. On one occasion he wrote an associate on the paper, "Your articles have stirred up the animals, which you as well as I recognize as one of the great ends of life." A notable bit of verse that expressed the admiration journalists felt for Dana, and was declaimed by them in the early days of my newspaper experience, was *The Man Who Worked With Dana on the New York* Sun.

Last but not least among Gotham's giants of the Fourth Estate, whose paper, the New York *World,* was always a favorite of mine, was Joseph Pulitzer. He came to this country as an immigrant from Hungary, managed in time to buy the St. Louis *Post-Dispatch,* with which he was highly successful, and then purchased the ailing New York *World.* That newspaper, under his masterful direction, was in the van of journalistic enterprise and editorial brilliance.

By his will he established the Columbia University School of Journalism and the Pulitzer Prizes. His sons failed to manage the *World* with their father's magic touch, and the paper declined gradually in revenue until, with the onset of the Great Depression, it was sold to the Scripps-Howard chain and vanished into the *World-Telegram.* When this great, crusading newspaper died, I felt as though I had lost one of my closest friends. Many other journalists were similarly grief-stricken.

Two southern editors of enduring fame have also interested me especially. They were Henry W. Grady of the Atlanta *Constitution* and Henry Watterson of the Louisville *Courier-Journal.* Grady and Watterson were the most celebrated southern journalists of the late nineteenth century.

Henry Grady was one of the enlightened young Southerners of the post-bellum years who sought to carry the region forward into a new era of intersectional amity, racial progress and industrial, agricultural and educational advancement. His first newspaper post was on a daily in Rome, Georgia, but he later acquired a one-fourth interest in the Atlanta *Constitution,* and it was there that his reputation, not only as editor but as orator, was made.

I was as impressed by Grady's public addresses as by his journalistic achievements. His orations were sensational in their impact. His address in 1886 on "The New South" to the New England

Society in New York, and that in 1889 on "The Race Problem in the South" to the Boston Merchants Association in Boston, made him virtually a national hero. But at the height of his fame, at age thirty-nine, when the country was ringing with his name, he came home from Boston to die. His untimely death was perhaps the greatest single tragedy that afflicted the South during the post-bellum years, with the exception of the assassination of Abraham Lincoln. The former Confederacy was struggling to recover from the devastation of war and Reconstruction, and Henry Grady's golden voice and able pen would have been enormously influential in helping to solve the region's extremely difficult problems.

Henry Watterson of the Louisville *Courier-Journal* had become a celebrity during the same postwar years that saw the climax of Grady's career. A Confederate veteran and typical goateed southern "colonel," Watterson lived until 1921, and retained the editorship of the *Courier-Journal* until shortly before his death. Writer of powerful, if verbose, editorials, a platform speaker of exceptional gifts, highly influential in the Democratic party and a colorful personality, "Marse Henry" was probably the best-known editor in America during the early years of the twentieth century. It made me envious to read that his editorial pronouncements received the rare accolade of being put frequently on the wire and sent all over the United States by the press associations.

Watterson had positive views on many subjects. Advocates of woman suffrage incurred his vehement wrath, and he termed them "Sillysallies" and "Crazyjanes." Prohibitionists, also among his pet abominations, were "red-nosed angels." Charged with failing to support certain Democratic candidates in his paper, Watterson retorted, "Things have come to a hell of a pass when a man can't wallop his own jackass!"

In the few years of his retirement, Marse Henry was relaxed and happy. Arthur Krock, his friend and confidant, reported that Watterson was wont to exclaim, as he sat amid his children and grandchildren, and looked back on his long and fruitful career, "I'm a free nigger at last, and will never be anything else, hallelujah!"

A balanced appraisal of the role of the *Courier-Journal* under

Watterson appears in one of the books on journalism that I have enjoyed most—Oswald Garrison Villard's *Some Newspapers and Newspaper-Men.* One must bear in mind while reading this volume that Villard, a grandson of William Lloyd Garrison, the abolitionist, was a pacifist, a Socialist, a prohibitionist and an idealist. These special characteristics color his estimates of Watterson and the other editors whom he discusses. But Villard is astonishingly well informed, and his book is highly rewarding.

One doesn't have to believe everything one reads in an antinewspaper tirade such as George Seldes' *Freedom of the Press,* published in 1935, to realize that there are aspects of the media that sorely need improving. There are rotten apples in every barrel, whether we are discussing newspapers, power companies, banks or labor unions. But it is possible to overemphasize the unfavorable side of the newspaper picture, as Seldes does, and thereby to create a largely erroneous impression.

Advertisers frequently manage to suppress news by exerting pressure on the paper's business office, according to Seldes. This undoubtedly happens, but how often? I believe the picture Seldes draws is greatly exaggerated, both for the time when it was written and even more for today.

For thirty-three years I was editor of the Richmond *Times-Dispatch* (1936–69). During that third of a century not one single advertiser approached me either directly or indirectly with a view to persuading me to alter my position on any issue in which the advertiser was involved. Unquestionably such efforts have been made in certain localities, but this is no longer true to the extent that it once was. For one thing, I am convinced that many advertisers realize that crude attempts to influence editors or publishers are often counterproductive.

Another statement by Seldes is that since the tobacco companies are big advertisers, "not more than ten per cent" of American newspapers carrying cigarette advertising will print an item critical of cigarette smoking. This is a serious overstatement. For example, it would be difficult to find a city anywhere in the world more dependent on cigarette manufacture than Richmond. Yet both Richmond papers have published regularly, in prominent positions, such critical declarations concerning the relation of cigarettes to health as have been issued by the U. S. Surgeon General and the American Cancer Society.

It also needs to be said concerning the Richmond papers that D. Tennant Bryan, their publisher, has insisted at all times that the news be printed, no matter who is involved. When relatives or friends of his have found themselves in embarrassing positions, and they would greatly have preferred that there be no publicity, their wishes have been disregarded.

Something approaching the ideal in guaranteeing a newspaper's independence may be said to have been reached in the case of the New York *World* under Joseph Pulitzer. Pulitzer made Frank Cobb, editor of the *World*, promise that if the paper's duty to its readers ever conflicted with Pulitzer's extensive investments, Cobb would disregard the investments. Most newspaper publishers have large financial interests in various directions. Hence one of the great obstacles to the operation of newspapers for the well-being of all the people, whether rich or poor, is that the average publisher experiences difficulty in maintaining a nonpartisan attitude where economic issues are involved.

One of the major complaints against newspapers, and it is well based, revolves about the fact that when a paper makes an error, it is often slow to print a correction. Furthermore, the correction seldom receives the prominence that was given the original item. Reacting to criticism, more and more papers are publishing corrections promptly and prominently. Some are also employing an ombudsman, i.e., a full-time employee charged with the duty of dealing with allegations of unfairness or inaccuracy. In some cases, the ombudsman is given free rein to criticize his own paper publicly in its columns. Greater prominence is also being given nowadays to letters from readers who take issue with the paper.

The increasing trend toward absorption of newspapers into chains is disturbing. Chains and conglomerates controlled 30 per cent of the nation's newspapers in 1960 with 46 per cent of the circulation. Today they own 59 per cent with 71 per cent of circulation.

There is also the unfortunate tendency of many papers to sub-stitute trashy "entertainment" for national and international news, in an effort to bolster falling readership and compete with television.

Although I have made some distressing observations concerning the undoubted shortcomings of newspapers, this should not dis-courage young men and women who have the proper determi-nation and zeal from entering the journalistic field. The above-mentioned criticisms are valid, but the balance is strongly in favor of a newspaper career for those who desire to pursue one. Today's excessive emphasis on investigative reporting will probably lessen ere long, and if it doesn't, those who enter the profession should attempt to bring this about. They should also strive to remedy the profession's other liabilities and deficiencies. It should be noted that women and blacks have a much better chance for employ-ment and advancement on newspapers than ever before, and this situation seems likely to improve still further.

Stanley Walker's book, *City Editor*, published in 1934, is perhaps the best analysis and exposition of the excitements of newspaper work. Walker, city editor of the New York *Herald Tribune* in its palmy days, was the most admired city editor in the United States. The city editor of a paper has charge of the local reportorial, rewrite and desk men.

"Jud" Evans, the highly original Richmond *Times-Dispatch* re-porter who was mentioned earlier in these pages, served a stint on the *Herald Tribune* under Walker. He wrote me that every item he turned in had to be written with as great care "as if it was to be chiseled on marble by Gutzon Borglum." Walker said in *City Editor* that "nothing can be too competently written for a news-paper." He resented the term "journalese" as "a sneering defense mechanism employed by windy professors. . . ."

No one should enter journalism unless he or she is consumed with a desire to do so, and is confident of being able to be one of the profession's better performers.

Roscoe Drummond, the columnist, has written concerning his newspaper career:

"I wouldn't change it for riches. I have found it exacting, exciting, exhilarating, rewarding and filled with satisfactions. . . . I've been at it for 44 years, and I can't wait to get to the office in the morning."

Since salaries on the news and editorial side of journalism are among the lowest in any profession, such a career should be pursued by only those persons with a substantial degree of dedication. Pay scales are higher in advertising and public relations, as well as on most college faculties. The problem of supporting a family and giving children a college education on a newspaper salary is a real one.

Yet the level of compensation on newspapers is much better today than it was in the early 1930s, when the Newspaper Guild was organized. At that time, the pay scale was outrageously low, and the guild performed a great service in forcing it up. I have never approved of the guild's affiliation with organized labor, for newspapermen should be objective in their reporting and commentaries, and they put themselves in an indefensible position when they join a labor union. At the same time, the Newspaper Guild, with all its faults and wrongheadedness, must be credited with compelling the publishers to provide something approaching adequate pay for their news and editorial employees.

Newspaper work is full of surprises, many of them pleasant and amusing, which helps to compensate for the lack of munificence in the salary department. Sir Philip Gibbs, the noted British reporter and correspondent in World War I, writes that on one occasion he was with a group of correspondents on a trip with King Edward VII through Scotland. The newspapermen were in the automobile immediately behind that of the King, and there was much speculation concerning their identity on the part of the crowds that lined the route. Finally one old farmer thought he had the answer.

"Eh mon," said he, as he stroked his beard, "they maun be the King's barstards."

With contagious enthusiasm, H. L. Mencken describes in his book *Newspaper Days* the joys and excitements that he experienced in the early years of the century as a reporter and news executive in Baltimore. In particular, he was deeply involved as city editor of the Baltimore *Herald* when the great Baltimore fire of 1904 broke out and raged for a solid week.

The first alarm reached him at his Hollins Street home at about 11:30 A.M. on February 7, and he relates that "it was not until 4 A.M. February 10 that my pants and shoes, or even my collar, came off again. And it was not until February 14 . . . that I got home for a bath and a change of linen."

Only a dedicated newspaperman could have endured such an ordeal and come out of it with even greater enthusiasm than when he went in. Mencken describes his early newspaper days as "the maddest, gladdest, damndest existence ever enjoyed by mortal youth." He relished "every minute of every day."

Those who are considering entering journalism should ask themselves whether they would have reacted similarly. If so, journalism is for them; if not, it probably isn't.

There are three principal phases of newspaper work—reporting and feature writing, copy editing and headline writing, and editorial writing.

The importance of copy editing and headline writing is perhaps not fully grasped by the average reader. The copy desk takes the raw material as received from the reporter or feature writer, tightens up the prose and corrects the spelling. Sometimes a rewrite man does the whole article over. A good copy editor can do much to improve the paper's quality. The same is true of a good caption writer, for a misleading headline can distort completely the meaning of the text beneath. I have had practically no experience in these phases of journalism.

Most of my newspaper years were passed in the writing of editorials. I greatly preferred it, as a career, to reporting, although I felt that reportorial experience was almost essential to good performance on the editorial page. I, of course, greatly enjoyed and profited from my early days as a reporter.

The editorial writer seeks to interpret and comment on events with a view to enabling the paper's readers to understand them. He should also endeavor to lead public opinion in the direction that he regards as in the public interest.

Henry Watterson once declared that the editor "should keep to the middle of the road, and well *in rear* of the moving columns." This is surprising advice with which I cannot agree. In fact, Marse Henry did not always follow it himself, for he was ahead of public opinion at times.

In an article "What's Wrong With Editorial Writing?" which I wrote at the request of the *Saturday Review,* and which appeared in that publication on February 24, 1945, I sought to explain why newspaper editorialists were being belabored and denounced from so many directions as reactionary, stuffy and largely unreadable. In a nutshell, I said that a prime reason was that most newspaper publishers are conservative businessmen, and many of them are not particularly well informed in the area of public affairs; that all too frequently, but with notable exceptions, they impose their views on their editors (it happened to me only very occasionally); that the great majority of publishers spend too little money on talent for producing the editorial pages, and that editorialists are often dull writers whose lucubrations concerning the passing scene are "flat, jejune and without sparkle." I expressed myself a bit more vehemently concerning these matters than I would today, in my mellow years, but I believe the thesis I set forth to be basically sound.

On another aspect of editorial writing, Tom Wallace, editor of the Louisville *Times,* once wrote, "Upon the honest editorial page in towns ranging from county seats upward; upon the honest editorial page, be it ever so humble, depends, more than any other single factor, the life of democracy." This is a pardonable bit of exaggeration, but it serves to bring sharply to our attention the basic importance of editorial writing. Any who desire to explore the subject further will find valuable insights in A. Gayle Waldrop's book *Editor and Editorial Writer.*

The statement is sometimes made that the era of "personal journalism" is over, and that we no longer think of great individual editors when we think of the papers on which they serve. It does appear to be true that no newspaper editor in this country today is as well known as the famous editors of years gone by. Papers nowadays tend to be anonymous corporations—or so it would seem. A century ago, or later, when a paper was a much smaller operation, one man pretty well dominated the scene, and it was much easier for him to become widely known. But in the recent past there have been editors of national stature, such as Erwin Canham, Hodding Carter, Harry Ashmore, Vermont Royster, Ralph Magill, James J. Kilpatrick and Jonathan Daniels. I discern no overriding reason why an editor, under existing conditions, cannot become nationally celebrated. Charles A. Dana expressed it well when he wrote, "Whenever in the newspaper profession a man rises up who is original, strong and bold enough to make his opinions a matter of consequence to the public, there will be personal journalism; and whenever newspapers are conducted only by commonplace individuals whose views are of no interest to the world and of no consequence to anybody, there will be nothing but impersonal journalism." Syndicated columnists did not exist in Dana's day, and they of course can readily achieve national reputations. But the door to fame is not closed to editors with ability, ideas and initiative.

Should a would-be journalist enroll in a school of journalism? There is much difference of opinion as to this, but the prevailing view, with which I concur, is that a course in one of the better schools is quite useful. Those schools not only instruct the student in the basics of newspaper work, but they also put strong emphasis on courses in the liberal arts—which is indeed essential to the best journalistic performance. The inferior schools are of no use whatever.

For more than a decade, enrollment in schools of journalism has gone steadily upward. Hence the difficulty of obtaining jobs on newspapers has increased, since too many graduates are applying for the available openings. Fortunately, enrollment in these schools seems to be leveling off. And the better schools of journalism are finding jobs on newspapers for most of their diploma recipients. For example, Virginia Commonwealth University in Richmond found places for all its 1977 newspaper graduates. However, locating openings on magazines is extremely difficult.

The best schools of journalism are turning out some well-trained prospects, but by no means all of their graduates have the needed qualifications. The quite appalling ineptitude shown by some of these in expressing themselves orally was touched upon recently by Angus McEachran of the Memphis *Commercial-Appeal* in the *Bulletin* of the American Society of Newspaper Editors. "Everything they say revolves around 'O.K.,' 'You know,' 'man,' and 'like,'" said he. And he elaborated:

"The following is drawn from a typical interview:

"Q. 'What makes you think you want to be a reporter?'

"A. 'O.K. Well, you know, man, ever since I was in the seventh grade, you know, I have loved writing, and like I think I have some talent. I like people, you know, and I like writing about them, O.K.?'

"Q. 'What books have you read recently outside of class assignments?'

"A. 'O.K., well, you know I have like everybody else read "Helter Skelter," which, man, you know I enjoyed very much. Then you know I read "All the President's Men." Like, man, I thought it probably overdramatized the job of reporters, you know, but like it was very well done.'

"When you run through more than 100 interviews in five days it gets a little wearing."

What is called "the new journalism" is an aspect of today's newspaper practice that should not be overlooked. Tom Wolfe, one of its ablest exponents, has written a book, *The New Journalism*, in which he sets forth its principal characteristics. A basic feature is that the reporter probes the subject in greater depth than is customary with the conventional type of newspaper story. To illustrate, Wolfe says:

"William Hazlitt is often mentioned as 'someone who was doing your "new" journalism 150 years ago,' and Exhibit A is his famous essay 'The Fight' concerning a bareknuckle prizefight between Bill Neate and the Gas-Man. What one finds in this piece is some vivid writing about the blows that were struck, the grimaces on the fighters' faces, and so on—and that is it. There is nothing that could not have been as easily observed . . . by any other Gentleman in the Grandstand, or in the crowd at ringside. . . . Hazlitt would have been too much of a gentleman, or too diffident, to do the sort of reporting that would have enabled him to bring the reader not merely inside the ring but inside the point of view of the fighters themselves, which is to say inside their lives—by following them through their training, going to their homes, talking to their children, their wives, their friends, as, for example, Gay Talese did in a story on Floyd Patterson. . . ."

In the new journalism, Wolfe goes on, the reporter "not only has to enter the bailiwick of the people he is writing about, he also becomes a slave to their schedules. [This] reporting can be tedious, messy, physically dirty, boring, dangerous even. . . ."

Such thorough probing has its undoubted merits, but the technique requires such vast amounts of time that it would seem to be better adapted to book or magazine writing than to the daily press. In my eleven years as a reporter I never found it possible to concentrate on a story in the round-the-clock-for-days-and-weeks-on-end manner described by Wolfe.

Newspaper training, whether of the old or new variety, is often a stepping stone to success in the book or magazine field. I have found it extremely helpful in my own case. The list of those who began in journalism and later became successful authors is a long one. Names that come readily to mind are Bruce Catton, W. J. Cash, William L. Shirer, John Gunther, Allan Nevins, Douglas S. Freeman, Barbara Tuchman and Clifford Dowdey.

In view of the enormous increase in the price of newsprint and other publishing costs, and competition from television, the question is being raised as to whether the newspaper can survive. The answer to this, I believe, is an unequivocal yes. True, it may survive in quite a different form from that which we now know, but certainly there will continue to be a demand for some sort of daily journal that can be read. The great advances made recently in the technical aspects of newspaper publishing, particularly in the field of electronics, make predictions hazardous as to the precise nature of tomorrow's newspaper. But there will be one; we may be sure of that.

And there will continue to be men and women who will not be happy except in pursuing newspaper careers. Reasons why this is so have been touched upon at some length in these pages, and are summarized in a statement by Ben Bagdikian, one of the most astute observers of journalism today. Bagdikian wrote concerning the satisfactions that flow from newspaper work:

"What never changes, is never overwhelmed or boring or taken for granted, is the learning of new things about life that continues all your days, and the fact that this never-ending voyage of discovery is your occupation. There are very few men and women in this world who can say that about their life work."

I find it impossible to improve on this description of journalism's joys, excitements and satisfactions.

15

L'Envoi

WILLIAM MCKINLEY WAS in the White House and Queen Victoria had been dead for only seventeen days when I was born in the first weeks of the twentieth century. More than three fourths of that century has now passed into history. I have witnessed two world wars, the Korean War and the war in Vietnam, not to mention the Russian Revolution, the Chinese revolution, the scientific revolution and the sexual revolution.

Empires have toppled, ancient dynasties have gone into oblivion, dozens of small independent countries have been created, the divorce rate has skyrocketed and men and women are living together without benefit of matrimony in a manner that would have scandalized our ancestors. Automobiles, airplanes, radio, television and antibiotics have been invented, abortions have been legalized and we have put men on the moon, but nobody has come up with a cure for the common cold. Racial segregation has been outlawed. Blatant and open obscenity in books, magazines, motion pictures and plays has reached heights, or depths, never conceived of in the past, and homosexuals are not only tolerated but are almost lionized in certain circles. "Chairmen" have been metamorphosed into "chairpersons," and there is even talk of women going into combat in the Army, Navy and Marine Corps.

The federal income tax, which did not exist until nearly a decade and a half after my natal year, 1901, now takes a whopping bite out of everybody's paycheck. Furthermore, the national debt is second only to the hydrogen bomb in its menacing dimensions.

It was just over $24 billion after World War I, but it is now approaching $800 billion, with no end in sight. The mere interest on this colossal debt is over $48 billion annually, and rising steadily.

An alarming aspect of American life is the widespread dishonesty, crookedness and cheating, and the "let's get ours while the getting is good" philosophy that seems to have taken possession of a large segment of this country's population. I have been deeply concerned with this trend for many years. The Watergate scandal and numerous other "ripoffs" are symptoms of a fundamental malaise.

This country is almost reminiscent of ancient Rome in the years of its decline. Our society is permeated with the rot of graft, thievery, apathy, immorality and cynicism. White-collar crime is rampant, and includes bribery, kickbacks, payoffs, embezzlement, pilferage, shoplifting and tax fraud. These offenses are increasing by about 10 per cent a year. As for violent crime, such as murder, rape, burglary, theft and aggravated assault, the rate has been astronomical for decades, until there are few, if any, more criminal countries on the globe than the United States.

Streets of many American cities are unsafe, even in the daytime. In the summer of 1976 my wife was mugged at 2:30 in the afternoon across the street from a busy Richmond shopping center. Three young blacks jerked away her pocketbook, knocking her down, dislocating her shoulder and causing her intense pain. The pocketbook, which was never found, contained valuable keys, licenses, charge plates, checks and considerable cash. Nobody was arrested. Such outrages occur practically every day in Richmond, often several times a day.

Confidence in our national government, from Congress to the White House, is at a low ebb. Not only Watergate but a whole series of other events in Washington have contributed to the skepticism with which our federal establishment is viewed. Congress looks the other way while a $13,000 salary raise for its members is put into effect; whereupon House Speaker "Tip" O'Neill says with a straight face that if only Congress had had a chance to vote, it would have beaten the raise overwhelmingly.

Flagrant dishonesty is rampant in most of our colleges and

universities. I have been convinced over a long period that cheating in school and college lies at the root of many of the evils that afflict our society. Young people get the habit of swindling their teachers, and as a consequence continue to swindle others in later life. And the lying and deception that has been a hallmark of "amateur" intercollegiate athletics for nearly half a century, with centers of higher learning and alumni groups conniving at violations of eligibility rules, cannot fail to undermine the integrity of those involved.

As long ago as 1940 I wrote a Richmond *Times-Dispatch* editorial captioned "Football—Wrecker of Honor Systems." It consumed practically the entire editorial space, and in it I gave chapter and verse on the manner in which young college athletes were signing untrue statements on their "honor" that they had never been paid for their "athletic skill or knowledge." I quoted a spokesman for the University of Chicago, which had just abandoned Big Ten football, as saying, "You can't play Big Ten football without being crooked, as far as the league's rules are concerned." At about the same time there were shocking revelations as to the widespread hiring of athletes in the Pacific Coast Conference. All this had occurred by 1939. A quarter of a century later, in 1965, Arthur Daley, prominent sports writer for the New York *Times*, blasted colleges and universities that teach young athletes "how to cheat, even before the kids have left high school." Almost simultaneously, Jesse Abramson wrote in the New York *Herald Tribune* that immorality "starts with colleges bidding for the blue-chip schoolboy athlete."

I followed up the above-mentioned editorial of nearly forty years ago with many others, dealing with cheating both in athletic and academic realms. In 1962 the U. S. Junior Chamber of Commerce launched a highly commendable nation-wide effort to curb cheating, with Richmond Jaycees taking the lead. I wrote two articles for national magazines in collaboration with the organization, and they were reprinted in several other publications. For a time it appeared that we might be making headway, but the whole thing seems to have had no tangible results. Cheating on both the high school and college levels apparently is as widespread as ever.

And the absurd scholastic requirements for athletes at some institutions are well illustrated in the prevalence of courses in physical education. A star pitcher at Virginia Polytechnic Institute and State University who was enrolled in such a course was quoted as telling the Richmond *News Leader* in the spring of 1977, "One of my classes started five weeks ago, and I've only been to it once."

Lack of parental control over children is a major cause of our current woes. Permissiveness is thriving on a grand scale, and boys and girls are left too largely to their own devices. Not only so, but the mother of a girl enrolled at one of the leading women's colleges in the East told me a few years ago that the chaplain there had said to the girls, "Tell your parents to go to hell." I was absolutely dumfounded. Some weeks later I asked the lady if I had understood her correctly. She said I certainly had, and that shortly after mentioning the matter to me, she had discovered that the chaplain at another eastern women's college had told the girls there the same thing. Now if religious leaders in colleges and universities are advising students in crude language to disregard their parents' instructions, how are children ever to be kept subject to parental discipline? Nor is respect for the clergy enhanced by such performances. It could be that these ecclesiastical attitudes—which, I must say, are unlike any with which I am personally acquainted—help to explain the writing in 1976 by a country singer of an almost sacrilegious song entitled "Dropkick Me Jesus (Through the Goal Posts of Life)." The song deals with a "lowly benchwarmer" who goes on to the big Super Bowl in the sky.

Such weird manifestations aside, there does appear to be ground for believing that Americans are becoming increasingly convinced of the importance of religion in their lives. Various religious leaders, both Protestant and Catholic, have expressed themselves recently as holding to this conviction. The trend contrasts with that of a few years ago, when the country seemed to be moving away from the church.

The proportion of Americans who feel that religion is increasing in influence has trebled since 1970, according to George Gallup, head of the American Institute of Public Opinion. A recent poll found that 31 per cent of adults in this country say they have experienced moments of sudden and dramatic "religious insight or awakening." This is an encouraging trend, and one that helps to counterbalance some of the other things that have been happening in the United States.

Another reason for rejoicing is to be found in the much more conservative attitude of the younger generation, especially those in college. A decade ago, during the Vietnam War, they were rioting, manhandling and spitting on deans, sitting down for days in the offices of university functionaries and otherwise indulging in mutiny and insubordination. Today, with occasional exceptions, they are behaving themselves about as well as collegians have been wont to do over the years. Gone are the arrogant demands, the shouted abuse.

Jamie Wyeth, the talented young artist and son of Andrew Wyeth, is one of those who has noted the sharp reversal in attitudes. "I'm constantly amazed at how extremism, which was so strong a few years ago, seems to have faded almost out of sight in this country now," he told *U.S. News & World Report* in the spring of 1977. "This is a much happier nation than it was in the 1960s, because we all seem to be more interested in getting along together again.

"Even some of my wildest young liberal friends, who were almost outside the bounds of society a few years ago . . . are working for change within the system, whereas they used to think our society had to be destroyed in order to make a clean start."

In fairness to today's youth, it should be said that even during the worst of the disorders in the 1960s, those young men and women were more idealistic and more socially conscious than the members of my own generation. In the days following the First World War, we youngsters were mainly preoccupied in looking out for our own interests and enjoying ourselves. It is to be doubted if such a thing as the Peace Corps could have gotten off the ground in that era. But half a century later much of young America was thinking in terms of how best to solve the problems of the poor, how to upgrade the Negro economically and educationally, how to promote a greater degree of social awareness on the part of business and industry. Many law students preferred to enter government service, rather than become attorneys for corporations. It appears that some of this high idealism has been receding of late, but a good deal remains.

In the realm of race relations, much progress has been made during the past two decades. We in the South were extraordinarily blind for many years to the injustices from which our Negro fellow citizens were suffering. It took the U. S. Supreme Court's landmark ruling of 1954 to provide a breakthrough, and to set in motion the forces that have corrected much of the unfairness. I believe that all American citizens are entitled to equality before the law, to equal opportunity and equal protection. This does not mean, however, that everything demanded nowadays on behalf of, or by, the blacks should be granted. For example, it is not even in their own best interests that unqualified blacks be admitted to educational institutions.

There is, furthermore, a vast deal of hypocrisy in the attitudes of leading white liberals who are making some of these demands. In the entire U. S. Congress in 1977 exactly one white congressman, Jenrette of South Carolina, was sending his child to a preponderantly black public school in the District of Columbia. Several score others were issuing pious statements advocating such a course, praising forced busing and denouncing those who failed to patronize the black schools of the district. Among them were Vice-President Walter Mondale and Senator Ted Kennedy, who had enrolled their children in private schools. A Washington reporter, Lawrence Feinberg, wrote, "There is no more articulate and uncompromising advocate of forced busing than a liberal with his child enrolled in a private school." And the Richmond *Times-Dispatch* commented, "Perhaps from his position of moral leadership as Vice-President, Mr. Mondale will one day explain why he does not want ordinary Americans to enjoy the privilege that his own family enjoys." In justice to President Carter, let it be noted that his daughter, Amy, is attending a public school in Washington.

While I rejoice that our black citizens are receiving far more equitable treatment than they were getting several decades ago, I cannot accept the current notion that all relations between the races in the early days of this century were bad, and are best forgotten. The fact is that there was often much warmth and affection in those relationships. Domestics who served in the same household for a generation or two were virtually like members of the family. Of course, they were in subordinate positions, they were not compensated adequately, and the desire of their descendants today to put that entire era out of their minds is understandable. But we who cherish the memory of those loyal and loving black men and women do not wish to forget.

In addition to the gratifying enhancement of our black citizens' status, there is cause for satisfaction in the fact that interfaith relations in this country have improved markedly. Protestants and Catholics are dwelling together in amity, and the virulent anti-Catholic prejudice that burst forth in the Hoover–Smith presidential campaign of 1928 was laid to rest long ago.

It would appear that anti-Semitism is also on the decline in the United States. Hitler's murder of six million Jews has had the opposite effect from that which he hoped to achieve, for it has created world-wide sympathy for this able and persecuted people. In addition, the National Conference of Christians and Jews has done much to allay anti-Semitism in this country. I have served on the board of its Richmond branch since 1946 in order to have a part in this activity. The organization operates quietly, usually without fanfare or publicity, and specializes in preventing interfaith conflicts before they occur. NCCJ's work in minimizing friction between Protestants, Catholics and Jews has been outstandingly successful.

I believe the South exhibits less interfaith and interracial prejudice than any other part of the United States. Once a stronghold of the Klan, it has risen in recent years above such narrowness and intolerance. In the field of race relations it is setting the pace for the nation. There is a consensus among militant blacks in the North and West that the South is making the soundest and quickest adjustment to the new dispensation, brought on by the Supreme Court's interracial decisions and by congressional enactments. For example, Ray Boone, vice-president of the *Afro-American* newspaper chain, said in 1977, "I believe the South will solve its race problems before the North largely because I know the Southern white man understands the problems of black people much more than Yankees." Many Negroes evidently agree with him, for instead of migrating northward and westward by the millions, as they were doing some decades ago, they are returning to the South. In the past few years there has been a net migration of Negroes into the land below the Potomac and the Ohio.

Forty years ago when the South was termed the nation's "Economic Problem No. 1" by an agency of the federal government, I joined the Southern and Virginia Policy committees in the hope of helping to remedy this deplorable situation. Today the region's economy is booming, along with its population. Per capita income has risen sharply, while the South's population achieved a net gain of more than five million persons between 1970 and 1975, more than the combined growth for the rest of this country, according to the U. S. Census Bureau. And whereas the northern states have appeared in all earlier tables with higher per capita incomes than the southern, Chicago's First National Bank recently published a survey which declares that when those incomes are adjusted for the cost of living in the two regions, and for state and local taxes, the South is seen to have a higher figure. For example, Alabama's adjusted per capita income in this table is $3,566 as against New York's $3,493. Thus it appears that the South will indeed "rise again," if it hasn't done so already.

There was once a wry saying that "southern hospitality has never extended to ideas." It had a measure of truth in past years, but not today. Dixie has become more open-minded, more cosmopolitan and is no longer culturally backward. When I wrote *Liberalism in the South* and *Below the Potomac*, back in the early thirties and forties, the southern literary renaissance was just getting up a substantial head of steam. Today the region's cultural revival is moving full speed ahead, and no informed person questions that the South's writers are as creative as those in any other part of the United States, perhaps more so. Similarly, the region has advanced spectacularly in the field of the arts. Mencken's scathing blast, "The Sahara of the Bozart," would make no sense nowadays.

True, "culture" is a rather nebulous term, and it embraces various facets of a region's life. Someone has defined culture amusingly as "anything we can do that monkeys can't." There are aspects of the South's cultural development, and the North's, for that matter, which are not resoundingly reassuring. Consider, by way of illustration, the fact that when Elvis Presley came to Richmond in 1976, about three thousand persons were waiting in line at the box office as the tickets went on sale, and some of them had been there since the previous day. The same thing could have happened—and probably has—in just about any other part of the United States.

Modern art is an aspect of culture that leaves many of us baffled and bewildered. Much fakery and humbug is involved, and numerous persons fear to express themselves forthrightly concerning this or that supposed "masterpiece," lest they be thought stupid or square. In his recent book *The Painted Word*, Tom Wolfe tells some hilarious truths concerning the spurious elements in modern art. Of course, this brought down on him the uninhibited wrath of the ultrasophisticates. A typical review of *The Painted Word* by one of these was that of John Russell in the New York *Times*, who declared, that "virtually every single sentence goes off the rails . . . most of the time . . . [Wolfe] doesn't know what he is talking about . . ." and "on the social level . . . Wolfe is still some way behind Molière, who died in 1673."

But Wolfe has a lot of intelligent people in his corner. Barbara Tuchman, the eminent historian, had dared some years previously (in the June 1967 *McCall's*) to denounce "the blob school, the all-black canvases, the paper cut-outs and soup tins and plastic hamburgers and pieces of old carpet" that are "treated as art, not only by dealers whose motives are understandable . . . not only by a gullible pseudo-cultural section of the public who are not interested in art but in being 'in' . . . but also, which I find mystifying, by the museums and critics."

And so the General Services Administration of our national government lays out $100,000 of your and my money in 1977 for a steel baseball bat weighing 40,000 pounds to ornament a federal building in Chicago!

Or consider the climactic masterpieces acquired by the Institute of Contemporary Art in London—a collection of soiled diapers, God help us, together with explicit pornographic photographs and instruments of flagellation. This truly memorable artistic display appeared in an institution that received an annual subsidy of $153,000 from the British Government, at a time when that government was teetering on the verge of bankruptcy.

I am by no means unsympathetic to all modern art. Some of it appeals to me strongly. For example, I consider Picasso's painting *Guernica* a powerful and moving depiction of one of Hitler's major atrocities, the bombing of a defenseless little Basque town by the Nazi Condor Legion. But when it comes to Picasso's ladies with three eyes and two noses, I draw the line. This artist left an estate officially valued at $250 million—an incomprehensible fact which others will have to explain.

In gratifying contrast to the unpatriotic riots and demonstrations by draft dodgers and their sympathizers during the Vietnam War, it appears that today in the United States we have a much more universal love of country. Then, young Americans were actually parading with the flag of North Vietnam, the Communist government that was torturing and killing Americans in faraway jungles beyond the Pacific. Such revolting spectacles are nowhere to be seen nowadays.

With many misgivings, we on the Richmond *Times-Dispatch* supported the Vietnamese war during most of that conflict, under the illusion that our President was telling us the truth. When we found that the facts were being grievously misrepresented, we stopped backing the war and urged that it be brought somehow to an honorable conclusion.

And with the fade-out of American youths cheering the reversals for American arms, a new and refreshing spirit has appeared. When the nation celebrated the two hundredth anniversary of the Declaration of Independence July 4, 1976, the "tall ships" in the Hudson River off New York, and television, seemed to bring the people of this country together. U. S. Senator Barry Goldwater was one of those who was greatly impressed. After witnessing the bi-centennial observance on TV, he remarked that "we're seeing a younger generation who knows that there's a lot of good about this country." He noted that during the Fourth of July observance "these kids that two or three years ago were tearing buildings down were out and cheering."

Yet Hollywood persists in producing films that are brazenly anti-American, and some of the stuff on television is equally slanted and misleading. "Left-wing twaddle" and "propagandistic rubbish" are the terms applied to this material by Tom Dowling of the Washington *Star*. He wrote not long ago that "Holly-wood's political activists are out there lounging around on the fashionable left side of the swimming pool and . . . they make bubble-headed movies explaining how this is a lousy country and it's going to get worse if we don't get rid of government." Dowling went on to describe the motion picture *Twilight's Last Gleaming* as "exactly the kind of heavy-handed propaganda movie Stalin might have commissioned had he been a Southern Califor-nia do-gooder."

I know of no better antidote to this sort of un-American drivel than the book *When Hell Was in Session*, by Rear Admiral Jeremiah A. Denton, Jr., a prisoner of war in the notorious "Hanoi Hilton" for more than seven years. The almost unbe-lievable courage and stamina with which he endured repeated tor-ture and long-continued starvation at the hands of the North Viet-namese Communists is an inspiration to all who read his grim story. When Captain Denton stepped off the plane that brought the first prisoners back from Vietnam, millions were watching on television. I choked up when I heard him say in a clear, strong voice:

"We are honored to have had the opportunity to serve our coun-try in difficult circumstances. We are profoundly grateful to our Commander in Chief and to our nation for this day. God bless America!"

Those words should go down in history as among the most in-spiring in our annals. And the bravery of Admiral Denton's lovely wife, Jane, in maintaining her morale during the long ordeal and never losing faith that someday her husband would return also deserves our fond remembrance.

On his retirement from the Navy, Admiral Denton accepted a position as assistant to the president of Spring Hill College, Mobile, Alabama. He is devoting much of his time to speaking and writing on behalf of traditional American values—patriotism, dedication and love of country. In addition, he has put together a remarkably effective organization called the Coalition for Decency, through which he is warring with the television networks on behalf of morality and the family. No better spokesman for these causes could be found.

Further inspiration is to be derived from the fortitude, endurance and patriotism shown by Commander Paul E. Galanti, a prisoner for seven years in Hanoi. Like Admiral Denton, Commander Galanti is an excellent speaker and writer, and in addresses and articles he rebuts the leftist propaganda that depicts the United States as an exploitive and second-rate society. "Every morning I wake up rarin' to go, and thank God that I'm an American," he wrote recently.

His charming wife, Phyllis, led the wives of the war prisoners in a weary round of petitions and appeals to the Hanoi Government for release of the men. She traveled to Stockholm and Paris in these efforts, and spunkily kept up her spirits. She and her husband live in Richmond, where their first child, a handsome boy, has been born.

The great Greek tragedian, Aeschylus, felt that, to prove his manhood, it was sufficient to say simply on his tomb that he had fought at Marathon. In like manner, it might be said that those Americans who resolutely endured the long years of loneliness, anguish and torture in Vietnamese prisons need no other evidence of their humanity and their devotion.

A naturalized American whose dedication and love of country is an example to his fellow citizens is Ernest M. Gunzburg of Richmond. A refugee from Nazi Germany in the 1930s, Gunzburg has spent much of his time and no little money in showing his gratitude for the opportunities that he has enjoyed in the United

States. He was with the U. S. Army in the D-day landing on Omaha Beach, June 6, 1944. "Appreciation of America Day," a ceremony on the steps of the Capitol in Richmond, was organized by him in 1976 as part of the bicentennial celebration. Always active in the annual naturalization ceremonies in Richmond, Gunzburg has helped to entertain the newly inducted citizens at luncheon on numerous occasions. In 1961 he organized a ceremony to express appreciation of the Jews for the courage shown by European gentiles in protecting them from Hitler's murder squads.

The patriotism exhibited by Ernest Gunzburg, Jeremiah Denton and Paul Galanti is reminiscent of Walt Whitman's lines in *Leaves of Grass*, a poem that Carl Sandburg said has "purpose, destiny, banners and beacon-fires":

> *And thou America*
> *Thy offspring towering e'er so high, yet higher Thee*
>   *above all towering.*
> *With Victory on the left and at thy right hand Law;*
> *Thou Union holding all, fusing, absorbing, tolerating all,*
> *Thee, ever thee, I sing.*

It is to be doubted if Walt Whitman was greatly concerned with whether world opinion was favorable to the United States when he wrote his famous poem. There is a large group of Americans who seem to think that this nation's vital interests should be sacrificed, rather than that world opinion should be offended.

Our government has been following this line for generations, and has handed out billions of dollars all over the globe; yet we are damned and reviled in both hemispheres. "Uncle Shylock" gets little or no thanks for all the aid that he has distributed gratis. The underdeveloped countries denounce him regularly in the United Nations.

I agree with those who say that the United States should not go overboard in trying to be loved, and that it should seek to cultivate a wider measure of respect.

When the Russians built the Berlin Wall, various pundits declared that they had made a terrible blunder, since world opinion would be turned against them. But the Soviets went right ahead, the wall grew more and more ominous and impregnable, and the brutality and suppression that it represents was, and is, obvious to all. What the rest of the world thought about it had no effect whatever on Russia's course of action, just as it had none when Soviet tanks crushed the Hungarians and the Czechoslovaks. The U.S.S.R. is more powerful today, and a greater threat to mankind than it has ever been. The government in Moscow looks out for its own national interests, and that is what the government in Washington should be doing. A reasonable concern for the rest of the world is all well and good, but putting world opinion ahead of everything is something else again. The British Empire under Queen Victoria, in the days of its greatest glory, won the *respect* of the world. Let's seek to do likewise and stop lying awake at night wondering whether the estimable burghers of Chad or Kamchatka are satisfied with our policies.

And now for some of my personal preferences, prejudices and shortcomings.

Greatly troubling me has been my lack of musical ability or appreciation. With a father and grandfather who were musically gifted, a half-uncle and aunt who were spectacularly endowed in this respect, a sister who displays both competence and understanding in the world of music, and several musically talented grandchildren, I fear that I come close to being what *Times-Dispatch* columnist Thomas Lomax Hunter called himself, "a musical moron." I revel in Strauss waltzes and such readily comprehended melodies as Schubert's "Serenade" and Chopin's "Funeral March," but the symphonies of Beethoven and the concertos of Bach are beyond my reach. This has long been among my major trials, for it cannot be doubted that one of the joys and opportunities of life has passed me by.

Fortunately I am more comprehending where literature is concerned. Reading has always been among my principal pleasures and diversions, and the great novelists, essayists, poets and historians have been my valued companions. Nonfiction rather than fiction has been my prime interest, since as a newspaper editor and amateur historian my concentration has necessarily been in that direction.

Literary appreciation and awareness adds a dimension to living, as should be obvious. The fact is perceptively noted by George Gissing in his classic but little-known autobiographical work, *The Private Papers of Henry Ryecroft*. "Why does it delight me to see the bat flitting at dusk before my window," asks Gissing, "or to hear the hoot of the owl when all the ways are dark? I might regard the bat with disgust, and the owl either with vague superstition or not heed it at all. But these have their place in the poet's world, and carry me above the idle present."

Dr. Samuel Johnson makes the same point: "There is as much difference between the lettered and the unlettered man as between the living and the dead. . . . Think merely how one's view of common things is affected by literary association. What were honey to me if I knew nothing of Hymettus and Hybla?"

One of the glories of our literature, the King James version of the Bible, has been mutilated almost beyond recognition by modern translators. They contend, and doubtless with reason, that in the King James Bible, the ancient Hebrew and Greek were not rendered into English with complete accuracy. But in attempting to correct this early seventeenth-century version of the Scriptures, they have virtually obliterated the majestic cadences and rolling rhythms that have made the King James as memorable as Shakespeare. At the same time, they have lowered the tone of the Bible approximately to that of street-corner conversation. It is a tragedy.

Also, it serves to illustrate the changing attitudes in our society. Another example of this is seen in the contents of the average novel today. Someone has said that a century or a half century ago, if a bedroom were involved in the plot of a novel, the story ended as the hero and heroine entered it. Nowadays, by contrast, the story begins in the bedroom and stays there. The result is that most modern novels are, for me, completely unreadable. I find them tedious and repetitious, with an obsessive concern for sexual relations, as though nothing else mattered, and language dealing with this subject that would almost make a bawdy-house operator blush. Yet some publishers are reliably reported to insist on at least one such scene in order to sell the book. It is a commentary on the taste of the reading public.

I occasionally read a French novel in the original, both for the pleasure it gives me and in order to maintain some familiarity with the language. A short time ago I read Henry Murger's *Scènes de la Vie de Bohème*, on which the opera *La Bohème* is based. It is a delightful account of artists and other Bohemians in the Latin Quarter of Paris, and their mistresses. These young men and women are quite obviously living together, and their amours, their adventures with landlords and other episodes of the Left Bank, as deliciously described by Murger, are amusing in the extreme. But the earthy details that permeate practically all modern novels *ad nauseam* are wholly absent. In other words, what I regard as good taste is observed throughout. In expressing such antediluvian sentiments I am aware that I am leaving myself open to the imputation of being totally out of tune with the best modern thinking, and a throwback to the nineteenth century.

As with the modern novel, today's legitimate theater and motion pictures serve to demonstrate the existence among us of drastically changed mores. Certain stage productions that have had long runs on Broadway would have been closed by the police as recently as two decades ago. As for the R- and X-rated motion pictures, they too would not have been tolerated in the 1950s.

On top of all else, blatantly pornographic publications are flourishing as never before. When vendors are arrested, the courts have a difficult time coping with the constitutional questions involved. But leaving all legal problems aside, the revolting character of these books and magazines is such that one finds it almost impossible to express one's disgust in words. This is especially true with respect to what is known as "kiddie porn," involving tens of thousands of children, beginning as early as age three. These boys and girls are bribed or coerced by degenerates and criminals into participating in sex acts of all kinds, natural and unnatural, some of which include animals.

Yet various judges and college professors have found that some of the most nauseating material of the "hard porn" publishers is "not obscene." I can only say that if it isn't, there is no such thing as obscenity. And everybody knows that there *is* such a thing, unless all standards of decency have been abandoned.

In expressing such dogmatic opinions I risk being called a person with a closed mind. I prefer to describe my posture as "holding to my convictions." The importance of maintaining an open mind is clear, and was impressed upon me as long ago as 1937 when I was attending a cocktail party at Harvard University.

Hugo Black had just been named to the U. S. Supreme Court, and had been revealed as a former member of the Ku Klux Klan. I took the position in conversation over martinis that this revelation should bar him from the bench. Professor Felix Frankfurter of the Harvard law faculty, who himself would be named soon to the court, argued that Black's former membership in the Klan ought not to bar him. It was sufficiently remarkable that Frankfurter, a Jew, was more forgiving of Black's one-time "klannishness" than I. In addition, events proved him right, since Mr. Justice Black became one of the ornaments of the nation's highest tribunal. During the conversation, Frankfurter and Professor Zachariah Chafee, another eminent member of the Harvard law faculty, were discussing whether Black had a closed mind on public questions. Black had been known as the most liberal member of Congress from the South. Frankfurter said to Chafee, "Zach, which do you think had the more fixed opinions when he went on the court, Hugo Black or John Marshall?" "John Marshall," replied Chafee. And he knew whereof he spoke, for Black became less liberal as the years passed, whereas Marshall never swerved from his conservative philosophy.

Occasionally I am asked whether in my retirement I miss the excitement of active journalism. The answer is that I don't. But this is because I have other things to occupy my mind, most particularly the writing of books. Were it not for that, I should greatly miss my one-time daily involvement with the march of events. But having spent forty-seven years on the Richmond papers, I was ready in 1969 to turn my attention to other things.

377

Writing for a newspaper has a certain impermanence about it, as noted long ago by others. "There is nothing as old as yesterday's newspaper" is a familiar saying. "Newspaper writing is like writing in the sand," said Dr. Douglas Freeman. Readers occasionally clip an article from the press that they like and put it in a scrapbook, but generally speaking the papers are thrown out each day with the garbage, or used to wrap fish or light the furnace.

Books, by contrast, are put together in more permanent form and are placed on shelves, where they may or may not be read. But they have a much better chance for survival than newspapers, which are fragile in the extreme, and largely inaccessible after the day of publication, except in the bound files of libraries. Hence the writing of books has an appeal that writing for the press cannot have. When one produces a book, one always hopes that it may contain material that is not wholly valueless, and that it will not simply gather dust on some remote shelf.

A most important contributing factor in my writing has always been the game of tennis. Had I not played regularly from about age ten down to date, I am sure that I would have produced less and of poorer quality. Nothing relaxes me or clears my mind as does tennis. Over the years when worried, harassed or tied in knots, I could relieve the tension with an hour or two on the courts. There is no therapy like it in the world. I banish all care from my mind, and think of nothing except hitting that ball. After three sets—only doubles nowadays, and no tournaments—I feel exuberant, ten or fifteen years younger, and renewed, mentally and physically. Since I am now seventy-seven, my tennis playing is regarded as something of a phenomenon in Richmond, and I am at times laughingly referred to as "King Gustav," the Swedish monarch who kept it up until age eighty-eight. I play three times a week in my retirement, on specific instructions from my doctor—it was formerly twice weekly—and frequently when I don't play, I walk two miles. But walking is far from being an adequate substitute; it doesn't leave me with the same sense of euphoria.

Speaking of walking, there was a prominent Methodist divine

in Richmond forty or fifty years ago, a prohibitionist and blue-nose, who was fond of telling the populace how to behave, with many "do's" and "don'ts," mostly the latter. He was opposed to almost every kind of activity on Sunday, however innocent. Somebody asked him what he felt was proper in the way of exercise on the Sabbath, and he replied, "You may walk briskly and with a purpose." I walk briskly, but my principal purpose is to get some fresh air and exercise.

Walking and tennis are helpful in keeping one's weight down. I weighed an even 200 pounds when we returned from an automobile trip to Canada's Gaspé Peninsula in 1946, but that was easily my all-time peak. I usually tipped the beam at around 190 during those years. About 1960 my doctor told me to lose fifteen pounds, which I did. My avoirdupois has been hovering for some time between 175 and 180, and I expect it to remain there. I am now six feet one inch, whereas in college I was six feet two and a quarter. The shrinkage is due, of course, to advancing age.

From the time when I joined the Richmond *News Leader* as a cub reporter in 1922 at age twenty-one, I was determined to remain in Virginia. I felt that the old Commonwealth was the place for me, the place where my forebears had lived and where I wished to stay. If I may offer a somewhat hackneyed comparison, like Antaeus, the legendary Libyan giant, whose strength was renewed when he touched the earth, I have drawn strength and inspiration from the soil of Virginia. Admittedly this is an old-fashioned viewpoint, reminiscent of earlier times when one's native state was exalted to much greater degree than is customary today. My great-grandfather's love of Virginia caused him to name his new-born son Virginius in 1835, as was noted in an earlier chapter. My father's devotion to his father resulted in my inheriting the name. Countless people have asked me how I happened to acquire it.

Being named Virginius involves a few problems, particularly in the area of spelling. The number of ways that Virginius can be misspelled is practically endless. I have a file that includes the following versions, all taken from letters addressed to me:

Virgina, Veretinius, Ziginius, Virgirnia, Virinius, Junius, Berginus, Virgenius, Verges, Virgininus, Vinginius, Virgna, Virginia, Viringuis, Virginios, Virginous, Viginius, Virginiuis, Rivinius, Virgirnis, Vurginius, Wirginius, Virginuis, Virgnus, Virniunius, Virgius, Virginias, Virginiua, Virg, Birgunius, Virgininius, Justinius, Mirginius, Reginos, Miss Virg, Miss Virginiu, Miss Virginia, Mrs. Virginia and Miss Virginius. There is so much uncertainty as to whether I am male or female that *Who's Who of American Women* forwarded the glad tidings in 1973 that I was being considered for inclusion in that estimable publication.

Furthermore, with a wife named Douglas, the confusion is almost endless. Which led Joseph Bryan III, in a clever rhymed Christmas greeting, to write:

> . . . *A mess of collards to the Fred Pollards,*
> *And cranberry sauce to Bonnie Ross!*
> *Good health to the Dabneys, Douglas and V!*
> *(D is the she and V is the he)* . . .

Back in 1901 when I was christened, my initials, V.D., were entirely respectable. But in more recent years they have become embarrassing and I no longer use them on handkerchiefs or cuff links. However, they are no more embarrassing than those of Winston Churchill or the late Virginia Congressman S. Otis Bland.

But let us return to my reasons for wishing to spend my life in Virginia. The people are one of the reasons, needless to say. Not all Virginians are charming, of course; in fact some of them are downright boorish and odious. But, on the whole, they strike a high average, and I am happy among them.

I make no defense of the "professional Virginian," that obnoxious and self-centered individual who finds nothing to criticize in the Commonwealth, and who spends much of his time knocking the inhabitants of all other states. Over the years, beginning with the article "Poor Old Virginia," which I wrote for the Baltimore *Evening Sun* in 1925 and to which earlier reference has been made, I have sought to point out the Old Dominion's weaknesses and to bring about constructive change.

Another reason why I prefer to live in Virginia is that its politics is probably the cleanest in the United States. The same may be said of Richmond's political climate; in Richmond's city hall graft and thievery are virtually unknown. There is rough and tumble "politicating" in Virginia, as elsewhere, for as the late Mayor Richard Daley of Chicago expressed it, "politics ain't beanbag." But the amount of crookedness is at an absolute minimum, and has been for generations.

There are some surprising points of view with respect to the most attractive aspects of life in the Old Dominion. J. St. George Bryan, among the state's great wits, once remarked, "Some people think the most enjoyable event that occurs in Virginia is a good old Virginia wedding. But give me a Virginia funeral, with the ladies crying upstairs into silk handkerchiefs and the men drinking good liquor in the basement."

The names of mountains, towns, counties, rivers and creeks in Virginia have a flavor all their own. Most of them have English or Indian derivations. Some, like Shenandoah and the Cumberlands, are musical; others, like the Mattaponi River, formed from the junction of the Matta, the Mat, the Po and the Ni, are quaint. Probably the most extraordinary names are borne by various creeks and rivers, such as Polecat, Toe Ink, Louse, Toots, Whiskey and Lickinghole creeks, Tin Pot Run and Stinking River. There is still a post office named Bumpass and another named Negro Foot, but Tightsqueeze changed its name to Fairview some years ago, to the dismay of thousands. It is to be doubted, however, if the Old Dominion can boast of place names as bizarre as Bug Tussle, Oklahoma, or 'T'ain't Much, Alabama.

My decision to remain in Virginia was made early, as previously noted. When I called on my former college-mate Reuben Maury, editorial writer for the New York *Daily News*, in the summer of 1926, I mentioned that I had just had an article accepted by the *American Mercury*. He was obviously surprised, and remarked, "Well, if you've had something accepted by the *Mercury* you certainly don't have to stay in Richmond."

But I *wanted* to stay in Richmond. A newspaper career there appealed to me far more strongly than one in New York, much as

I enjoyed being in New York briefly in those days. As a long-term proposition, I had never found the fleshpots of Gotham particularly tempting. Besides, too many young Southerners were being wooed away from their native habitat. This was a major reason why the South had fallen behind the rest of the country.

In 1928 I was interviewed by *Haldeman-Julius Monthly*, a long-since defunct publication. The interviewer wrote, "Virginius Dabney's reason for being in the Old Dominion is a very obvious one. It is that he is a part of it. I doubt that he could write anything that wouldn't betray him to be a Virginian. And when he debunks Virginia, he is more Virginian than ever."

This may have been intended as a compliment, although it is no secret that a fair number of people from other parts of this country regard Virginians as a supercilious and conceited lot, concerned mainly with their ancestors and looking down their noses at lesser breeds.

About forty years after the above-mentioned interview appeared I was standing at the registration desk of the Palace Hotel in Helsinki, Finland. I had just arrived and had uttered not more than half a dozen words to the clerk when a young man who was standing nearby turned to me and said, "Are you from Virginia?" He was a recent University of Virginia graduate from New York who had recognized my Virginia accent as soon as I opened my mouth.

A reviewer of my history of Richmond wrote in 1977 concerning the author of that opus, "With the possible exception of Robert E. Lee, he probably has a stronger feeling for Virginia than any other man raised south of the Potomac." I never expected to be mentioned in the same breath with General Lee, and the statement seems otherwise to be an exaggeration, but I'll not argue with anybody who accuses me of affection for Virginia.

That affection is felt by others and evidently transcends oceanic barriers, for on April 9, 1965, exactly one hundred years after Lee's surrender to Grant, the following advertisements appeared side by side on the front page of the London *Times*:

"ARMY OF NORTHERN VIRGINIA—In affectionate remembrance of

Robert Edward Lee, General CSA, and the brave men who surrendered with him at Appomattox Court House on April 9,
1865."

"In memory of those who stood at Appomattox—and those
who died before—9th April, 1865."

Many non-Virginians surrendered at Appomattox, of course,
but the accolade seems significant.

Which brings to mind the beautiful tribute paid Virginia's role
in the Civil War by another Englishman, Colonel G. F. R. Henderson, biographer of Stonewall Jackson. Colonel Henderson
wrote:

"Far and wide between the mountains and the sea stretches the
fair land of Virginia, for which Lee and Jackson and their soldiers,
one equal temper of heroic hearts, fought so well and unavail-
ingly. Yet her brows are bound with glory, the legacy of her lost
children; and her spotless name, uplifted by their victories and
manhood is high among the nations. Surely she must rest content,
knowing that so long as men turn to the records of history will
their deeds live, giving to all time one of the noblest examples of
unyielding courage and devotion the world has known."

I confess to being greatly moved by those words. Admittedly,
too, I have tried to aid in establishing historical priorities for Virginia, especially when our New England friends have made what I
regard as extravagant claims. Among these is their contention, advanced innumerable times down the years, that practically everything worthwhile in this country stems from the Pilgrim Fathers
and Massachusetts Bay.

Let us freely acknowledge that the *Mayflower*, which brought
the Pilgrims to Plymouth, and the more important, but little-
known, *Arbella*, which brought the Puritans to Massachusetts Bay
a decade later, were significant in American history. But one
would never know from reading the paeans of praise constantly
wafted aloft for these early New Englanders that Jamestown was
settled thirteen years before either of their colonizations began.
Or that the Jamestown colonists brought the English common
law to these shores; or that the first legislative assembly in the

New World met at Jamestown in 1619, the year before the *Mayflower* sailed from England.

The Puritans of Massachusetts Bay were pioneers in education, and in the development of the town meeting. They also set an example for future generations of fortitude and granitelike character. But their contribution has been vastly exaggerated. Consider the words of one of America's foremost historians, the late Charles M. Andrews of Yale University, a *Mayflower* descendant and winner of the Pulitzer Prize for his writings on the colonial era. In his book *The Fathers of New England*, Dr. Andrews wrote concerning the Pilgrims:

"Their intellectual and material poverty, lack of business enterprise, unfavorable situation and defenseless position in the eyes of the law rendered them almost a negative factor in the later life of New England. No great movement can be traced to their initiation, no great leader to birth within their borders, and no great work of art, literature or scholarship to those who belonged to this unpretending company. The Pilgrim Fathers stand rather as an emblem of virtue than a molding force in the life of the nation."

Andrews analyzed the contributions of both Plymouth Rock and Massachusetts Bay in an address to the Colonial Society of Massachusetts in 1932. This internationally recognized authority said:

"It has been customary . . . to extol the political and social principles of both Pilgrims and Puritans as of great significance, in that they anticipated the doctrines which were destined . . . to become the warp and woof of our American system of government. I doubt this. . . . Nowhere in their writings or applications of policy can we find any generalizations foreshadowing the ideals of the later American republic. . . . None of them would have subscribed to our American doctrines regarding church and state, popular government or religious freedom."

I have been unable to ascertain the nature of the reaction in Boston and its purlieus to these heretical statements. I wrote an article for the New York *Times Magazine* in 1957 calling Dr. Andrews' assertions to public notice, but the citizens of Back Bay appear to have paid little or no attention. Yet Dr. Andrews was not alone in expressing such views. Another celebrated American historian, James Truslow Adams, was writing in a similar vein at the period. But neither man seems to have changed the thinking of New England or the nation as to where the foundations of America were laid. Our country remains the "land of the Pilgrims' pride," not of the Jamestown settlers.

Both Virginia and Richmond are making important forward strides, culturally and economically, after a considerable period when they were clearly in the doldrums. Both are managing to retain much of their ancient charm as they move into the new age.

One of Richmond's chief attractions for me is the fact that all three of our children and their spouses have elected to live there, along with the ten grandchildren. This is good fortune beyond all reckoning. I know of few parents who enjoy such incredible luck. And as the climax of my blessings, there is the fact that I have had my lovely and forbearing wife for well over half a century.

As I conclude these reminiscences there come to mind the words of Sir William Osler, who once voiced a prayer that has appealed to me strongly. In it the noted British physician expressed the hope "that as the years go by, I may be able to bear success with humility, the affection of my friends without pride, and so when the day of weakness and sorrow comes, to meet it with the courage of a man."

I look back over my life of more than three quarters of a century, and it is obvious that I have lived in one of the most exciting eras in the history of the world. Wars and revolutions and popular uprisings have changed the map almost beyond recognition, long-submerged races and peoples are rising to influence and importance, scientific breakthroughs have carried man across new frontiers, and ideological and social upheavals have introduced lifestyles that contrast sharply with those that have gone before.

The closing years of the twentieth century and the opening years of the twenty-first can be among the most momentous and most splendid of all. Undoubted dangers confront us, but we have confronted dangers many times in the past. Russia looms ominously on the horizon, but exactly the same thing was said in the mid-nineteenth century. The West survived and went on to greater glories.

The days that are gone inspire us, but let us not be overly concerned with them. In the words of a philosopher whose name is unknown to me, "Take not from the past its ashes but its fires." The future beckons; let us be worthy of it.

Appendix

THE SELL-OUT TO HITLER

Richmond *Times-Dispatch*, September 20, 1938

THE year 1938 will mark the beginning of the end of the British Empire, the decline of France as a world power, and the rise of a German Empire far mightier than that of CHARLEMAGNE. Those are the fateful conclusions to which we have been driven by the events of yesterday in London and Paris, where the British and French governments capitulated ignominiously and completely to the demands of the Nazis, and set about the business of dismembering not only the last obstacle in HITLER's path to the Black Sea, but the last stronghold of freedom in the heart of Europe.

HITLER stands on the threshold of greater triumphs than he has yet known, and his contempt for the great democracies has been justified. With unerring prescience he divined that despite all their protestations and their proclamations, their conferences and their communiques, Britain and France would not fight, when the acid test came. Those who counted on them to meet the issue squarely have had to admit that HITLER knew his antagonists. With that same genius for making the right decision at the right time which has made possible his rise to power, the *Fuehrer* of what will soon be a Reich of 78,000,000 armed, disciplined and practically invincible Germans, has once more forced London and Paris to give way before his sword-rattling. It was the last call for them, and they failed to heed it. One finds it difficult to see how anything can stop Nazi Germany now. Central and Southeastern Europe are as good as gone, and thereafter it will again be "Berlin to Baghdad"—and beyond.

The shades of DRAKE and MARLBOROUGH, NELSON and WELLING-
TON must be wringing their hands in anguish at the spectacle which
the great empire they helped to build has made of itself. The English
boasted that the sun never set on that empire, but the empire's sun is
setting now. MAJOR GEORGE FIELDING ELIOT of the United States
Army Reserve, a recognized authority on military matters, wrote in
April of this year:

"Once Czechoslovakia has succumbed, the German outposts will
stand at the mouths of the Danube and the Dniester. . . . And this
means not only a vastly more powerful Germany, a Germany possessed of reserves of foodstuffs and minerals and above all of that essential of modern warfare, petroleum: it also means a German fleet in
the Black Sea; it means German pressure on Turkey and eventually on
Iraq and Persia; it means German accomplishment of the final objective of the *Drang nach Osten* policy, the acquisition of the short-line
to the Indian Ocean via Mosul and Baghdad to Basra; it means, in fine,
the end of British dominance in the Near East and within a measura-
ble period of time, in the Indian Ocean. It means, therefore, nothing
less than the destruction of the British Empire: or its preservation at
the price of a long, bloody war."

MAJOR ELIOT, it will be noted, thinks the empire *may* be saved, at
terrific cost. He is far from certain. But it seems fairly obvious that
the cost will be infinitely greater five or ten years from now than it
would be today, when Germany cannot stand a long war. Once the
Reich secures the resources of the old Austro-Hungarian Empire and
the Balkans, it will be the most formidable fighting machine the
world has ever seen. The Germany of 1914 held out for four years
against overwhelming odds. The Germany which CHAMBERLAIN and
DALADIER have now helped to bring into being will be vastly more
terrible.

Chamberlain's Difficult Decision

True, it was a tremendously difficult decision which the British and
French governments had to make. They were uncertain, in the first
place, of their own people. CHAMBERLAIN had to decide whether the
British would "go along" in a general European war, which on the
surface would be fought to save Czechoslovakia, even though the un-
derlying issues went far deeper than that. There was also the extremely serious question as to the dominions. They can stay out of
any war in which the mother country becomes involved. It was not
certain that they would go in this time.

Similarly, DALADIER knew that there is internal dissension in France, that the country's financial position is far from strong, and that, as in England, a large element is opposed to going to war over Czechoslovakia, or any questions growing out of that country's plight.

Russia, whose behavior has been decidedly enigmatic during the crisis, and from whom little has been heard, was not obligated to attack Germany, in the event of an invasion of Czechoslovakia, unless France did so. Besides, there was no assurance that Russian troops would be allowed to traverse Rumania in coming to Prague's aid, and the extent to which Russia has been weakened internally by the wholesale purges of the past year or two is unknown.

These and other factors had to be weighed carefully by MESSRS. CHAMBERLAIN and DALADIER and their colleagues. It was not an easy decision to make, but there is a grave question whether in the end, the decision they made will not be seen to have been the greatest blunder Britain and France have committed in modern times. If they had told HITLER flatly that they would not allow him to encroach upon the sovereignty of Prague in any way, and that his insistence upon such a course would mean war, the chances are that he would not have attacked. He knows that Germany today cannot stand a prolonged struggle with powers which can blockade his coasts and shut off his supply of food and raw materials.

Another reason why, in our opinion, he would not have attacked is that he could probably have achieved the gradual downfall of Czechoslovakia through economic and political pressure, albeit his victory would have been more gradual and less spectacular than it now turns out to be. As it is, he has forced both Britain and France to back down publicly before him, thereby enormously enhancing his prestige both inside and outside Germany, and correspondingly damaging the prestige not only of Britain and France, but of democracy as a form of government and a way of life.

This latest capitulation of the great democracies before the Fascists is the worst of a series. First there was the unhampered repudiation of the disarmament clauses of the Versailles Treaty by HITLER in March, 1935. A year later, HITLER sent the German Army into the Rhineland, and no one raised a finger to stop him. He was permitted to manhandle the minorities in the so-called Free City of Danzig, to insult the high commissioner of the League of Nations, and otherwise to defy Britain, France and the rest of the League. He seized Austria in March of this year, and now he will smash Czechoslovakia. All these things have been accomplished without the firing of a shot.

In 1935–36, MUSSOLINI likewise defied the same powers, when they tried to stop his seizure of Ethiopia. For a time it seemed as though collective action would be effective, and the League of Nations appeared to be functioning smoothly in the application of sanctions. But Britain backed down before the *Duce's* apparent determination to fight, and the League's effort turned out to be a dreadful fiasco.

On top of all this, a rebellion was staged against the Spanish government in July, 1936, with the active assistance of Italy and Germany. Some months later, Soviet Russia came to Madrid's aid. Here again the Fascists were allowed by Britain and France, under the guise of a "nonintervention committee," to ship troops by the tens of thousands, and vast quantities of planes and other supplies, to FRANCO. The CHAMBERLAIN government not only connived at all this, under the guise of "nonintervention," but actually failed even to protest when MUSSOLINI's planes sank dozens of British merchantmen who were exercising their right, under international law, to carry supplies to the legal government of Spain.

And now comes the crowning diplomatic and political defeat of Britain and France—their sell-out of the Central European republic for whose creation they were responsible, a republic which, under huge difficulties, has bravely maintained a regime based on liberty and democracy in a part of Europe where such ideology has been all but blotted out.

Did It Prevent War?

It is being said, of course, in some quarters that the sell-out was justified because it prevented a European war. The argument is open to question. THE TIMES-DISPATCH is as strongly opposed to war as any newspaper in America. It believes that war should be avoided whenever that can be done with justice and honor. But in the present instance, we do not think it has been avoided with justice or with honor, and neither are we convinced that it has been avoided permanently. If Britain and France had told HITLER to take his hands off Czechoslovakia, he might not have fought, and even if he had, they could have beaten him in the long run. But now, if they have to fight him in, say, 1945, it is highly probable that they will lose in the end. Even if they win, it will be after a far longer and bloodier struggle than would have been necessary now. Germany could have been starved and blockaded into submission, even if the fortifications which are nearing completion had kept the invader from her soil.

As it is, the evil day probably has merely been postponed, and at the same time, millions of Europeans who believe in intellectual liberty, in orderly government by law, in parliamentary institutions, in freedom of speech, of religion and of the press, have been left helpless before the onrushing Nazis. The refugee problem created by the appli-

cation of Nazi *Kultur* in Germany and Austria now is about to become doubly acute, as Nazi pressure upon Hungary and the Balkans
forces those states into the German orbit, and makes them subservient
to the Nazi philosophy.

Aside from the fact that the United States should be interested in
doing what it can to offer these refugees a haven, this country is still
more largely concerned, on its own account, with the developments
which have just taken place in Europe. For since those developments
have greatly weakened the prestige of democracy in the world, it
behooves the people of America more than ever before to preserve
their democratic institutions, and to guard them zealously against the
rising tide of Fascism.

We believe that one result of the sell-out of Czechoslovakia to
HITLER will be a great strengthening of isolationist sentiment in the
United States. Many Americans who might have been inclined to
come to the aid of Britain and France in a war with Germany and
Italy, if Britain and France had themselves exhibited a willingness to
go the limit for the preservation of democracy on the Continent, will
now feel that Britain and France are not worth it. They have retreated
time and again before the dictators, and now, in the most crucial
test of all, they have retreated again.

War is terrible, but there are some things in the world worth
fighting for. Liberty is one of those things. If CHAMBERLAIN and
DALADIER and the other so-called "realists" aren't willing to put
up a battle for the preservation of liberty in those parts of the world
which thus far have escaped the blight of Fascism, and prefer, instead, to sign agreements with medieval fanatics who admit openly
that they break such agreements whenever they can get away with
it, they need not count on any help from this side of the water. They
have made their bed. Now let them lie in it.

THE CONSERVATIVE COURSE
IN RACE RELATIONS

Richmond *Times-Dispatch*, November 21, 1943

THE TIMES-DISPATCH advocates abolition of the segregation law on
streetcars and buses in Virginia because it considers this the truly
conservative course. Such abolition would be tangible and convincing
evidence that the whites of Virginia desire to work with the Negroes

in eliminating injustices, arriving at amicable solutions of interracial problems, and relieving interracial tension.

Southern Negro leaders are genuinely and sincerely anxious to co-operate with Southern white leaders, and they want to avoid the inter-racial friction which would be sure to arise, if more radical Negroes from the North should gain a foothold among the colored people of this section. Many Virginians probably do not know it, but we have now arrived at the point where radicals from the North will find it easy to secure a large following in the South, unless reasonable and proper concessions to the colored people are made.

Repeal of the segregation law affecting streetcars and buses through action of the Virginia Legislature probably would be the greatest sin-gle step toward better race relations taken in any Southern State for decades. It would buttress the case of the Southern Negro leaders as hardly anything else could do. These leaders have had to take im-portant risks in keeping Northern extremists of their own race from forcing themselves into Southern interracial affairs, and the white masses of the South should respond accordingly. If they do not re-spond, and the Southern Negro leaders become convinced that it is hopeless to expect any concrete advances for their people from the Southern whites, they will be compelled, through lack of any alterna-tive, to turn to Harlem for guidance.

These things are said from a knowledge of the facts. They are not surmises or guesses. The Negro leaders of the South are looking to the white leaders of the South for help—now. They are ready and anxious to work with us and to continue to maintain cordial relations with us, if we will let them. They have not issued any threats or ulti-matums, but they have made it clear, in a thoroughly friendly and dignified fashion, that unless we meet them halfway, it will be dif-ficult, if not impossible, for them to retain control over their people. The colored masses of the South are in ferment, and they see radical spokesmen in the North demanding the complete abolition of all dis-crimination overnight. The conservative Negroes of the South realize that they cannot maintain their positions of leadership, under such circumstances, if they are unable to deliver any worthwhile conces-sions.

Not Asking "Social Equality"

They are not asking for an overnight revolution in race relations, or anything remotely approaching it. They wish to obtain for the South-ern Negroes a better share in the good things of life—better education, better health, better welfare, better jobs, better opportunities. They are not seeking "social equality," but equality before the law.

How do we know what these Negro leaders are asking? Because we have been meeting and conferring with them for the past year, trying to learn their point of view, seeking to find out what the white South can do which will enable these Southern colored men and women to keep control of the situation in this region, and prevent the Northern radicals from coming in with their drastic proposals, proposals which are so apt to produce violence.

A highly important movement began in October, 1942, when nearly threescore colored leaders from the South met at Durham, N. C., in an effort to draw up a statement which would allay the growing suspicion and tension between the races. *They deliberately excluded from that gathering all Negroes from north of Mason and Dixon Line, because they were determined to work this thing out with the Southern whites, and to devise a Southern solution for the problems confronting them.*

Among those who took leading parts in that Durham meeting were DR. GORDON B. HANCOCK, of Virginia Union University, Richmond; DR. P. B. YOUNG, editor and publisher, Norfolk *Journal and Guide*; DR. LUTHER P. JACKSON, Virginia State College for Negroes, Petersburg; WILLIAM M. COOPER, Hampton Institute; PRESIDENT RUFUS E. CLEMENT, of Atlanta University; PRESIDENT F. D. PATTERSON, of Tuskegee Institute; DR. CHARLES S. JOHNSON, of Fisk University, Nashville, and others.

The "Durham Statement," which they issued, was a landmark in Southern race relations, and probably the most important document of the kind since the War Between the States. It set down the things which the Negroes of the South would like to expect from the whites of the region.

The statement was a challenge to the whites, and they responded by holding a meeting of their own in Atlanta. That meeting was attended by more than 100 men and women from all over the South, with RALPH McGILL, editor of the Atlanta *Constitution*, presiding. This gathering, which included many prominent white Southerners, unanimously adopted a statement which said that the Durham manifesto "is so frank and courageous, so free from any suggestion of threat or ultimatum, and at the same time shows such good will, that we gladly agree to co-operate." Many more Southerners signed the Atlanta statement, after it was printed and circulated. Among them was GOVERNOR COLGATE W. DARDEN, JR., of Virginia.

As a result of the Atlanta parley, representatives of that conference and of the Durham conference met in Richmond on June 16, and conferred jointly. DR. GORDON B. HANCOCK, of Richmond, prominent colored sociologist and columnist for the Negro press, sounded the keynote, as follows:

"If Negro leadership in the South is to survive, the South must cease waiting for outside sources to extort from it in the courts concessions that should be made without a fight. If Negroes are forced to look elsewhere for leadership in critical times, then they are going to be inclined to look elsewhere at all times. . . .

"Negro leadership in the South can be strangled or strengthened. . . . If the South resents interference from outside elements, then there must be a greater liberalism in the South in dealing with Negro leadership; and interracialism must not be synonymous with a 'motion to lay on the table' every proposal for social and economic advance. . . . It makes a world of difference to the cause of race relations whether the capital of the Negro race is in New York City or Atlanta."

Please note that last sentence: "It makes a world of difference to the cause of race relations whether the capital of the Negro race is in New York City or Atlanta." DR. HANCOCK and his associates in this movement are trying to keep that capital in Atlanta. They can do it, if we will help them.

It was in the hope of carrying this process further that another joint conference was held in Atlanta in August. At that time, committees of about 20 members from each race, presided over by DR. HOWARD W. ODUM, of the University of North Carolina, and DR. CHARLES S. JOHNSON, of Fisk University, drew up a plan for establishing a Southern regional council which would seek to achieve fairness and justice for colored citizens. That council now seems on the verge of formal establishment. It will function in every Southern State, and have its headquarters in Atlanta, according to present expectations. It will have as its prime objective the creation of public sentiment on behalf of reasonable concessions to the colored citizens of the South, to the end that harmonious relations may be promoted and bitter clashes prevented.

Those who say that public discussion of this problem "merely stirs it up" and "does more harm than good" apparently are not familiar with the foregoing facts. Actually, the issue had become acute even before the Durham conference a year ago, and it has remained acute ever since. It has now reached something closely approaching a crisis. The time has come when the white South must do more than issue pious statements about loving and understanding the Negro, if it wishes to build a firm foundation for amicable race relations in this region.

394

Here in Virginia such relations can be promoted and cemented in several practical ways. In addition to the repeal of the segregation law for streetcars and buses—on the ground that it fails to segregate and is a constant source of friction and ill-feeling—colored policemen should be appointed for the colored sections of our cities, and the Piedmont Sanatorium at Burkeville, for tuberculous Negroes, ought to be given an all-Negro staff at the earliest possible time.

Three Things for Virginia

If these three things could be achieved in Virginia, it would mean an immense deal to those conservative Negro leaders of the South who are earnestly desirous of working with the white leaders of the South, and who, at risk to themselves, have deliberately excluded the colored radicals of the North from their councils. Approximately 15 Southern cities have Negro policemen now, and they are proving highly satisfactory to the white police chiefs. Georgia, Kentucky, Maryland and West Virginia have State hospitals for Negroes with all-Negro staffs. The segregation law on streetcars and buses has broken down, and is to all intents and purposes almost a dead letter.

So there is nothing radical or revolutionary in what we are proposing. The overwhelmingly favorable response in letters received from white Virginians in nearly all walks of life to our suggestion for repealing the segregation law as to urban carriers shows the trend of thought in the State.

It is noteworthy that this favorable response was elicited without the full explanation of our proposal which this editorial seeks to give. Some of those who have written us in advocacy of repeal knew the history of the conferences in Durham, Richmond and Atlanta, and the earnest and sincere effort which the Negro leaders in this region have been making to arrive at satisfactory solutions of this problem. Others responded favorably and instinctively without being fully aware of the related facts.

These Virginians were, and are, convinced that obvious injustices and sore spots should be obliterated at the earliest possible moment, in the interest of fairness to the 10,000,000 Negroes who live below Mason and Dixon's Line. They realize that tension exists, and they are anxious to lessen it in any legitimate way.

We respect the views of those who disagree with us, of course, but we trust they are now aware that the alternatives which confront this section are as follows: We white Southerners can remedy the evident injustices in the treatment of the Negroes, and thereby win their confidence, respect and co-operation, or we can refuse to do anything, and repeat the old nonsense to the effect that "the problem will solve itself, if people will only stop talking about it." THE TIMES-DISPATCH is fully convinced, from long and careful study, that the former course is the only course, and that the best way to provoke bitter race clashes in this region over an indefinite period is for the whites to turn their backs on the legitimate appeals of the Negroes for justice. The crisis is upon us, and we shall ignore it at our peril.

WE WILL NOT BE INTIMIDATED

Richmond *Times-Dispatch*, March 15, 1948
(Winner Sigma Delta Chi national editorial award, 1948)

The Virginia House of Delegates has passed a resolution instructing the State Corporation Commission to investigate Richmond Newspapers, Inc. This absurd action was taken in retaliation for criticisms leveled at members of the General Assembly, and more particularly members of the House, during the session just ended.

The Times-Dispatch does not intend to be silenced by any such political skulduggery. This newspaper has spoken its mind freely during the recent session of the State Legislature, and it will continue to speak its mind. No threats from any section of the State, or from any branch of the General Assembly, nor yet from the Democratic machine, will influence its course.

The issue here is far bigger than the question whether a Richmond newspaper should criticize the Virginia Legislature. One of the constitutional bulwarks of free peoples is involved.

George Mason's immortal Bill of Rights, which is a part of the Virginia Constitution, and has been virtually copied in the Constitution of the United States, as well as in the constitutions of the other 47 states, says (Article 1, Section 12, Virginia Constitution):

"That the freedom of the press is one of the great bulwarks of liberty, and can never be restrained but by despotic governments. . . ."

The laws of libel, both criminal and civil, are always available, of course, to any citizen who is aggrieved by improper newspaper criticism.

There are all kinds of newspapers, just as there are all kinds of people, but once freedom of newspapers or individuals to criticize public figures is hampered or curtailed, the first step toward dictatorship has been taken.

In country after country where the liberties of the people have been quenched, under Fascist, Nazi or Communist rule, one of the first steps has always been the smashing of the independent press.

The Second World Congress of the Communist International had this to say:

"Only when the proletarian dictatorship has deprived the bourgeoisie of such powerful weapons as the press, the school, parliament, church, the government apparatus, etc., only when the final overthrow of the capitalist order will have become an evident fact—only then will all or almost all the workers enter the ranks of the Communist Party."

Adolf Hitler said in *Mein Kampf*:

"It [the State] must not let itself be misled by the boast of a so-called 'freedom of the press,' and must not be persuaded to fail in its duty and to put before the nation the food that it needs and that is good for it; it must assure itself with ruthless determination of this means for educating the people."

Here in America there have been examples of interference with liberty of newspaper expression by officials or legislatures. One of the earliest occurred at the end of the eighteenth century, when the Richmond *Examiner*, a Jeffersonian organ, was attacked under the notorious Sedition Act for its political editorials. The effort to stifle the *Examiner* was unsuccessful.

The late Huey P. Long, as Governor of Louisana, had his servile legislature impose a ruinous tax on all the Louisiana newspapers of large circulation because they had criticized his administration and exposed its rottenness. The tax was pronounced unconstitutional by the Supreme Court.

Frank Hague, the Jersey City boss, struck at the *Jersey Journal* by firing any county or city employee seen reading the paper, and by bringing about the withdrawal of certain advertising.

Similar techniques have been employed both in this and other countries. Those who employ them violate one of the principles on which American liberty has been founded, a principle for which oceans of blood have been spilled.

The resolution of the House of Delegates is a threatening gesture designed to arouse public prejudice. It is not motivated by ethical intent to correct economic injustice; its purpose is to gag the press.

So long as this newspaper is in the hands of its present ownership and management, it will not be gagged.

It will fight fiercely the concentration of governmental functions in a few hands and the making of governmental policies by a small group of insiders.

It will not be muzzled by the House of Delegates, or any other agency.

The Times-Dispatch will not be intimidated.

CLAGHORN, THE DIXIE FOGHORN

Richmond *Times-Dispatch*, March 22, 1948

For years, yes decades, we've been battling to bring some measure of rationality into the fried-chicken-watermelon-mammy-magnolia-moonlight-mockingbird-moon-June-croon school of thinking on Southern problems, and now we've run up against the toughest proposition yet. We refer, of course, to that bombastic, bumbling, *brou-ha-ha* of the air waves, Senator Beauregard Claghorn, "from the Deep South, that is," whom a writer in *Life* has just referred to as "the most quoted man in the nation."

This amazing character on the Sunday evening Fred Allen program must have given millions in the North and West the notion that Southern Senators spend their time in making frightful puns, and bellowing "That's a joke, son!"; and in such professionally Southern deliverances as: "When in New York Ah only dance at the Cotton Club. The only dance Ah do is the Virginia Reel. . . . The only train Ah ride is the Chattanooga Choo-Choo. . . . When Ah pass Grant's tomb Ah shut both eyes. Ah never go to the Yankee Stadium! Ah won't even go to the Polo Grounds unless a southpaw's pitchin'.'"

All this is amusing, certainly, to Southerners who know what nonsense it is. The rambunctious Claghorn, with his ridiculous rodomontade, is a caricature that Dixie can appreciate, because it realizes how absurd most of the "Senator's" antics are. The only disturbing thing about the business is that so many who never have seen a Southerner in the flesh will think that Claghorn is a typical citizen of this region, and that we all go around roaring in the Claghorn manner.

It's bad enough to struggle with the periodic emanations from Tin Pan Alley which hymn the wonders of Ca'lina, Virginny, Texas, Alabam' or whatnot, the latest being an eruption of "Atlanta, Gee Aye" in the familiar rosies-posies-Dixie tradition. But Tin Pan Alley must now take a back seat on the presence of Allen's Alley. This latter agency of enlightenment has created a character whose doings and sayings are something we haven't experienced up to now. Claghorn is a laughable cuss surely, but he threatens to keep us all explaining for the rest of our lives that his outlandish and his preposterous dithyrambs about the South bear no more relation to reality than Mortimer Snerd's obtuseness on the Bergen-McCarthy program is typical of the average countryman.

We Southrons have been kept sufficiently busy asserting to our Northern friends that we aren't all morons and degenerates, à la Tobacco Road, or banjo-picking mammy-singers à la Al Jolson, but now we have to go around protesting that we aren't all raucous nitwits and foghorns like Senator Claghorn, "from the South, that is." Gad!

'LEFTWINGERS' HEARST AND PEGLER

Richmond *Times-Dispatch*, March 11, 1955

W. R. HEARST, the elder (father of the HEARST who wrote the excellent recent series on the Soviet Union in THE TIMES-DISPATCH), clamoring in 1918 for instant recognition of the blood-stained Bolshevik government in Russia. WESTBROOK PEGLER clamoring just as loudly in 1938 that "the working masses of Spain had a right to rebel" in the Spanish civil war, and denouncing FRANCO's backers.

Fantastic? Untrue? Not at all. This is precisely what happened in both instances.

MR. HEARST *did* write a prominently displayed editorial in the New York *American* for March 1, 1918, in which he termed the Bolsheviki "the representatives of the most democratic government in Europe," and demanded that they be recognized immediately.

MR. PEGLER *did* write a column, published in THE TIMES-DISPATCH on April 27, 1938, in which he spoke sympathetically of the Loyalist cause and denounced the elements behind FRANCO.

A telegram from us to MR. PEGLER asking for any comment he cared to make brought no comment. W. R. HEARST, JR., when asked concerning his father's views in 1918 on recognizing the Bolsheviki, simply said that his father soon changed his mind.

The HEARST newspaper chain is today as vigorous a foe of communism as there is in the United States, and there is no more unrestrained critic than PEGLER of those who sympathized with radical causes back in the 1930's.

MR. HEARST's paean of praise for the Bolsheviki is quoted in the February 26 issue of *The New Yorker* as part of A. J. LIEBLING's article on "The Wayward Press."

PEGLER's column on the Spanish civil war was exhumed by us from dusty TIMES-DISPATCH files, and it shows WESTBROOK in a surprising light. Part of his column is directed to criticism of the Catholic Church in Spain. We are not discussing here the propriety or accuracy of these criticisms, but merely pointing out that they were made by PEGLER.

After attacking "those members of the Spanish clergy and the well-born Spaniards of the Catholic faith who neglected a duty that was placed upon them," and adding: "To them, originally, rather than to the mobs which raged in the early days of the war, I would charge the blame for the slaughter of the priests and nuns," PEGLER went on:

> I ask whether it is now intended to drive the Spanish masses back to the church at the point of FRANCO's bayonets, some of them in the hands of Mohammedans, some in the hands of pagan Nazis, without as much as a gesture from the church to punish or rebuke its guilty and negligent servants.

There hasn't been anything of this nature in PEGLER's column for a long time, needless to say. PEGLER has a right to change his mind over a period of more than a decade and a half, of course. But what do the junior Senator from Wisconsin and the House Un-American Activities Committee think of one who was so militantly sympathetic to left-wingers only 17 years ago?

And while we are on this subject, have you forgotten what PEGLER wrote about FRANKLIN ROOSEVELT (yes, FRANKLIN ROOSEVELT) two days after the Pearl Harbor attack? He said ROOSEVELT had been "right all along" about the threat of war, praised the President's speech of 1938 urging "a quarantine for aggressors," and termed him "the one man responsible for the vast improvement of the military fitness of the United States."

Of course, WESTBROOK PEGLER is as far from being pro-ROOSEVELT or a sympathizer with Spanish leftists today as could well be imagined. Yet it all goes to show how unfair it is to write off as a "Red" or a "Communist" anybody who, for example, favored recognition of Russia in 1918 or 1933, or who was sympathetic to Loyalist Spain.

"Oh, that mine adversary had written a book," was the cry of JOB back in Old Testament days. Those who write books take the risk, as JOB realized, of being quoted later to their embarrassment. So do writers of newspaper editorials and columns—as the elder HEARST and WESTBROOK PEGLER could testify.

MENCKEN—FLAILER OF THE 'BOOBOISIE'

Richmond *Times-Dispatch*, January 31, 1956

H. L. MENCKEN, flailer of "porcine politicians," "prohibitionist soul-savers," "tinpot evangelists," "wowsers," "fundamentalists," "Babbitts," and "the booboisie," is dead. He died in his sleep, after some years of semi-invalidism in which he found it impossible either to read or write. Such a fate for a man whose life had been wholly concerned with either reading or writing was tragic. He might have been happier had he died from the stroke which felled him in 1948.

"Imagine my day," he said to an interviewer just two years ago at his lifelong home on Hollins Street, Baltimore. Gesturing toward the book-lined walls of his study, he added: "I can't read any of them. I wish it were all over."

Yet he managed to derive a certain pleasure from life. Gone were the days when he managed to launch about one savage attack per week against Rotarians or other symbols of what he regarded as American middle-class "oafishness," against prim lady essayists or other prudish litterateurs, against mountebanks, dervishes or other "frauds." Yet when he relaxed in his declining years, with a glass of his favorite lager in one hand and his favorite cigar in the other, he was not unhappy.

In his heyday he had "set fire to more stuffed shirts than anybody in modern times," in the appraisal of one newspaper editor. His had been the mocking voice of a whole generation of young intellectuals, who religiously read and wrote for the *American Mercury*, after MENCKEN and GEORGE JEAN NATHAN founded it in 1924. Much that MENCKEN derided should have been derided—Ku Kluxers, lynchers, fanatical prohibitionists, Comstocks—all excrescences of the 1920's. When he swung his meat ax on them, they knew they had "had it." But MENCKEN overstated his case against practically every object of his wrath, with the result that he roused thousands to fury.

His essays on the contemporary scene were interlarded with such terms as "hogs," "swine," "tub-thumpers" and "imbeciles." Such pungent words begat words equally pungent, and MENCKEN was widely and fervently assailed as a "rantipole," a "vulture," a "hyena" and a "jackass." None of which disturbed him even mildly. On the contrary, he published an entire volume of epithets hurled at him, under the name of *A Schimpflexicon* (Dictionary of Abuse).

Despite his intemperate assaults on many aspects of our culture, especially Southern culture, HENRY MENCKEN was a force for progress in certain respects. As a furious foe of "uplifters," he would have denied the imputation in sulphurous language, but the fact is that his blasts made people think. His searing essay on the South, *The Sahara of the Bozart* (1920), brought many Southerners to the verge of apoplexy, but the Southern literary renaissance got under way shortly thereafter.

MENCKEN had many imitators, but as a journalist and essayist he was unique. His three volumes of memoirs are delightfully Menckenesque, and his *The American Language* is a scholarly work in the field of philology.

MENCKEN came upon the American scene at the very time when his type of withering skepticism had maximum impact upon his generation. But when the Klan faded out, prohibition was repealed, and prudishness largely disappeared from American letters, he found himself with few flaming issues with which to belabor the "booboisie." Then came his illness.

His final years were what, with his fondness for the phrases of his ancestral Germany, he might have termed a *Totentanz* or a *Goetterdaemmerung*. But—let it be said for the record—in his prime he put on a gaudy show.

A GREAT VIRGINIAN PASSES

Richmond *Times-Dispatch*, August 10, 1959

The most distinguished religious leader Virginia has produced, and one of the most beloved, is dead. BISHOP HENRY ST. GEORGE TUCKER's death marks the passing of a truly great man, and one whose humility and lack of ostentation were matched by his intellectual brilliance and his broad humanitarianism.

President of the Federal Council of Churches while serving simultaneously as presiding bishop of the Protestant Episcopal Church in the United States, HENRY ST. GEORGE TUCKER combined in his person two of the most exalted ecclesiastical offices in the world. So greatly was he admired and loved that when his six-year term as presiding bishop of his church expired, it was extended, in order that he might be retained in the position for three more years. He had been virtually drafted for the post in the first place. His nomination came from the floor, after three other nominees had been formally announced.

From his student days at the University of Virginia and at the Virginia Theological Seminary, St. GEORGE TUCKER was marked for notable achievement. His scholastic record at both institutions was almost fabulously brilliant.

At the seminary, for example, he took an examination in Greek, and inadvertently translated the wrong chapter of the New Testament— one which the class hadn't even studied. Next day the professor called him aside and said:

> MR. TUCKER, you ought to be given 100 on this examination, but since you translated the wrong chapter, I felt obliged to cut your mark to 99¾.

Yet St. GEORGE TUCKER was no book worm. Although 6 feet 2 inches tall, and weighing less than 150 pounds he played "center rush," as it was then called, on the University of Virginia football scrubs, opposite the powerful NATHANIEL B. "BULL" EARLY, one of the most devastating linemen in Southern gridiron history. How young TUCKER managed to survive this experience is a mystery.

"My body was one vahst mahss of bruises," said the Bishop years afterward in describing the ordeal, using the delightful "broad A" which always characterized his speech.

St. GEORGE TUCKER was also a tremendous swimmer and mountain climber. His exploits in both spheres are well-nigh legendary. When serving in Japan for 24 years, he climbed most of the high mountain peaks (he went up Fujiyama a dozen times).

An exceptionally strong swimmer, he was once called on, as a youth, for a stunt at Virginia Beach. He swam out beyond the breakers with an umbrella and a volume of Plato, and floated for half an hour, perusing his Greek while shielded from the sun's rays!

BISHOP TUCKER's service in Japan for nearly a quarter of a century, during 10 years of which he was Bishop of Kyoto, caused him to be recognized as one of the foremost figures in the missionary field. Many of his experiences there are described with characteristic modesty, and an all-pervading sense of humor, in his charming volume of reminiscences, *Exploring the Silent Shore of Memory*.

One episode in Japan—which he, of course, never mentioned—occurred after he had brought food to famished Japanese in a remote region. Years later, when another missionary spoke to these Japanese of Jesus, they said:

"We know of Him. He was with us during the famine and fed us."

Those who were privileged to know BISHOP TUCKER, to experience the sweetness, the winsomeness of his truly Christ-like character, know that this account has the ring of absolute truth.

He was, indeed, one of that rare company of men who are endowed with the divine spark. His missionary zeal has been compared to that of St. Paul, and his concern for the poor and the disadvantaged to that of St. Francis of Assisi. Both comparisons are apt.

Born into a family which has contributed much to the greatness of America, his humility was that of the true aristocrat. To his heritage from the Washingtons and the Tuckers he added an aristocracy of personality, intellect and integrity.

One of the noblest of Virginians has gone "to where beyond these voices there is peace."

A MAN FOR THE CENTURIES

Richmond *Times-Dispatch*, January 25, 1965

Sir Winston Churchill is dead. The matchless orator, the brilliant winner of the Nobel Prize for Literature, the incomparable leader of men has breathed his last.

Who can forget the Battle of Britain when Churchill carried the British people through that ordeal of smoke and flame on his broad shoulders? The incarnation of John Bull, in his flat-top bowler hat, giving the V-sign amid the rubble of London, Coventry or Bristol, he was an inspiration to the free world.

The British Expeditionary Force had staggered back from Dunkirk, and many in other lands were saying that it would be hopeless for Britain to resist the terrible German war machine, which had crushed Poland, France and the Low Countries in a matter of weeks.

But they reckoned without Winston Churchill, Britain's indomitable leader. Thomas Jefferson once wrote that "torrents of sublime oratory" poured from the lips of Patrick Henry in the great days of the American Revolution. Words no less sublime poured from Churchill as he nerved the people of Britain for the greatest ordeal they had ever faced.

"I have nothing to offer but blood, toil, tears and sweat," he told the cheering Commons, as he took the helm of state. Inevitable disaster apparently loomed across the English Channel, and Goering's supposedly invincible *Luftwaffe* prepared what was to be the fatal blow.

The blow fell, but the British, standing amid their burning cities, and lifted to well-nigh incredible heights of valor by Churchill's words, fought back desperately, bravely and successfully. In doing so, they gave the United States and the entire free world time to prepare.

When Hitler double-crossed the USSR with the Nazi invasion of

Russia in 1941, CHURCHILL was the first to proclaim that Britain must stand beside the Soviet Union until HITLER was crushed. But once the hated swastika had been erased from the brow of Europe, CHURCHILL began giving close attention to Stalin's ruthless expansion in various directions, and to his total disregard of the pledges he had given his allies.

The great Englishman's "Iron Curtain" speech at Fulton, Mo., in 1946 was one more evidence of his firm grasp of the realities. It shocked many into an awareness of the true situation and accurately called the turn on the lamentable course of events for all the postwar years. WINSTON CHURCHILL was the first so clearly and frontally to expose the Kremlin's sinister plans.

It is impossible to comment adequately in a brief space on the career of so many-sided a man. Future generations will remember him not only for the courage with which he inspired his fellow-countrymen in their darkest hour, but also for the rolling cadences of his prose, both in his oratory and in his memorable works of biography and history; for his sparkling ripostes on the floor of the Commons, which skewered many an opponent; for his deep devotion to his "darling CLEMENTINE," his Pixie-like smile, and his ever-present cigar.

WINSTON CHURCHILL was not only a direct descendant of the DUKE of MARLBOROUGH, in whose palace at "Blenheim" he was born; he was also half American, the son of beautiful JENNIE JEROME of New York.

Americans, therefore, have a right to special pride in his truly epochal career. But the whole human race should walk a little straighter, in the knowledge that the species was capable of producing WINSTON LEONARD SPENCER CHURCHILL—a man not only for all seasons but for all the centuries.

KKK KARPETBAGGERS

Richmond *Times-Dispatch*, September 7, 1965

Virginia has been completely free for many years from the affliction of the Ku Klux Klan, but this aggregation of krackpots, klowns, and kooks is apparently trying to get a foothold in the Old Dominion, with a North Carolina karpetbagger leading the effort.

Virginians have been too savvy in the past to be taken in by this outfit but some softheaded individuals are reported to have chipped in with "donations" when the boys in the 50-cent chemises burned a fiery cross near Victoria, Lunenburg county, on Saturday night.

Every gang of kluckers that comes along is always the only true, original, genu-wine, 100% American Ku Klux Klan. There are usually several Klans operating simultaneously in the South, each hungry for the swag in initiation fees. If enough fatheads can be duped into putting up $10 or whatever the going fee is for wearing a nightshirt in the dark of the moon, the crusade is a huge success.

One can never be sure when the name of the Klan is mentioned in connection with crimes of one sort or another which Klan is meant. Perhaps it is the one suspected of complicity in the murder of the three civil rights workers in Mississippi; or the one whose members were charged with slaying a Negro lieutenant-colonel from ambush as he drove through Georgia en route from a military assignment; or the one whose konklaves were alleged to have been represented in the slaying at night on a lonely Alabama road of a woman worker for civil rights.

Or perhaps it is the Klan with three members who got 20 years each in Alabama in 1957 for mutilating an innocent Negro who, they admitted, had done nothing whatever. Or possibly the one in North Carolina, some of whose top officials went to jail.

It was also a North Carolina KKK outfit which boasted a "grand wizard" a few years back yclept the Rev. JAMES (CATFISH) COLE. The Rev. CATFISH had a lovely little police record which included two convictions for simple assault, one for being drunk and disorderly, one for assaulting an officer and resisting arrest, and one for making false statements to obtain a chauffeur's license.

Other sterling patriots are running the Klan in North Carolina today, but they may have a bit of difficulty living down the foregoing facts.

The overall reputation of the Klan is such that BARRY GOLDWATER flatly rejected its support in last year's presidential campaign. Virginians, we believe, can be counted on to adopt a similar attitude. They have been getting along very well for a long time without any of the KKK's klaptrap. They will continue to do so.

A HALT MUST BE CALLED
OR ANARCHY LIES AHEAD

Richmond *Times-Dispatch*, April 29, 1968

The United States is on the threshold of anarchy. Unless those in responsible positions in the federal government and on our college campuses assert themselves at once, and in no uncertain terms, this country is entering its most dangerous period since the Civil War.

The "Poor Peoples Campaign" is to begin today, with massive "dislocation" promised for the coming weeks. Those responsible are playing with dynamite.

Will our federal authorities, and particularly Atty.-Gen. Ramsey Clark, at last move forthrightly to stop lawlessness before it gains any momentum? Or will they continue to temporize with looters, arsonists, disrupters of the public business, sitters-down in public thoroughfares, and so on?

If genuine firmness is not shown now, it may well be too late. There is an ugly mood abroad in the land, and lawless elements are being allowed to run wild. Further indulgence of these hoodlums will merely encourage them to go even further in the direction of law-breaking and violence.

The college students who are behaving in this fashion represent only a tiny minority of any student body, as Dr. Louis B. Wright, director of the Folger Library in Washington, pointed out in an address last week at the University of Richmond. Yet he warned solemnly against existing trends.

Dr. Wright spoke advisedly. A former professor himself, the holder of a Ph.D. and 28 honorary degrees from this country and Europe, he knows his way around in academic circles as few men do.

Conditions have become far worse since Dr. Wright spoke here last week. A veritable epidemic of collegiate hoodlumism has broken out all over the place.

This sort of thing doesn't have to be tolerated by college and university presidents. Why, for example, should President Kirk of Columbia University knuckle under to the demand by a violent element that plans for a gymnasium be discontinued? Who is running Columbia, the administration, or these arrogant students?

On top of everything else, Stokely Carmichael and H. Rap Brown, the two most notorious racial agitators of all, who were forbidden by campus police to go on the Columbia campus, broke through the police line and got in anyway. They departed later, unpunished.

And get this: Although President Kirk's office had been wrecked by student vandals, *faculty members threatened a lie-down to prevent police from clearing occupied buildings.* Dr. Kirk thereupon warned all police away!

This situation at Columbia is among the worst of all, if not the worst, but plenty of others might be cited. And this type of near-anarchy is spreading. As stated above, a halt will have to be called, or the situation will become increasingly hopeless.

Every time a group of determined student agitators finds that they can obtain concessions by bullying tactics such as Hitler's Nazis used, further such tactics become inevitable.

If chaos is to be prevented, college and university presidents and trustees, federal and state authorities, and local police will have to make it abundantly clear that nobody—*nobody*—in this country is going to violate the law with impunity—the late MARTIN LUTHER KING to the contrary notwithstanding. Otherwise we are in for endless riots, burnings, looting, sit-downs, and seizures of property.

The mealy-mouthed permissiveness which we are seeing is making this country a laughing stock in the eyes of the civilized world. A halt must be called, or we shall all suffer, the poor as well as the rich, blacks as well as whites.

Obituary by Virginius Dabney,
Richmond *Times-Dispatch*, September 8, 1929

ELLEN GLASGOW'S PET SEALYHAM TERRIER HAD CANINE PERSONALITY

"JEREMY," WHO DIED THURSDAY, WAS VERY INTELLIGENT; DEATH SINCERELY MOURNED

"Jeremy," the pedigreed Sealyham terrier belonging to Miss Ellen Glasgow, of Richmond, is dead. The little dog, which always greeted visitors to the picturesque old Georgian mansion, at 1 West Main Street, and was such a favorite with them, died Thursday night after a long illness. He was 8 years old.

Miss Glasgow rushed back to Richmond from Maine in order to be with "Jeremy" in his last hours. The internationally famous novelist was on the verge of a nervous collapse, from worry over "Jeremy," when she left for the North a month ago, and it was only because of fear of a breakdown that she was persuaded to go.

The little Sealyham was in the last stages of pneumonia when Miss Glasgow reached his bedside, but he was able to recognize her. That night he died. He was buried in the flower garden of one of his devoted admirers.

"Jeremy," it is agreed by those who knew him, was a dog of extraordinary intelligence and vital personality. Miss Glasgow and Miss Anne Virginia Bennett, who lives with her, regarded him as a member of the family, and their grief at his passing is as genuine as if he had been a near relative.

Appendix

Welcomed Guests.

He possessed an almost human understanding, which was well-nigh uncanny at times. It was his habit to greet visitors to the Glasgow home at the door, and accompany them into the parlor. When a party was being held, "Jeremy" was the first to go downstairs and welcome the guests.

It was his custom, when a guest came to stay at the house, to accompany the visitor upstairs to his room, and to sit with him for a few minutes, apparently in order to make him "feel at home."

On one occasion, when a caller, who was not liked by a certain member of the household, came to the house, "Jeremy" treated him with his accustomed cordiality, but when he went back upstairs, he crawled apologetically into the presence of the person who disliked the visitor, for his remarkable intuition had told him of that dislike. And afterwards, whenever that person called, "Jeremy" repeated the performance. He was always cordial, but he was always apologetic when the caller had left.

Dr. James Galloway, who treated "Jeremy" in his last illness, who is credited by Miss Glasgow with having prolonged his life considerably, and who sat up with him all night many times, stated that he had never seen a dog with such an extraordinary personality.

He underwent a major operation last December, and seemingly was quite well for several months thereafter. But certain tissues had been injured, and another operation had to be performed on July 21. Pneumonia developed some weeks later, and death resulted.

"Jeremy" had the best medical attention procurable from both physicians and veterinarians. Specialists from New York and Philadelphia were consulted by long-distance telephone. Everything known to science was tried in an effort to save his life.

Not only are Miss Glasgow and Miss Bennett grief-stricken over his death, but "Billie," Miss Glasgow's little French poodle, wanders about the house distracted. "Billie" was the only dog "Jeremy" ever had any use for.

He first saw "Billie" about six years ago near the Glasgow home, and apparently was attracted to him, for afterwards, whenever "Billie" came near, "Jeremy" uttered a friendly bark, and "sidled up" to him. Later "Jeremy" began "inviting" him into the house. He would bark at "Billie" from an upper window as he passed the house, and then run down to the front door, and accompany him upstairs.

Finally, after this had been going on for about a year, arrangements were made by Miss Glasgow to buy "Billie" from his owner, and he was added to the entourage at 1 West Main Street. The two dogs became almost inseparable. They went driving in the car at least twice a day, if not oftener, and played about the house together. "Billie" looks very forlorn, now that his playmate is gone.

Dog of Fine Lineage.

"Jeremy" was a dog of fine lineage, having descended from six generations of champion Sealyhams. His sire was the great champion, Barberry Hill Gin Rickey, the best of the breed in his day, and his brother was Barberry Hill Bootlegger, another noted champion.

While Miss Glasgow and Miss Bennett are confident that "Jeremy" would have taken many prizes, if he had been given the opportunity, they never exhibited him because they could not bear separation from him for a sufficient length of time to do so.

Index

Index

Index

415

Index

Index